The Imperialist Imagination

Social History, Popular Culture, and Politics in Germany
Geoff Eley, Series Editor

A History of Foreign Labor in Germany, 1880–1980: Seasonal Workers/Forced Laborers/Guest Workers, Ulrich Herbert, translated by William Templer
Reshaping the German Right: Radical Nationalism and Political Change after Bismarck, Geoff Eley
The Stigma of Names: Antisemitism in German Daily Life, 1812–1933, Dietz Bering
Forbidden Laughter: Popular Humor and the Limits of Repression in Nineteenth-Century Prussia, Mary Lee Townsend
From Bundesrepublik *to* Deutschland: *German Politics after Unification,* Michael G. Huelshoff, Andrei S. Markovits, and Simon Reich, editors
The People Speak! Anti-Semitism and Emancipation in Nineteenth-Century Bavaria, James F. Harris
The Origins of the Authoritarian Welfare State in Prussia: Conservatives, Bureaucracy, and the Social Question, 1815–70, Hermann Beck
Technological Democracy: Bureaucracy and Citizenry in the German Energy Debate, Carol J. Hager
Society, Culture, and the State in Germany, 1870–1930, Geoff Eley, editor
Paradoxes of Peace: German Peace Movements since 1945, Alice Holmes Cooper
Jews, Germans, Memory: Reconstruction of Jewish Life in Germany, Y. Michal Bodemann, editor
Exclusive Revolutionaries: Liberal Politics, Social Experience, and National Identity in the Austrian Empire, 1848–1914, Pieter M. Judson
Feminine Frequencies: Gender, German Radio, and the Public Sphere, 1923–1945, Kate Lacey
How German Is She? Postwar West German Reconstruction and the Consuming Woman, Erica Carter
West Germany under Construction: Politics, Society, and Culture in Germany in the Adenauer Era, Robert G. Moeller, editor
A Greener Vision of Home: Cultural Politics and Environmental Reform in the German Heimatschutz *Movement, 1904–1918,* William H. Rollins
A User's Guide to German Cultural Studies, Scott Denham, Irene Kacandes, and Jonathan Petropoulos, editors
Catholicism, Political Culture, and the Countryside: A Social History of the Nazi Party in South Germany, Oded Heilbronner
Contested City: Municipal Politics and the Rise of Nazism in Altona, 1917–1937, Anthony McElligott
The Imperialist Imagination: German Colonialism and Its Legacy, Sara Friedrichsmeyer, Sara Lennox, and Susanne Zantop, editors
Mobility and Modernity: Migration in Germany 1820–1989, Steve Hochstadt
Framed Visions: Popular Culture, Americanization, and the Contemporary German and Austrian Imagination, Gerd Gemünden
Triumph of the Fatherland: German Unification and the Marginalization of Women, Brigitte Young

The Imperialist Imagination

German Colonialism and Its Legacy

Edited by Sara Friedrichsmeyer, Sara Lennox,
and Susanne Zantop

Ann Arbor
THE UNIVERSITY OF MICHIGAN PRESS

Copyright © by the University of Michigan 1998
All rights reserved
Published in the United States of America by
The University of Michigan Press
Manufactured in the United States of America
♾ Printed on acid-free paper

2001 2000 1999 1998   4 3 2 1

No part of this publication may be reproduced, stored in a retrieval system, or transmitted in any form or by any means, electronic, mechanical, or otherwise, without the written permission of the publisher.

A CIP catalog record for this book is available from the British Library.

Library of Congress Cataloging-in-Publication Data

The imperialist imagination : German colonialism and its legacy /
    edited by Sara Friedrichsmeyer, Sara Lennox, and Susanne Zantop.
       p. cm. — (Social history, popular culture, and politics in
    Germany)
    Includes bibliographical references and index.
    ISBN 0-472-09682-6 (acid-free paper)
    ISBN 0-472-06682-X (pbk. : acid-free paper)
    1. Arts, German. 2. Arts, Modern—20th century—Germany. 3. Exoticism in art—Germany. 4. Imperialism in art. 5. Colonies in art. 6. Germany—Colonies—Africa—History. 7. Nationalism—Germany—History. I. Friedrichsmeyer, Sara. II. Lennox, Sara. III. Zantop, Susanne, 1945– IV. Series.
NX550.A1 I53 1999
325'.343—ddc21   98-25522
                                                              CIP

Contents

Introduction   1
Sara Friedrichsmeyer, Sara Lennox, and Susanne Zantop

Part 1. Colonial Discourse in the New Empire

Nietzsche's Colonialist Imagination: Nueva Germania,
Good Europeanism, and Great Politics   33
Robert C. Holub

Orientalism, Imperialism, and Nationalism:
Karl May's *Orientzyklus*   51
Nina Berman

Engendering German Nationalism: Gender and
Race in Frieda von Bülow's Colonial Writings   69
Friederike Eigler

National Identity, Nomadism, and Narration in
Gustav Frenssen's *Peter Moor's Journey to Southwest Africa*   87
John K. Noyes

The Talk of Genocide, the Rhetoric of Miscegenation:
Notes on Debates in the German Reichstag Concerning
Southwest Africa, 1904–14   107
Helmut Walser Smith

On Colonial Spaces and Bodies: Hans Grimm's
Geschichten aus Südwestafrika   125
Thomas Nolden

Part 2. Imperialism without Colonies

Formalism to Psychoanalysis: On the Politics of
Primitivism in Carl Einstein   141
Andreas Michel

Mapping the Native Body: On Africa and the
Colonial Film in the Third Reich 163
Sabine Hake

Reading the Face of the Other: Arnold Zweig's and
Hermann Struck's *Das ostjüdische Antlitz* 189
Leslie Morris

Blacks, Germans, and the Politics of
Imperial Imagination, 1920–60 205
*Tina Campt, Pascal Grosse, and
Yara-Colette Lemke-Muniz de Faria*

Part 3. Imperial Fantasies after 1945

Of Seeing and Otherness:
Leni Riefenstahl's African Photographs 233
Lisa Gates

White Ladies and Dark Continents in
Ingeborg Bachmann's *Todesarten* 247
Sara Lennox

Imagining Migrants' Literature:
Intercultural Alterity in Jeannette Lander's
Jahrhundert der Herren 265
Leslie A. Adelson

Christoph Hein's *Horns Ende:*
Gypsy Essences and German Community 281
Sara Friedrichsmeyer

Ethnic Drag and National Identity:
Multicultural Crises, Crossings, and Interventions 295
Katrin Sieg

Epilogue: "Land of Truth—Enchanting Name!"
Kant's Journey at Home 321
Willi Goetschel

Bibliography 337

List of Contributors 359

Index 363

Introduction

Sara Friedrichsmeyer, Sara Lennox, and Susanne Zantop

Cultural Studies and German Colonialism

German cultural studies comes belatedly to the investigation of colonialism and postcoloniality. Only in the mid-1980s did significant numbers of German Studies scholars begin to explore the texts and experiences of minorities in contemporary Germany, and few analyses of German colonial and postcolonial discourse appeared in either the Federal Republic or the United States before the early 1990s (Bitterli; Bader and Riesz; Horn). But since the beginning of this decade, U.S. scholars, often influenced by the sophisticated investigations of colonial and postcolonial topics within Anglo-American cultural studies, have played a vanguard role in opening up this new area for scholarly investigation within German Studies. Their pathbreaking work has been presented in papers at the conferences of the Modern Language Association, the American Historical Association, and the German Studies Association, as well as in books like Arlene Teraoka's *East, West, and Others: The Third World in Postwar German Literature* (1996), Nina Berman's *Orientalismus, Kolonialismus und Moderne: Zum Bild des Orients in der deutschen Kultur um 1900* (1997) and Susanne Zantop's *Colonial Fantasies: Conquest, Family, and Nation in Precolonial Germany, 1770–1870* (1997). That three German journals—*KultuRRevolution, Neue Rundschau,* and *Das Argument*—have recently devoted special issues to colonial and postcolonial topics suggests that these have also captured the interest of a wider circle of scholars and intellectuals within Germany itself. The present collection of essays grows out of such discussions both here and in Germany. It comprises, we believe, one of the first interdisciplinary collections in English or German to focus entirely on German colonialism and its aftermath, and brings to German Studies a range of scholarly investigations that model how postcolonial theory and analysis might be applied in a German context.

Although colonial and postcolonial studies have been the focus of special issues of prestigious scholarly journals like *Critical Inquiry, Social Text, Diacritics, Ariel, Yale French Studies, PMLA,* and *Signs,* the definitions of these terms are by no means uncontested even within Anglo-American cultural studies. Most commentators, however, date the emergence of the approach from the appearance of Edward Said's *Orientalism* (1978); as Patrick Williams and Laura Chrisman, editors of *Colonial Discourse and Post-Colonial Theory,* have observed, with this book Said "single-handedly inaugurates a new area of academic inquiry" (5). Informed by an eclectic appropriation of Gramsci and Foucault, Said's interrogation of how the West has produced knowledge and other forms of representation about the Middle East, that is, the "Orient," has deeply influenced the subsequent development of the field. Although the expansion of postcolonial studies has been accompanied by a not unsurprising blurring of the term "postcolonial," most scholars would agree with the definitions of postcolonial literature and theory offered by Bill Ashcroft, Gareth Griffiths, and Helen Tiffin, editors of *The Post-Colonial Reader:* "Post-colonial literatures are a result of [the] interaction between imperial culture and the complex of indigenous cultural practices . . . Once colonised peoples had cause to reflect on and express the tension which ensued from this problematic and contested, but eventually vibrant and powerful mixture of imperial language and local experience, post-colonial 'theory' came into being" (1). Their formulations emphasize the breadth of the field: "[P]ost-colonial theory involves discussion about experience of various kinds: migration, slavery, suppression, resistance, representation, difference, race, gender, place, and responses to the influential master discourses of imperial Europe such as history, philosophy and linguistics, and the fundamental experiences of speaking and writing by which all these come into being. None of these is 'essentially' post-colonial, but together they form the complex fabric of the field" (2).

Postcolonial scholars draw on a range of theoretical models, including various new versions of Marxism; Foucault, Derrida, and other poststructuralists; Fanon and other critics of imperialism; Freud, Lacan, and other cultural critics influenced by psychoanalysis; feminists; race theorists; new historicists, cultural materialists, and experimental ethnographers; and radical geographers. To be sure, some of the most distinguished practitioners of these approaches now question the utility of so diffuse a term as "postcolonial." Ella Showat and Robert Stam argue, for instance, that, when it is applied to a wide range of spatially and temporally distinct phenomena—white settler colonies like Canada and Australia, "third world" countries that gained independence after World War II, the "third world" diasporic presence within "first world" metropolises—"the all-inclusive formulation homogenizes very different national and racial formations, obscures power relations between colonizer and colonized, and collapses diverse chronologies by designating formerly colonized countries which achieved independence at very different historical points or even the entire period of world history since European colonization began" (37–39). Similarly, Anne McClintock protests that, though the emergence of postcolonial subjects speaking in their own voice drew the preeminence of the West into question, the use of the term "postcolonial" threatens to reestablish that hierarchy: "If postcolonial theory has sought to challenge the grand march of Western historicism and its entourage of binaries (self–other, metropolis–colony, center–periphery, etc.), the term postcolonialism nonetheless reorients the globe once more around a single, binary opposition: colonial–postcolonial" (10–11). Yet even scholars who acknowledge the legitimacy of such critiques also concede that the new method has evolved by necessity to address a definitively new set of global and local relations. They also acknowledge that the postcolonial condition, itself a hybridized, syncretic product of local and global processes, elicits and necessitates quite heterogeneous responses. What may, however, unite postcolonial scholars and writers is their effort to draw into question the binary categories in which the West has described itself and its others.

This brief sketch of some of the components of postcolonial studies begins to explain why the approach has been so slow to gain a foothold in Germany. Most obviously, Germany's short period as a colonial power, from 1884 to 1919, has seemed to make the entire question of colonialism far less relevant to Germany than it was for countries that enjoyed centuries of imperial prestige and then endured protracted and costly struggles over decolonization. To be sure, the German experience was less historically significant than those of the generally acknowledged imperial powers, but although its overseas empire was not as impressive geographically or as profitable economically as that of other colonial powers, the German colonial empire did have historic importance, not alone for Germany but for the colonies as well. Nevertheless, even historians in Germany have traditionally accorded little attention to Germany's colonial past; similarly, when scholars today turn to the subject of eighteenth- and nineteenth-century imperialism, they most often focus on Great Britain and France, ignoring the expansionist German and Austro-Hungarian empires. It is not surprising, then, that postcolonial theories and analyses have in general been developed with little substantial reference to the German colonial experience (cf. Said, *Culture* xxii–xxiii).

A further reason for contemporary Germany's seeming lack of interest in postcolonial studies underscores other differences between Germany and its imperial neighbors. If "postcolonial literature" means writing by formerly colonized people in the language of their colonizers, there are apparently no postcolonial texts in German—partly as a consequence of German language policy in the colonies, which in some instances may have favored keeping the number of literate "natives" small. Even if postcolonial writing also refers to texts by white settlers, the German-speaking whites who still remained in the formerly German colonies when they gained their freedom after World War II also appear not to have written texts of belles lettres. Nor has there been until very recently a diasporic presence of formerly colonized peoples in Germany to remind Germans of the past violence that Europeans had inflicted on non-European peoples, what Homi Bhabha has called "colonials, post-colonials, migrants, minorities—wandering peoples who will not be contained within the *Heim* of the national culture and its unisonant discourses but are themselves the marks of a shifting boundary that alienated the frontiers of the modern nation" (*Nation and Narration* 15). Moreover, while many minority intellectuals in other Western European countries and the United States have been educated and now teach at elite Western universities, giving them privileged access to metropolitan discourses, there is no equivalent of these nomadic stars in Germany. Minorities in Germany, the "guestworkers," for example, have instead been concentrated at the bottom of the German economy, while Germany's citizenship laws, conferring automatic citizenship only on those of German "blood," have made it impossible for Germany's immigrant population to amass the political power that could force German politicians to attend to their interests and needs.

The German focus on the Holocaust as the central and unavoidable fact of German history may also have occluded Germans' view of European colonialism and their own complicity as Europeans in it. To be sure, various traditions of German thought insist on connections between colonialism and National Socialism. In *The Origins of Totalitarianism* Hannah Arendt explored how imperialism's political self-legitimation laid the groundwork for fascism (and Stalinism), and the German student movement underlined connections between neoimperialism and fascism (the chant "USA-SA-SS" was a favorite at anti-Vietnam demonstrations). In addition, many historical studies have also pointed out continuities between German colonial and Nazi policies and practices. Nevertheless, the postulate of the singularity of the Holocaust has been fundamental to postwar West German politics. The Federal Republic's unqualified embrace of Western values after the "aberration" of National Socialism was therefore taken as proof that Germany had earned the right to rejoin the family of nations. As Jürgen Habermas put it, "The unreserved opening of the Federal Republic to the political culture of the West is the great intellectual achievement of the postwar period" (39). From a non-European perspective, however, European policies seem less benign and differences between the European powers much smaller. As Andreas Huyssen has observed: "The decision to opt for a European identity in order to avoid the Germanness in question, so typical of postwar intellectuals, was and remains a delusion. . . . Rather than representing an alternative to nation, Europe was always its very condition of possibility, just as it enabled empire and colonialism" ("Inevitability" 71). But so long as the options are postulated to be Europe or Auschwitz, that critique of the European legacy remains difficult for Germans to advance.

Thus, whereas postcolonial theory is premised upon the decentering of Europe and of universalizing categories as well as upon an attentiveness to the differences those categories have suppressed, such a paradigm shift has made few inroads into Germany. It is possible that the German indifference or hostility to postmodernism or poststructuralism (as well as other new theoretical models inflected by poststructuralism), both of which Neil Lazarus has recently asserted to be fundamental to postcolonial analysis, may also be related to the absence of strong minority voices in Germany who might raise objections to universalistic paradigms. Certainly the relationship of postcolonialism to postmodernism's and poststructuralism's challenges to the universalizing master narratives of the West is a highly complex and contested one, and there may be good reason for formerly colonized peoples to remain suspicious of postmodernism's political implications. But on the other hand, as Robert Young argues in *White Mythologies: Writing History and the West,* poststructuralism, and with it, postmodernism, may be understood as a response—displaced into the realm of theory—to real political challenges to the hegemony of the Western colonial powers by national liberation movements in the colonies, and specifically the Algerian war of independence against France. "Postmodernism," Young argues, "can best be defined as European culture's awareness that it is no longer the unquestioned and dominant center of the world" (19). The enthusiastic embrace of postmodernism and poststructuralism in some parts of the U.S. academy might then be related to the U.S. defeat in Vietnam, as Michael Geyer has proposed, as well as to the success of various ethnic groups here in insisting on multiple histories and literary canons. Certainly it is clear that many white American feminists turned to poststructuralist categories in order to retheorize female identity after U.S. women of color had criticized the essentializing paradigms of the women's movement of the 1970s.

Until very recently, Germans have not had to confront a challenge of similar proportions. So influential a figure as Habermas can thus propose that the postmodern threat to Enlightenment universalism comes entirely from the right. As Cornel West observed some years ago, Habermas's thought is Eurocentric in the best and worst senses; though he affirms the values of emancipation, liberty, and fraternity, he has no critique at all of the ways in which European hegemony is as much a project of domination as of emancipation. Or, as Huyssen has put it, Habermas's failure to grasp the ambiguity of the project of modernity, which he reduces merely to its rational Enlightenment components, "is a view which results from the blind spot of the European enlightenment, its inability to recognize heterogeneity, otherness, and difference" ("The Search" 40). If Young is correct to argue that in postwar French theory it is the "sovereign self of Europe which is today being deconstructed, showing the extent to which Europe's other has been a narcissistic self-image through which it has constituted itself while never allowing it to achieve a perfect fit" (17), that theoretical project has still made little headway in Germany.

With this volume of essays we hope to help promote an investigation of these and other theoretical debates that have raged for more than a decade within Anglo-American cultural studies as a consequence of its encounter with postcoloniality. Certainly these essays begin to fill a gap in German cultural studies by providing information about the German colonial experience and the ways in which German colonial fantasies affected notions of Germanness and of German cultural and national identity. Exploring the German experience with colonialism can address Paul Gilroy's recent call for "comprehending Fascism in ways that allow the colonial adventures of European states to be more important than they have appeared to be when Fascism was presented as Europe's private internal drama" (26). An emphasis on the heterogeneity of the German experience as well as the degree to which Germanness has always been constituted in relationship to non-German others can also help to explode "the myth of homogeneity" in which German culture has long remained trapped (Peck, *Natives* 99). In the realms of theory and of practice, studies such as those in this volume may pose a challenge to any easy reliance on universalizing models of inclusion by revealing that Enlightenment values can be criticized from both the left and right. Perhaps, by encouraging Germans to attend more carefully to Germany's location within a postcolonial world, essays such as these may ultimately have a salutary effect even on German cultural production itself. As Peter Schneider has argued: "A significant portion of French and British cosmopolitanism is due to their colonial history and their laboriously achieved disengagement from it. The corresponding background is missing in Germany. One could partially explain the continuing German provincialism with the fact that the Germans never managed a comparable colonial history, and, at a time when other peoples had begun to put such a history behind them, tried to catch up in the most horrifying way in the middle of Europe" (489).

Finally, understanding German culture as embedded within a larger postcolonial context might help Germans and scholars in a variety of fields to envision a new, different Germany analogous to the Britain Catherine Hall imagines: "The post-colonial moment in Britain is the moment after Empire when British identities have to be imagined anew, when 'we' are no longer the centre. A moment of potential, when 'we' could recognise the inequalities associated with the different raced and gendered ways of belonging to the nation/state, when 'we' could build a different kind of future which was inclusive rather than exclusive, when whiteness would not be a condition of belonging" (76). In Germany, as Lora Wildenthal has argued, the "repression of [the colonial] past has permitted the widespread belief there that 'Germandom' has survived 'untouched' by Africans, Asians and Pacific Islanders" ("Race, Gender" 281). *The Imperialist Imagination,* intended as a contribution to the long-overdue examination of the relevance of Germany's colonial adventures and fantasies for an understanding of the German past and present, will, we hope, help to make such an allegation no longer possible.

The German Colonial Empire

What would German history look like if it were informed by the assumption that "colonization was never simply external to the societies of the imperial metropolis . . . [but that it] was always inscribed deeply within them" (Stuart Hall, "Post-Colonial" 246)? In a recent reassessment of imperial Germany published in the same series as this volume, Geoff Eley identifies "the post-Saidian critique of colonial and racist forms of thought in the Western cultural tradition" as a component of "a still-emergent cross-disciplinary formation, cultural studies . . . whose future influence promised to be great" (31). Certainly there is a significant store of historical studies on Germany's colonial period, but to date little of that historical scholarship has been influenced by such newer approaches.[1] Though

---

1. Currently, according to the *African Studies Newsletter,* four dissertations on German colonialism in Africa are under way or completed: Krista O'Donnell, "The Colonial Women Question: Gender, National Identity and Empire in the German Colonial Society's Female Emigration Program, 1896–1914" (SUNY Binghamton); Daniel Walther, "Creating Germans Abroad: The Politics of Culture in Southwest Africa, 1894–1939" (University of Pennsylvania); Lisa Marie Gates, "Images of Africa in Late Nineteenth- and Twentieth-Century German Literature and Culture" (Harvard University); and Karin Schestokat, "German Women in Cameroon: Travelogues from Colonial Times" (University of Southern California).

historians have taken account of the role of forces supporting colonization in imperial Germany—the German Colonial Society, the Pan-German League (cf. Chickering)—as well as the function of the lost colonies within Nazi ideology (Smith, *Origins;* Schmokel), it does not appear to us that a postcolonial perspective has yet begun to play anything like the transformatory role in German history that women's and gender studies have already performed (see, e.g., Quataert). Yet as this volume begins to show, the colonies and Germany's others have helped to shape a German "imperialist imagination" more powerful and more pervasive than hitherto recognized.

Before analyzing the "imperialist imagination," however, it is important to recall Germany's colonial ventures, which, we argue here, so profoundly affected German self-perceptions.[2] Though the Kaiserreich under Bismarck and subsequent chancellors was a somewhat hesitant colonial power, and although the aristocracy and the Junkers were not eager supporters of overseas acquisitions, German-speaking peoples over time have exhibited a long history of imperialist enthusiasm. In fact, a popular volume on colonial history published in the mid-1980s begins by discussing—with evident pride—"Two Thousand Years of German Colonial Endeavors" (Graudenz and Schindler 11). As W. O. Henderson observed earlier, quoting the geographer Heinrich Schmitthenner: "'There are colonies which are territorially contiguous with the Mother Country, and there are colonial activities without the flag. Colonization does not emanate from the State alone but from the colonizing activities of the race.' From this point of view the Germans are a colonizing people with centuries of experience. They have traditions of settlement, missionary work and commercial activity which go back far beyond the short-lived colonial empire of 1884–1919" (*Studies* 112). While the raids of marauding Germanic tribes cited as evidence by Graudenz and Schindler (12) may not count as colonialism proper, the Teutonic knights of the Middle Ages began the drive to the East, and German involvement in more specifically colonial ventures dates back at least to the fifteenth and sixteenth centuries, when thousands of Germans took part in the conquest and colonization of the "New World"—as adventurers or mercenaries in Spanish and Portuguese expeditions, as merchants outfitting ships or trading in slaves, as scientists, explorers, or interpreters.[3] Beginning in 1499 the rich merchant houses of

---

2. The following presentation of Germany's colonial history is strongly indebted to the studies of Woodruff Smith and Horst Gründer.

3. Bartolomé de las Casas's documentation of Spanish crimes against indigenous peoples, published in 1545, includes a special condemnation of "animales alemanes," German merchants supposedly more bestial than their Spanish counterparts (see Zantop, *Colonial Fantasies,* chap. 1).

the Fuggers and Welsers financed expeditions and brought German miners and African slaves to South America. In return for massive loans to the crown, they were rewarded by Emperor Charles V with territories and imperial trading privileges (which they eventually lost). In 1657 the Bavarian Johann Joachim Becher called for the founding of German colonies in South America. Perhaps even more important for the fostering of a German colonial tradition were the colonial experiments of Prussia, beginning in the late seventeenth century when the Great Elector of Brandenburg successfully established several forts on the coast of West Africa and leased part of the West Indian island of St. Thomas from Denmark. Prussian interests were expanded when Frederick the Great established the Asiatic-Chinese Merchant Society in 1751. In the main, these undertakings were short-lived and/or unsuccessful, due to the lack of financial and human resources.

In the late eighteenth century, when France and England were amassing their colonial empires, there were no similar ventures in German-speaking lands, in part because their "particularist" forms of government offered no political or economic base for large-scale overseas acquisitions. While little colonial activity can be noted in the years from 1750 to the 1850s, a number of famous and not-so-famous Germans—including Georg Forster and Alexander von Humboldt—undertook voyages of scientific discovery to Africa, South America, China, Australia, and New Zealand. In the nineteenth century Germany's population growth (and its several failed revolutions) also led millions of Germans to emigrate to the New World, where they established German settlements in both North and South America. In the same period, missionaries set about to bring Christianity to the "natives," and merchants established outposts in territories that were later to become German colonies. The activities of these explorers, settlers, missionaries, and merchants helped to keep the "colonial idea" alive.

State-sponsored colonialism began, however, only after German unification. Although he had earlier resisted overseas expansion, Bismarck rather suddenly reversed himself, plunging the nation into what A. J. P. Taylor has called "the scramble for Africa" (3). German colonialism began with a "protective" gesture: in a telegram of 24 April 1884 to the German consul at Cape Town, Bismarck officially proclaimed that the areas of Southwest Africa granted to tobacco merchant Adolf Lüderitz by local chiefs were now under the protection of the German government.[4] It was an action that set a precedent; despite Bismarck's explicit instructions

---

4. German colonies continued to be called "Schutzgebiete"—protectorates—until they were removed from German control, though they increasingly took on the configuration of the colonies of the other European powers.

to the contrary, the self-styled colonial explorer Carl Peters soon declared the coast of East Africa to be a German protectorate. Bismarck himself ordered a German gunboat to secure Togo and Cameroon as protectorates in the summer of 1884, and in the Pacific he mainly claimed areas in which German commercial interests were already active. At the Berlin West Africa (Congo) Conference of 1884–85, the Western powers agreed to regularize the procedures for colonial occupation in Africa and confirmed its subdivision among themselves—a great diplomatic success for Bismarck. By 1885, then, Germany had acquired its entire, not unsubstantial, colonial empire: four African territories (Southwest Africa, Togo, Cameroon, and German East Africa) and several territories in the Pacific (northeastern New Guinea, part of Samoa, the Bismarck, Marshall, Caroline, and Mariana Islands, and Kiaochow on the Shantung Peninsula in China).

Why Bismarck changed his mind about German colonies is still a matter of conjecture. In his useful summary of the motivations that historians impute to Bismarck, Woodruff Smith notes a desire to sow discord between the two major colonial powers, Britain and France; a need to protect Germany's mercantile interests or to signal Bismarck's own shift from a free-trade to a protectionist economic policy; or even an attempt to divert attention from the domestic problems of the newly industrialized nation, the latter a view supported by Smith. Bismarck himself favored classical trading colonies, where commercial interests would incur most of the expense and effort and German government intervention would only be required to insure internal peace and fend off threats from other colonial powers. But from the 1860s onward, a variety of organizations had been founded in Germany to promote a quite different notion of colonization: emigrationist or settlement colonialism. Especially among the lower-middle classes, hard-hit by the depression that began in 1873, support for emigrationist or settlement colonization seemed to combine a solution to the economic distress and dislocation caused by industrialization with an appeal to German nationalism: in the white settler colonies that the colonial associations promoted, especially after they combined to form the German Colonial Society, industrious German farmers could preserve the traditional (i.e., preindustrial) life-styles and virtues they associated with Germanness.

Other motives also reinforced the drive for colonies. There was in the newly unified Germany a rising enthusiasm for empire as many of its citizens sought for their new nation an identity commensurate with that of other imperial powers, and who, now that German supremacy had been established on land, looked to other continents for their next conquests. Yet another sizable voice for colonial expansion was linked to nationalist sentiments on the part of those who had left Germany before it became a nation and who, after 1871, wanted to be part of the Reich. As a consequence of his ability to obscure exactly what kind of colonization he advocated, Bismarck was able to gain crucial middle-class support from these and other groups, forge cross-party alliances, and build consensus in a divided nation for his own domestic aims and policies.

German conduct within the colonies depended very much on the nature of the land and specific German interests. As Winfried Baumgart puts it, colonial policy until 1914 "remained a haphazard and improvised affair" (158). Unlike Britain, which wished to convert the rest of the globe to the English way of life, and France, committed to its *mission civilatrice,* Germany's policy aims in the colonies were almost exclusively economic. In these ambitions they were sorely disappointed: with the exception of tiny Togo, Samoa, and Kiaochow, none of the German colonies ever turned a profit. The goals of the emigrationist colonialists, as represented by the German Colonial Society, were also only minimally met, since, with the partial exception of Southwest Africa, none of the African territories was really suited for settlement. At the height of Germany's colonial period there were never more than 20,000 Germans in Africa, a minuscule figure when compared to the number of emigrants to the Americas.

With a climate unfit for European settlers, Togo was nonetheless termed Germany's "model colony," both because it consistently produced a trade surplus and because major military efforts to suppress indigenous uprisings were unnecessary. Nonetheless, its allegedly "humanitarian" governor pacified Togo's interior by force, created concentration camps for political prisoners, and conscripted forced labor for public works projects, flogging and fining those who refused to work.[5] Cameroon's political and economic structures were less congruent with German economic interests. Trading companies attempted to establish European-run rubber and cocoa plantations on land in the interior confiscated from Africans and employing African forced labor (under conditions that led to a death rate sometimes as high as 30 percent [Gründer, *Geschichte* 151]). Frequent military campaigns were necessary to subdue resistance in the interior and break the trade monopoly of coastal peoples, who, according to Cameroon's first governor, were the "laziest, falsest, and meanest rabble on whom the sun ever shone, and it would certainly have been best when the country was conquered in 1884 if they had been, if not exterminated, at least expelled from the land" (quoted in Smith, *Empire* 80). A number of well-publicized incidents of brutality by the colonial government (includ-

---

5. Donna J. E. Maier has also determined that the use of slave labor persisted and possibly increased in Togo for at least the first fifteen years of German rule (73–91).

ing flogging naked Dahomey women before the eyes of their men [Gründer, *Geschichte* 139]) aroused indignation even within Germany, in part because the use of force inevitably produced resistance that had to be subdued by expensive colonial troops. Thus, toward the end of the colonial period, colonial officials began to experiment with systems of indirect control, "an outgrowth," Smith observes, "of the whole thrust of German official colonial theory since the 1880s: govern as cheaply as possible, consistent with limited economic aims, and if possible, govern indirectly through those organized structures with a stake in development, whether white or black" (*Empire* 89). By the end of the German colonial period in Cameroon, European schools there (much to the displeasure of Cameroon's small group of white settlers) had produced a small Germanized African elite that could enter the lower ranks of the German administration.

The situation in the two larger African colonies was much more volatile. Both German East Africa (parts of present-day Tanzania and Kenya plus Ruanda and Urundi) and Southwest Africa (present-day Namibia) were sites of continued clashes between colonial forces and the indigenous populations. In East Africa, Carl Peters, a proponent of massive white settler colonization, insisted on risking confrontation with the African population by claiming enormous quantities of land and exercising tyrannical rule. Peters was finally removed from power and imperial office in 1896 when it was revealed that he had executed his African mistress and her lover in a fit of jealous passion. But even after his removal, East Africa witnessed a series of uprisings, the most important of which was the "Maji Maji" revolt (1905–7), which resulted in the deaths of 75,000 to 100,000 Africans. Though the German government invested vast sums in East Africa, especially to build several railways into the interior, its policies of encouraging large European-led plantations on which Africans were coerced to work and, in areas with few white settlers, forcing cash-crop production by African peasants also contributed to indigenous unrest. After 1907, when a reform administration assumed control of colonial affairs in Berlin, colonial officials tried to deter excessive exploitation of African labor, preserve cultural systems, and promote peasant agricultural production. This "negerfreundliche" ("pro-Negro") policy (Gründer, *Geschichte* 164) swiftly ran into opposition from growing numbers of German settlement colonists—who in 1913 still numbered only 882, out of a total white population of 5,336—and their supporters in the Reich, a tension that persisted until World War I.

As the only German colony that ever attracted significant numbers of white settlers (though in 1911 still amounting to no more than 16,947),

Southwest Africa was a site of particular antagonism between Germans and Africans. The German Colonial Society encouraged (male) farmers to settle in Southwest Africa, while its Women's League sent German women there to marry them. The territory of Southwest Africa had been populated by several different, semi-nomadic peoples with quite different social forms, the largest groups among them the Herero and the Nama. The Germans tried to govern by playing the Herero and Nama off against each other, subjecting, as a SWAPO history of Namibia puts it, "a number of distinct societies to a single system of exploitation" (9). Since cattle-raising was the only form of agricultural activity successfully undertaken by the settlers, they soon entered into competition with the Herero for lands and cattle; beginning in 1897, the Herero were gradually removed to reservations. As the SWAPO account observes: "By 1903, more than half the Herero cattle had passed into the hands of the settlers, whose farms were encroaching alarmingly on Herero pasture land" (13). The combination of these social and economic pressures on the Herero led them to declare war on the Germans in January 1904, and they were soon joined by the Nama, who had been engaged in guerrilla warfare against the Germans throughout the 1890s. An expeditionary force of 14,000 troops under the command of General Lothar von Trotha undertook to exterminate the Herero, and to "settle" the native question once and for all. Historians have debated whether this campaign should be termed genocidal, and any consensus would seem to depend mainly on how genocide is defined.[6] Probably German officials had not decided upon a deliberate policy of genocide at the outset of the war, but by October 1904 von Trotha had issued his infamous extermination order:

> The Herero nation must leave the country. If it will not do so, I shall compel it by force. Inside German territory every Herero tribesman, armed or unarmed, with or without cattle, will be shot. No women and children will be allowed in the territory; they will be driven back to their people or fired on. These are the last words to the Herero nation from me, the great general of the mighty German emperor. (SWAPO 13)

The Herero retreated into the Kalahari desert, where the vast majority died of starvation and thirst. By 1906 less than 20,000 of the original 80,000 remained, and most of them were confined in concentration camps to be used as cheap labor. The Nama held out longer, but by 1907 over half

---

6. Dedering offers an account of the most recent debate on this subject.

of them were dead. The Germans, then, had succeeded in killing over 60 percent of the African population of what is today southern and central Namibia. As the official German war account boasts:

> This bold enterprise shows up in the most brilliant light the ruthless energy of the German command in pursuing their beaten enemy. No pains, no sacrifices were spared in eliminating the last remnants of enemy resistance. Like a wounded beast the enemy was tracked down from one water-hole to the next, until finally he became the victim of his own environment. The arid Omaheke was to complete what the German army had begun: the extermination of the Herero nation. (SWAPO 15)

To be sure, von Trotha's policy aroused controversy in Germany: he was recalled in 1905 and demoted. Nonetheless, after the war all Herero and Nama wealth and property were confiscated, and the "natives" were permitted to own farm animals and land only by permission of colonial authorities, so that most were forced to engage in wage labor for whites and to carry a work book (*Dienstbuch*) and pass (the model for the pass system of South Africa's apartheid regime). The racism of the settlers seemed only to intensify after the Herero-Nama war; an acting governor of the colony responded to expressions of concern in the Reichstag about the treatment of Africans by asserting that the interests of the Reich and the colony would be best served by rejecting any "humanitarian claptrap" (Drechsler 274).

In contrast to its African colonies, Germany's tiny possessions in the Pacific attracted little attention in Germany. With the exception of Samoa and Kiaochow, they were also a financial burden on the German government. In Samoa, German business interests had been active and profitable for over a century before official colonization began. The explanation given in 1897 for the acquisition of Kiaochow, Baumgart quips, "was that Germany needed a coaling station for her navy—which at that time hardly existed, but which was then created, as A. J. P. Taylor put it, in order to protect the coaling station" (154). The naval base then established was intended mainly to facilitate German economic penetration into China and, unlike the African colonies, attracted the investments of prominent German commercial interests. The German colonial administration drew heavily upon the Chinese administrative system already in place and was thus able to govern with little expense; profitable mining and railroad enterprises were also established on the Shantung peninsula. As Smith notes, like Togo, Kiaochow became a "'model colony' in miniature" (*Empire* 113). New Guinea, on the other hand, constituted more of a liability than an asset. Despite efforts to establish a variety of plantations, copra (whose value on the international market declined during this period) remained the major commodity produced in New Guinea. The colony also proved quite unsuitable for white settlement, achieving a white population of only 1,137, most of whom were missionaries.

Although colonialism continued to present more problems than it resolved, in the years before World War I the German Foreign Office committed itself to the idea of colonial expansion, envisioning as a parallel to *Mitteleuropa* (the central European economic union that was one of Germany's war aims) a *Mittelafrika* that would stretch across the Congo basin and unify the German colonial empire in central Africa. Attempting to protect the black labor force essential to the economic future of the colonies, reformists succeeded in pushing a resolution through the Reichstag stating that "native rights should be respected in labor recruitment, that unjustifiable coercion of natives should be abolished, and that education and example should be used to effect social change in the colonies" (Smith, *Empire* 219). But that resolution (in any case without binding force) became moot with the outbreak of war in 1914. Until mid-1917, Germany's war aims included *Mittelafrika*, an expanded Togo, Nigeria, and a variety of islands for naval bases in the Atlantic and Pacific. From mid-1917 onward, a more conservative German government called for an even larger African empire, but placed its main emphasis on expansion into eastern Europe, where German settlements were to relieve overpopulation in Germany itself.

The war quelled any attempts at expanding or even retaining the colonial empire. Instead Germany lost its colonies, one by one, to the victors. The Pacific colonies had been abandoned almost immediately and were occupied in 1914 by the British and Australians with little opposition. Kiaochow was taken by the Japanese after a month's siege. Togo capitulated on 25 August 1914 and its mandate was divided between Britain and France. After a fairly effective defense, Cameroon surrendered in 1916 and also went to France and Britain. Southwest Africa was conquered by South African troops in 1915 in a campaign that gave South Africa a claim to the territory and also made the reputation of General Jan-Christian Smuts, later South Africa's prime minister. In 1918 Southwest Africa became a South African mandate, not achieving its freedom until 1991. Only in East Africa were the Germans, employing the first integrated army of colonial warfare, able to mount a successful resistance, not yielding to English troops until after the armistice on 25 November 1918. Most of East Africa became a British mandate, though Ruanda and Urundi went to Belgium, and Portugal received a small triangle in the south. Though Germans at Versailles agitated for the return of their colonies, the Allies, supported by a wartime propaganda campaign that documented German brutality toward its colonial subjects, instead declared the colonies League of Nations mandates to be overseen by the victor powers. The Versailles Peace Treaty, ratified by the Weimar government on 10 January 1920, stipulated that Germany relinquish all rights to its colonies (Para. 119). On 3 March 1920, 414 Reichstag deputies (including even the Social Democrats, who had initially rejected colonialism) voted to oppose the loss of colonies, while only seven accepted the verdict. Indeed, colonialism had become a national project.

During the Weimar Republic the colonialist mentality survived across the political spectrum. All parties, with the exception of the KPD and most of the USPD, supported a demand for the return of the colonies, and German revanchists denounced the "myth of Germany's colonial guilt" (*Kolonialschuldlüge*). Though the Colonial Office was dissolved, its affairs were transferred to a Central Colonial Administration that was given "the task of pursuing the further development of the former protectorates, the development of the colonial question in general, and the possibility of regaining colonial possessions" (Gründer, *Geschichte* 217). Though the political leaders of Weimar were not interested in the annexation of territories in Europe, they did consider colonies necessary for Germany's resumption of its proper role as an economic world power. Annexationism or inner colonialism (what Smith in *The Ideological Origins of Nazi Imperialism* calls "Lebensraum imperialism") survived across the political right because it simultaneously appealed to big business interests and to the right's own antisemitic, anti-industrial, antimodern, romantic agrarianism. Though the attention of the radical right increasingly focused on Europe, some groups, notably the Colonial Society, whose leaders now consisted mainly of retired colonial officials, continued to argue for overseas colonization. At the Berlin Colonial Week and Exhibition in 1925, Foreign Minister Stresemann launched the expansionist slogan "Volk ohne Raum," and a year later Hans Grimm's novel of the same name—which was published in 1926 and by 1935 had sold 315,000 copies—helped to popularize such radical right positions. The absorption of right-wing colonialist positions into National Socialism was made easier by the fact that a number of eminent members of the colonial movement joined the Nazi party in the 1920s. After the Nazi takeover and *Gleichschaltung,* the Colonial Society was reorganized according to Nazi principles, and its second in command was made head of the Colonial Policy Department (*Kolonialpolitisches Amt*) of the Nazi government.

What the Nazis (or Hitler) really thought about overseas colonization is not completely clear. Helmuth Stoecker notes that "historians, especially in the Federal Republic of Germany, have sometimes doubted if the

German fascists pursued any colonial aims outside Europe in earnest, citing their cautious approach and the seemingly contradictory statements made by Hitler before coming to power and in the years immediately afterwards" (*German Imperialism* 337). For instance, the third point of the Nazis' first programmatic statement, their party program of 1920, is clearly imperialist in aim, demanding "land and soil (colonies) for the nourishment of our people and for the settlement of our excess population" (Smith, *Origins* 239). *Mein Kampf*, however, is pervaded by anticolonialist sentiment, condemning demands for the return of the colonies as "nothing but silly gossip, without so much as a thought of practical application" (635). Smith maintains that Hitler "originally thought of colonies in the conventional migrationist sense, and like most other Nazi leaders . . . came to the conclusion that such colonies made much more sense in Russia than in Africa." In general, however, the Nazis were convinced that Germany would eventually need an extensive overseas empire to guarantee its access to raw materials, markets, and investment areas, and they renewed the call for a *Mittelafrika* that would transcend the bounds of the prewar colonies. "By the 1940s," Smith concludes, "the eventual acquisition of an empire that would span the continents was a widely accepted goal of Nazi policy" (*Origins* 250).

In the first years after their seizure of power, the Nazis, not wanting to antagonize Britain, were cautious about raising the question of the colonies. But from 1935–36 onward, they frequently broached the issue in diplomatic discussions while also intensifying colonial propaganda. That did not mean, however, that colonies were at the top of their agenda; when in 1938, shortly before the annexation of Austria, the British offered Hitler African colonies in return for détente in Europe, Hitler dismissed the offer out of hand. Once war was declared, however, the colonial issue again moved to the forefront; through the summer of 1940 Hitler was willing to make the return of the colonies along with the recognition of the division of Poland the price of peace, while officials within the Nazi government developed elaborate plans for an administration of the colonies at war's end. Colonial policy was to be founded on a policy of paternalistic apartheid, as articulated in the so-called German Colonial Catechism: "The principle of the separation of races applies in the German colonies. Aiding the welfare of the natives is one of the primary tasks of all German colonial activity. The separate folkish nation of the natives, their customs and mores and legal institutions, will be honored insofar as they do not offend the German concept of morality" (Schmokel 161). Only losses on the eastern front persuaded Hitler in January 1943 to issue instructions suspending the activities of the Colonial Policy Office "for the duration of the war" (Stoecker, *German Imperialism* 416).

They were to be suspended forever. Postwar Germany, intent on rebuilding the country, harbored no colonial desires. In fact, as Uwe Timm has put it, after 1945 "it proved quite useful not to have colonies any longer . . . Those countries that Germans had only recently envied for their colonial possessions, England, France, Portugal, were now involved in costly and bloody wars of liberation, in Vietnam, Indonesia, Kenya, Angola, and Algeria." Thus "instead of making war, the new German state, the Federal Republic, made business" (7). Colonialism became a thing of the past, little studied and barely remembered. A German radio reporter could thus recently declare, "for historical reasons, Germany is less interested in Africa than England or France, because Germany, after all, was never a *real* colonial power" (*Tagesspiegel,* emphasis added).

The Imperialist Imagination

To understand how "real" and long-lived German colonialism was—not just for the colonized, but for German society itself—it is necessary to go beyond historical facts and programmatic statements to investigate the mentalities and imaginary configurations that persisted throughout the colonial period and lingered long after. A recent survey of European colonialism by Jürgen Osterhammel concludes its presentation of colonial structures, epochs, and theories with a call for precisely such an investigation (112). As he suggests, colonialist thinking is deeply embedded in the mind-set of colonizing nations. It manifests itself in a variety of ways: as the construction of an inferior otherness, of a colonizing "mission" and mandate of guardianship, and as the utopian notion of a natural order to be achieved through "cultivation" (114–18). The productivity of a focus on symbolic constructs, on the imaginary, has been amply demonstrated by Benedict Anderson (*Imagined Communities*) and, more recently, Jacqueline Rose (*States of Fantasy*), both of whom have convincingly argued that national identity is the product of collective, albeit largely unconscious, efforts to imagine and define national interest, national desires, and a collective will. Rose proposes that the "unconscious dreams of nations" emerge from narratives that construct social relations, that fantasy produces social realities, and that social realities in turn create their own "fantasies." In Rose's words: "Fantasy is not . . . antagonistic to social reality; it is its precondition or psychic glue" (3).

Since the *Wende,* a number of studies have focused on the elusive nature of national identity in European contexts. A recent German study of "nationalism, masculinity, and xenophobia in the patriotic discourse of German writers of the eighteenth century," according to the subtitle of the anthology *Machtphantasie Deutschland,* corroborates Rose's approach.

Its editor, Hans Peter Herrmann, suggests that an exploration of literary discourse, of the fantasy life of German authors, leads us to the earliest stirrings of an exclusionary, xenophobic national identity in the mid-1700s, "at a time when a German nation, even a German nation-state as a real historical formation could not even be predicted" (8). Basing their own studies on the work of Anderson, Ernest Gellner, George Mosse, and Klaus Theweleit, Herrmann and his collaborators conclude that "patriotism" as a collective, wish-fulfilling fantasy "existed before its object, the fatherland, existed" (19). Analogously, we propose that a colonialist mindset existed before the desired object, the colonies, came within Germans' reach. And because German colonialism as an intellectual concern developed toward the end of the eighteenth century at about the same time that the French Revolution was reinvigorating the desire for German nationhood, the dream of nation and the dream of colonial possession became inextricably intertwined. It is our contention that the coincidence of these two desires—for nation and for empire—had distinct and broad ramifications for Germans in their attempts to understand themselves as a political entity. Further, we argue that it was the parallel failure of these dreams that has made the German search for identity, for Germanness, so pervasive and has led to the preoccupation with national identity that has shaped, even plagued, so much of subsequent German history. Indeed, Germany's inability to form a nation until 1871 and its "belated" colonialism created complex, interrelated "states of fantasy" (Rose).[7]

Unlike in England or France, nationalism along with the dreams of empire that supported it was in Germany a middle-class phenomenon (Greenfeld 293). The architects of German national identity did not come from the aristocracy and the ruling elites. In the German-speaking principalities it was instead the educated middle class, the *Bildungsbürgertum*, who assumed the leadership in urging and molding the German national consciousness. Members of this group brought into being and controlled the press; they helped to mold a reading public and began the quest for a national literature that would help shape a national identity; they gave the impetus to conceiving of a fatherland that would be administered like colonized territory (and vice versa); they "imagined" nation as plantation. Like patriotism, and linked to it, colonialism developed, then, as an imaginary, phantasmagoric configuration, a discourse of the intellectual elite who engaged in the construction of a symbolic national-colonial identity as it confronted a deficit in real political power.

An attention to colonial fantasies in conjunction with fantasies of

---

7. All students of German colonialism stress its "belated" nature. The term implies, we believe, that there was a proper moment for colonialism—an assumption we would like to contest.

nationhood and Germanness before the formation of empire gives insights into thought patterns that span several hundred years: myths and legends that emerged in Germany alongside European expansionism, that outlasted the years of failed colonial endeavors and forced colonial abstention, and that accompanied or obscured colonial practice. These fantasies were reinforced after imposed decolonization in the 1920s and 1930s and are in some ways operative in the minds of many Germans even today. Exploring these fantasies that have demonstrated such a remarkable continuity in the face of political disruptions can help to answer questions that have repeatedly preoccupied historians and critical observers of contemporary Germany, namely, How did European colonialism affect the self-perceptions of Germans and their sense of nationhood? How has "Germanness" been defined? What influence did colonial practice have on thinking in Germany even after the colonies were relinquished? What are the connections between colonialist thinking and practice and National Socialism? And to what extent do colonial thought patterns reverberate even in today's relations between Germans and so-called foreigners?

As Susanne Zantop has argued, colonial fantasies and colonialist projections already occupied the imagination of writers even in the many German states that comprised the Holy Roman Empire (*Colonial Fantasies*). Despite or because of the absence of state-sponsored colonial activity, stories of imaginary enterprises proliferated, especially tales of racial conflicts and ideal race relations, set in actual or fictitious colonies, in which "German" protagonists were able to exhibit the qualities that marked the superiority of German colonizers. These narratives were inserted into travelogues or anthropological treatises; they appeared in forms such as epic poems, plays, novellas, or *Singspiele;* they were contained in tropes or images, mini-narratives of their own kind (e.g., virgin islands, devouring jungle). As fantasies of German difference they reinforced the posture of the "disinterested," "objective" observer whose colonial abstinence entitled him to criticize the excesses of others. Moreover, predating German colonialism by centuries, colonial fantasies generated a colonialist predisposition and the "colonial legend" of the moral, hard-working German colonizer of superior strength and intelligence who—unlike other colonizers—was loved like a father by his ever-grateful native subjects. As stories of benign patriarchal relations, these colonial fantasies reflected the fantasy of the *Vater Staat* who—through the *Landesvater*—would take care of his obedient "children."

Despite continuities in the definition of a putative "German" colonizer, the three moments in Germany's colonial history—the precolonial, colonial, and postcolonial periods—produced very different fantasies. In the eighteenth century, in the wake of Defoe's *Robinson Crusoe,* myriads of German Robinsonades followed their Germanized protagonists to distant islands, usually in the Caribbean or the "South Seas," where they would establish model colonies based on morality, hard work, frugality, and other Christian virtues. From Schnabel's *Die Insel Felsenburg* (Rock Castle Island, 1745) and Joachim Heinrich Campe's *Robinson der Jüngere* (Robinson the Younger, 1779) to Albrecht's *Die Kolonie* (The colony, 1793), benign German Robinsons worked in unison with obedient natives, creating perfect miniature fatherlands in exotic settings. In these texts, the colony functioned as an idealized version of the home, providing outlets for political unrest under absolutism. The relations between men and women/children, between Europeans and natives, were inevitably governed by enlightened rule, creating a "familial" order that nevertheless affirmed "natural" hierarchies.

Toward the end of the eighteenth century a second master fantasy gained ground, embodied in the metaphor of the "marriage" of cultures. This fantasy of harmonious colonial relations emerged as European colonialism witnessed its first challenges: the successful independence movement in North America and the anticolonial uprisings in the Caribbean and on the South American continent after the 1780s. Embodied by such fictional or historical pairs as Incle and Yariko, John Smith and Pocahontas, Alonso and Cora, or John Stedman and Joanna, these colonial narratives envisaged harmonious colonial relations between conqueror and native princess, loving master and obedient "slave," that would base colonial takeover not just on collaboration, education, and respect for the rule of law, but on "love," that is, on natural attraction and the "natural" subjection of the weaker to the stronger (Zantop, *Colonial Fantasies,* chap. 7). German writers seemed to display a particular predilection for these happily ending love stories into which they could smuggle "German" protagonists—men who domesticated and cultivated their new possessions, thereby transforming them through hard work into productive spaces: fertile fields and fertile wives. These fantasies, too, seemed to have been exacerbated by a rejection of revolutionary solutions and a concomitant desire for "familial," patriarchal relationships—within the family, within the nation, and among states—that is, for relationships that accepted the "natural order" as a given.

German tales of natural attraction between colonizer and colonized quickly gave way to tales of violence and separation when the New World colonies began their struggle for decolonization. Marriage fantasies receded to make room for fantasies of separation (e.g., Kleist's "The Betrothal in Santo Domingo," Caroline Auguste Fischer's "William the Negro," or Theodor Körner's "Toni"). These divorce fantasies, however, were short-lived. In fact, the years from 1820 onward (the first "postcolonial" period as far as the Americas are concerned) generated "neocolonial" fantasies, as the newly independent nations became, once more, objects of European imperialist designs. Again German writers, stimulated this time by the German "Columbus," Alexander von Humboldt, and his travels and explorations of South America, participated actively in the imaginary conquest of new terrains. But this time the moral-outsider position gave way to a more participatory, predatory stance. As fantasies of patriarchal or marital relations, so popular in the eighteenth century, faded into the background, Columbus dramas, in which a visionary heroic male figure "discovers," explores, and takes possession of virgin territories, assumed center stage. These fantasies of a "Second Discovery" emerged in a context of rapid industrial-capitalist expansionism and the rise of the colonial movement in Germany after the 1850s, which writers reproduced by returning often to somewhat anachronistic, preindustrial forms of "conquest."

These German precolonial fantasies not only underscored the rising "desire" for colonies, they also set the stage for articulating and justifying this desire during colonialism proper, the period with which the contributions in this volume begin. As Baumgart asserts, the colonies were considered an important factor in German *Weltpolitik,* a term that came into use in the 1890s to designate Germany's new conception of itself as equal to the other world powers (152). Many thinkers of the time linked imperialism and national aspirations. Friedrich Naumann, for example, in answer to the question "What is nationalism?"—a question he himself raised in 1897—maintained: "It is the motive power of the German people to spread its influence all over the globe. . . . You must conquer something, anything in the world to be something" (quoted in Baumgart 153). Colonialism, that is, the power to conquer, possess, and exploit "unclaimed" territory, was thus intimately tied to ideas of national identity and self-worth, of power and superiority on the international plane. Proof of the masculinity and maturity of a nation, the violent acquisition of colonies was considered the "natural" right of the stronger over the weaker, of the more advanced over the less advanced, of the *Kulturvolk* over the *Naturvolk* (Stoecker and Sebald). As a corollary fantasy implied, the *Kulturvolk* had to prove its superiority by transforming arid space into fertile grounds, deserts into blooming gardens, that is, by domesticating the wilds and making them "his own." This imperial assertiveness vis-à-vis colonizable continents also translated into national fantasies, in which "colonial mastery" extended over national "slaves": the working class, women, minorities (McClintock).

Throughout the colonial period, German colonialist literature reiterated a basic pattern, that of the colonialist male hero who "discovers" and appropriates unclaimed territory, who settles down and renders it fertile, and who thus demonstrates over and over again his physical, mental, and cultural superiority (Warmbold). If precolonial fantasies had focused on ideal colonial relations and were set mostly in the New World, colonial fictions written during Germany's brief colonial interlude were inclined to stress the hardships and challenges of the actual "colonial adventure" in Africa. These narratives of the newly acquired lands provided not just a space for relating practical experiences, but a sense of the liberation and mastery men as well as women felt as they engaged in what they considered to be a specifically German civilizing mission. More often than not the emancipatory tendencies of texts (concerning gender, not race) were subsumed into and suppressed by their nationalist ideology. While women's colonial narratives—for example, those of Clara Brockmann, Margarete von Eckenbrecher, and C. Falkenhorst, or the diaries, travelogues, or novels of Frieda von Bülow, to name just a few—purported to paint a realistic picture of life in the colonies, they too were imbued with fantasies of the physical and moral superiority of Germans and with stereotypical depictions of indigenous groups. In the works of both male and female writers, the question of German identity in international competition continued to form an integral part of the colonialist imagination: as *Musterknabe* (model child) among the European nations, Germany could produce only *Musterkolonien*—models of German probity, cleanliness, and industry.

Unlike precolonial literature, colonial literature did not idealize the relations between Germans and "natives" or envisage a "marriage" between cultures. Instead, as Wildenthal has argued, the colonies forced Germans to think about the relationship between "Germanness," "whiteness," and "color." Colonial fictions consequently reinforced a kind of *Berührungsangst* and tendency toward homosocial society that had also been discernible in earlier fantasies (e.g., the Robinsonades in the wake of Campe's *Robinson the Younger*); Hans Grimm and Frieda von Bülow, for example, viewed cross-racial liaisons with suspicion and represented them as problematic, sinful, and fated, if they represented them at all. In German accounts, the colonial "romance" took place between colonizer and land, with the indigenous peoples functioning only as a useful labor force, to be contained yet hardly desired.

Colonial fantasies thus constituted a kind of projection surface that allowed for the insertion of different, even conflicting desires and interests. They made possible the conceptualization of a preindustrial Germanness that preserved the traditional German values of patriarchal peasant families deeply connected to the land. They also promulgated sexualized images of strong states using their surplus energy, that is, surplus population and industrial strength, to "generate" daughter colonies that would remain part of the "family." Such colonial fantasies could comfortably accommodate a *Blut und Boden* ideology and could also serve as a terrain onto which the need for more *Lebensraum* could be projected. For women settlers like Frieda von Bülow, they could become the vehicle for dreams of control over their own lives, dreams of mastery in which slaves, not women, occupied the position of the despicable others.

"Postcolonial" German texts, that is, literature and film produced *after* the Germans had been forced to relinquish their colonies to the victors of World War I, continued this obsession with Germanness as masculinity, strength, and superior civilization. If the colonial latecomer had earlier wanted to prove to the world his national maturity by exhibiting greater colonial prowess, now the disappointment over having been deprived of that opportunity translated into fantasies of past glory and imaginary restitution. From Hans Grimm's *Volk ohne Raum* (A people without space, 1926) to the contributors to series such as "Deutschlands Kolonialhelden" (Germany's colonial heroes, 1932–33), "Afrika-Bücherei" (Africa library, 1942), or the eighty-eight titles of the "Kolonial-Bücherei" (1940–42), popular writers tried to keep the colonial idea alive. They fictionalized past colonial ventures such as the Welser's Venezuela interlude or the Great Elector's attempts to establish a colony in Africa, and they glorified recent colonial struggles and their often dubious leaders, such as the notorious Carl Peters. Since, unlike in the Spanish, French, or British colonies, decolonization was not achieved by an armed uprising of the colonized, the fantasy of Germans' greater colonial skills and the undying gratitude of "their" former native subjects—particularly the "loyal Askari"—could remain intact throughout the Nazi period, inspiring films such as *Germanin, Ohm Krüger,* or *Carl Peters.*

The German colonial fantasy could survive even World War II and the Holocaust. It survived because of the concentration on reconstruction and despite (or because of?) "a rather significant lapse in the production of literary texts on the formerly colonized" (Streese, "Writing the Other's Language"). The lack after 1945 not just of literary texts, but of historical information altogether, led to a general amnesia about colonialism, which allowed the colonial legend to survive practically intact. As Uwe Timm has put it, referring to the time between 1945 and 1980: "In the public consciousness, the German colonial past is, if at all, still present today in the same way as before 1945: as the legend of the hard-working Germans who built roads and railroads in Africa and taught the blacks their ABCs. That this legend survives so stubbornly can probably also be explained by the fact that—after the horrors of German fascism—Germans thought that in this area at least they had an edge on other peoples" (7). The legend was not disturbed even in the 1960s, when, due to the Vietnam War and the student movement, writers of the New Left took up the issue of colonialism—this time from a critical perspective (Lennox). The fictions and docudramas of the 1960s, however, focused not on German colonies or German perpetrators, but on revolutionary struggles in Latin America and the Caribbean and on U.S. imperialism. Colonialism and decolonization were, it seemed, problems *others* faced, whereas Germans could, once again, occupy the position of moral arbiters and theoreticians of world history that they had designated for themselves in the eighteenth and nineteenth centuries. Despite their denunciation of imperialism, texts produced during this time therefore lack an important component of postcolonial writing: the profound self-questioning and decentering of Europe and the European perspective. As Konstanze Streese has pointed out, it is not until the 1980s that a critical awareness of Germany's colonial legacy began to affect the deep structure of colonial fantasies themselves, as in Uwe Timm's *Morenga* (1978)—an exploration of the Herero and Nama Wars in German Southwest Africa—and Hans Christoph Buch's *Die Hochzeit von Port-au-Prince* (The Wedding of Port-au-Prince, 1984), where Buch's exploration of family history in Haiti leads him to one incident among many in Germany's nineteenth-century gunboat diplomacy. Both texts raise the issue of Germany's complicity with European and U.S.-American imperialism, albeit in different ways, and challenge the legend of the benign, superior German colonizer; they are, however, exceptions in postwar literature. To date, and despite constant reminders that colonialist-racist thinking has not abated in German lands, a critical interrogation of the colonial and imperial fantasies that have populated German self-perceptions for centuries, and continue to populate them, has otherwise not been undertaken. There are signs, however, that this amnesia will soon be overcome. The critical attempts mentioned in the first section of this introduction, the dissertations and studies that are currently under way, and, we hope, the contributions in this volume will all help to lay bare the contours of Germany's imperialist imagination.

About the Contributions

We have structured this anthology in three parts, concentrating first on the colonial period itself, then on the period between World War I and 1945 when the "lost" colonies remained an issue, and concluding with the period from 1945 to the present during which the imperialist imagination took more subtle forms. The first part focuses then on colonial discourse in the new German Empire and begins with an investigation of a figure who, because of his fervent antinationalism, is usually not discussed in this context. Based on a reinterpretation of *Beyond Good and Evil,* Robert

Holub argues that the "paralysis of will" that Friedrich Nietzsche's politics were aimed at overcoming was in fact related to the European "disease" that had supposedly kept the most civilized European nations from fulfilling their destinies as masters of the earth. Three investigations of literary texts follow, texts that to varying degrees became a part of what we today would call late-nineteenth-century popular culture. Nina Berman examines a cycle of Orientalist novels written during the 1880s by the prolific and extremely popular author Karl May. Placing these adventure novels against the background of German imperialist aspirations in the Balkans, she argues that German Orientalist discourse is not merely an abstract conceptualization of self versus other, but a discourse of power and appropriation. Frieda von Bülow's audience was more limited, but her colonial writings, as Friederike Eigler demonstrates, are important for understanding the ambivalence of colonial discourse when gender becomes a factor. In her male protagonist, von Bülow embraces a "true" German national identity based on racism and traditional gender roles; yet in creating a heroine who opts for an independent existence as a planter, she undercuts the patriarchal underpinnings of the colonialist project. John Noyes bases his investigation of Gustav Frenssen's *Peter Moor's Journey to Southwest Africa* in the nineteenth-century understanding of nomadism as, on the one hand, connected to positive human qualities such as *Wanderlust* and, on the other, a marker dividing primitive tribes from developing civilizations. Frenssen's project, according to Noyes, was to distinguish his protagonist's travels from the "aimless" wanderings of African natives destined for extermination. This part concludes with Helmut Walser Smith's analysis of the relationship between power, culture, and the rights of peoples to exist as nations as these intertwining issues emerge in two public debates: one on the near annihilation of the Herero and Nama nations and the other about mixed marriage and miscegenation in the colonies. He argues that the notion in these debates about a homogenizing German *Kultur,* articulated by intellectuals across the political spectrum, was only a thin veil for a discourse of extinction.

The contributions in the second part again represent a variety of disciplinary perspectives and document a neocolonial preoccupation with fantasies of German identity after the loss of the colonies. In the late 1920s and 1930s, Hans Grimm was a leading propagandist for the return of the former German colonies to Germany. By analyzing his *Geschichten aus Südwestafrika* in the context of popular colonialist propaganda and pseudoscientific writings of the time, Thomas Nolden demonstrates that Grimm intended the themes of his short stories—their "negative ethnicity," their gendered images, and their spatial structures—as constituent elements in the development of German national identity. Carl Einstein's pathbreaking work on African art is the subject of Andreas Michel's investigations. Beginning with Torgovnick's thesis that Western art history has been driven by an unacknowledged emotional interpretation of the primitive in modernity, he demonstrates that Einstein deliberately discussed African sculpture in formalist terms in order to destabilize those Western bourgeois conceptions; yet Michel provides evidence that Einstein too partakes at times of a primitivist discourse at odds with his analytical writings. Leslie Morris's study of *Das ostjüdische Antlitz* by Arnold Zweig and Hermann Struck is a reminder of the various forms the German drive for a national and/or cultural identity could take. Reading Zweig's explanatory texts to Struck's lithographs of the Eastern European Jews they encountered as German-Jewish soldiers stationed in Eastern Europe during World War I, Morris argues that Zweig, in representing the "Ostjude" as an "Ur-Jude," constructs him also as an other, thereby perpetuating many of the same myths about Eastern European Jews as did philosemitic and antisemitic propaganda. Working with recent studies on fascist aesthetics in the visual arts, Sabine Hake examines images of blackness and of German colonialism in Nazi films as displacements of the struggle for *Lebensraum* in Eastern Europe. The history they present, she argues, attempts to legitimate Nazi ideology and policies while at the same time providing a heroic narrative in which fantasies about body, identity, and race could be inscribed. From their perspectives as historians, Tina Campt, Pascal Grosse, and Yara-Colette Lemke-Muniz de Faria document German responses to blacks and Afro-Germans in three different periods and analyze the effects of the continuing equation of blackness with foreignness. Their discussion of the Weimar years focuses on the German response to the African colonial troops of the French occupying army; of the Nazi years, on the lives of African colonial immigrants; and of postwar Germany, on German pedagogical approaches to Afro-German children.

The third part addresses the less direct forms in which an imperialist imagination has manifested itself since 1945, the common denominator of which continues to be the defining of German national identity through the construction of foreign others. Part 3 opens with Lisa Gates's investigation of Leni Riefenstahl's African photographs from the 1970s and 1980s. Challenging Susan Sontag's undifferentiated linking of these works with a fascist aesthetic, Gates argues for a discussion of these photographs of the Nuba and Masai—almost exclusively young, nubile men with bodies resembling those of classical gods—in the context of the pornography debate and insists that definitions of pornography should include power imbalances based on race as well as on gender. Sara Lennox's focus is an unpublished fragment from the Ingeborg Bachmann archive in which an African student rapes an East Prussian countess and is thereby responsible for her sexual awakening. Virtually alone among postwar women writing in German, Bachmann, Lennox maintains, explores the racialized foundations of Central European femininity; yet by continuing to project white fantasies onto black figures, she remains captive to the racist structures her work attempts to critique. Leslie Adelson locates her discussion of a novel by Jeannette Lander in the context of international discussions of the fluidity of ethnic identities that have been largely unheeded in the scholarship on migrants' literature in Germany. By fostering a comparison between the gender subordination of its contemporary German protagonist in Sri Lanka and the early medieval heroine Genoveva of Brabant, the text, according to Adelson, insists on the positionality of life stories conditioned by the history of colonialism and its legacy. Turning to an often overlooked racial group, Sara Friedrichsmeyer discusses Christoph Hein's representation of Gypsies and Gypsiness in *Horns Ende*. She argues that Hein's attempt to fight age-old negative stereotypes is undermined by his representation of Gypsies as a homogeneous ethnic group—existing outside of political, historical, and social developments—who can serve as a positive model for the kind of solidarity he finds missing in his own East German society. Turning to contemporary theater, Katrin Sieg investigates the relationship between national identity and what she terms ethnic drag. In her discussion of Indian clubs and parades, cross-racial casting, and Karl May festivals, she insists on the links between systems of oppression and underscores the multiplicity of axes along which the fiction of the nation is generated. The final contribution in the volume takes us back to the late eighteenth century, raising a question that could be considered an important challenge to all the other contributions. In his examination of Kant's critique of colonialism, Willi Goetschel focuses on the four narratives Kant inserted into his *Critique of Pure Reason*, arguing that here Kant compares colonialism with the acquiring and producing of knowledge, that any conceptualization implies the intellectual appropriation of and competition over "foreign" territory. Not everyone will agree with Goetschel's contention that moral categories hamper the discussion of colonialism, but many may find it provocative.

With this volume we do not intend to imply that all German-speaking writers, artists, and thinkers in the past two centuries have been enmeshed in the kind of "us versus them" thinking that supports an imperialist imagination. Yet, these contributions leave no doubt as to the pervasiveness of the model. They reveal the connections between German concepts of nation and German concepts of colony; they investigate "Germanness" from the perspective of the "racial" and cultural ideas that developed from the eighteenth century onward and continue to affect the laws of German citizenship. They point to continuities—for example, in the fantasies of

Germans' special ability to cultivate and colonize, in fantasies of order, industry, and benign paternal rule—and to historical discontinuities that challenged these fantasies, such as the wars of displacement or extermination leveled against various African populations; British allegations and the loss of colonies during World War I; the revelation of atrocities committed during the Holocaust; and, finally, the sometimes quite subtle xenophobia that persists in Germany even today. A focus on the imagination, on Germany's relationship to its imaginary others, may help us understand how colonialist thinking came into being before colonial practice, how it survived colonialism, and how the specifics of the German colonial and postcolonial experience facilitated the survival of thought structures that are still discernible today. It may help us resolve the question of whether German colonization "formed part of a much more extensive historical process entailing the partial Westernization of the entire world," as Arthur Knoll and Lewis Gann maintain (xiii), or whether it exhibited a specific line of development that led from late-eighteenth-century patriotism to German imperialism under Bismarck and from thence to Hitler, as both Hannah Arendt and Helmut Bley have proposed. In 1991, in the wake of aggression directed at minorities in Germany, Sheila Mysorekar, a member of the Initiative of Black Germans, declared in *Der Spiegel* that Germans "have not progressed one step beyond colonial times" (23 December 1991, 56–57). We hope that scholarly efforts such as those in this volume will help to render verdicts such as hers soon obsolete.

Part 1
Colonial Discourse in the New Empire

Nietzsche's Colonialist Imagination: Nueva Germania, Good Europeanism, and Great Politics

Robert C. Holub

It may come as a surprise that Nietzsche had any views at all on the growing German colonial movement of his times. After all, he reminds us repeatedly that his thinking is untimely, that he does not follow current events, and that he does not even read the newspaper. His statement in *Ecce Homo* that some people are born posthumously (6: 298) was undoubtedly self-referential.[1] In fact, however, he often expressed positions on the central issues of his time: although his remarks are neither extensive nor particularly well informed, we find frequent reference to contemporary concerns, such as socialism and workers' organizations, the growing women's movement as it was spreading across Europe (see Holub "Women's Question"), and antisemitism as it coalesced in Germany in

---

1. He also includes this remark in the preface to *The Antichrist* (6: 167), and in a letter written to Carl Fuchs shortly before the composition of *Ecce Homo* he remarks: "Some are born posthumously" (8: 403). Although parenthetical citations refer to the *Studienausgabe* of Nietzsche's works, I have consulted the following translations, modifying them when accuracy was wanting: *Human, All Too Human* (*Menschliches, Allzumenschliches,* 1878–80), tr. R. J. Hollingdale (Cambridge: Cambridge UP, 1986); *Daybreak* (*Morgenröthe,* 1881), tr. R. J. Hollingdale (Cambridge: Cambridge UP, 1982); *The Gay Science* (*Die fröhliche Wissenschaft,* books I–IV, 1882; book V, 1887), tr. Walter Kaufmann (New York: Vintage, 1974); *Beyond Good and Evil* (*Jenseits von Gut und Böse,* 1886), tr. Helen Zimmern (Buffalo: Prometheus Books, 1989); *The Genealogy of Morals* (*Zur Genealogie der Moral,* 1887), tr. Francis Golffing, with *The Birth of Tragedy* (Garden City: Doubleday, 1956); *Ecce Homo* (*Ecce Homo,* 1908), tr. R. J. Hollingdale (Harmondsworth: Penguin, 1979); *The Portable Nietzsche,* tr. and ed. Walter Kaufmann (New York: Viking, 1954) (includes *Thus Spoke Zarathustra, Twilight of the Idols, The Antichrist,* and *Nietzsche contra Wagner,* plus selections from other writings, notebooks, and correspondence).

1880 (see Holub "Jewish Question").[2] His comments on the colonial movement, like his remarks on most social issues, are somewhat sketchy and do not evidence an intimate knowledge of the subject. Moreover, they have to be understood in the context of the nineteenth-century discourse on colonialism. In the books and essays that appear today on German colonialism, scholars usually focus on the German procurement and governance of African and Pacific colonies from 1884, when Germany began to acquire Togoland, Cameroon, Southwest Africa, German East Africa, and New Guinea,[3] until 1919, when it lost its small colonial empire. Most accounts dealing with the 1870s and 1880s concentrate on a limited number of topics: the debates internal to Germany, the founding of various colonial societies that agitated for an overseas empire, or the men who themselves traveled to the colonies and made German imperialism a reality. Obviously the discussions and events that ushered in the era of German colonial power reached their height during the years that Nietzsche was composing his major works, and they were significant for him, at the very least as a background for his own comments on the course of German global politics and its relationship to a problematic nationhood.

But the colonial mentality hardly exhausts itself in this official story of colonization. Just as important for Germany, and more important for Nietzsche, were efforts of small groups of Germans to colonize other parts of the globe. The main way in which Nietzsche became involved in colonialist discourse was through one of these efforts, undertaken by Bernhard Förster, who married Nietzsche's sister Elisabeth on 22 May 1885 (Richard Wagner's birthday)[4] and moved with her to Paraguay in February of the next year. Indeed, Förster and others of his ilk appear to have believed that the recently established German Empire was moving too slowly and too hesitantly toward colonialism. In a work published in 1886 Förster emphasizes that he had broached the topic at an earlier date, but only in the mid-1880s did it become easier to speak of these matters in public (*Deutsche Colonien* 1). He also stresses the un-German proclivities of the dominant political scene. Förster's remarks make us conscious that colonialism in general became an acceptable part of discourse in the German political public sphere only after 1880, and that many colonialists

---

2. My recent monograph on Nietzsche, which is a preliminary study for a longer work, endeavors to locate him more firmly in the context of nineteenth-century thought and society.

3. In 1897 Germany acquired Kiaochow; in 1899 Samoa.

4. The significance of this day for the wedding did not escape Nietzsche, who wrote to Franz Overbeck on 7 May 1885: "My sister will be married on the 22nd of May; you understand the date" (7: 46). Nietzsche had been estranged from Wagner and the Wagnerians—at least in his own mind—since the inauguration of Bayreuth in 1876.

considered themselves, and not the German Empire, to be the true bearers of Germanness. It is not hard to understand why Förster held such views. He considered the Germany of his time too Jewish, too urban, and too materialist; his ideology, which is part of a larger reaction to the advent of modernity to which his brother-in-law—in a different manner—also objected, is thus simultaneously conservative in many of its tenets and utopian in its tenor. It combined themes of Wagnerian derivation, such as vegetarianism, antisemitism, and antivivisectionism, with a quasi-socialist longing for community, a rejection of private property, and a Protestant reliance on productive, hard work. Because the Germany of his time appeared no longer to favor these positions, colonialists like Förster could not depend on the "step-fatherland" as their only support. It was not important for him that a colony be controlled by Germany, but rather that the colony be thoroughly German: "Whether colonies are founded in direct dependence on the German Empire or under foreign domination seems to me a matter of indifference: a colony that develops with vitality will know how to preserve its national and economic rights under a foreign flag, and a colonial land politically dependent on the motherland will, if it progresses with vigor, in any case come to the point where it frees itself and becomes independent" (*Deutsche Colonien* 8). Förster's need to escape Germany was therefore a peculiar type of self-exile: it was meant not so much as a rejection of German nationalism and the German nation as an affirmation of a more authentic nationalist spirit.

Both Förster's colonial venture and the official colonialism of the Second Empire thus revolve around a nationalist sentiment that Nietzsche abhorred and that predisposed him against all varieties of the colonialist mentality. With regard to Förster's particular project, however, his assessment was negatively overdetermined. Not only was Förster a fervent advocate of Aryan supremacy; not only did Förster take away Elisabeth, Nietzsche's "beloved llama"; he was also associated with the dreaded Wagnerian cultural cause. Indeed, Förster's first discussion of colonization for a wider audience appeared in the *Bayreuther Blätter* in 1883. A confused concoction composed of cultural criticism, racist prejudice, and Christian ethics, it begins by connecting Wagner to the question of colonization: "Wagner could become the unique artist, the purveyor of our hearts, he can become the reformer of his mistreated people above all because his being represents the most successful, the most fortunate, and generally the most valid incorporation of the type of the Aryan race" ("Ein Deutschland" 44–45). Because colonization is ultimately concerned with preserving German culture, which is simultaneously a matter of the health and vitality of the *Volk,* Förster continues, Wagner's activity coincides with his own in proposing the establishment of German colonies. Supplementary to this nationalist and cultural justification for colonization, Förster also supplies an explanation that Nietzsche could validate. In what may be an argument drawn from his future brother-in-law's writings, Förster contends that every organism, if it is vital and viable, exhibits the tendency toward the expansion, the enlargement, and the augmentation of its being. Arguing by analogy, he maintains that Germany, if it is to remain vital, must seek to expand itself, enlarge itself, and augment itself through the founding of colonies. In Nietzsche's notebooks written at about the time of this essay we find the following remark: "The individual is an ovum. Colony formation is the task for every individual" (10: 664). And in a passage written a few years earlier he notes, "A society must strive to become over-abundant [*überreich*] (over-population), in order to produce a new one (colonies), in order to divide into two self-sufficient beings. Attempts to give an organism duration without the goal of reproduction destroy it, are unnatural—as are today's clever 'nations' of Europe" (9: 491). In one regard, Nietzsche's infrequent comments on colonies in his notebooks thus exhibit a framework similar to Förster's. Although he rejects the national and racial superiority of Germany, he reasons, as Förster does, that colonization is a natural proclivity of groups, analogous to the biologically based reproduction of an organism.

The story of Förster's colonizing efforts has been told several times (Podach 139–76; Peters 85–125; Janz 415–21 et passim), most recently by Ben Macintyre in his journalistic account *Forgotten Fatherland*. Nietzsche's reaction, however, has been generally ignored, or else reduced to a wholly negative assessment. In fact he was not as ill-disposed toward the Paraguayan settlement as one might have anticipated. Indeed, at one point he appears to have considered himself a potential emigrant. A central factor in Nietzsche's thinking about a possible change of domicile was climate, a veritable obsession during the last decade of his sane life. His letters from the 1880s are replete with remarks about the percentage of sun and cloudiness, barometric readings, precipitation amounts, and atmospheric "electricity" in various locations he was considering for domiciles. In February of 1883, shortly after Förster had left for South America, he wrote to Heinrich Köselitz that "the old Deluge-Europe [*Sündflut-Europa*] will kill me yet: but perhaps some one will help me and drag me to the highlands of Mexico" (6: 333). The thought of emigration persisted, and in a letter to his sister from the following August he complains of the exceptionally poor weather, in particular the heavy cloud cover, which makes him "another person, morose, extremely malicious against myself, as well as against others." His solution to the problem is "still" (*immer noch*) "the valley of Oaxaca in Mexico, which has ca. 33 cloudy days in a year, the rest of the time day and night pure, cloudless Engadine weather, ca. 220!; while Sils has 80 pleasant days in a year. (The altitude is the same as here [he is writing from Sils]; there is a Swiss colony; the costs are exceptionally inexpensive.)" (6: 431).[5] It is therefore not completely inconceivable that Nietzsche himself, in times of the great physical discomfort he attributed to the European climate, considered the possibility of emigration. In July 1885, a few months after Förster's return to Germany, he wrote to Overbeck that he had many worries, "to be sure also a few strange desires, especially concerning the new world in Paraguay. At a moment's notice Europe can become impossible for me; and think of it, perhaps there in that distant land there is a tree branch for such a lost bird like me" (7: 61–62). It is difficult to ascertain how serious Nietzsche was about leaving Europe, but if we take him at his own word, he ultimately rejected any thoughts of emigration on chiefly climatological grounds:

> I have considered extensively the thought of colonization in Paraguay, not without the ulterior motive of whether I might not find for myself an asylum there. With regard to this prospect I have come to an unconditioned "no"; my climatic needs contradict. Otherwise there is a great deal that is reasonable in the entire matter; Paraguay is a wonderful piece of earth for German farmers—and a Westphalian or Pomeranian can sail there in good confidence as long as he does not have exorbitant expectations. (7: 97)

In the same letter Nietzsche also expresses concern that Paraguay might not be the right place for his sister and brother-in-law either, and that he, like his mother, is extremely apprehensive about the entire matter. But Nietzsche's initial reactions are quite favorable, and had Förster chosen a drier, sunnier climate for his New Germany, it is possible that this self-proclaimed "good European" would have become one more of the millions of Germans to leave the fatherland for the New World in the second half of the nineteenth century.[6]

---

5. In a draft of a letter to Overbeck Nietzsche asks: "Should I consider resettlement in Mexico?" (6: 426). It is perhaps interesting to note that Nietzsche had determined on the basis of his "climatological studies" that Barcelona was the best European city for him (6: 350). That this obsession with climate was not a passing fancy is indicated by a letter of June 1888 to Meta von Salis in which he provides a chart of five Italian cities that includes for the month of January the number of bright days (*heitere Tage*) and days of rain, and the percentage of cloudiness (8: 336).

6. Obviously climate was not the only factor that prevented Nietzsche from emigrating. Besides the ideological differences he harbored with Förster, we can imagine that an educated European like Nietzsche would not have felt very comfortable in the woods without a library, with few books, and without the possibility of intellectual engagement. He indicated as much to his mother: "For myself I am even too aristocratically minded to place myself legally and socially on the same level as 20 families of farmers: as he [Förster] has it in the program." Significant perhaps is that he recognizes that the person with the strongest will and the most

During the last four years of his sane life, Nietzsche began to pay attention to colonial affairs in Paraguay, even reading newspapers (a phenomenon of modern life he despised) to gather information (7: 172, 293). His interest in South American colonization, and his attempt to assess the possibilities for the future success or failure of Förster's colony, may have been motivated by more than simply an interest in his sister's welfare. Although most commentators have claimed that Nietzsche wisely rejected offers to invest in the colonial enterprise, it is not clear that he did so because of either the principled objections he harbored or his skepticism about its prospects. The evidence is sketchy, but suggests other motives were at play. Elisabeth must have approached her brother with an investment proposition while she and Förster were still in Germany, since Nietzsche mentions it in a letter to her in Naumburg shortly before her departure for South America (7: 147). Once she arrived in Paraguay, she approached him with a concrete investment plan to purchase land and cattle, and informed him that he could keep the livestock himself or have Förster and herself integrate it into their herd, which will be branded "Eli." In total she requests from him 6,000 marks. She also proposes an alternative plan: she and her husband are prepared to borrow the same sum of money at 8 percent interest. Two days later Förster writes to "his dear brother-in-law Zarathustra" and includes a map of the area so that Nietzsche can see where his property would be (3,4: 213–15). Nietzsche appears to have been at least mildly interested in such an investment, but after consulting with his Basel colleague Overbeck (7: 272), who was overseeing his precarious pension in Basel, he decided an investment was too risky (7: 278). A short time later Nietzsche had another opportunity to invest in Förster's colony. In late November of 1886, Förster put his signature to an agreement that secured land for Nueva Germania, and in the next few months, buoyed by optimism and prospects for enormous success, Elisabeth and her husband set about attracting emigrants and capital to their colony. She was able to secure money from her mother and various friends, as well as from Förster's family, and in this context she must have again written to her brother.[7] He responds that he is entirely disin-

---

cleverness will gain the upper hand, and that German men of learning like himself are badly prepared in these two areas. He also objects to Förster's dogmatic vegetarianism, believing that carnivores make better colonizers: "a vegetarian diet like the one Dr. F[örster] wants makes such people only more excitable and bad-mooded. Look at the meat-eating English: they are until now the race that has founded colonies the best. A phlegmatic disposition and roast beef—up to now they were the recipe for such 'enterprises'" (7: 54). Nietzsche's repeated discussions of why he should not leave Europe for Paraguay indicate, however, that he must have taken the proposition of emigration fairly seriously.

7. We have Nietzsche's response, but not Elisabeth's letter requesting money.

clined to give any money because his own position is too insecure and theirs is not yet secure enough. But he adds that on the suggestion of their mother he has made 800 thaler available to them that was tied up in the house in Naumburg.[8] As a postscript to the letter he sends his best wishes to Förster on the occasion of his land acquisition, adding the maxim, "anyone who possesses, is also possessed" (*wer besitzt, ist auch besessen*), which carries the same pun in English as in German (8: 85). Elisabeth expresses disappointment that her brother "wants to remain a poor man" and annoyance that he could think she would advise him to invest in something that was less than a sure thing.[9] She presents the investment as a unique situation with a finite window of opportunity since "the colonists in our colony will increase the value of their land threefold and fourfold, but through their own personal efforts." A few months later she gives him a piece of land (3,6: 296), but the remainder of their correspondence contains no mention of investment.[10]

What do these refused investment opportunities tell us about Nietz-

---

8. From the correspondence it is not entirely clear to whom this money belonged. It appears that Nietzsche has freed up some part of Elisabeth's share in the house, since in her response to her brother she expresses disappointment that he has not seen fit to invest.

9. Of course it was anything but a sure thing. Förster committed suicide in 1889 when he failed to keep his part of the contractual agreement, which committed him to attracting 140 families to Nueva Germania, and a few years later Elisabeth severed ties with the colonialist project, turning her attention to a more promising and personal venture: promoting the celebrity of her insane brother's works.

10. The enmity between Nietzsche and his sister has been much overstated in the literature. It is certain that Nietzsche suppressed some rather aggressive feelings toward both his sister and his mother. We certainly see evidence of aggression in the various draft letters to Elisabeth, but it is not unimportant that the actual letters usually have a much different tone. He continued to send his sister his published works and to keep her informed about his activities and mutual friends. For her part Elisabeth harbored genuinely positive feelings for her brother. Although some critics have claimed that Elisabeth was trying to wring money out of her poor brother for an enterprise she knew would fail, the evidence in letters does not support such a claim. Rather, Elisabeth continues throughout to respect her brother and his works, although she, like Förster, appears to believe that as an academic and philosopher, he was much removed from the practical life they had chosen. Elisabeth is generous in her praise of her brother (although sometimes one wonders how well she understood his writings), concerned with his health, and generally complimentary to him. In a letter written in January 1888 she comments enthusiastically about his latest musical composition, "Hymn on Life" ("Hymnus an das Leben"), and even suggests, probably with some irony, that it could perhaps become the national anthem of Nueva Germania (3, 6: 146). Although she objects to Georg Brandes and his promotion of her brother, possibly because Brandes was a Jew, she nonetheless expresses delight ("In my heart I am boundlessly happy for you") that through Brandes Nietzsche is beginning to win the acclaim that he deserves. There were no doubt strains in the relationship starting with the affair around Lou Salomé, but the proximity of the siblings should not be turned into an animosity that was not the dominant tone in their relationship.

sche's views of colonization? Do they reflect his own precarious financial situation or a distrust of the colonial enterprise? Are they evidence for a dislike of Förster's colony, or of colonizing efforts in general? Did his contact with Nueva Germania affect his views on politics and the geopolitical goals of Germany and Europe? These questions are difficult to answer with certitude. We know for certain that Nietzsche disliked the nationalist, socialist, and antisemitic ideology behind Nueva Germania, and to the extent that the actual colonialist enterprise entailed one or more of these reactive tendencies, Nietzsche cannot be considered a proponent of German colonialism. Nonetheless, Nietzsche is hardly an opponent of colonialism, and with regard to Förster's enterprise, he remained surprisingly affirmative. Supported by his sister's overly optimistic reports on the success of the undertaking, Nietzsche frequently expresses admiration and a certain amount of pride in the colony. As late as June 1888 Nietzsche informs Köselitz of a long passage in his sister's letter describing the ceremonious inauguration of Nueva Germania, adding, "The matter is really taking on a magnificent dimension" (8: 332). Only in the last few months of his sane life did Nietzsche begin to have serious doubts about the soundness of Förster's business dealings. In one of his last letters to Overbeck from Christmas of 1888 he remarks that "in Paraguay things are as bad as possible. The Germans who were lured over there are furious and demanding their money back—but there is none. Brutalities have occurred; I fear the worst" (8: 549). Since Nietzsche opens this letter with the statement that "in two months I will be the first name on earth," it is difficult to know how conscious he was of the actual situation in Paraguay, but it is evident that before he fell completely into insanity he recognized the imminent collapse of Förster's project.

Nietzsche's personal involvement with the colonial imagination has a philosophical counterpart in his writings. His contact with Nueva Germania through his sister was, as we have seen, marked by a certain ambivalence; although Nietzsche did not disagree with colonization in principle, he objected to many principles on which this particular colony was founded. Nietzsche's own thinking about colonies, which was never very developed, is contained primarily in remarks surrounding two slogans that became prominent in his writings during the 1880s: the "good European" and "great politics." The first of these slogans appears earlier in Nietzsche's thought. In *Human, All Too Human* Nietzsche argues that the development toward a European union is an inevitable consequence of modernity. Working against this Europeanizing tendency are nationalism and national hostilities, which by comparison are artificial and benefit ruling dynasties, as well as "certain classes of business and society." Nietzsche continues, "once one has recognized this fact, one should not be afraid to proclaim oneself simply a *good European* and actively to work for the amalgamation of nations" (2: 309). In other works Nietzsche uses the "good European" as a foil to the detested features of contemporary life. In a note from 1884 he writes that the good European is "against equality, against moral tartuffism, against Christianity and God" (11: 150). In the preface to *Beyond Good and Evil* good Europeans are opposed to Jesuits and democrats, as well as to Germans, and likened to "free spirits." The European is synonymous with the "supra-national" (11: 229), and Europeans are the "super-race" (*Über-Rasse*) (11: 136); Europeanism signals the overcoming of various epistemological, ethical, and political transgressions of the nineteenth century:

> Looking at nature as if it were proof of the goodness and governance of a god; interpreting history in honor of some divine reason, as a continual testimony of a moral world order and ultimate moral purposes; interpreting one's own experiences as pious people have long enough interpreted theirs, as if everything were providential, a hint, designed and ordained for the sake of the salvation of the soul—that is *all over* now, that has man's conscience *against* it, that is considered indecent and dishonest by every more refined conscience—mendaciousness, feminism, weakness, and cowardice. In this severity, if anywhere, we are *good* Europeans and heirs of Europe's longest and most courageous self-overcoming. (3: 600)

In this passage we find an unusual mixture of qualities possessed by the good European: antireligious and antiprovidential, the "Europeans of the day after tomorrow" (5: 151) are also beyond ethics and opposed to modern social degenerations such as feminism. The "higher men" that Nietzsche foresees emerging to dominate European affairs will be entrusted with revitalizing characteristics that persist subterraneously. In various passages Nietzsche suggests that some core of Europeanness has been temporarily negated by Christianity and its attendant morality. In contrast to the Greeks, in whom "morality thrived in the *ruling* castes" (11: 56), in Europe the hypocrisy he associates with Christianity has emanated from the lower classes, from slaves and oppressed peoples. Occasionally in European history—for example in the Renaissance or in figures such as Napoleon—we have witnessed a reemergence of the proper European spirit. For the most part, however, the good European, like his cousin the superman (*Übermensch*), is a project for the future,[11] a higher type of human being whom we must consciously create.

---

11. Nietzsche makes it clear that the reemergence of good Europeans involves an overcoming of nationalism in *Beyond Good and Evil:* "Indeed, I can imagine dull, sluggish races which, even in our fast-moving Europe, would need half a century to overcome such atavistic attacks of patriotism and cleaving to one's native soil and to be restored to reason, I mean to 'good Europeanism'" (5: 180–81).

The expansion of Nietzsche's reflections from German and European problems into world affairs occurs only in his writings of the 1880s. In an unusual passage from his pre-*Zarathustra* period, Nietzsche comments in *Daybreak* on the miserable conditions of the working class in Europe, claiming that no ameliorative measures could turn this form of slavery into something desirable. His solution, which was the remedy realized by millions of Germans during the late nineteenth century, is emigration: "Outside of Europe," he insists, "Europe's virtues will accompany these workers on their wanderings; and that which at home began to degenerate into dangerous ill-humor and inclination for crime will, once abroad, acquire a wild beautiful naturalness and be called heroism" (3: 184–85). If we substitute "Germany" for "Europe," the sentiments here approximate the reasoning we find a few years later in Förster's essays and pamphlets. Nietzsche's compassion for the workers, his opposition to state and business, and his deprecation of Europe mimic colonialist rhetoric. Although one can hardly imagine that the lower classes to which Nietzsche refers are included in his notion of "good Europeans," they do appear to have inborn European characteristics Nietzsche hopes will thrive in foreign climes. He even suggests, as Förster does later, that colonization could have a salutary impact on Europe. The benefit, however, would not necessarily result from the repatriation of the workers, but rather from the clearing of the air, the eradication of overpopulation, and the elimination of the European habit of overreflection. Nietzsche also suggests that to solve the problem of a depleted work force, Europe could import Chinese, who will bring with them "the modes of life and thought suitable to industrious ants" and thus "contribute to the blood of restless and fretful Europe something of Asiatic calm and contemplativeness and—what is probably needed most—Asiatic *perseverance*" (3: 185).

In this early reflection on colonization, Nietzsche's focus is ultimately the health of Europe. In later passages, most of which were composed after 1884 and thus after the actual beginnings of the German colonial empire, it is clear that Nietzsche's thoughts turn to a European subjugation of the world. Toward the middle of the decade we find more frequent comments about European colonies. In his notebooks in the spring of 1884 he writes: "The way Europeans found colonies proves their predatory nature" (11: 56); "Europeans betray themselves in the way in which they have colonized" (11: 53); and "one can assess the character of Europeans according to their relationship to foreign countries, in colonization: extremely cruel" (11: 61). Here we again encounter the suggestion that Christian ethics and moral platitudes are a veneer, that a European essence manifests itself only in unusual circumstances and outside of the continent, which has been too long subjected to the "civilizing" influence of Christianity and a morality of pity and compassion. Although these statements, taken out of context, could be employed to condemn European colonialism, Nietzsche is actually affirming the cruelty and aggressiveness of imperialism. We should note that the German term Nietzsche uses for "predatory nature" (*Raubtier-Natur*) appears in other Nietzschean contexts without any pejorative sense. In many writings from the 1880s the beast of prey (*Raubtier*) is contrasted with the despised herd, the domesticated animal that human beings have become under the leveling influences of the Judeo-Christian heritage and a politics of democracy. We must evaluate similarly Nietzsche's identification of the good European with the criminal, who also has a positive valence in Nietzsche's works.[12]

Other texts from the 1880s indicate that these colonialist criminals and predators are in fact synonymous with the "good Europeans." Sometimes the European colonial project is justified in terms of a biologistic analogy. In the notebooks from 1888 Nietzsche claims:

> The right [*Recht*] to punish (or to social self-defense) has become the word "justice" [*Recht*], indeed, only through a misuse: a right is acquired through contracts—but self-protection and self-defense are not based on a contract. At least a people ought to consider with just as much justification its need for conquest, its craving for power, as a right, whether it be with weapons, with trade, commerce, and colonization—a right to growth, so to speak. A society that rejects war and conquest for all times and instinctively is in decline: it is ripe for democracy and shopkeeper regimes. (13: 379)

In this passage Nietzsche contrasts democracy and the shopkeeper mentality—frequently described derogatorily in *Zarathustra*—with aggressive colonialism, interpreting European expansion as a natural right to self-preservation. In other remarks Nietzsche uses a historical view to discuss the desired course for European domination of the world. In *The Gay Sci-*

---

12. For example, in notes made in preparation for the fourth part of *Zarathustra* Nietzsche wrote: "the good European 'I have committed all crimes. I love the most dangerous thoughts and the most dangerous women'" (11: 348). Beginning in the late 1870s, in much of Nietzsche's writings the criminal becomes synonymous with the original thinker, the destroyer of accepted norms, or the creative man; the fact that a person is called a "criminal" is society's method of concealing and canceling this originality and iconoclasm. "One conceals that in the criminal there can be demonstrated a great deal of courage and originality of thought, independence" (9: 127). Or in *Zarathustra,* where Nietzsche makes the etymological connection between breaking (*brechen)* and committing a crime (*Verbrechen*): "Behold the good and the just! Whom do they hate most? The man who breaks their tables of values, the breaker [*Brecher*], the lawbreaker [*Verbrecher* = criminal]; yet he is the creator" (4: 26).

ence, under the general heading "Our faith that Europe will become more virile," Nietzsche praises Napoleon as a continuator of the Renaissance, a destroyer of nationalism, and an enemy of modern ideas; he is someone who

> brought back again a whole slab of antiquity, perhaps even the decisive piece, the piece of granite. And who knows whether this slab of antiquity might not finally become master again over the national movement, and whether it must not become the heir and continuator of Napoleon in an affirmative sense; for what he wanted was one unified Europe, as is known—as mistress of the earth. (3: 610)

Finally, in other rare passages Nietzsche's thoughts include concrete references to geopolitical considerations. In a reflection from the summer of 1885 Nietzsche looks past national wars and newly created empires to his real concern: a united Europe. Citing the forerunners in this quest for unity ("Napoleon, Göthe, Heinrich Heine, Stendhal, Beethoven, Schopenhauer," and perhaps Richard Wagner [11: 583]),[13] Nietzsche sketches an economic situation that is already familiar to us. Commerce and trade, as well as monetary concerns, will compel the disintegration of national boundaries, as European nations pursue a greater part in world trade and commerce. But further measures will have to be undertaken when the stakes rise.

> In order to enter into the struggle for the rule of the earth with a good chance of success—it is obvious against whom this struggle must be waged—Europe will probably need to reach a serious "understanding" with England: it needs England's colonies for that struggle just as much as today's Germany, to practice its new role as mediator and broker, needs Holland's colonies. No one really believes any longer that England itself is strong enough to continue to play out its old role for another fifty years; it is being destroyed by the impossibility of keeping the *homines novi* out of the government, and one must not have such a change of parties in order that such protracted things—today one has to be a soldier first not to lose his credit as a merchant. Enough: in this, as in other things, the next century will be found in the footsteps of Napoleon, the first and most anticipatory man of modern times. (11: 584)

---

13. Nietzsche's list of his contemporary "good Europeans" includes Jakob Burckhardt, Hans von Bülow, Hippolyte Taine, Gottfried Keller, Bruno Bauer, and Richard Wagner, all of whom, as he boasts in a letter to Georg Brandes, are his readers (8: 205).

Nietzsche's fragmentary vision, although confused and sketchy, is clear about certain priorities. At stake is the domination of the earth by a European, not a national, ruling caste (11:72), which will assert its domination, as Napoleon did, through military conquest in order to secure economic supremacy. These "good Europeans" will have no need for a "public sphere" or parliaments (11: 584); casting off the veneer of civility resulting from the Christian ethics of brotherly love, they will rule by authoritarian means that may well entail the conquest and subjugation of peoples.

The tasks Nietzsche sets for his "good Europeans" can be summed up in another Nietzschean concept: "great politics." But we have to exercise caution when regarding this notion in Nietzsche's works. "Great politics" was appropriated by Nietzsche from the political sphere existing in Germany during the Bismarck era, and often he employs it to refer to the foreign policies of the Second Empire, rather than to his own, more grandiose designs.[14] The initial instances of "great politics" in Nietzsche's writings are thus informed by his own ambivalent relationship to the Second Empire and to the nation-state as a political entity. In *Human, All Too Human,* for example, the preoccupation with "great politics" diverts energy from other endeavors in which a people might engage. Nietzsche reasons that even worse than this sacrifice of time and energy is the loss of individualism that politicization brings with it: "There occurs a spectacle played out continually in a hundred thousand simultaneous acts: every efficient, industrious, intelligent, energetic man belonging to such a people lusting after political laurels is dominated by this lust and no longer belongs wholly to his own domain, as he formerly did" (2: 315). Nietzsche's objection to Bismarckian "great politics" is thus an extension of his objection to politics and nationalism in general. He closes this aphorism, entitled "Great Politics and What They Cost," questioning whether the "inflorescence and pomp of the whole" is really worth the sacrifice, especially "if all the nobler, tenderer, more spiritual plants and growths in which its soil was previously so rich have to be sacrificed to this coarse and gaudy flower of the nation" (2: 316).

Like most concepts that Nietzsche develops in his writings, "great

---

14. As Peter Bergmann points out, the term in English may hide the associations that Nietzsche was trying to counter, as well as those he was trying to promote: "In German the term has a familiar, majestic ring, one rooted in the then fashionable conviction of the primacy of foreign policy, of a higher form of politics specifically addressing European and world power conflicts in contradistinction to a presumably lesser form of politics dealing with internal matters" (162). Looking back at the Wilhelminian period in the 1920s, German historians published documents under the title "The Great Politics of the European Cabinets, 1871–1914" (*Die grosse Politik der europäischen Kabinette, 1817–1914*), and this usage captures the semantic field in which we should locate the term.

politics" in this negative sense fits into a complex mosaic of terms and ideas. It refers not only to current events and to a particular psychological constellation, but also to a system of values and to a religious outlook. In his later work, when Nietzsche was most concerned with the development and mutual conditioning of morality and religion, he locates great politics of the unfavorable, Bismarckian variety within the nexus of the Judeo-Christian heritage and an ethics of *ressentiment*. In *The Genealogy of Morals* "great politics" is equated with a politics of revenge, part of a Judeo-Christian value system that has come to dominate modern civilization and has furtively manifested itself in the nationalism and petty political attitudes of Bismarck's Germany (5: 269). Because many of the phenomena Nietzsche identifies are symptoms of the identical value system, he can easily move back and forth from religious and ethical reflections to comments on current politics. Thus in *Twilight of the Idols* Nietzsche embarks on a discussion of the "spiritualization of sensuality" and the emergence of Christian "love," but winds up speaking about the foreign policy of the Second Empire. Just as a political party needs oppositional parties in order to achieve self-definition, so too Germany requires enemies, both external and internal, in order to assert itself. Great politics is tantamount to Judeo-Christian ethics translated into geopolitical terms: "A new creation in particular—the new *Reich,* for example—needs enemies more than friends: in opposition alone does it *feel* itself necessary, in opposition alone does it *become* necessary" (6: 84). The modernity that Nietzsche opposed with his "good European" appeared in many guises, and as the 1880s progressed the "great politics" proclaimed by the newly unified Germany became for Nietzsche one of modernity's most loathsome manifestations.

At about the time that Germany was acquiring its first colonial possessions and Nietzsche was being introduced to colonization through his brother-in-law, we encounter the first mention of an alternative type of "great politics." In the positive, Nietzschean sense, we find its first occurrence in the notes Nietzsche penned during the late spring and early summer of 1885, when he comments laconically: "Furthermore, the higher Europeans, precursors of *great politics*" (11: 532). It is a bit difficult to tell what Nietzsche has in mind with his "great politics" at this point, but it is evident that the term is already closely associated with the elitist Europeanism he advocated throughout the 1880s. In notes written a few months previously, possibly composed in connection with a plan for a continuation of his *Untimely Meditations,* Nietzsche lists five topics and an introduction that include many of his favorite themes of these years: "hierarchy of men," "knowledge as the will to power," "beyond good and evil," "the hidden artists," and "the hammer." Among these topics is "great politics" (11: 484). In another note from 1885 he endows "great politics" with class distinctions and a direct geopolitical dimension: "The new philosopher can emerge only in connection with a ruling caste, as its highest spiritualization. Great politics, world hegemony up close; complete lack of principles for it" (11: 533–34). This field of association continues to surround "great politics" in Nietzsche's writings and correspondence for the next three and a half years, although the term itself coexists uneasily in many texts with the negatively valenced, Bismarckian "great politics."

Nietzsche's own notion of "great politics" gradually begins to predominate in his writings of the late 1880s, becoming one of a series of themes that encapsulates the final phase of Nietzschean thought. As such, it is closely related to other concepts of this period and serves as the shorthand for an antinationalist politics that has world-historical, as well as global, dimensions. In a passage from his last notebook, composed in December 1888, Nietzsche entitles the first page "great politics" and explicates as follows:

> I bring war. *Not* between nation and nation: I have no word to express my contempt for the despicable interest-politics of European dynasties, which makes a principle, indeed nearly a duty out of the incitement to arrogant selfishness of peoples against each other. *Not* between classes. For we have no higher classes, therefore also no lower ones: what is today on top in society is condemned physiologically and moreover—what is proof of this—has become so impoverished in its spirit, so insecure, that it professes the *counterprinciple* of a higher type of man without scruples.
>
> I bring war directly at odds with all the absurd coincidences of nation, class, race, occupation, education, culture: a war as if between rising and falling, between the will to life and *vengeance* against life, between uprightness and deceitful mendacity. (13: 637)

"Great politics" in the Nietzschean sense of the term is a political program that institutes his philosophical regime. It cancels nationalist and class-based conflicts, but eliminates neither domination nor differences, since it advocates a hierarchical order (*Rangordnung*) based on Nietzschean philosophical tenets. In a continuation of this passage, "great politics" assumes a more ominous stance with regard to humanity. In keeping with the biologistic turn in his later writings, Nietzsche advocates the breeding of a higher form of human being, and his wording slips into a rhetorical register that is unfortunately familiar to us from eugenic nightmares of the twentieth century. He demands "merciless severity against anything degenerate and parasitic on life—against anything that destroys, poisons, slanders, ruins . . . and that sees in the destruction of life the indication of a higher type of soul." At another point he writes that great politics "puts a ruthless end to everything degenerate and parasitic" (13: 638). In such passages Nietzsche's "great politics" converges with the more familiar colonialist imagination. Although it is too laden with biological assumptions to be considered a direct reference to any specific venture in foreign policy, "great politics" nonetheless contains imperatives for global action and harbors implications for the entire human race. Despite his rejection of the antisemitism and nationalism on which much colonialist rhetoric was based, Nietzsche's rhetoric resonates with the writings of contemporaries he would have otherwise despised.

Infrequently in his published works Nietzsche made the connection between "great politics" and the colonialist imagination more explicit. The locus classicus for this connection occurs appropriately in *Beyond Good and Evil,* where the struggle for world domination, for the hegemony of Europe over a vast colonial empire, is viewed as an essential question for the nineteenth century. Nietzsche observes a "paralysis of will" spread unevenly across Europe. This "European disease" is most prevalent where civilization has prevailed longest; significantly France, and not Germany, is deemed the worst of the infirm nations, while in Germany, especially northern Germany, and in England, Spain, and Corsica, Nietzsche finds that "the power to will and to persist" is somewhat stronger. Surprisingly, Russia, "that immense middle empire where Europe as it were flows back to Asia," exhibits the most strength in Nietzschean terms. It is difficult to determine precisely what is driving these evaluations, but it may be that the nations and regions Nietzsche deems strongest in terms of will are those that have been least affected by the domesticating ethical practices of Judeo-Christian doctrine. Although Nietzsche foresees only an augmentation of sickness, with its attendant "parliamentary imbecility" and "the obligation of every one to read his newspaper at breakfast," he has hopes that Russia will become such a danger that European nations, in order to counter the Russian threat, will be compelled to band together and carry out their appointed task:

> . . . to *acquire one will,* by means of a new caste ruling over Europe, a persistent, dreadful will of its own, that can set its aims thousands of years ahead; so that the long spun-out comedy of its petty-stateism, and its dynastic as well as its democratic many-willed-ness, might finally be brought to a close. The time for petty politics is past; the next century will bring the struggle for the dominion of the world— the *compulsion* to great politics. (5: 140)

As this passage indicates, Nietzsche's negation of virulent nationalism does not mean that he opposed European domination of the earth. What he opposes, instead, is that this domination be accomplished under the auspices of nations ruled by political parties and informed by public debate. Consistent with the "beast-of-prey" morality that we encounter in his ethical writings, the "good European," practicing "great politics," will have the task of subjugating the entire earth.

Nietzsche's thoughts on colonialism cannot be separated from tenets that he developed elsewhere in his works. It is essential that we consider the will to power, biologism, and the transvaluation of values, as well as Nietzsche's heavy reliance on antinationalist, antistatist, antidemocratic thought, if we are to understand his fragmentary and sporadic comments on colonies and global politics. But it is also important to recognize that his remarks cannot be separated from the events of his epoch. No German could fail to notice the nationalism of the Second Empire and the building pressure for Germany to enter into the race for colonial possessions. No German could have ignored the mass exodus of Germans from their native soil for a better life in the Americas and the propaganda for creating a new and better Germany on foreign territory. And no one living in Europe during the last quarter of the nineteenth century could be blind to the global political situation in which one continent had gradually gained supremacy over most of the remainder of the earth. Nietzsche's timeliness lies in his attentiveness to these tendencies of his era. With his sister and her husband he was compelled to enter into a private and ongoing discussion about the possibilities and hazards of colonial life in Paraguay. Nietzsche's untimeliness—if we grant him this ascription—involves his unusual way of approaching the problems posed by foreign affairs and world politics. Eschewing the nationalist, mercantile, and utopian/idealist approach to colonization, he developed, along the lines of his own philosophy, a conceptual framework that entailed a geopolitical perspective. In the "good European" he found a term for a future elite that could overcome the nation-state, create a superior cultural life, and achieve domination of the world. With "great politics" he offered an alternative to parliamentary life and actual colonial fantasies, as well as a vague blueprint for global conquest on a grand scale. The visions Nietzsche harbored were certainly unrealistic for his own times, but their "untimeliness," their opposition to and negation of accepted norms of nineteenth-century European thought and realities does not imply that they offered, or still offer, an acceptable alternative. As deleterious as actual developments have been for the Third World, it is difficult to locate features of Nietzsche's "untimely" colonial imagination that would have mitigated the oppression and inequities still rampant in our own postcolonial reality.

Orientalism, Imperialism, and Nationalism: Karl May's *Orientzyklus*

Nina Berman

> But their own coming [*the colonizers'*] *too was not a tragedy as we imagine, nor yet a blessing as they imagine. It was a melodramatic act which with the passage of time will change into a mighty myth.*
> —Tayeb Salih, Season of Migration to the North

I

Over the last few years, German cultural critics (e.g., Klotz; Noyes; Wildenthal; Zantop) have increasingly investigated the formative role literary and nonliterary texts played in the construction of colonialist consciousness and the establishment of colonial rule. German orientalist texts, however, have only rarely been analyzed in the context of the power relations between German-speaking countries and Middle Eastern, Northern African, or Asian countries. To this day, German orientalist texts are generally treated as "exoticist" pieces of literature that negotiate domestic issues. Their connections to actual political and economic events taking place in the countries thematized in the exoticist texts were and still are usually neglected. In fact, several scholars have even set out to prove that Edward Said's model of orientalism, which examines European cultural representations of the Orient in their ideological significance for existing power relations, does not apply to German texts, mostly because German political and economic interests in Oriental countries are allegedly absent or insignificant (Fuchs-Sumiyoshi; Amman 12; Heizer 13). The fact that Said's model makes the nexus of colonialism and nationalism a precondition for the emergence of orientalist texts partially explains the persistence of this approach. And, indeed, neither Germany nor the Habsburg Empire had colonies, and they only rarely made territorial claims, in the Middle East and Northern Africa,[1] that is, in those areas to which the German word "Orient" generally refers. (The meaning of the German word "Orient" thus differs from its meaning in French, British, American, and other cultures where it is more inclusive, referring to the Far East as well [Nina Berman, *Orientalismus,* Introduction].) Furthermore, a German nation-state has existed only since 1871, which—according to the Saidian model—left German-speaking countries without "national" interests in Oriental areas until that moment.

Said restricts his own examination of German orientalism to the period *before* the emergence of a German nation-state; he focuses almost exclusively on the "first two-thirds of the nineteenth century" during which, he maintains, "at no time in German scholarship . . . could a close partnership have developed between Orientalists and a protracted, sustained *national* interest in the Orient" (*Orientalism* 19). "Nation," as Said understands it in this passage, is synonymous with the nation-state. But other definitions of "nation" also exist. A people in search of an identity might define itself as a nation (for instance as a *Kulturnation)* even before the actual establishment of a nation-state. Nationalism precedes the founding of a nation-state (Hobsbawm 10), and it might be argued that national interests precede the nation-state as well. Said concedes that German orientalism shared "a kind of intellectual *authority* over the Orient" (19) with its British, French, and American counterparts. But his focus on the connection between colonialism and nation-state leads him to disregard other models of political and economic hegemony in which Germany and Austria might be implicated. Since the Middle Ages, German-speaking countries had maintained strong and continuous political and economic ties to the Middle East; the Crusades and the expansion and then the fall of the Ottoman Empire were also of crucial political, economic, and ideological importance. The analysis of this interdependency clearly disproves Said's claim that "the German Orient was almost exclusively a scholarly, or at least a classical, Orient" (19). Nonetheless, in this essay I do not reject Said's larger model of orientalism; rather I propose modifying his model to include other forms of orientalist discourse that are not colonialist in the traditional sense. I thus extend here the approach taken by Lisa Lowe and others, who have sought to establish a more differentiated understanding of orientalizing strategies (ix ff.). Although the other

---

1. Germany showed strong interest in Moroccan territory, especially because of its ore deposits. The "1. Marokkokrise" (1905–6) and the "2. Marokkokrise" (1911) were resolved quickly; the provisions of the conference of 1911 allocated to Germany a large chunk of the French Congo in exchange for the acknowledgment of French authority over Morocco.

forms of orientalism I examine here are not dependent on the presence of a colonial occupying army or an administering bureaucracy, they nevertheless display structural and functional similarities to the orientalist representations generated by the culture of colonial powers.

These preliminary remarks are important for what follows in two ways. In order to understand Karl May's *Orientzyklus,* the focus of this investigation, we need to acknowledge the history of the political and economic relationships between German-speaking countries and the Middle East/Northern Africa. We also need to explore the early years of the Wilhelminian Empire that form the backdrop to May's orientalist novels, a time of intense debates about national identity as well as the period in which Germany emerged as a colonial power. Although no German-speaking country established a colonial regime in the Middle East or Northern Africa, the German and the Habsburg Empires of the late 1900s extended their economic and political influence into the territories of the Ottoman Empire in significant ways. The six-volume *Orientzyklus* by May, one of the most widely read authors of German popular culture, attests to these developments. The following analysis will focus on several central issues: What does May's *Orientzyklus* tell us about contemporary power relations between Germany and the Middle East/Northern Africa? How does the text teach colonialist attitudes, and how does it lay the ideological foundation for what I would call a nonoccupational imperialism? Furthermore, how does the text participate in debates on national identity in the newly founded German Empire?[2]

The popularity of May's writings among the German peoples is unparalleled; the more than fifty million volumes printed in German since 1892, not including publications in widely circulated journals and calendars (Tschapke), have been read by approximately 175 million readers (Schulte-Sasse 101). This popularity makes the study of May's works especially compelling, since their influence on the creation of a colonial, orientalist, and national consciousness is unsurpassed by that of any other German-speaking writer of the nineteenth and twentieth centuries.

II

Before undertaking an analysis of May's *Orientzyklus,* which was published in the 1880s, I suggest a closer look at the critical historical background. Two factors are crucial for understanding May's novels: German emigration in the nineteenth century and the genesis of German colonial-

---

2. Previous research on May's *Orientzyklus* either has not asked these questions or has dealt with them in inadequate ways. Compare, for example, the anthology by Sudhoff and Vollmer.

ism, of the "colonial idea." Both explain the dynamic movement across space, the preoccupation with non-European cultures, and, as will become evident, the attitudes toward those cultures that are present in the *Orientzyklus*.

The immediate historical context of the novels was shaped by particular events in the Balkans and in the Middle East. Numerous military confrontations between the Ottoman Empire and Austria and Russia contributed to the gradual decline of the Ottoman Empire. A series of political crises (e.g., the Crimean War of 1853–56) culminated in the "Balkankrise" of 1875–78. The conference at which the peace treaty was negotiated convened in Berlin (hence the name "Berliner Kongreß") in 1878, and Bismarck led the negotiations. The treaty had important repercussions for the peoples living in the Balkans, the European powers, and the Ottoman Empire; its stipulations and political implications inform the ideological underpinnings of May's *Orientzyklus*.

The period during which May composed and published his *Orientzyklus* saw the political and economic intervention of European powers in territories of the Ottoman Empire both in its European part and also in Northern Africa: Britain bought shares in the Suez Canal in 1875 and occupied Egypt in 1882; the French, in Algeria since 1830, occupied Tunisia in 1881. German economic and political interests in the Ottoman Empire manifested themselves mainly in three areas: military advice, arms deals, and the pursuits of German financial institutions.

Some of these activities predated the establishment of the German nation-state. Prussian military advisers had repeatedly helped to train and restructure the Ottoman army throughout the nineteenth century. In 1798, Oberst von Goetze was the first in a series of advisers who were invited by the Ottomans to redesign the Turkish army (Kössler; Wallach; Trumpener). The arms dealer Alfred Krupp had been in touch with Ottoman envoys since the 1860s and was able to finalize his first major arms sale in 1873. Increasing military cooperation between Germany and the Ottoman Empire resulted in numerous contracts for Krupp and other German businessmen, enabling Germany to acquire a monopoly on arms trading with the Ottoman Empire (Kössler 106–25). By the late 1880s, toward the end of the period in which May's *Orientzyklus* was published, German financial institutions had a controlling interest in economic projects in the territories of the Ottoman Empire. In 1888, for example, a treaty was concluded that guaranteed the *Deutsche Bank* control over the building of the Trans-Anatolian Railway, a project essential to the expansion of trade relations between East and West (Kössler 125–43; Grunwald; Rathmann). All in all, Germany played a significant role in what Roger

Owen calls the "single international regime of powers" whose "primary aim . . . was to safeguard the position of those who held shares in the Ottoman public debt [the Ottoman Empire had declared bankruptcy in 1875], but in time a second aim came to assume increasing importance: that of opening up the Turkish economy to further European economic penetration" (192).

May's *Orientzyklus* was thus written at a time when Germany was expanding economically and politically. It was becoming a colonial power in Africa and, to a lesser degree, in Asia, and it was becoming an important economic and political force in other areas, such as the territories of the disintegrating Ottoman Empire.

III

The contents of the six volumes of Karl May's *Orientzyklus,* encompassing more than 3,000 pages in the critical edition by Hermann Wiedenroth and Hans Wollschläger, were first published in the weekly magazine *Deutscher Hausschatz in Wort und Bild* (VII–XIV) between 1881 and 1888. The cycle consists of an extended detective story whose plot can be summarized in a few sentences: the first-person narrator, a writer whose German name has been arabicized to "Kara Ben Nemsi Effendi," finds the corpse of a French merchant in the Schut mountains of Algeria. The protagonist's interest in solving the mystery of the merchant's murder leads him, an eccentric Englishman, and an increasing number of Middle Eastern (mostly Arabic) companions who join the search with a variety of motives, to uncover a criminal organization spread throughout the Ottoman territories. In attempting to track down the criminal organization and its leader, the group tours almost the entire Ottoman Empire: from Northern Africa into Arabia, on to Istanbul and into European Ottoman areas. The heroes face spectacular adventures that have captivated millions of German (and non-German) readers across the boundaries of class, gender, ethnicity, and age. The story ends with the defeat of the "Schut," the leader of the criminal organization who is pursued and dies along with his horse when they plunge together into a wide chasm. After other members of the organization are captured and punished, the heroes return to their respective countries. A relatively short appendix to the novel about a visit of Kara Ben Nemsi to Halef and his family was written in response to requests from May's audience.

This summary, however, does not do justice to the complexity of the novels. A closer look at the text shows that what at first seems to be simply a suspenseful adventure and detective story turns out to be an intricate narrative functioning on various levels. In the course of the *Orientzyklus,* the narrator and self-proclaimed writer Kara Ben Nemsi Effendi—who initially said he had come to the Orient to pursue his anthropological interests and engage in exciting adventures—develops into a prototypical colonizer. He intervenes in local matters with the support of his accomplices and repeatedly brandishes his whip, one of the most powerful symbols of colonization. Precisely this development of the protagonist is what teaches the reader how to think and act like a colonizer, a Eurocentrist, and a racist. To understand this "didactic" aspect of May's writings, I will focus my investigation here on Kara Ben Nemsi's metamorphosis, on his relationship with his Arab friend and servant Hadschi Halef Omar, and on his treatment of the local inhabitants of Middle Eastern and Northern African territories. As I will demonstrate, it is May's use of narrative strategies that is responsible for his text's forceful colonialist, orientalist, and nationalist message.

How is Kara Ben Nemsi introduced to the reader? May's creation of a first-person narrator suggests to the naive reader a congruence between the author and the protagonist. Indeed, for decades May's readers, eagerly awaiting new publications, believed him to be traveling abroad, while he was actually consulting dictionaries, travelogues, and archaeological treatises about the countries he visited solely in his imagination. Only in 1899 did he actually journey to Africa and Asia, and this extended trip of sixteen months then had a significant effect on him. In conjunction with scandalous (and protracted) lawsuits challenging May's claim that his travel tales were based on actual experience (Wollschläger 77ff.; Heermann 277ff.), his first-time encounter with Asian and African realities during the journey of 1899–1900 drastically altered the author's depiction of the colonial world.

In addition to staging public announcements and performances, May fabricated a public image of himself by inserting features into his texts that suggested that his narrative was autobiographical. In the *Orientzyklus,* for example, May's own name is hidden in an arabicized name given to the protagonist by Halef (I: 52, 55):[3] Kara Ben Nemsi Effendi—if one accepts the name as an Arabic construction[4]—means "Master (or Sir) Karl, son of

---

3. The titles of the novels are *Durch die Wüste* (I), *Durchs wilde Kurdistan* (II), *Von Bagdad nach Stambul* (III), *In den Schluchten des Balkan* (IV), *Durch das Land der Skipetaren* (V), and *Der Schut* (VI).

4. The Arabic word "nimsa" or "nemsa" means "Germany" and also—in its modern sense—"Austria"; more common, however, are the terms "almaniya" or "jermaniya." The arabic "ibn," which means "son" and is rendered here as "Ben," generally precedes the name of the father. May's construction, which defines genealogy in terms of nationality rather than in terms of personal ancestry or tribal belonging, does not reflect Arabic traditions but reveals a great deal about German identity construction.

Germany." The protagonist is, like May himself, a writer (I: 277).[5] He further identifies himself as belonging to the tribe of the "Saxaly" (IV: 58; also I: 24), implying that he—like May, who was born in Ernstthal—comes from Saxony. Furthermore, May's eclectic writing style seems to support the claim to authenticity: he mixes fiction with facts, presenting a considerable amount of accurate information about geography, languages, customs, and political conditions. May even uses footnotes in his travel narratives, thus appealing to scholarly authority. The desire to be considered learnedly sound is also apparent in May's promotion of himself to "doctor of philosophy": books in his library carry a stamp saying "Karl May, Dr. phil., Dresden, Prinzenstr. 4."

So the fictional writer from Saxony sets out to tour the Ottoman Empire. He claims that he wants "to get to know this land and its inhabitants" (I: 227). Apart from his anthropological and literary interests, Kara Ben Nemsi admits to his passion for adventure: "I came to Africa and also to this country to see its inhabitants and to do great deeds" (I: 272; see I: 299). The protagonist has multiple motivations, then, for his exploration of Oriental countries and their peoples. His apparent orientophilia is demonstrated not only by his adoption of an Arabic name but also by his wearing of Arabic garb. Kara Ben Nemsi goes native; he joins the group of famous cultural cross-dressers, fictional and nonfictional, who precede and follow him. Like Lord Byron, Sir Richard Burton, T. E. Lawrence, and Isabelle Eberhardt, like Rudolph Valentino as Ahmed ben Hassan in *The Sheik* (1921) and like Kim in Rudyard Kipling's eponymous novel (1901), he adopts non-European clothing in order to immerse himself in a foreign culture.[6] The costume proves successful: Kara Ben Nemsi passes for an Arab on numerous occasions, and he is taken for a Muslim by Arabs, Kurds, and Turks alike. This metamorphosis is further facilitated by Kara Ben Nemsi's ability to speak the languages of different regions of the Orient, including some of the tribal dialects. He even prides himself on reciting passages from the Koran in the dialect of the Koreish, the tribe of the prophet Muhammad (VI: 136).

Cultural cross-dressing can symbolize the desire for immersion into a foreign culture; it can suggest a willingness to open oneself up to a different civilization. On the other hand, cultural (and gender) cross-dressing can be used for strategic purposes, as a vital tool allowing one to enter another culture (not to mention individual motivations for cross-dressing, which can, of course, be myriad). As Marjorie Garber has shown, cross-

---

5. All translations from May's texts are mine.
6. In his song from the 1970s, "Guck mal, ach ne, sieh mal da, Mann aus Alemannia," Reinhard Mey has portrayed this desire to pass as a local inhabitant as typical of German tourists. I am grateful to Steven P. Scher for bringing Mey's song to my attention.

dressing is a means of both empowerment and subversion. She emphasizes that its power lies exactly in the impossibility of locating the cross-dresser. As she says of Dorothy in Sydney Pollack's film *Tootsie* (1982): "'Dorothy's' power inheres in her blurred gender, in the fact of her cross-dressing, and not—despite the stereotypical romantic ending—in *either* of her gendered identities" (6).

This also holds true for Kara Ben Nemsi, who not only passes for an Arab, but whose power is augmented by the fact that he cannot be clearly identified: "One thought I was a grandiose prince, and another took me to be the son of a Persian sovereign. A third swore I was an Indian magician, and a fourth screamed at the top of his lungs that I was a crown prince from Moscow and had come to conquer the land for Russia" (V: 24). This ambiguous identity has different, though generally positive, consequences for the protagonist. Though his ability to pass as a local inhabitant or even as an Ottoman official is sometimes useful to him, the fact that ultimately he is not Oriental is advantageous in other situations. This ambivalence makes possible unrestricted operation in a gray zone, creating the basis for Kara Ben Nemsi's interventions into local matters as well as his expedient withdrawal from them. The protagonist's cross-dressing thus represents a model for strategic behavior vis-à-vis the "natives."

As Homi Bhabha has shown, the appropriation of the colonizer's symbols by the colonized subject can be a means of questioning the authority of colonial power ("Signs"). Appropriation and mimicry, however, not only potentially empower the colonized, but also pose the question of the colonized's own identity. Bhabha suggests that behind the mask there is no authentic self, which means that identity itself needs to be redefined ("Of Mimicry"). Kara Ben Nemsi's—the colonizer's—mimicry raises similar questions: cross-dressing and imitation may be powerful tools, but they also draw attention to the protagonist's identity. Though Kara Ben Nemsi is not forced to face himself, and the success of his cross-dressing is undeniable within the framework of the novels, the reader may be inspired to ask further questions. Just as the spy—another parallel figure bearing structural similarities to that of Kara Ben Nemsi—is always potentially a double agent and in danger of crossing over (Garber 234–66), so likewise does Kara Ben Nemsi's position display an irritating ambivalence. It is interesting to note that Karl May the author, who represented himself as Kara Ben Nemsi and Old Shatterhand in his public performances, was forced to confront the significance of his own cross-dressing in painful encounters with reality in later life.

This ambivalent cultural identity, which the protagonist exploits to great effect, is accompanied by a similarly ambivalent gender identity. Several of May's self-portraits as Kara Ben Nemsi Effendi demonstrate this gender uncertainty: pieces of clothing like scarves, cloaks, embroidered blouses, and veils and accessories like necklaces or bracelets can be read in the context of Western culture as signifiers of femininity. In the novels themselves, which do not include examples of these visual self-representations, an ambivalent gender identity is created primarily via the relationship between Kara Ben Nemsi and Hadschi Halef Omar, whose "friendship" contains strong homoerotic elements. Although the ending -*a* feminizes the protagonist's German name, it is generally Halef who is associated with stereotypical female attributes. He is smaller and weaker than Kara and is often ridiculed for his sparse beard, a strategy that—as Susanne Zantop argues in a different context—feminizes the other in order to prove his natural inferiority ("Dialectics" 306ff.). Halef appears naive, intellectually underdeveloped, ignorant, and innocent, and his actions are generally determined by Kara Ben Nemsi's decisions. The bedouin Halef obeys his master, and if he does not, he has to face the consequences (see IV: 432ff.; VI: 43ff.).

The narrator describes his relationship to Halef in terms that recall a love relationship. For example, Halef supposedly does not know if he loves his wife or Kara Ben Nemsi more (III: 492), and Kara Ben Nemsi often uses romantic language to acknowledge their mutual attraction (III: 136; VI: 532). They spend many sleepless nights together—talking, of course—but the intimacy suggested goes beyond the level of friendship (VI: 498). Eve Kosofsky Sedgwick's concept of "male homosocial desire" may most aptly describe their relationship—a relationship between ("heterosexual") men that can be erotically charged without necessarily involving sexual acts. As Arno Schmidt has shown in a somewhat homophobic study, May's works are filled with homoerotic metaphors—perhaps an explanation for why they were such a success with his predominantly male audience.

Most importantly, the relationship between Kara and Halef reproduces the patriarchal model of heterosexuality. Kara is active, dominant, intellectual, and thus stereotypically male, while Halef is presented as passive, weak, ignorant, and, by implication, feminine. The heterosexual model of domination and submission is then transferred onto the relationship between Europe and the Middle East: Kara Ben Nemsi as the representative of Europe and Halef as the representative of the Middle East personify the colonial paradigm. The strategy of feminizing other cultures is—as Nancy Hartsock, Peter Hulme, and others have demonstrated—one of the central features of colonial discourse. In May's *Orientzyklus,* Kara Ben Nemsi and Halef model what May intends as exemplary behavior: they teach their audience how to act like colonizers, how to treat their colonized subjects, and what to expect of them.

Kara Ben Nemsi is revealed, then, as an ambivalent character whose blurred cultural and gender identities enable him to obtain what Said calls "*positional* superiority" (*Orientalism* 7). This positional superiority functions as a premise for Kara Ben Nemsi's intervention in local Oriental matters. It is not only ambivalence, however, that creates the basis for intervention. Nor is it physical strength; rarely does the protagonist succeed in actions that are based on crude force. Rather, the omnipotence of this superman from Saxony is based on knowledge, psychological analysis, tricks, and the possession of powerful weapons.

The use of knowledge to gain positional superiority is the most prominent of those tools, and the didactic nature of this strategy—"mit erhobenem Zeigefinger"—may be typical of the German approach to colonial rule. Kara Ben Nemsi, the foreigner, seems to be more familiar with local geographies, religious beliefs, and customs than the local inhabitants themselves are. In a paradigmatic scene, Kara Ben Nemsi lectures the leader of a group of bedouins about the relevance of seasonal weather conditions for battle strategies: what effects hot weather has on the vegetation, which tribes would be migrating in response to hot weather, and what repercussions that would have for the army of the enemy. The sheikh, who has spent all his life in the region, then asks the writer from Saxony how to proceed and how long it would take to get to a certain point, revealing his astonishment at the German's thorough knowledge: "Master, you are a great Emir. [At this point, May does not explain the Arabic word that means "prince." He had translated the term in a footnote added to a preceding passage.] You come from a faraway country, and you know this area better than I!" (I: 470).

The sheikh's amazement is understandable. He is unaware of the military maps, history books, and geographical information about his country that are available to readers in the West. This fictional situation repeats actual confrontations between colonizers and colonized peoples; first came the geographers and anthropologists, who then gave way to military and economic interventionists. The complicity between scientists and colonizers has been explained most forcefully by Said and has since been further analyzed by cultural critics such as Mary Louise Pratt. Kara Ben Nemsi uses knowledge acquired by Orientalists to obtain exactly the kind of positional superiority that Said so convincingly describes in *Orientalism*.

This nexus of power and knowledge becomes even more obvious when one looks at the protagonist's use of his knowledge about Islam. The exemplary situation in which Kara Ben Nemsi lectures Arabs, Kurds, and Turks about their religion begins with the words: "You are wrong. Your Koran says . . ." (I: 159). In fact, May conveys correct as well as incorrect information about Islam, as has been demonstrated in a meticulous study by Inge Hofman and Anton Vorbichler. More significant, however, than the truth value that may or may not be present in May's writings is how the narrator employs his knowledge strategically. At times, he points out similarities between Christianity and Islam (I: 90); in other situations he poses as an enlightened and tolerant person: "Leave my faith to me, and I will leave you yours!" (I: 15; see III: 105). But often Kara Ben Nemsi uses his (true or false) information about Islam to criticize and scold Muslims for their behavior. For example, he reprimands a Muslim for drinking alcohol (IV: 167). The protagonist's didactic and condescending attitude functions as a powerful tool for mocking and humiliating the "natives." And Kara Ben Nemsi knows the power of his arguments. In a typical scene, the narrator says to a Muslim man: "Doesn't your Koran say that Allah has foreordained the length of the life of a human being from the beginning?" The next sentence reveals the narrator's awareness of the impact of his words on the Muslim: "This made him visibly uncomfortable" (IV: 233).

The protagonist uses his knowledge about local customs such as the treatment of guests (I: 299) or the status of women (I: 26) in a similar way. Often, locals are presented as ignorant and superstitious, and they fall prey to the tricks of the enlightened protagonist. Kara Ben Nemsi pretends to be a doctor and is revered by villagers for the common-sense cures he provides, which—as the narrator reveals to the readers—could only mystify ignorant Orientals (I: 440; II: 182ff.). To Kara Ben Nemsi's omniscience are added many skills: he is also able to make champagne (I: 446), detect a secret code (II: 84–88), and decipher a cryptic message (V: 450).

Furthermore, the protagonist has the ability to read people's characters based on their outward appearance and behavior. Physical characteristics, mimicry, and body language are decoded by the protagonist's analytic gaze in a way that renders his enemies helpless and defenseless. May's prose reveals the influence of physiognomic theories asserting that human character and behavior could be determined on the basis of physical appearance, like Johann Kaspar Lavater's *Physiognomische Fragmente zur Beförderung der Menschenkenntnis und Menschenliebe* (4 vols., 1775–78) and Georg Christoph Lichtenberg's *Über die Physiognomik* (1778), which suggest that psychological conditions determine physical features (Gündogar 69ff.).[7] In addition, May's writings also display the influence of contemporary racist theories, like those of Comte de Gobineau's multivolume *Essai sur l'inégalité des races humaines* (1853–55)—which attempts to prove the "superiority" of the Aryan races—as well as traces of the emerging science of psychology (see II: 48; IV: 255; V: 448; V: 449). Kara Ben Nemsi is

---

7. Lavater's work was composed in partial collaboration with Herder and Goethe.

empowered by the knowledge he derives from these theories and is thus able to manipulate and dominate Oriental peoples.

Manipulation and trickery are powerful tools used by the protagonist throughout the novels. He exploits the purported ignorance and superstition of locals by pretending to be possessed by the "Evil Eye" (V: 361–62) or by claiming that Halef and other members of his group have become invulnerable by eating one chapter of the Koran per day (V: 59ff.). That claim is even "supported" by an incredible hoax (V: 95ff.) in which Kara Ben Nemsi uses fake bullets to prove the heroes' invincibility to an entire village. The tale of this performance immediately becomes widely known, and, as a result, the heroes are feared by the local population wherever they go.

Intimidation by means of superior weapons, a frequent theme in the text, makes the novels resonate strongly with actual historical events, such as the arms deals of Krupp and other traders. In an exemplary scene, Kara Ben Nemsi warns the local inhabitants of the power of miraculous European weapons. The unbelieving comment of a local man reflects the respect that guns and revolvers elicit: "Shall I let my people ridicule and mock me? How could you have so many bullets in your gun?" (III: 116).

In sum, Kara Ben Nemsi's positional superiority is based upon the ambivalence of his identity, his use of knowledge, psychological analysis, trickery, and superior weaponry. The authority he acquires by these means enables him to operate without restrictions. It motivates local leaders to choose him as the organizer of a rescue action (I: 121), and it allows him to act as a spy in the context of a major military battle (I: 311) and to function as a military adviser (I: 344). Kara Ben Nemsi masters several languages, he understands behavioral codes, he knows the ethical and religious customs, he intervenes in local matters, and he rules over the fate of local inhabitants; in short, he is a self-appointed master and judge, who derives his legitimacy from belonging to Western culture and who establishes his authority by using the tools of knowledge and power provided by his culture.

Kara Ben Nemsi thus teaches May's readers lessons that are fundamental to the contemporary imperialist agenda in Germany and Europe. The connection to Germany's concurrent economic expansionism into the territories of the Ottoman Empire becomes even more apparent if one looks at Kara Ben Nemsi's behavior toward the inhabitants of specific regions in the Balkans. As Kara Ben Nemsi gains power with every page of the *Orientzyklus,* his behavior and practices change. Most striking is his use of the whip, which gradually emerges as the legitimate and most efficient way of dealing with Turks, Albanians, and other peoples. While this conduct demonstrates the evolution of Kara Ben Nemsi from neutral writer and anthropologist to colonizer, it is also important to understand whom Kara Ben Nemsi is treating in what ways.

In May's novels, the peoples of Northern Africa and the Middle East do not appear as a homogeneous lot. Homogenization, the erasure of individuality—which has been identified as one of the strategies of orientalist and colonialist discourse—is in fact not at work here. Rather, the peoples of the Middle East and Northern Africa form a conglomerate of distinct communities. Individual figures in the *Orientzyklus* come to symbolize typical characteristics of their people; but even when Kara Ben Nemsi encounters persons whose behavior does not correspond to the stereotypes attributed to their groups, the exception only serves to justify the prejudice. The narrator describes various ethnic and religious communities in ways that enable the reader to construct a hierarchy of Oriental peoples based on an evaluation of their behavior, values, beliefs, customs, and actions. This hierarchy consists of images that range from the noble savage to "barbaric," "fanatical," "corrupt," and "decadent" nations. The inhabitants of northern Africa and the Middle East are treated by Kara Ben Nemsi according to this hierarchy, and his interactions with the specific peoples hence vary quite dramatically. Apart from its relevance for understanding the connections of May's *Orientzyklus* to the contemporary political and economic context, an analysis of this hierarchy also demonstrates how the novels participated in the contemporary debate on national identity. The presentation of positive and negative characteristics that are (or are not) exemplary for the German community serves to define an ideal of Germanness. May's *Orientzyklus* therefore achieves that formative dimension which Homi Bhabha has described in his analysis of the discourse about national identity in *Nation and Narration*.

At the top of the scale are the Yezidis, a religious community living in northern Iraq, whose faith blends elements of the Muslim and Christian religions. The narrator portrays the Yezidis, who are also known as "Devil Worshippers," as a modest, honest, clean, orderly, happy, and peaceful community. He repeatedly likens their values to European ones (II: 10) and draws analogies between Christian and Yezidi culture (I: 530, 534). It becomes evident that the Yezidis meet certain standards that make them a model for notions of ideal Germanness. The Germans' identification with the Yezidis, for instance, is underlined in the following quote: "The Devil Worshippers are slandered because they are better than their slanderers. If they were more numerous and not as scattered, they could become the Germans of Asia" (I: 526). According to a definition by Michael Makropoulos, who differentiates between the "other" and the "strange," the "strange" is "an extract of the problematic self" (7). In May's descriptions of the Yezidis, the "Devil Worshippers" lose the threatening aspect of being "strange," because May's narrator makes the other familiar via the deployment of images that resemble the ideal self instead.

Less favorable but still generally positive is the narrator's treatment of the Arab bedouins, who appear as the noble savages of the desert. Their value system is based on trust and honesty, and they hold courage, hospitality, family, friendship, and love in high esteem. May's Arabs like to talk, to embellish, to exaggerate, but the narrator treats these weaknesses with sympathetic forbearance. Kara Ben Nemsi develops close friendships with Arab characters. Furthermore, his name and garb seem to suggest that he identifies strongly with Arab culture. However, differences among individual tribes arise, and the narrative distinguishes between good and bad bedouins (see I: 249, 409ff.). Nonetheless, in contrast to the more critical depiction of the Arabs of the cities, the nomadic bedouin community is represented as cultivating values like hospitality and friendship that Kara Ben Nemsi considers fundamental for human relationships (see I: 293ff., 323ff.). May's image of Kurdish peoples parallels that of the Arab bedouins in many respects (see II: 162ff.).

Somewhat less approving is the portrayal of Chaldean Christians, which resonates strongly with the Nietzschean contempt for weakness and imperfection (see II: 104–5, 399, 408). May's representation of Jewish peoples can at best be described as ambivalent. It does not reflect the tone of the contemporaneous antisemitism debate, yet the repeated use of stereotypes in the description of Jewish peoples reveals the influence of antisemitic beliefs (see III: 41ff.).

Turkish people are characterized as corrupt, decadent, unpredictable, filthy (II: 152; IV: 306), stupid, and comical (II: 28). Describing a scene where Turkish soldiers are asked to line up in order to pay reverence to Kara Ben Nemsi, the narrator comments: "The soldiers attempted to comply with this demand, but they formed a sort of crooked line, which at the end turned into a bent tail" (II: 161). This tableau of disorder parallels the scenes in which the protagonist demonstrates how powerless the Turkish authorities are. In numerous cases, Kara Ben Nemsi counteracts, bypasses, or ignores Turkish administrators. This image of Turkish peoples differs from the one prevalent in the sixteenth and seventeenth centuries, which associated Turkish people with violence, irrationality, and sex, as can be observed in texts by Luther and Lohenstein. W. Daniel Wilson has shown that the new, less intimidating representation evident in May's writings was born in the eighteenth century, when the threat of the Ottoman Empire slowly receded and European countries moved into ascendency (11ff.).

The image of Persians is similarly negative (the leader of the criminal organization turns out to be Persian), but the peoples at the very bottom of the hierarchy are Greeks, Armenians, and Albanians. Unlike the Turks, whose decadence is often excused by either corrupt leadership, the negative effect of the Islamic religion, or European involvement (suggesting the existence of an "authentic" Turk), the Greeks, Armenians, and Albanians of the *Orientzyklus* are innately corrupt, brutal, reckless, and unscrupulous. Employing the rhetoric of physiognomy and racism, May relates the "malicious" characters of these peoples to their physical appearance: "His wide chest, his long face with its appalling hook-nose suggested that he was an Armenian" (IV: 255). The members of the criminal organization that Kara has been pursuing all through the Ottoman Empire derive predominantly from these ethnic groups.

In his portrayal of Oriental peoples, May reflects attitudes toward the disintegrating Ottoman Empire that were—with occasional exceptions—for the most part prevalent in Germany at the time. By comparing May's texts to sources upon which he possibly drew: encyclopedias (e.g., *Brockhaus*), periodicals (e.g., *Zeitschrift der Deutschen Morgenländischen Gesellschaft, Das Ausland, Deutsche Rundschau für Geographie und Statistik*), newspapers (e.g., *Leipziger Illustrirte Zeitung*), historical writings (e.g., works by Leopold von Ranke and Friedrich Christoph Schlosser), archaeological reports (e.g., A. H. Layard's accounts), and geographical manuals (e.g., works by Friedrich von Hellwald), it becomes evident that the author was participating in dominant discourses that aimed at defining and ultimately controlling Oriental cultures.

But what accounts for the differences in the treatment of Oriental peoples? The historical context for the hierarchy of peoples previously outlined is, as I observed earlier, the Balkan Crisis of 1875–78 and German economic interests in this area. The closer Kara Ben Nemsi comes to European Ottoman territory, the less favorable his judgment of the inhabitants becomes. The pursuit ends in the Balkans. These areas had been at the center of the Berlin Treaty of 1878, which had enabled European powers to redistribute Ottoman territory. The groups directly affected by the treaty's provisions, the Ottomans and the Christian peoples of the Balkans striving for independence, were only marginally involved in the decision-making process. The decrees of the treaty brought national independence for Romania, Serbia, and Montenegro; Bulgaria remained tributary to the Ottoman Empire to which it also lost Macedonia as well as Eastern Rumelia, which gained autonomy in domestic affairs. Furthermore, the treaty assured territorial gains for Russia, the Austro-Hungarian Empire (which occupied Cyprus and Bosnia-Herzegovina), and Great Britain. In addition, several stipulations furthered the expansion of European economic interests: the Ottoman Empire, Serbia, and Bulgaria were obliged to establish a railway system through their countries and to distribute commissions for its construction to the European powers. This measure would subsequently enable the economic infiltration of these countries and their connection to the European trade system (Hösch 136ff.).

In the following years, Germany and Austria-Hungary became significant trading partners of the Ottoman Empire. Between 1888 and 1893, the volume of German exports to the Ottoman Empire increased by 350 percent, while imports from Turkey to Germany surged by 700 percent during the same period (Schöllgen 80; Birken). By the end of the 1890s, Germany was the third most important trading partner of Ottoman and Northern African territories, lagging only behind Britain and France. By contrast, the German Empire's trade with its colonies was of marginal importance (Schinzinger; Gann), which demonstrates that the economic returns on nonoccupational imperialism at times surpassed the payoff from colonies.

The negative depiction of the peoples in the Balkans and in the European Ottoman Empire is thus not coincidental, but can be explained by German political and economic interests in those territories. The writer and anthropologist-turned-colonizer Kara Ben Nemsi acts in an authoritarian way in those territories where supposedly chaotic conditions call for authority from the outside. Commenting on lawless conditions in the Balkans, Kara says, "Is it amazing, then, when the traveler in such areas makes his own law since he can't find it otherwise?" (V: 135). To this day, foreign interventions are legitimized in similar ways.

IV

On 26 March 1899 Karl May left his home near Dresden to embark on a sixteen-month journey that took him through Northern Africa and Asia. During his first real "Oriental" journey, Karl May encountered the peoples and places he believed he had come to know through his intensive studies. After several months of traveling, May suffered two nervous breakdowns, one in Sumatra, the other in Istanbul. These breakdowns resulted from a twofold confrontation with reality: at home in Germany, several journalists had staged a press campaign against May, accusing him of fraud and questioning the authenticity of his accounts. In addition, May was compelled to see his fictional creations in a new light as a consequence of his personal encounter with the realities of Northern Africa and Asia.

Confronted with these challenges, May underwent a fundamental transformation. He returned to Germany and in 1901 wrote *Et in terra pax* (which was later renamed *Und Friede auf Erden!*), a scathing indictment of colonialism and white Christian supremacy. May had been asked to write this volume for an anthology intended to glorify German participation in the suppression of the Chinese Boxer Rebellion. Joseph Kürschner, the editor of *China: Schilderungen aus Leben und Geschichte, Krieg und Sieg* did not at all expect that May would deliver a gospel of world peace instead. According to Wollschläger, May submitted the novel in small installments, and when Kürschner belatedly noticed the subversive nature of the text, he asked May to bring the novel to a conclusion immediately. In his preface to the anthology, Kürschner apologizes to his readers for the content of the novel. He allegedly even denied May his honorarium (Wollschläger 88–89). It is telling, though, that May's later works, which, like *Und Friede auf Erden!,* employed a mythical and at times overwrought symbolism, never achieved the popularity of the earlier novels, such as the *Orientzyklus* or the first three volumes of the *Winnetou* tetralogy. With those earlier texts, however, May shaped (and continues to shape) German attitudes toward other cultures.

Engendering German Nationalism: Gender and Race in Frieda von Bülow's Colonial Writings

Friederike Eigler

Frieda von Bülow, considered to be the founding mother of German colonial literature, began publishing her colonial novels in the early 1890s, approximately five years after the establishment of the first German colony in East Africa. Whereas initially German colonial ambitions had encountered little enthusiasm among the German people and were only reluctantly supported by the Bismarck administration, during the 1880s and early 1890s the "colonial idea" was actively endorsed by colonialist associations intent on securing Germany's "place" among other colonial empires (Westphal 108–10). It was promoted by fervent colonialists such as Carl Peters, with whom Bülow had become acquainted during her extended stays in German East Africa and on whom she modeled Ralf Krome, the male protagonist of her novel *Im Lande der Verheißung: Ein Kolonialroman um Carl Peters* (In the promised land: A colonial novel about Carl Peters, 1899).[1] The publication of Bülow's first colonial novels thus coincided with the beginning of an era that saw increasing political,

---

1. Peters, a fervent defender of colonialism and an admirer of the British empire, was instrumental in transforming the German settlement in East Africa into a German colony by resorting to dubious negotiating methods with Arab and African leaders and to the violent suppression of contentious "natives." Initially he met resistance from the Bismarck administration, which was hesitant to enter into competition with the British empire over the appropriation of colonies. Eventually Peters managed to gain official support for establishing a colony in East Africa, but his relationship to the German government continued to be fraught with tensions.

economic, and military support for the German colonies.[2] Her last colonial novel was published in 1899, at a time when the German Reich was fully committed to its colonial conquests and had repeatedly intervened with military force in order to suppress uprisings by the Arab and African populations (Westphal 336–42). My analysis focuses on one of Bülow's earliest colonial novels, *Der Konsul. Ein vaterländischer Roman* (The consul: A patriotic novel, 1891), and on her last one, *Im Lande der Verheißung*. These two novels bracket the decade of the 1890s, that is, the period in which Germany became firmly entrenched in its colonial politics. Read a century later from a feminist and postcolonial critical perspective, Bülow's representations of German colonialism provide rich material for exploring the complex interplay between the "personal" and the "political" in colonial terms.

The scarce research on German colonial literature that exists to date generally fails to give Bülow's colonial writings any serious attention.[3] Joachim Warmbold, for instance, in one of the more recent studies of German colonial literature, forgoes any closer analysis of Bülow's texts; instead, he dismisses her colonial novels as light fiction, oblivious to the "reality" in the African colony. In contrast to Warmbold's approach, which is marred by a problematic notion of colonial "reality" and by a strong gender bias,[4] Werner Glinga provides a more balanced and careful assessment of Bülow's novels. He calls the female protagonist in *Im Lande der Verheißung* an "Effi Briest under colonial conditions" (274) whose unhappy marriage results in her idealization of and erotic attraction to the colonialist Krome. While Glinga reads *Im Lande der Verheißung* as a feminist novel "in the sense that the main problem of the protagonist is women's emancipation" (274), he also comments on her blindness to the

---

2. Not until the so-called Congo Conference organized by Bismarck in 1884 and the ensuing "scramble for Africa" among European colonial powers did Bismarck fully support the establishment of German colonies (Westphal 118).

3. Sander Gilman (*On Blackness* 119–28) and Martha Mamozai (175–76, 200–201) refer to Bülow's colonial writings only in passing. Exceptions are Helga Thorson and Barbara Kratzer, whose presentations at the 1994 MLA convention integrated feminist and (post)colonial theories and offered more careful readings of Bülow's novels.

4. Warmbold spends more time detailing Bülow's life than exploring her literary works (68–94). He reduces Bülow's colonial novels to a mere reflection of her biography (88–89), attributes the fact that she wrote colonial novels solely to the influence of Carl Peters (76–80), and claims that her novels are of neither aesthetic nor ethnographical value (89–93). He criticizes her lack of interest in the indigenous people, but he fails to observe that this Eurocentric perspective is a central characteristic of most colonial literature. The gender bias in his approach is most obvious when one compares his often biting comments on Bülow's novels with his critical yet respectful assessment of Gustav Frenssen's colonial best-seller *Peter Moors Fahrt nach Südwest* (95–124).

"enslavement of others" in the colony. (In supporting German colonialism Bülow found herself in accord with most other European women, including most women active in the women's movement, who, as is well documented, either tolerated or supported colonial expansionism well into the twentieth century.)[5]

The point of departure for my own analysis is the contradiction that Glinga notes between the novel's demand for emancipation of colonial women on the one hand and its denial of self-determination in the representation of indigenous peoples on the other. Glinga can view this inequity as the novel's fundamental "contradiction" because he considers the novel's representation of the personal realm to be separable from its treatment of the sociopolitical setting of the German colony. In contrast, I do not assume that these arenas are two separate spheres but explore instead how the personal is implicated in the political and vice versa. What appears to be the novel's demand for emancipation, I argue, is inextricably linked with the protagonist's romanticized vision of colonial conquest, a vision that does not merely ignore but helps to legitimize the subjugation of the indigenous. Rather than searching for representations of colonial "reality"—the guiding principle of Warmbold's approach—I explore how the gendered and racialized identities Bülow constructs in the "personal" realm relate to the "political" realm, that is, the realm constructed by the colonial and nationalist discourses that inform her novels. Specifically, I discuss how her representation of the "personal" realm of gender and race relations is pervaded by the colonial/nationalistic practices of appropriation and exclusion and, conversely, how her representation of the "political" realm, via colonialist and nationalist discourses, relies on racial and gender stereotypes.

For readers unfamiliar with Bülow's colonial writings, I begin with some general comments on her novels and with a brief discussion of the discursive strategies she employs in the representation of other races. Bülow's early colonial novel, *Der Konsul*, and her last colonial novel, *Im Lande der Verheißung*, are both primarily written from the perspective of the main female characters and portray their attraction to colonial men against the backdrop of the transformation of the German settlement in Africa into the colony "German East Africa." *Der Konsul* depicts the con-

---

5. Even among women who participated in the international conventions of the women's movement, there was little solidarity with or even interest in the plight of native women in the colonies (Mamozai 234–47). In her study of women's role in German colonialism *Schwarze Frau, weiße Herrin,* Mamozai details how German women—with rare exceptions such as Rosa Luxemburg, who was highly critical of German colonialism (214)—supported the colonial cause both in Germany and in the colonies.

sul's ultimately unsuccessful attempt to enlarge German territory to the north by "negotiating" with the Arab governors, whose control over the coastal area is increasingly weakened by the advancing European empires. *Im Lande der Verheißung* is set against the background of the already established German colony.

The novels' embrace of colonialist discourse can be observed in the ways they represent the relationship between colonizers and colonized and, even more importantly, in discursive strategies that de-emphasize the existence of the Arabs and Africans. These novels contain few comments about the African population that go beyond passing references to their roles as house servants. Their lack of attention to other aspects of colonial life can be attributed, at least in part, to their gender-specific narrative perspective, since colonial women were for the most part confined to the traditional gender roles of wife and mother. While women did not participate in the actual colonial expansion and military subjugation of the native populations, they did participate in what Achille Mbembe has called the "intimate tyranny" at work in everyday life in the colony (Horton 25).

The novels' mere passing references to indigenous peoples can be seen as a strategy that, according to Chris Tifflin and Alan Lawson, characterizes colonial literature in general: colonial writers, they argue, contributed to the success of actual colonial conquests by "conceptually depopulating countries . . . by looking through the native and denying his/her existence. These were necessary practices for invoking the *terra nullius* upon which the now-disputed legality of imperial settlement (as opposed to 'invasion') was based" (*De-Scribing Empire* 5).

Bülow's novels do contain some images of relatively peaceful German interaction with both the African and Arab populations. However, these idealized representations are disrupted by references in the later novel to the colonialists' use of physical and military force against Arabs and Africans. The presentation of the "friendly takeover" of Arab-controlled land in *Der Konsul,* for instance, contrasts with the Arab uprising and its military suppression by the German colonial powers alluded to in the last part of *Im Lande der Verheißung.* There the novel justifies the Germans' use of military force by portraying the Arabs as the "real" aggressors who attack unarmed German settlers (215, 229) and subject Africans to inhuman slavery, that is, it projects the "origin" of aggression and racially "motivated" exploitation onto the "other."

Comments by Krome, the central figure in *Im Lande der Verheißung,* who defends "harsh" treatment of the Africans against criticism from European "apostles of humanity" (248), also disrupt the images of peaceful life in the colony. In this portrayal of Krome, Bülow draws upon the history of Peters, who in 1887 was convicted of killing two of his black servants out of personal revenge.[6] The novel elevates the homicides from the personal to the larger political realm, justifying them as acts necessary for colonial expansion and glorifying Krome's accomplishments as "creator" of German East Africa (40, 347–49). The historical facts of the case are separated from the figure of Krome and projected onto a minor figure (whose name, "Kramer," retains the relationship to Krome). The German settlers are portrayed as being critical of their companion's arbitrary and excessive violence not because of humanitarian concerns but because of their fear of the Africans' revenge. They do not question either the right to or necessity of corporal punishment for Africans (106–7). Bülow's selective and skewed reworking of the historical murder case against Peters thus contributes to the idealized representation of Krome, obscuring the extent to which colonial aspirations are based on the control or elimination of the indigenous.

In both examples—the German suppression of the Arab uprising and Krome's trial—the novel justifies the use of force by German colonialists and projects the use of excessive and arbitrary violence onto another "race" (here, Arabs) or a minor colonial figure (who is presented as the violent exception to the rule). Bülow's comments about the forceful subjugation of the indigenous people occur in contexts that play down or justify these violent acts; yet for today's reader these references effectively disrupt the myth of a humane German colonialism, a myth that Bülow's colonial writings generally seek to uphold.

Beyond openly legitimizing the colonial cause, both novels resort to a highly effective strategy of displacing the major conflict inherent in all colonial expansionism from an interracial plane onto an intranational one. The leading colonialists, who are the main protagonists in both novels, are portrayed as being in constant "battle" with the officials and politicians in the German Reich. The German Reichstag is portrayed as wavering in its support of colonial efforts and is thus made responsible for any failed "mission." This displacement has the effect of obscuring Germans' forceful control of the indigenous people and instead foregrounds the fervent nationalism of the colonial rulers.

---

6. The timing of the trial against Carl Peters—a year and a half after the double murder had come to the attention of the Reichstag—suggests that it was primarily the result of partisan politics in the Reichstag (Peters 79–94). From this vantage point, Peters's conviction can be seen as a mechanism to preserve the pretense of the legality of colonialism. The scapegoating of Peters obscures the fact that the violent subjugation of the native population is at the core of colonialism and not just the faux pas of an individual who oversteps his orders from back home.

The nationalism projected in Bülow's novels is informed by notions of racially and morally "pure" Germanness. Within these constructions of Germanness, women characters assume a special role, a role that lends itself to a discussion of the racial and sexual politics that underwrote the colonial conquest. Like more established colonial empires, Germany increasingly promoted the "import" of German women to its colonies in an effort to assure the racial "purity" of its colonial ruling class.[7] Any sanctioning of interracial sexual relations and their offspring was seen as threatening the continuation of white domination (Mamozai 127–33). Thus some postcolonial critics argue that European women in the colonies inherently occupied a double role: they were subject to the sexual/racial politics of patriarchal society that instrumentalized them for the sake of continued white male domination, while, at the same time, they were participating subjects in the colonial cause (cf. Stoler, "Rethinking"; Sharpe 225). This assessment of the conflicting roles white women assumed in the colonies provides a partial explanation for the central "contradiction" between female emancipation and women's racism that Glinga observes in Bülow's novels. But beyond identifying and criticizing the racist stereotypes on which Bülow's characters draw, it may prove more productive to explore what kind of conflicting roles the main female characters in Bülow's novels play and how exactly they negotiate the "inherent" double position—both as subject to the sexual politics and subject of the racial politics in the colonies.[8]

When the German woman Maleen joins her husband in German East Africa at the beginning of *Im Lande der Verheißung*, the male characters immediately assign to her the role of improving standards of moral and social conduct. The comment that the German men run wild (*verwildern*) without "German ladies" (291) is a euphemistic allusion to the sexual abuse of native women that was common practice in all colonies (Mamozai 277–85). The term *verwildern*, which purports to be concerned with the moral conduct of colonial men, is indicative of the racist subtext of this moral discourse; it stamps the indigenous as "savages." Indeed, there are several instances where Bülow employs the pejorative term *Wilde* in reference to the Africans (152, 156).

While the construction of Germanness as racially and morally "pure"

---

7. German women in the *Frauenbund der deutschen Kolonialgesellschaft* supported this policy by recruiting and preparing women for life in the colonies (Mamozai 198–201).

8. My analysis of race and gender stereotypes in Bülow's novels is informed by Homi Bhabha's call for an exploration of stereotypes as symptoms of ambivalent attitudes toward the "other," often combining fear and desire. This approach seems more promising in addressing the tenacity and pervasive attraction of stereotypes than their mere identification and dismissal ("The Other Question" 69–70).

dominates the later novel, it is affirmed only initially and then disrupted in the earlier one. *Der Konsul* introduces the character of Josefa in the most stereotypical terms as an exotic woman from Bohemia who looks like a "gypsy" and is "beautiful as sin itself" (60–62). The novel portrays the new consul Silffa as fighting off Josefa's sexual advances and as longing for Nelly, the sister of one of the settlers, whom he envisions to be an "educated, polite German girl" (65). Although the character Nelly in fact deviates from the consul's projection of ideal femininity, the novel's narrative perspective initially constructs her as racially and morally superior to Josefa. Nelly is portrayed as adopting a "male" gaze vis-à-vis Josefa: she emphasizes Josefa's physical features, and imagines and disapproves of her presumed promiscuity. The distance between these two women is gradually overcome, however, by Nelly's attention to and appreciation of aspects other than Josefa's appearance, for example her courage and care for others (175), and eventually Nelly accepts Josefa's different life-style and moral standards (266).

In a scene that represents the turning point in their relationship and that effectively explodes the binary opposition between the moral superiority of "racially pure" Germanness and the moral inferiority of "mixed race," Josefa rescues Nelly from being sexually assaulted by a group of drunken Germans. Josefa is portrayed as courageous—she confronts and successfully challenges the male assailants—and as independent—she challenges bourgeois morality that produces women like Nelly, who blame themselves for being sexually harassed (181). The figure of Josefa and the representation of the Germans' assault on a woman of their own "race" undercut two central aspects of colonial discourse: first, the instrumentalization of white femininity to signify the "heart" of Western civilization, requiring special protection in the colony; and second, the myth of the black male sexual threat to white femininity, a myth that was used to legitimize the subjugation of entire peoples (cf. Williams and Chrisman 193). This scene can be read as one of the few examples where Bülow's novels adopt a counterhegemonic position by exposing the extent to which nationalist and colonial discourses rely on mechanisms of denial, projection, and "othering."

In contrast to this early novel, the novel Bülow wrote eight years later, at the height of Germany's colonial expansionism, reaffirms the colonial discourse of *racial* superiority. *Im Lande der Verheißung* exposes, however, the gender bias that informs the discourse of *moral* superiority. The character Ralf Krome puts Maleen, who has joined her husband in the colony, in a double bind by stressing on the one hand her positive effect on moral decency in the colony and expressing his erotic interest in her on the other. When Maleen, who returns his feelings but remains faithful to her husband, learns that Krome is involved with Maria, a young woman of "mixed race," the latent tensions between white and nonwhite women that the novel has alluded to all along come into the open. Maleen's rage is primarily directed against Maria; her description abounds with racist stereotypes (e.g., "wild cat," "narrow-eyed, dull-witted young savage"— "Wildkatze," "schmaläugige, blöde, junge Wilde" [152]). But, as Maleen's own thoughts indicate, her emerging racism and her moral outrage are inseparable from her frustration about her own socially proscribed desire for Krome. Indeed Maleen's statement, "and this lucky woman Maria was free. She did not have to lock her burning heart in seven iron shields" ("und diese glückliche Maria war frei. Die brauchte nicht ihr heißes Herz in sieben eiserne Panzer zu schmieden" [154]), indicates that her jealousy has been replaced by her envy of Maria's perceived sexual freedom. Vis-à-vis Krome, Maleen assumes the "moral voice" that he had personally assigned to her. Though he promises to stay away from Maria, he justifies his interest in her by reference to the distance Maleen keeps from him and the need to find respite from an "excessive exertion of energy" ("Übermaß an Kräfteanspannung" [161]). This constellation can be read as an indication of how the gender- and class-specific dimensions of the moral double standard—characteristic for nineteenth-century patriarchal society—play out in the colonial situation: in order to ensure white domination, the seemingly privileged role of moral authority is assigned to the middle-class European woman, a role that has the effect of reinforcing the regulations and strictures placed on feminine desire (Mamozai 145; Sharpe 224).

For the character Maleen, the restrictions on feminine desire are represented as a reverse enactment of the "feminization of the Orient," the (pre)colonial fantasy so widely documented in Said's seminal study. From the point of her first encounter with Krome, Maleen fights off a tropical infection that stands in metaphorical relation to her desire for Krome. When Maleen eventually "succumbs" to a severe fever, she welcomes the release from moral responsibility that accompanies this tropical disease (191). Maleen's unconditional surrender to her desire for Krome mimics the sexual permissiveness she projects onto the woman of "mixed race." As a consequence, her fever can be read as the orientalization of her (feminine) desire.

Ironically, however, Maleen has to explain to Krome how to "read" her illness: she informs Krome of her surrender in a mediated and displaced manner, through a written declaration of love that he finds by mistake when he visits her sickbed. Since her surrender to Krome can only come via the disguise of a disease, Krome, who has a profound dislike for the sick and weak,[9] loses his romantic interest in the "real" Maleen. Instead, he carries her written declaration of love with him when he sets off to defend "his land" against the Arab uprising. Thus Maleen's attempt to redirect Krome's attention remains unsuccessful. His visit does not end with the promise of commitment to and love for Maleen but instead with his renewed commitment to the conquered land. This displacement can be read as staging the classic trope of colonial virility, that is, the encoding of the conquest of foreign lands in sexual terms (cf. Kolodny; Zantop, "Domesticating").

The representation of this encounter between Krome and Maleen epitomizes the imbrication of traditional gender roles—"feminine" submission and "masculine" control—within the colonial discourse. But while the novel's ending repeats and reinforces the representation of the psychic economy of the colonial man, it seems to open up a new space for the colonial woman. Both characters are portrayed as sustaining their romantic feelings for one another despite, or perhaps because of, the other's absence. At their last meeting, which takes place after both Maleen's husband and brother have died and after she has returned from an extended stay in Germany, Krome is taken aback by Maleen's age, and he concludes that from now on he will "continue to fight with free arms—and admire a feminine ideal—merely from a distance" (405). These comments make explicit what was already implicit in Krome's escape from the sick Maleen. The novel projects the image of a fervent colonialist who channels his energy in the aggressive appropriation and/or annihilation of the "foreign," finds "respite" in sexual encounters with women of "inferior race," and upholds his image of the "pure white woman" against any real interpersonal involvement.

While Krome exhibits little character development, the character of Maleen undergoes significant changes, moving from a state of almost total dependency toward relative autonomy and self-sufficiency. This emancipatory move continues to be framed, however, by colonial and national discourses. For instance, the novel inflects Maleen's emotional disengagement from Krome with clear nationalistic overtones; she disapproves of Krome's contempt for the German state, which failed to support his colonial acquisitions, and of his decision to work for the British empire instead. In contrast to this unequivocal adoption of a nationalist perspective, Maleen's decision to stay in German East Africa in order to cultivate

---

9. In an unusually drastic manner, the narrator comments on Krome's dislike for the sick and weak: "he would poison the terminally ill if it were permitted" (195). For today's readers, this comment clearly recalls Nazi attitudes and crimes.

the colonial land is more ambiguous and provokes a number of conflicting readings. The novel's ending suggests Maleen's liberation from patriarchal control while stressing at the same time her active participation in colonial activities.

Her personal emancipation accompanies her decision to give up Krome and continue her independent life as a single woman in Africa instead of returning to Germany. Contrary to colonial conventions that promoted traditional gender roles reinforcing women's dependency on men, Maleen takes charge of the land she inherited from her brother. In this particular instance, the novel posits the colony as imaginary space for female emancipation. The ending foregrounds a liberating tendency that had been present in the novel throughout but that was enmeshed with the representation of traditional gender roles. Maleen's decision to marry Dietlas, for instance, was motivated by her wish to join him in German East Africa, a place onto which she had projected her desire for meaningful life and work. This romanticized vision of the colony is shattered by the "reality" of her marital life, in which her husband restricts and controls all of her movements. Maleen's heroic horseback ride—which she undertakes during her husband's absence in order to warn nearby farmers of an impending Arab uprising—represents an attempt to break out of the role assigned to her (216–22). This act of transgression is immediately condemned by her returning husband who threatens to send her back to Germany. Maleen's attraction to Krome is, however, not only motivated by her oppressive marriage and by the attention and respect she receives from Krome, but also by her "passionate wish to be a man" (64). Thus, at the novel's beginning she envisions her liberation from social strictures placed on women by identifying with a male figure who embodies colonial virility. Read within this larger context, her retreat to farm life portrayed at the end of the novel seems to indicate a path toward independence that is no longer male-identified.

By envisioning an African farm as the site of woman's partial liberation, Bülow relies on a literary topos that reappears in the colonial writings of other women authors, for example, in Olive Schreiner's *The Story of an African Farm* and Isak Dinesen's *Out of Africa*. In a suggestive study of Schreiner and Dinesen, Susan Horton explores the role Africa played in each woman's psychic economy, reading Dinesen's representation of Kenya and Schreiner's of South Africa as one piece of "the very artful bricolage that was their work of self-construction" (xii). Similar to Dinesen and Schreiner (Horton 60), Bülow uses the topos of the African farm as a means of creating physical space around the female protagonist. This position of relative safety enables Maleen to interact with her African workers as well as with other white farmers in a relationship of mutual respect and support.[10]

In contrast to Horton, who is concerned with the spaces these colonial women create for themselves in their representations of Africa, Glinga in the study previously mentioned is concerned with discrepancies between these literary appropriations and colonial "reality." The topos of an African farm, Glinga maintains, represents a "myth which sums up the whole delusion of settlers' romanticism" (273). Paradoxically, this myth, created mostly by European women writers, projects onto the African farm a state of relative freedom at a time when the very conditions the women (and their protagonists) sought to escape had produced the enslavement of indigenous peoples. The demands for emancipation in *Im Lande der Verheißung* thus remain ambivalent at best: by projecting an idealized image of a colonial "family" headed by Maleen, the "caring mother" (361, 362), the novel romanticizes and justifies colonial exploitation. Taking Glinga's critique even further, I read the myth of an African farm as the feminine-coded counterpart to the trope of colonial virility mentioned earlier. Maleen's embrace of the "German land" is erotically charged and displaces her love for Krome (404). Although she liberates herself from her personal dependency on him, Maleen fulfills the "conqueror's" legacy by adopting the role of caring "mother"-colonizer toward the colonial land and the African workers. The myth of an African farm completes the colonial and nationalist aspirations represented (and ultimately betrayed) by Krome.[11]

Im Lande der Verheißung can be read, as I have suggested, as a text that enacts and exposes how patriarchal discourse is intertwined with nineteenth-century colonial ideology and how European women were coopted in the effort to expand white (male) domination in the colonies. The novel includes critical comments on gender-specific mores and social norms that restrict white women's lives, but its demands for an emancipatory vision depend on continued colonial practice. This support of colonialism is univocal, the only exception being an intertextual allusion to a dissenting voice that was more fully developed in the novel *Der Konsul*.

---

10. Horton attributes to Africans the roles of an "audience" for women's identity formation and of a shield against Europeans who infringe on these women's personal spaces (72). In order to avoid stereotypical representations and projections, Horton take pains not to make any statement about colonial "reality." She fails to note, however, the extent to which her approach enacts a discursive appropriation of the Africans by looking exclusively at their importance for the identity formation of white colonial women.

11. Mamozai maintains that European women, in return for the special recognition they received in the colonies, often became fervent nationalists (152).

Among several intertextual references in *Im Lande der Verheißung* to the earlier *Der Konsul* (which Bülow had written eight years before) is a brief encounter in Cairo of Maleen and her brother with the former German consul in East Africa and his wife Nelly (the latter two are the protagonists of *Der Konsul*). When the group receives news about the killing of the members of a German colonial expedition in East Africa, Nelly suggests that the price Germany pays for the colony is too high, while Maleen responds with a patriotic defense of the colonial cause (305). This brief exchange introduces a sentiment that—together with Nelly's more fully developed position in *Der Konsul*—throws the representation of a seemingly closed ideological system in *Im Lande der Verheißung* into critical relief. Nelly is as little concerned about the plight of the indigenous people as any of the other characters. But from the outset she is critical of the new consul's idealism and the patriotism with which he sets out to reform moral and social conduct in the settlement, to establish a sense of national identity among the settlers, and to transform the settlement into a German colony. In one of their most contentious exchanges, Nelly accuses Silffa of what she considers to be a typically masculine tendency to project a bloated sense of self onto patriotic or nationalist beliefs.[12] The lexicon Nelly employs to describe patriotism and nationalism has imperial connotations: she talks about *expanding* one's spheres of power and fame by *including everything* that one claims to be part of *one's own*. In her critique of the consul, Nelly refers to the gendered nature of nationalism; the significance of these comments extends, I would argue, beyond the situation in which they are spoken and indicts the colonial cause.[13] Silffa's response falls short of addressing the substance of her critique; instead he praises her sharp mind but rejects her critique as destructive (*zersetzend*, 73), asserting the superiority of even the most stupid deed over reflective inactivity (77).

Nelly's critique and Silffa's reaction to it recall a moment of critical reflection by Silffa himself, a character who otherwise embodies "action" throughout the novel. Just after his arrival in Africa, the consul observes the daily activities of some Africans and compares their seemingly contented life with the proletarian struggle for survival in German cities. He muffles his ensuing doubts about the superiority of Western concepts of

---

12. "Their whole patriotism does not impress me one bit. The word patriotism is always supposed to provide the cover-up and pretense for the most presumptuous egotism. If the self-love of you men is no longer satisfied with glorifying your own person, then you quickly extend the concept of your sphere of power and glory by including everything conceivable as yours. And that's what you then effusively call 'nation' or 'fatherland.'" (72)

13. Nelly's critique resonates with the argument of Patrick Williams and Laura Chrisman, who relate nineteenth-century colonial discourse to the "crisis of masculinity" that, in their view, was triggered in part by women's demand for, and partial success in, attaining social advancement.

progress and culture with a vague reference to the inevitable course of history, whereupon the narrator comments: "Silffa preferred to avoid a train of thought that threatened to paralyze him and to make him reactionary" (37–38). This comment draws attention to the fact that the consul avoids any thoughts that may force him to reconsider the entire colonial endeavor, including his own activities as German consul. Here the novel's narrative perspective comes closest to endorsing a critique of Western imperialism, a stance that corresponds to the critical position attributed to Nelly. The evolving narrative affirms the validity of colonial *activities,* but dissenting voices continue to inhabit Silffa's mind (he recalls Nelly's critique repeatedly later in the novel) and undercut the colonial ideology generally embraced by the novel.[14]

In his dismissal of Nelly's critical comments, Silffa resorts to an opposition that privileges masculine-coded "action" over "thought," coded as both unfeminine and effeminate. Silffa regards Nelly as "ruled by intellect," thus "unfeminine" (74). But the novel portrays "thought" and "reflection" as betraying not only the "natural" gender characteristics of woman, but also of man. The opposition between virility and the lack thereof governs the discourses on colonialism and nationalism in both novels. Yet in the early novel *Der Konsul,* this opposition is refracted by voices that question the superiority of (colonial) activity over (anticolonial) reflections, while in the later novel this opposition is univocally reaffirmed: *Im Lande der Verheißung* repeatedly contrasts the *activity and virility* of the colonial man (epitomized in Krome) and the *passivity and impotence* of scholars, lawyers, and politicians in Germany. While the former supposedly fight for the "true" German nation, the latter either pursue lofty and inconsequential ideas or attempt to control and restrain the colonialists by appealing to "false" humanist ideals (70–71, 382, 400–401).

Silffa's and Krome's disregard for parliamentary processes in the name of German nationalism is not just a critique of the Prussian "spirit of submission," a reading that the novel's narrative perspective suggests. Instead, the colonialists' defiance amounts to the wholesale rejection of the legal and political institutions of the German nation-state and to the embrace of totalitarian principles.[15] In Bülow's novels the tensions

---

14. Even though Nelly changes considerably in the course of the novel, she reaffirms her general skepticism toward patriotism at the very end of the novel (256).

15. Hannah Arendt's early and comprehensive study of imperialism in *The Origins of Totalitarianism* (1951) analyzes the historical conditions and political effects of European colonialism in the light of Nazi Germany and the Holocaust. According to Arendt, the inherently totalitarian tendencies of imperialism include rule by decree, control by an "enlightened" few, and racism. By contrast, the modern nation-state is founded on legal and political principles—whose historical realization has remained incomplete and fraught with contradictions—that guarantee its citizens certain irrevocable rights as well as some degree of political representation and participation (218–57). According to Arendt, tensions between the

between the colonists and officials in Germany have no larger political ramifications, in part because Silffa eventually submits to state authorities and Krome leaves Germany for the British empire. Historically speaking, however, Silffa's and Krome's antistate attitudes reverberate with the strong colonial and antidemocratic sentiments that were spurred by Germany's defeat in World War I and the ensuing loss of all German colonies which was part of the Versailles Treaty. These volatile sentiments contributed to the real dismantling of the Weimar Republic under the banner of "true" German nationalism.[16]

I have called Bülow's representation of the colonialists' fight against parliamentary control a "displaced" struggle because it foregrounds the nationalist efforts of "true Germans" and obscures the "other" battle against the indigenous population in the colonies. Around 1900 this alignment of German nationalism with colonialism in Bülow's novels is likely to have had the effect of strengthening national support for the German colonies. But the antistate "heroism" embodied by Krome and its racial and gendered subtexts also prefigure the kind of nationalistic discourse that—under a different set of political and historical circumstances[17]— became dominant in Nazi Germany.[18]

The notion of German nationalism in these two novels is grounded in an opposition that associates everyone who appears to hinder the nationalist project of colonialism with deficient masculinity or, in Nelly's case,

---

colonies and the European metropolis were characteristic of all empires and resulted from the fundamental incompatibility of imperialism and the nation-state/nationalism.

16. According to Arendt, there is the constant risk that nationalism may align itself with imperial aspirations resulting in the destabilization of the nation-state and its democratic dimensions. She sees Germany as a prime example of this alignment and attributes it to Germany's delayed and only partially successful creation of a nation-state as well as to its late entry into and early "exit" from colonial expansionism (250–54).

17. By opening up this historical perspective, I do not subscribe to a monocausal approach that sees Nazi Germany in a linear progression from Germany's "thwarted" colonial period. Arendt's study is an excellent example of an approach that looks carefully at the historical emergence of what she terms totalitarian aspects while at the same time accounting for the historical specificity and complexity of each period. This does not prevent her, however, from resorting to her own set of racist stereotypes in her assessment of the African peoples.

18. The political implications of the novels' privileging of action over thought as well as the corollary of antidemocratic sentiments come to the fore in the preface to Carl Peters' collected works, published in Nazi Germany (1943). The editor Walter Frank idealizes Peters as embodying action and turns even his writings into "deeds," claiming that they were inseparable from "blood-red experience" (*blutrotes Erleben* vi). Commenting on Peters's release as civil servant that cut short his "career" for the German Reich, Frank writes: "This is how Carl Peters fell. He survived the spears of the Massais and the poison arrows of the Warombos. But he was defeated by the poison arrows of the German politicians and the spears of the privy councillors and lawyers" (11).

with deficient femininity. This gendered opposition intersects with a revealing racial opposition in *Der Konsul*. Among the novel's most stereotypical representations is that of the Galician Jew Nathanael Lindenlaub, who associates with the beautiful, "gypsy-like" Josefa and who is described as smart but submissive and avaricious (30, 40). Silffa's ambition to build a strong patriotic community extends to Lindenlaub, to whom, in a tirade of antisemitic stereotypes, he attributes "extreme submissiveness, detestable self-contempt, cowardice" ("hündische Unterwürfigkeit . . . ekelhafte Selbstverachtung . . . Feigheit" [42]). In an attempt to explain these "characteristics," Silffa rejects, however, an explanation based on race alone and subscribes instead to a historical explanation: "because for centuries the Jews, an intellectually superior and richly-endowed race, were oppressed and abused by less refined peoples" (42). In a sudden shift, he then compares the Germans to the Jews or, to be more precise, the Jews remind him of the "Germans' position regarding foreigners." The German phrase ("die Stellung der Deutschen den Ausländern gegenüber" [42]) can be read in two different ways: as a reference to the inferior position of the Germans or to their perceived inferiority. On the one hand, the shift to the Germans' inferiority undercuts Silffa's portrayal of Lindenlaub and turns it into a reflection on Silffa's racist *perception* of a Jew. The comparison between Jews and Germans, when considered within the context of the entire novel, suggests, on the other hand, that Silffa's real concern is the inferior status of the German nation among other European nations, especially with regard to its "hesitant" and "weak" colonial politics and to its "submissive" approach to more established colonial powers, in particular Great Britain. Thus Silffa's antisemitism can be explained as the projection of the perceived flaws of his own people onto the other, the German-speaking Jew. This reading is confirmed by the scope and success of Silffa's nationalist mission, which explicitly includes Lindenlaub: in two separate but analogous processes, the consul succeeds, at least partially, in strengthening the "sense of self and dignity" of both the German settlers and Lindenlaub (116, 236). But despite Silffa's appropriation of Lindenlaub for the nationalist project of uniting the settlers in the name of greater ideals—the nation, the people, the fatherland (176)—the novel's stereotypical portrayal of "the Jew" persists.

Recent theories of the nation and nationalism suggest that these seemingly contradictory processes of "othering" and "appropriating" are both intricate parts of the modern concept of nation that emerged in late-nineteenth-century Europe (Hobsbawm, Anderson). This new concept of nation had not only ethnic but also territorial and political implications and was increasingly propagated by the political right. Right-wing movements in France, Italy, and Germany defined their respective nations in opposition to "foreigners" and resorted to essentialist notions of race and ethnicity in their call for ethnic and linguistic purity. Historians like Eric Hobsbawm, Ernest Gellner, and Benedict Anderson stress the artificiality of the very concept of "nationality," and Anderson defines the nation as "imagined community."[19] In order to illustrate that nationality is neither an inherent nor essential characteristic, Hobsbawm provides examples of people with multiple national self-definitions that vary according to their position vis-à-vis "other" ethnic groups (6–9). From the perspective of post-Saussurian critical theory, Hobsbawm's notion of nationality can be regarded as a shifting signifier that acquires its meaning differentially, that is, only in opposition to other groups. This theoretical position accords with the novel's representation of national identity: the consul constructs, on the one hand, a notion of (superior) Germanness in opposition to "the Jew"; on the other hand, Silffa enlists Lindenlaub in his effort to create a sense of national loyalty among the German settlers. Silffa urges Lindenlaub, for instance, to replace the French term for his restaurant with the German *Gastwirtschaft* (41), a request Lindenlaub is portrayed as fulfilling with so much devotion that this "national" act of purifying the German language is simultaneously used to reinforce the previously employed antisemitic stereotypes. These seemingly contradictory practices of appropriation and exclusion both contribute to the generation of a sense of national identity.

In a similar vein, the entire novel can be read as staging German nationalism in the making. Silffa literally creates a sense of national identity among the settlers by evoking a notion of national pride that supplants individual pride and a notion of communality that transcends the centrifugal individualism he initially witnesses in the settlement. Beyond evoking this utopian national community through mere rhetorical persuasiveness, Silffa promotes a sense of national unity by advocating the singing of German songs, the purification of the German language, regular attendance at German church services, as well as social gatherings for Germans (*Stammtisch*). The novel's ending can be read as exposing the artificiality of the project of nation-building: the sense of national loyalty Silffa managed to establish among the settlers falters as soon as he is replaced. Thus *Der Konsul* foregrounds the extent to which the nationalist project Silffa promotes is based on an "imagined" community and not on any preexistent entity.

---

19. Anderson defines the modern nation as an "imagined political community—and imagined as both inherently limited and sovereign" (617). See Bhabha ("DissemiNation") for a critique of Anderson's tendency to naturalize and nationalize the "space of the imagined community" (157–61).

In sharp contrast to the early novel, Bülow's last colonial novel represents German nationalism as a phenomenon that pervades and shapes life in the colony, a phenomenon that is no longer questioned but embraced by all the main characters (as opposed to the disruptive voice of Nelly in the earlier novel). This presentation of a naturalized notion of German national identity and nationalism in the late novel can be attributed in part to the different political circumstances of the late 1890s, that is, Germany's firm political and military commitment to its colonies. In this regard *Im Lande der Verheißung* stages the amnesia that became characteristic for twentieth-century nationalism (Anderson 5): the relatively recent history of the modern concepts of the nation and national identity—whose emergence as an "imagined community" the early novel details—is "forgotten" and replaced by a long, fabricated history of the nation used to "justify" new political and territorial demands (Hobsbawm 14).

While the later novel works within an established nationalist framework, the earlier novel displays the inner workings of emerging nationalism and the extent to which it relies on racial and gender stereotypes. The projection of what Silffa perceives as the Germans' weakness onto "the Jew" intersects with the novel's projection of "debilitating reflection" into realms that are coded as unfeminine or effeminate. Silffa's strong nationalistic and colonial ambitions are masculine-coded and can be read as an attempt to compensate for these perceived flaws. His success as German nationalist and colonialist depends in part, however, on the continued suppression, projection, and debasement of these characteristics in the "other" ("the Jew," the "unfeminine" woman, the "effeminate" scholar, the lawyer, the politician, etc.). Both novels include voices that disrupt and thereby partially expose these mechanisms when they concern gender relations. The novels' narrative perspective fully embraces these strategies of othering, however, when it concerns the representation of other "races."

A century later, postcolonial critic Homi Bhabha—drawing on Frantz Fanon and Julia Kristeva, among others—argues that the only future of modern society and the nation-state lies in the disruption of its presumed homogeneity and unity by feminist and minority discourses ("DissemiNation" 152–57). The need for this disruption is borne out by Germany's "postcolonial" history.

National Identity, Nomadism, and Narration in Gustav Frenssen's *Peter Moor's Journey to Southwest Africa*

John K. Noyes

One of the strangest moments in German colonial literature—and it has some very strange moments—is the closing paragraph of Gustav Frenssen's novel *Peter Moor's Journey to Southwest Africa* (1906). Over the course of two hundred pages, Frenssen relates the adventures of a young soldier, Peter Moor, who joins the German Protectorate troops and leaves home to help suppress the uprising of the Herero and Nama against German colonial rule in 1903–4. The plot covers the rebellion and its suppression by the German occupation forces, a particularly brutal chapter in the history of European colonialism. By the end of the short campaign, 65,000 Herero, or four-fifths of the entire population, had died, either killed by German troops or forced into the desert where they died of starvation. The novel follows the adventures of Peter Moor from the time when he enlists in the Protectorate forces through his journey to the colony, his experiences of hardship and heroism in the battle of the Waterberg, the defeat of the Herero on 11 August 1904, and his return home.

The entire book is narrated in the first person by Peter Moor. Peter tells of his youth in Schleswig-Holstein, his astonishment at the idea of traveling to Africa, his expectations and disappointments when he does so,

---

Versions of this article have been presented to a number of diverse audiences: the MLA convention (1994), the History of Sociology and African Studies workshops at the University of Chicago (1995), and a German Department seminar at New York University (1995). I would like to thank participants in these discussions for their valuable comments, many of which have been incorporated (as creatively as possible, I hope) in this essay. Unless otherwise noted, all translations are my own.

his fears and triumphs during the campaign, and his return home. He speaks and listens, allowing others to speak through him. He serves as a collecting point for the voices whose dialogues construct the novel's ideology.

In the final paragraph, Peter tells how he arrives back home in Hamburg after having survived his many ordeals. I will quote this paragraph in full:

> When I was sauntering along the Jungfernstieg in my worn-out, dirty cord uniform, with dark, sunburnt face, a middle-aged man came up and joined me, and asked me all sorts of questions as we went along. In the course of the conversation it came out that I had heard of him in my father's house, for he had known my father from childhood. I related to him all that I had seen and experienced, and what I had thought of it all. And he has made this book out of it. (243)

This paragraph narrates its own impossibility. By relating Peter's adventures in the first person, Frenssen's realist prose seeks to establish, as realist prose does, the unity of narrated subject and narrative voice. Theories of deictic functions developed by linguists like Émile Benveniste or Roman Jakobson help us to conceive of this convention of realism: the narrative voice, speaking in the first person, requires that the participant of the narrative event, or the subject of the enunciation, be identical with the participant in the narrated event, or the subject of the enounced—both are Peter Moor. This unity, and with it the narrative pact we have established with Peter Moor throughout the book, is shattered in a single sentence. In the final sentence, the subject of the enunciation tells us that he is not Peter Moor, but the man that he met on the docks. However, he continues to speak in the first person with the voice we have come to ascribe to Peter Moor. The message is clear: "I, Peter Moor, am not Peter Moor, and I never was."

What Frenssen evidently intends with this paradoxical overlay of the narrative voice is a heightened realism. Eyewitness reports, such as those he collected while researching the novel, are often told to a third party. But the truth value of these reports relies on the identity of the narrating subject, the individual who experienced the events related. As soon as the eyewitness is replaced with a fictional character the reality effect of speech threatens to collapse. Frenssen obviously intends to end his tale with a flourish of realism by turning Peter Moor into a witness of the Herero Rebellion. My argument is that he in fact accomplishes the opposite, and that this is not necessarily due to narrative incompetence, but to discrepancies in the place of narration and the place of experience.

Gustav Frenssen was born in Schleswig-Holstein in 1863 and, after ten years as a pastor in Hemme, became an overnight sensation with the publication of his third novel *Jörn Uhl* in 1901. Written in the immensely popular genre of the *Heimatroman,* or regional novel, this book told the interminable tale of a farmer's son struggling to realize the inherent potential of his hearty, down-to-earth, country stock, while at the same time freeing himself from the social ghetto in which his community had been confined. In its first three years, *Jörn Uhl* sold 130,000 copies, making its author the most widely read contemporary German writer. And by the time Frenssen wrote *Peter Moor's Journey to Southwest Africa,* he was also the best paid. In 1906, the first 120,000 copies of his fourth novel *Hilligenlei* earned him 220,000 marks in royalties. Frenssen's winning formula was a mixture of Charles Dickens, Wilhelm Raabe, and Theodor Storm, stirred together with a dash of moral commentary and cooked over the fast growing fire of national and regional sentiment. Why then would such an experienced realist writer allow his prose, and with it his hero, to collapse as it does at the end of *Peter Moor*?

There are a number of answers to this question. There is an anecdotal answer: in shattering Peter Moor's fictive subjectivity, Frenssen is dramatizing the writing of his own novel. Frenssen never saw Southwest Africa with his own eyes. Instead, he interviewed returning soldiers and studied military documents, using these narratives to compile a kind of memoir of the "Universal Soldier" in Africa. His plot is historically accurate, if we are prepared to overlook its obvious ideological bias, and his landscape is convincing (perhaps a little too convincing) for those who have seen what is now Namibia. But the narrative voice of the soldiers could enter the book only through Frenssen's mediation. In order to allow the soldiers to speak with a single voice, Frenssen had to construct Peter Moor, and collecting the voices of his comrades is one of Peter's primary functions in the book. In order to write as if he had seen Southwest Africa, Frenssen had to speak with Peter Moor's voice, wearing his narrative persona like a mask. In the final sentence, Frenssen, the middle-aged man on the quay, removes the mask and reveals his identity. What he was obviously hoping for was the kind of reality effect we find at the end of *Candid Camera,* when the host points straight at us and says: "See the hidden camera? All those viewers (readers) out there have seen through my mask all along, but now the game is over. This is where reality begins."

In this essay I would like to pursue another, less anecdotal explanation of why Frenssen deconstructs his own narrative perspective in the way he does. My explanation begins at the moment when the book is closed and reality begins. I will attempt to show that the contradiction expressed in the final sentence has to do with the vital function the book accords to the idea of returning home and narrating. It has to do with this moment when narrative is cashed in for reality. When the witness returns to tell his story, he reassembles the fragmented wandering subject, the nomadic subject, as a stable national subject.

The reality Frenssen constructs as a frame for his narrative of adventure in Africa is the fiction that had made him successful—a fiction of regional and national identity in the first few decades of the newly constituted German Reich. Well before the Nazis pushed "degenerate" art aside and elevated *Blut-und-Boden* kitsch to the status of official romance, the regional novel was telling tales of nation and race bonded in idyllic communion by the irrational power of the soil. In the years of Frenssen's greatest successes, the regional novel was the German reading public's favorite subgenre. The term *Heimatkunst* (regional art) had been coined in 1895 by Adolf Bartels, the literary historian whose racist polemics against Judaism would later make him one of the Nazis' authorities on ethnic cleansing in art. When Bartels set about defining *Heimatkunst* in 1900 in his journal *Heimat,* he came up with a vague notion of robust writers "who have sucked their best powers from their native soil, who have created local art, real art, and often art of stylistic greatness" (15). This image of the rough and ready poet with his mouth to the ground was as powerful as it was ridiculous. Everywhere writers were beginning to conjure up the hidden powers lying just under the topsoil. Later, as the Nazi tide swept Germany, second-rate writers like Konrad Beste would swoon in ecstasy at the "dull sound" of a fertile young woman jumping from a wagon onto the "swollen earth . . . Still his senses reeled from this thud, this satiated encounter of woman and earth" (125).

This obsession with regional flavor might appear anathema to colonialism, but it was in fact just the opposite. There are two reasons for this. First, these satiated encounters with local soils were mass-distributed in book form to German-language readers of every provenance, creating the kind of imagined national reading community described by Benedict Anderson. Bartels stated this quite clearly when he claimed that "without a strong underlying feeling of *Heimat* there is no real feeling for nation" (18). For Bartels it is evident that German nationalism needs regional sentiment if it is to prevail against the liberal bourgeoisie and the "Internationalism of Social Democracy" (18). Regionalism created imaginary national communities struggling against the most vociferous opponents of colonialism at the time. The second reason for regionalism's colonialist overtones was that it allowed subjects not simply to act as if they belonged to imagined national communities, but also to admit that their community was imaginary. Or, to put it differently, it attached national identity to individual subjectivity, so that those who left home for colonial territories could tell themselves that their national identity, because it was a state of mind or a level of consciousness, could be carried with them, like their passports. This was one of the interesting side effects of the regionalist-nationalists' irrational mythology of soil. Once again, we have only to read Bartels:

> Of course the new *Heimat*-feeling was strongly opposed to the barren rationalism and radicalism of our time, and to the modern plebeians. By joining ranks with what is primeval, powerful and great on home soil, it became essentially aristocratic. At the same time, it tended to preserve whatever was particular and valuable in all regional compatriots [*Heimatgenossen*], and to make as many of them as possible into strong and free people. And in this way, people were gradually elevated above the local and the regional-national to a new *German* world-citizenship. Those who love their *Heimat* and yet give it up will do everything they can to conquer a new, real *Heimat* in the wide world. Not *ubi bene, ibi patria* but *ubique patria*. (18–19)

These two nationalist-colonialist effects of regionalism form the foundation of Frenssen's novel. After the book is closed, *Peter Moor* has been a thrilling and enticing detour from the security of home, a departure, but also a return. Peter leaves home as a product of Schleswig-Holstein's soil, but he carries with him his national identity, and he returns a German. When Frenssen writes about adventure in a German colony, his problem is one of the central problems in the ideology of white settler colonization—how is it possible to think about leaving home, traveling through a distant land, and returning with a national identity? Frenssen's story may be set in Africa, but it is about constructing a place called home and naming it in national terms.

The opening paragraphs of the book tell us that home has become a problematic place for Frenssen. The initial problem is that European expansionism produces European desire as a negation of home—a process described by Klaus Theweleit (I: chap. 2). As a child, Peter wants to be a coachman or postman, which pleases his mother. Later he wants to go to America or become a sailor, whereupon his mother scolds him and weeps. The alternative to a life of wandering, living away from family and nation, is living at home in the face of death. This realization comes on the day after he leaves school, when, standing at the anvil in his father's shop, the apprentice says to him: "See! there you stand, and there you will stand till you are gray" (1).

The initial problem in performing national identity lies in the double bind facing the national subject. Either he takes on the sedentary life, a precharted itinerary whose goal is death, or else he becomes a wanderer, violating national territory in search of a subjective identity divorced from (and therefore measured according to) nation and family. These are the two possibilities Frenssen tries out in the opening paragraphs of the book. At the heart of national identity the narrative uncovers on its first page a multiple loss which is death, loss of family ties, and loss of territorial fixity. This multiple loss becomes the narrative's problem. It is then mapped onto the colony of Southwest Africa, where it is revealed as a doubt concerning the ability of the wandering subject to bear with him the traces of national identity. For a naive young man in the age of German colonialism the idea of white settlers in Africa prompts astonishment. When Peter hears that "in Southwest Africa the blacks, like cowards, have treacherously murdered all the farmers and their wives and children," he is "completely bewildered" and asks: "Are those murdered people Germans?" (6). The astonishment expressed here concerns the ability of the family to dislocate with respect to territory and still be spoken of in terms of national identity.

The question that Frenssen finds himself posing is: what is it about traveling subjects that allows them to carry their national identity with them into distant parts of the world? Frenssen is concerned with the construction of subjectivity in the Aristotelian sense, as *subjectum*, the instance that remains unchanged in changing circumstances and is therefore the founding instance of knowledge. But where Aristotle looks to morality to stabilize the subject, Frenssen casts his faith in nation and its institutions.

One of these institutions is the family. Fifty years after Frenssen published *Peter Moor*, Frantz Fanon described the European family as "a miniature of the nation" (141). This is the belief Peter must enact in order to feel responsible for the dead families in Africa. Once he is convinced that their dislocation does not affect their national identity, he sees it as his duty to fight in the campaign. This is the decisive moment in the ideology of national identity—the moment when the astonishment over mobile national subjects is overcome, and the white settler family is reinstated as Fanon's encapsulated nation. And yet, doubt concerning the markers—the visibility—of national identity persists: "As I went along I looked at the people who were passing, and I wondered if perhaps they knew and if they could see in us that we were going to the Southwest to be revenged on a heathen people for the German blood that had been spilled" (7).

How is such a fundamental doubt to be countered? The first solution that the narrative attempts is simple—the invisibility of national identity both inside and outside the national territory is easily remedied by the excessive attention paid to description of uniforms, which are after all the most blatant markers of national identity. In this way, an affective relation of the subject to national territory is constantly constructed and reconstructed as a visible attribute, an aspect of the novel that Alan Bowyer discusses. This allows Peter's desire for mobility as an escape from sedentary life to be recast as a mobility in the service of national identity, extending national identity beyond the boundaries of national territory.

However, the attempt to map national identity onto national territory is problematic enough that this is not sufficient. First of all, in the 1890s, German national identity is still fragile enough that the narrator needs constantly to remind us that it is the sum of a series of provincial identities. The book is littered with references to individuals as Schlesians, Bavarians, Thuringians, people from Holstein, Berliners and the like, always within the greater (Bartelsian) context of being German. But here the campaign against the Herero seems to cement this fragile bond, and in the same way that English history happened overseas (as Salman Rushdie tells us),[1] the history of German territorial bonding could use the African landscape to represent itself as already secure.

Second, in order to be presented as a stable unity, national identity requires a historical perspective in which it appears as part of a long process of territorial expansion. This becomes the central problem of the narrative from the moment Peter sets sail for Africa. For Peter, wandering that acquires territory is a part of his historical heritage, and it is easy for him to imagine his own departure in this vein. On passing the shore of England he muses on how "his forefathers had, thousands of years ago, traversed the same rough way that we now followed," and he imagines "the wild struggles that they had to go through before they had built their huts and found a home on these forbidding shores" (15). By analogy, Peter's own departure involves him in a teleology of sedentary life, being understood as an extension of national territory.

In spite of these strategies, the integrity of national subjectivity remains fragile and endangered in the face of mobility throughout the book. For the wandering national subject, there is no guarantee that the departure into the unknown will partake of the teleology of sedentary life. The mobility of soldiers attempting to seize territory far from home with the express aim of rendering it habitable for white settlers seems to work against the relations of subjectivity to territory that constitute sedentary life. If we believe Deleuze and Guattari, it even seems to approximate the mobility of the "nomads" they are fighting against (see chap. 12: "1227: Treatise on Nomadology—The War Machine"). For Peter Moor, subjective identity becomes cast between two regimes: that of sedentary life, with its predictability and stasis,

---

1. See Homi Bhabha's reading, particularly chapter 8: "Dissemination. Time, Narrative, and the Margins of the Modern Nation."

and that of the wandering soldier-adventurer, risking death for the sake of returning to sedentary life. This is where the idea of the return becomes so vital. At all times, the departure from national territory is threatened by the possible loss of national identity. This becomes apparent later when we are introduced to another German wanderer:

> He was born in Nuremberg and had spent his childhood there. When he was fifteen years old he had left his home because of a stepfather, and since that time had wandered restlessly over the world. He had travelled out to South America from Bremen as a steward, had gone straight through to Chile, had seen Samoa, and had been a waiter in San Francisco. There he had enlisted in the United States Navy, but not for long. A few hundred marks in his pocket had enabled him to travel from New Orleans to Australia to dig gold, but he found little or none. When Australia was enlisting volunteers to fight against the Boers, he had come over as a trimmer, but to help the Boers. (*Peter Moor* 119)

This is the fear that haunts Peter's departure—that it might fall into a mode of wandering like the preceding, in which national identity is violated and the wanderer pays with a loss of subjective integrity. The aimless wanderer is accordingly rejected by the narrator:

> I believe there are not many Germans who wander so restlessly and madly and with such foolish good-nature through the world. The whole life of such is passed running indiscriminately, at the first impulse of a restless, unstable mind, into the right or wrong path, and after that course is run, plunging without reflection or regret at the next object which comes just then into their field of vision ... It is bad when a human has no control over his life. (119)[2]

---

2. Unrestrained wandering in the name of avarice was also an important theme in the ongoing conflict between British and German ideologies of colonialism. One example is the claim that the British had acquired perversion—and more specifically, homosexuality—in their imperialist nomadism. Sander Gilman speaks of the popular German argument that the British fail to retain the requisite detachment fitting to a civilizing race in their imperialist activities. The reason is that they "are perverted because they have internalized in their wanderings all the perversions of the world" (Gilman, *Disease* 159). This deep-seated perversion arising out of British imperialist experience leads to a "brutalization of the masses [which] is nothing more than misdirected sexuality in a society deeply embedded in all the perversions of the earth" (Moeller van den Bruck 251. Quoted in Gilman, *Disease* 159).

With the introduction (and immediate dismissal) of this character the distinction between Peter's campaign (which is also Germany's) and the pointless wandering outside of national identity is firmly put into position. This wanderer passes his life outside of the determinations of national identity because his wandering is irrational, indiscriminate, and uncontrolled. It cannot partake of a sedentary teleology and cannot acquire territory. Instead of an extension of national territory, it becomes a madness, an immorality and a flight. It becomes nomadic.

Having established the negative of Peter's departure and wandering, the book now sets about accomplishing two things. It projects this negative onto the "natives"—the "enemy"—and it establishes the criteria whereby Peter, and those like him, can guarantee themselves that their wandering is not nomadic. In other words, it attempts to disavow the nomadism it has uncovered at the heart of colonial expansion by projecting it onto colonialism's disinherited victims.

Throughout the book, the narrative wrestles with the grounds for distinguishing between the "natives" and the Germans. Both the ideological message of the novel and its imagery center upon constructing the criteria for this differentiation. Ideologically, the moment of unveiling comes in a passage that is invariably cited in discussions of the novel. In the middle of the campaign, Peter joins the old soldiers at the fire one evening as they discuss the enemy. Dialogically, various subject positions for German colonizers are tried out. The rebellious Africans are compared to North Germans rebelling against "foreign oppressors" in 1813. Then, as this comparison requires, they are described from the perspective of the missionaries as "our dear brothers in the Lord." The contradictions between this point of view and the actual interests at stake in white settler colonization are then voiced:

> And there were soldiers, farmers, and traders, and they said: "We want to take your cattle and your land away from you and make you slaves without legal rights." Those two things didn't go side by side. It is a ridiculous and crazy project. Either it is right to colonize, that is, to deprive others of their rights, to rob and to make slaves, or it is just and right to Christianize, that is, to proclaim and live up to brotherly love. (77–78)

The resolution to this dilemma comes immediately, univocally and unproblematically:

> They are not our brothers, but our slaves, whom we must treat humanely, but strictly. These ought to be our brothers? They may

become that after a century or two. They must first learn what we ourselves have discovered,—to stem water and to make wells, to dig and to plant corn, to build houses and to weave clothing. After that they may well become our brothers. (78)

Ideologically, the solution to a very real and much-debated contradiction in colonial discourse is solved from the point of view of white settler colonization. On the surface, this is all that the novel has to say. On closer examination, however, *Peter Moor* tells a different story, in which the claims of the African to land ownership are not so easily dismissed. Here it is not enough for the soldiers to repeat the ideology of colonial land theft. The narrative must construct both an African subjectivity to which land ownership is denied, and a German subjectivity to which it accrues.

The criteria that the soldier mentions in denying brotherhood to Africans center around the performance of civilization. This performance is reducible to those technical modifications of the environment that form the basis of sedentary life. By choosing the performance of sedentary life as a way of dismissing the African struggle for land ownership, Frenssen is addressing a set of assumptions that, at the time, provided a powerful and contentious means of conceptualizing the native's relation to territory—and hence the native's rights to land ownership. This was the doctrine of African nomadism. In a large number of texts from various discourses associated with German colonialism, we encounter a tension between two modes of subjective mobility. On the one hand, subjects in motion are depicted as national subjects. Their relation to territory is understood to be sedentary and capable of being formulated in terms of ownership. On the other hand, subjects in motion are depicted as nomads, for whom the relationship of subjectivity and territory is purely accidental. Their relation to territory can be described in terms of land utilization but not of ownership.

This dichotomy must be a familiar one for any reader of colonialism's documents. It is, however, necessary to resist its simple mapping onto a dichotomy of colonial settlers and disinherited natives. Of course the distinction between settlers and natives came increasingly to approximate that between national subjects and nomads; however, this was only possible through an act of disavowal. One of the features, one might even suspect one of the purposes, of this dichotomy was to banish traces of nomadic subjectivity as they were seen to reside at the heart of civilized man in fin-de-siècle Europe. In the late nineteenth century, the concept of nomadism came to be discussed not only as a social form, but as a psychological constitution. And as a psychological state, it threatened to undo the nation-building activities of imperial man. By the time Frenssen writes *Peter Moor,* the understanding of nomadism as a mode of production adequate to a particular environment has been eclipsed by the suspicion that to be a nomad is to possess a specific psychological constitution, and that this renders the subject unsuitable for sedentary life, uncivilized, and perhaps even uncivilizable.

Once it becomes understood in terms of *psyche* and not *socius,* nomadism no longer haunts civilization as a sociopolitical limit, but as a historical and moral limit. Nomadism emerges as a disavowal of contradictions, which the mobility of the European traveler introduced into the relationship of subjectivity to territory; and, in this disavowal, it is projected onto specific ethnically defined groups. Here it becomes a theme that has important consequences in administration and policy-making. In various medical, ethnographic, and administrative discourses it would seem as if the two modes of subjective mobility are quite distinct, and that it is unproblematic to project national and nomadic mobility onto settlers and natives respectively. However, works such as *Peter Moor* testify to a profound discontent concerning the nature of this distinction and the ways it can and cannot be projected onto settlers and natives.

Since the time of antiquity, the social order of the nomad had been discussed as the barbaric negative of the *polis,* as its horror and its repressed sense of community.[3] The image of nomadic hordes as a barbaric limit of civilization continued throughout the age of German colonialism. Encyclopedias and textbooks during the age of empire liked to paint pictures of nomadic hordes sweeping civilization before them by their "speed of travel and great barbarity, paired with stamina, courage and the consciousness of having nothing to lose" (*Meyers Konversations-Lexikon*). They are "warlike and disposed to raiding, which makes them dangerous neighbors for sedentary nations" (*Brockhaus' Konversations-Lexikon*). At the same time, however, a new picture of nomadic herders gradually arises, primarily out of a closer concern for their pastoral activities. From this perspective, the wild barbarians become passive and aimless herders. They are described as "primarily occupied with cattle-raising." They have "no fixed place of dwelling, but wander around from place to place seeking pasture for their herds" (*Brockhaus*). By the time Frenssen wrote *Peter Moor,* nomadism had become a common scientific term, describing, as the anthropologist Neville Dyson-Hudson has pointed out, a vague intersection of pastoralism and spatial mobility (3).

Beginning in the late eighteenth century, the conceptualization of activity and passivity begins to change, and the mobility of nomads comes

---

3. I am indebted to Bernd Hüppauf for this observation. See also Leed 236–37 and Numelin.

to be articulated as a psychological condition independent of environmental or socioeconomic conditions.[4] In an article in *The American Anthropologist* of 1894, for example, the anthropologist Otis T. Mason isolates objective and subjective impulses for the migration of peoples. Within the subjective impulses, he attempts to distinguish two kinds of nomadic peoples: those who migrate because of an inner strength, a drive that compels them to expand into new territory; and those who move out of weakness, who are driven, forced out of submissiveness and cowardice to abandon their territory.

In this view, nomadism becomes a metaphor for colonial struggles: activity becomes a strength of the mobile European, and passivity becomes a determining condition of the noncivilized nomad. Subjective passivity, cowardliness, and degeneration are easily projected onto the "primitive" races, while history seems to prove that the active and mobile races are entitled by the laws of nature to occupy the land they have seized. But this metaphor required a dual disavowal. The barbaric nature of imperial expansion had to be purged from colonial ideology, and the colonial settler's brand of pastoralism had to be clearly distinguished from the African pastoralist's passive dependence on cattle. This disavowal found a comfortable place in prevailing ideologies of historical progress. If the history of the civilized West could be told as a process of sedentarization, then nomadism was either the barbaric roots out of which civilization had emerged, or else it occupied the geographical limits of the civilized world. The aggressive, active nomad was relegated to prehistory, and the passive, primitive nomad was placed outside history. For civilization to imagine itself as sedentary, it has to imagine nomadism as elsewhere and else-when.

The argument that colonization successfully overcomes nomadism can be encountered in numerous guises in the second half of the nineteenth century, and it is at all times easily reducible to a plea for subjectivity as

---

4. The attempt to develop a psychology of territorial mobility is part of the wider ethnological tendency to psychologize the forms of human culture. For example, in his highly influential *Allgemeine Culturgeschichte der Menschheit,* G. Klemm divided the human races into "the active and passive nations." For Klemm, the active races are the wandering, conquering races, while the passive races tend to remain sedentary. What is important in the present context is that he enhances his physiological description of the two races with general psychological portraits. The mentality of the active nations is characterized by "the will, the striving for mastery, independence, freedom," while the passive nations are prone to "ennui, reluctance toward exploration, thinking, and mental progress" (196). Klemm does not attempt to map this schema onto active and passive nomadism. However, various similar conceptual pairs and their psychological correlates appear to have served to psychologize the nomad as inherently aggressive well into the age of German colonialism. See for example the opposition of "raw, freedom-loving nomads" who live in the steppes and the "hard-working but unwarlike" inhabitants of the lowlands, mentioned by T. Achelis (50n1).

national identity. According to the discourses of medicine, law, and the philosophy of history in the age of colonialism, the accession to subjectivity could be measured in terms of sedentary life. That is, the markers of subjectivity tended to require the performance of an attachment to national territory, an attachment that could be understood not only as socioeconomic, but as a libidinal and moral commitment to nation. The late-nineteenth-century European had an almost Herculean capacity for telling and retelling himself the story of his own civilization as a common commitment to a shared territory. Moritz Lazarus and Hermann Steinthal stated an ethnological commonplace of the time when they described in 1860 how communities of peoples had come to emerge from a shared consciousness, which in turn had arisen out of a shared territorial origin and "proximity of dwellings" (37). The conviction that culture requires both sedentary habits and a consciousness of subjectivity's attachment to territory is plainly evident in discussions surrounding the territoriality of wandering peoples in nineteenth-century Europe. An important subtext in late-nineteenth-century discussions of nomadism was the prevalent attempt to grasp the nature of Gypsies—as described by Katie Trumpener—and Jews in terms of homelessness. Jews presented the prime example of a people who had moved across territories for thousands of years without being able to settle, and therefore were treated as though they had no claims to original culture.

Histories of sedentarization distinguished the aggressive expansionism of the German nation from that of nomadic groups by constructing a teleology in which nomadic expansionism culminated and concluded in the state. Condorcet had named the building block of the state the "family, settled upon the soil" (22). And according to Auguste Comte, the "prime human revolution" is the "passage from nomadic life to the sedentary state."[5] The continued adherence to this view in the second half of the nineteenth century owed much to Edward Westermarck's *History of Human Marriage,* a work that inspired Linus W. Kline's theory of sexual nomadism, in which wanderings were initiated by men in search of brides. In this context it became common to describe the emergence of the civilized state as a sedentarization process initiated by the imperatives of sexual relations.

In the first few pages of his best-selling book *Psychopathia Sexualis* (1886), the immensely popular psychologist Richard Krafft-Ebing describes the role of sexual instinct in the emergence of sedentary civilization. For Krafft-Ebing, the seeds of civilization are sown when women cease to be hunted as sexual objects and begin to exercise choice in the

---

5. Cited in Centre national de la recherche scientifique, 1986.

selection of sexual partners. This introduces the art of wooing, with its attendant idealization, modesty, and ethics of love. Instead of joining the roving bands of savages to pursue his animal instincts, man learns to appeal to woman's desire. And since, as every good fin-de-siècle scientist knew, woman desires nothing more than motherhood and home, man's nomadic sexuality begins to succumb to woman's sedentary morality. Man and woman bond to form a couple, and the household emerges as the building block of civilization. This dual process of sedentarization and moralization is for Krafft-Ebing the driving force in the history of civilization. Civilization emerges when roving bands of savages give way to Fanon's miniature European nations.

For Krafft-Ebing it went without saying that the prehistory of Western civilization could still be encountered among "savage races" existing in his day—the "Australasians, Polynesians, Malays of the Philippines" (2). This historical myth was also used to distinguish the pastoralism of large-scale farming in the colonies from the nomad's irrational and passive economy. This is directly related to land cathexis. The European liked to imagine himself as emotionally bound to the soil in the way a "savage" could never be. Ernst Bloch has observed that the European's love of wandering, his *Wanderlust,* was regarded as an integral part of European (and particularly German) national identity. A writer as influential as Herbert Spencer could claim that civilized man has inherited a certain restlessness from his nomadic ancestors (556). But it was this consciousness of having descended from, but also having overcome, nomadism that distinguished the European's *Wanderlust* from the primitive pastoralist's wanderings. European national identity meant inserting the subject into a historical progression, relegating European nomadism to the distant past. Writing in 1937, Ragnar Numelin put it like this: "While the civilized races have learnt to foresee wants of the future, and have established a system of agriculture which provides food for everyone and leaves a part of the population free to pursue other occupations, the primitive peoples take no thought of tomorrow, and the search for food becomes a hand-to-mouth matter which occupies the attention of every member of the community" (69). Arguments like Numelin's make it clear that what the passive nomad was seen to lack was a historical consciousness.

The belief that civilization emerged from and constantly struggled against a primitive nomadism was to play a decisive role in discourses of colonialism. Since it was widely felt that European civilization emerged through a process of sedentarization, moralization, and rationalization, nomadism came to be seen as both an external and an internal limit to civilization. Thus it was easy to understand colonialism as a suppression of nomadism in the name of civilization. For Krafft-Ebing, the process of civilization "is hastened whenever nomadic habits yield to the spirit of colonisation, where man establishes a household. He feels the necessity for a companion in life, a housewife in a settled home" (3).

Let us return now to *Peter Moor*. In light of the theme of nomadism as previously outlined, it should be clear that the projection of nomadic wanderings onto the natives was an easy task for Frenssen. The second move, which attempts to tie the mobility of the European subject to a sedentary national identity, is more difficult. The nomadic quality of wandering is a constant threat to Peter and his companions. The terrain he crosses is determined by a topography revolving around indeterminately positioned water holes and fading wagon tracks, rendered alien by a strange night sky, inhospitable desert and featureless bush all around. This—and the significant fact that he had never seen the landscape he was describing—makes it difficult for Frenssen to present his protagonist as the master of the territory he crosses. This is compounded by the fact that, at times, the landscape begins to captivate him—to master him. In the better moments of his wandering, Peter experiences this landscape as sheltering, and understands this feeling as a reemergence of his own nomadic heritage—a reawakening of "the experiences of the forefathers, which sleep a long sleep through generations and again raise their hoary heads in the fancy of the child who is again led in the same ways and by-paths" (141). Considering where Peter experiences these fantasies of captivity, these forefathers become ambivalent representatives of a mythological prehistorical unity of humankind—a unity that negates any difference between his identity and that of the nomadic enemy. In this respect, his cathexis onto the African landscape seems to be characterized by the same ambivalence that Homi Bhabha claims for Goethe's Italy: it is both a metaphor for national identity and an invocation of a temporality in which nation becomes impossible (*The Location* 143).

The strategy that soon emerges in the book for converting the nomadism of wandering into a sedentary excursion is to measure it in terms of a distance from home. For example, when Peter lands in Madeira, his comrades advise him: "You must get a souvenir to take home, Moor. Perhaps the insurrection will be over and we shan't land. If you say afterwards at home that you were with us and have nothing to show, no one will believe it" (25). Whereupon Peter reflects upon his experiences, thinking to himself: "Keep your eyes open and see what you can; who knows if you will ever again get so far from home" (26). This strategy would be too obvious to warrant mention were it not that distance from home soon emerges not only as a geographical quantity, but more importantly as a potential for narrative. The farther Peter wanders from home, the greater the narratability of his experiences. As the troops ride on the train to

Windhoek, they "didn't say much. Many were probably at home in thought or saw themselves coming home and telling of all the wonders they had seen" (43). To comfort themselves during thirsty marches they imagine how "after a few days we'll travel back to the coast and we'll start for home! What shan't we have to tell about in this monkey-land!" (74). And while recuperating from illness in camp, Peter and his comrades speak of home: "Probably the topic turned no less than fifty times upon the subject of our dismissal and return home. That was our favorite theme! Home! What happy faces they would wear there. What shouldn't we have to tell?" (110). As the novel progresses, home becomes increasingly important as the place that authorizes subjective mobility while retaining the integrity of national identity. This is possible only because home is the place where narration is possible.

The importance of subjective mobility and its attendant modes of narration would later be theorized by Walter Benjamin. According to Benjamin, the authority of narration in Western culture rests upon specific modes of relating subjectivity to territory. On the one hand, "people imagine the storyteller as someone who has come from afar," a figure whose "archaic representative" is the "trading seaman"; on the other hand, "they enjoy no less listening to the man who has stayed at home," typified for Benjamin by the "resident tiller of the soil" ("The Storyteller" 84–85). Expanding on Benjamin's analysis, one can argue that those who stay at home are sedentary by performance, while those who return from far-off places are sedentary by desire. Indeed, it could even be stated that their departure and return creates desire and attaches it to the place of home. And they are the ones who can tell tales of far-off places—they are the ones who master that transformation of moving bodies into the written word whereby subjectivity becomes national. The narrative moves of sedentary man authorize subjectivity by attaching it—by performance or by desire—to a particular place. The narration of sedentary performance and sedentary desire masters the dispersal of bodies in time and space by relating subjectivity to territory. In the narration of subjectivity's territoriality, territory is produced as the place in which narration becomes possible, and subjectivity is produced as the totality of bodily dispersals that narration authorizes. By the time Benjamin wrote, this project could only express a nostalgia for subjectivity's lost (and fictional) totality. And yet, for this very reason, it continued to possess force in a number of discourses, not least the revivalist discourses of colonialism.

In constructing his protagonist as a wanderer who returns home to narrate, Frenssen has already condemned his Herero natives to nomadism, to voicelessness, and to extermination. Two main thematic clusters serve this purpose. The first centers on the markers of sedentary life that were mentioned at the beginning of this essay: primarily houses, gardens, and wells. This process begins by describing the violence of the Herero as an antisedentary violence, aimed at houses and gardens. The very first sign of the natives is "when we arrived at our first stopping-place which the negroes had destroyed. They had burnt out the modest house, torn down the tin roof, smashed the little household furniture, and taken everything else with them" (46). Later on, the soldiers come across "a stately farmhouse [that] had been totally ruined by the blacks: the windows had been torn out; the heavy, well-made furniture had been smashed to pieces; and many books were strewn about, soiled and torn" (56). In contrast, the German houses that still stand testify to the success of the Fanonian family-as-nation:

> As we rode by the first house that wasn't roofless, and hadn't burnt-out window-holes, we admired it very much, and when we noticed that proper furniture, a table and chairs, were standing on the open veranda, we stared in astonishment and turned in our saddles to look till we had passed. With wide eyes we gazed into the garden, which in former years the colonist had laid out with great care . . . And there in the shade of the veranda stood a German woman, and she held a little child on her arm. (127)

The second thematic cluster that distinguishes the nomadic natives from the sedentary Germans is the marks they leave on the earth. Following a strong convention of the time, Frenssen has the Germans mark the earth with their blood and their graves, and he interprets these marks for his reader, explaining that they signify ownership. Joachim Warmbold puts it concisely when he states that "nothing can illustrate the claim of German settlers to their new homeland, nothing the claim of the German Empire to its 'protectorates' more convincingly, according to Frenssen, than 'the fact that of all the non-European continents the soil of Africa has drunk the most German blood, German sweat, and German tears'" (86). Of course, Frenssen knew perfectly well that if he wanted to count the pints, there was no question that the land was soaked not with "German blood" but with "Herero blood." But this is not his intention. The point he wishes to make is that German suffering and death mark the earth as German territory, because he can narrate its claim to territory. Herero death and suffering mark the earth in the same way their cattle marked it—trampled flat by the flight of nomads:

> The next morning we ventured to pursue the enemy . . . The ground was trodden down into a floor for a width of about a hundred yards;

for in such a broad, thickly crowded horde had the enemy and their herds of cattle stormed along. In the path of their flight lay blankets, skins, ostrich feathers, household utensils, women's ornaments, cattle, and men dead and dying and staring blankly. (189)

From there it is but a short step to the final few pages of the book and the conclusion that the Herero "deserved death before God and man, not because they have murdered two hundred farmers and have revolted against us, but because they have built no houses and dug no wells" (233). Here the extermination of the Herero follows so easily from their nomadism, because in the absence of narration, wandering leads only to death. This is the same abyss that Peter has already glimpsed in the aimless wandering of his German comrade and in the precharted monotony of life in the old world.

And yet, even as ideologically blatant and narratologically blunt a work as Frenssen's novel enacts the failures of its own attempt to construct national identity by a disavowal of nomadic mobility. As has been shown, the novel struggles constantly to dispel fundamental doubts concerning national identity. As it draws to a close, these doubts are increasingly transposed onto the narrative that national identity authorizes. The moment at which the fantasy of white settler colonization as a transfer of sedentary national identity to Africa reaches its apogee is also the moment at which its impossibility as a personal experience is most evident. A wounded guardsman speaks this fantasy and impossibility:

> The guardsman was leaning against his horse. He had a severe pain in his chest, and in a distressed voice said: "When we were sitting by our fire there in the south, our captain said that two million Germans would live here, and their children would ride safely through the country and visit their playmates, stopping on the way to water their horses at these water-holes and at many new ones which would be dug everywhere. But I shall not see anything of it; I am sick, very sick. (233)

On the journey home one young man who has lost a leg in the campaign "said he could now sing the song that they often used to sing in the village school: 'For all I am and have, I thank thee, my Fatherland'" (241). National identity and sedentary life reveal themselves as fantasies that are purchased with the death of the individual. Finally, the closing paragraph of the book brings a complete collapse of the sustained effort on the part of the narrator to actualize the authority that national identity has vested in him—the attempt to convert nomadic desire into a sedentary performance of national identity. The final sentence could have been part of the preface, dedication, or signature of the book, but where it stands it serves only one function—to demonstrate the breakdown of the subjective integrity upon which the narrative authority of the wandering European depends. If we accept Homi Bhabha's argument that national identity is an attempt to unite in narrative the subject positions of enunciation and the enounced (which he calls the performative and the pedagogical), then what Frenssen has demonstrated at the end of his book is the impossibility of this project (Bhabha, *The Location* 149–51).

In the relation of the subject to national territory, late-nineteenth-century European discourse executed another of its many attempts to gather together the fragmenting European subject. It did this by constructing a series of subject positions in which the relation of a unitary subject to a unitary territory failed, and by projecting these failures of national subjectivity onto the native. In order to produce the wandering European subject as a sedentary being, it was necessary to produce the settled African as a nomadic being. The European traveler acquired subjectivity by moving in a field whose spatiality was determined by distance from home—a distance that was measured as a potential for return and a potential for narration. And yet, as Benjamin tells us in "The Storyteller," the beginning of our century is characterized by the loss of this ability to convert departures and returns into narration. The more acutely this loss was felt, the more powerful its projection onto the native. While colonial expansion removed Africans from their land, colonial ideology told a story about nomadic Africans who depart without returning; and while colonialism obliterated the voices of Africans, it visualized them as those who cannot narrate the experience of wandering. This projection was articulated as a dialectic of European and non-European subjectivity, but it was enforced by embodying the problematic aspects of national subjectivity in the person of the "native." The nomadic native becomes the object and the victim of European man's self-perception as a castaway in a hostile world, a world where subjective unity undergoes a radical dispersal, that Benjaminian world in which the only constants are the sky and the fragility of the human body.

The Talk of Genocide, the Rhetoric of Miscegenation: Notes on Debates in the German Reichstag Concerning Southwest Africa, 1904–14

Helmut Walser Smith

> *Of course we are for humanity with respect to human beings of all kinds; but in contradiction to some of the orators preceding me, I would conclude by abjuring the interested authorities: Do not apply too much humanity to bloodthirsty beasts in the form of humans.*
> —Graf Ludwig zu Reventlow

> *I have not held a speech in favor of the Hereros; I have repeatedly emphasized that they are a wild people, very low in culture.*
> —August Bebel

Between Graf zu Reventlow, a conservative, and August Bebel, the parliamentary whip of the German Socialists, a wide, unbridgeable political chasm existed. Indeed, in the German Empire it would be difficult to find two people who more fundamentally disagreed on questions of economics, politics, and the fundamental rights of human beings. They also disagreed on German colonial policy: Reventlow—a racist, reactionary in the ordinary sense—supported all measures that increased German power in the world; Bebel—a democrat and humanitarian—criticized German colonial policy from the start. Yet across these differences they could find some measure of common ground in the terms, the images, and the categories they used to describe the Herero—a nation then in armed revolt against

German colonial rule in Southwest Africa. Reventlow saw in them "bloodthirsty beasts in the form of people"; Bebel believed them to be "a wild people, very low in culture."[1]

One might see in this common ground the terms of a discourse of rule, shared across the political spectrum, and part of a larger, seamless orientalism that insisted on the silence of colonized peoples, denying them, literally and figuratively, their humanity. Here one could point out the common referent, the image of the primitive, as well as the common assumption that cultures are to be conceived on a vertical axis, organized according to cultural development, and, depending on attributed position in this hierarchically conceived order, subject to rule, whether in the name of world power politics or in the name of a larger humanity. This interpretation would not be wrong.[2] But it would be blind to a salient difference: to wit, that Bebel, his image of the primitive notwithstanding, attributed humanity to the Herero, and Reventlow, precisely because of his image, did not.

In this essay I propose to examine the racist assumptions and images that undergird parliamentary debates concerning German colonial policy from 1904 to 1914, specifically focusing on discussions of German Southwest Africa (now Namibia) and more specifically still on discussions concerning two events that I consider touchstones for understanding not only German attitudes toward black Africans but also for understanding the emergence of twentieth-century racism. These events, which I will describe in closer detail in the course of the essay, are (1) the German army's brutal annihilation of the Nama and Herero between 1904 and 1907 and (2) the attempt to outlaw and to render juridically null and void marriages between white men and black women in Southwest Africa and the related attempt to deprive children of such interracial marriages of their fundamental rights.

The near genocide of the Herero and Nama has been described in the specialist literature on German colonial policy as well as on the history of Namibia.[3] Yet this massacre, and the problem of interracial marriage, have remained curiously unintegrated into our understanding of racist ideology in late-nineteenth-century Germany. They are also inexplicably absent from mainstream accounts of the *Kaiserreich*, both those written from a "critical" perspective as well as those written in a tone more empa-

---

1. *Stenographische Berichte über die Verhandlungen des deutschen Reichstages* (hereafter VdR). 1903–5, vol. 1, 60th meeting (*Sitzung*), 17.3.1904 (dates are rendered European style, day first), p. 1900 for Reventlow's citation; p. 1891 for Bebel's citation. Unless otherwise noted, all translations are my own.

2. See Stoler for criticisms of this approach (135–36) and, for more detail, Thomas.

3. See Bley, Drechsler, and, specifically for the war, Bridgman.

thetic with the past, or, to be more precise, with the Germans of the past. Thus, for example, the new permanent exhibit of German history in Berlin passes over the near genocide without a word. Yet these events are important in their own right—decisive, of course, for the history and peoples in Namibia, but important as well for understanding the colonial imagination in imperial Germany and for the way in which this imagination structured the wider fields of German and European racism. In what follows, then, I propose to consider the parliamentary discussion of these two events as a prism through which to understand the range, intensity, and figurative language of racial thinking in the Empire in the decade before World War I.

The scope of this racial thinking was, I shall argue, very wide; it stretched across the political spectrum and shaped, for both left and right, images of the black African. Political positions were not irrelevant to this shaping, but they did not structure patterns of perception so self-evidently as one might suppose. The analytical distinctions, I would argue, are not simply from right to left, from conservative to Catholic Center to liberal to socialist, though the spectrum of party politics is certainly germane as well. Instead, the more decisive distinction involved one's sensitivity to the modern, even revolutionary character of the spectacle of an advanced state annihilating a people. And this sensitivity rested, in its turn, on one's idea of acceptable sacrifices to progress as well as on one's perception of whether the Herero and Nama were as human as white people.

I

For the German military they were not. Between 1904 and 1907, the German colonial army decimated the Herero and Nama in a series of protracted battles, driving them to the Kalahari desert, where, in all likelihood, most of them died of thirst, starvation, and disease (especially typhus). Helmut Bley, who has written the most detailed account of German colonial policy in Southwest Africa, estimates that the Nama lost close to 50 percent of their people, the Herero 75 to 80 percent. Moreover, a very large number of people of both nations, including women and children, died not in the open field, but in prisoner-of-war camps (150–51). This massacre, which in the summer of 1995 became the object of demonstrations in Namibia demanding reparations and restitution from the Federal Republic of Germany, was not simply a case of *à la guerre comme à la guerre,* as Bernhard Dernburg, the Colonial Minister, allegedly put it.[4] Rather, the massacre resulted from what came to be known as General

---

4. Cited by Ledebour in VdR, vol. 228, 40th meeting, 3.5.1907, pp. 1451–52.

von Trotha's extermination order. This order stated, inter alia, that: "Any Herero found within the German borders with or without a gun, with or without cattle, will be shot. I shall no longer receive any women or children; I will drive them back to their people or I will shoot them."[5]

The internal politics of this order—the terms of its public declaration, and the Chief of the German General Staff Count von Schlieffen's criticism of it (on grounds of expediency, not principle)—are quite complex (Bridgman 130–32). Here we are only concerned with this order as an object of political debate in the German Reichstag. For the order, and one's position on it, constituted a barometer for political sensitivity to a phenomenon that, as Hannah Arendt rightly insisted in *Origins of Totalitarianism,* constituted something new in the modern world: states eradicating peoples, or, as she described it, "administrative massacres." In such massacres—whether perpetrated by the British in India, the Belgians in the Congo, or the Americans in the Philippines—white men reduced Indians, Africans, or Filipinos to the status of "natural" human beings. Consequently, as Arendt pointed out, the victims lacked "a specifically human reality, so that when European men massacred them they somehow were not aware that they had committed murder" (192).

In German Southwest Africa the indigenous uprisings, or wars of liberation, commenced in 1904 and lasted with interruptions until 1907. From the standpoint of the Herero, the wars cost roughly 60,000 lives; from the standpoint of the Nama, roughly 10,000—but one cannot know exactly. From the German standpoint, they cost 676 dead, 907 wounded, 97 missing (Bridgman 164).[6] The uprisings—wars would be the better word—thus constituted conflagrations of considerable magnitude, with more blood shed in the desert and the bush than in any war on German soil since the Napoleonic invasions. As such, these wars were also the object of considerable public discussion and parliamentary debate.

Within the Reichstag, the German parliament elected by universal manhood suffrage, the political parties defended—to the last—the right of German troops to quell what they saw as illegitimate rebellions. Only the Social Democrats, and in particular August Bebel, perceived the uprisings as a revolt for freedom, a notion that derived partly from his understand-

---

5. The date of the order is 2 Oct. 1904; it is reprinted and discussed in Bridgman (127–28).

6. Both in Germany and South Africa, there has been considerable debate concerning the extent of Herero and Nama losses, with some historians arguing (with, to my mind, insufficient evidence) that the losses have been dramatically overestimated. See, for a review, Dedering. For the argument that genocide did not take place, see Spraul. It should be noted that whatever the actual numbers were, contemporaries, including the representatives of the Reichstag, assumed that a large-scale massacre had, in fact, taken place.

ing of the Social Democratic conception of the universal rights of man, and even more, I think, from his public insistence that the Nama and Herero each constituted a people, a nation, a *Volk*. To attribute nationhood meant to attribute collective rights and collective agency. Bebel argued that the Nama and Herero rebelled "as any other people" would whose property had been taken away. He thus assumed structural equivalence with European nations, even when he conceded that the Nama and Herero existed in closer proximity to barbarism, and, as such, were legitimate objects for "cultural raising."[7] Bebel's critique was not, therefore, of colonial rule, but of its harshness. And he did not criticize the right of the German army to defend German life and property in Southwest Africa, but rather the way in which the rebellion was suppressed, which he considered "not just barbaric, but bestial."[8]

This speech, which detractors denounced as "a hymn of praise to the Herero," proved particularly provocative. One representative expressed disbelief that such sentiments could even be uttered in the German Reichstag.[9] Why, one may ask, should it be that a reasoned call for restraint should be so roundly decried? The standard answer, a partial explanation, refers to the German tradition of militarism, which included a deep suspicion of parliamentary criticism of the army, "the insulated body," as one military leader put it, "into which no one dare peer with critical eyes" (Craig 247). Militarism, in this sense, best describes Dernburg's defense against parliamentary criticism of the German army's *Konzentrationslager* (the term is from the debate) on Shark Island off the Southwest African coast, where only 245 Nama and Herero prisoners (of 1800) survived. The rest were left to die of malnourishment, typhus, and exhaustion.[10] According to Dernburg, the commanding officer of the troops in Southwest Africa would necessarily insist that, as commander, he could not take responsibility for prisoners without further burdening the German taxpayer and without endangering the long-term prospects of the war. To this Dernburg, the Colonial Minister, could only acquiesce. He could express regret at the brutality with which the prisoners on Shark Island were treated, but he, a civilian minister, could not interfere in the prosecution of war.[11] But militarism only partly explains Shark Island and why it did not become, as Zabern did in 1913, a well-publicized clash between parliament and the military. As in Bebel's provocative speech, something more was at stake: the perception, shared across a large range of the political spectrum,

---

7. VdR, 1903–1905, vol. 1, 60th meeting, 17.3.1904, p. 1890.
8. VdR, 1903–1905, vol. 1, 60th meeting, 17.3.1904, pp. 1891–92.
9. VdR, 1903–1905, vol. 1, 60th meeting, 17.3.1904, p. 1894.
10. VdR, vol. 228, 40th meeting, 3.5.1907, pp. 1399, 1452.
11. VdR, vol. 228, 40th meeting, 3.5.1907, pp. 1451–52.

that black Africans, a different race, were not just a different people; they were not a people (a *Volk*) at all; and for some, they were not people, that is, humans. This, I would submit, made all the difference, for Bebel's speech constituted a provocation not because of its antimilitarism, but because in it he employed inversions that revealed central assumptions about the humanity of the Herero—whether and in what sense they were people—and therefore questioned the meaning and legitimacy of the near genocide that had occurred.

The most important inversion concerns the image of man and beast. For government officials as well as for National Liberal and conservative politicians, it was axiomatic that the Herero revolt resulted in greatest measure from the inbred "dissoluteness" (*Zügellosigkeit*) of the Herero; as such it was a revolt against civilization. Moreover, and precisely because the Herero were a "wild people," the way in which the German troops dispatched them derived not from German shortcomings, but from the nature of the opponent. As Karl Schrader, a left-liberal representative, put it: "In the midst of a revolt, one is not inclined to mild treatment of wild people, and, often enough, it is hardly appropriate."[12] The language is important, precisely because Schrader was not the most extreme in his denigration of the Nama and Herero. More measured than National Liberals and conservatives to his right, he criticized von Trotha's order and insisted, in contrast to von Trotha, that "these people are also human," and that, as a consequence, one should take care to be "humane," and that, as a further consequence, women and children should be spared.[13] Schrader thus left open the question of whether "these people could ever be educated to civility."[14] Still, they were a people, if not on the same order as, say, French, Italians, or Germans.

From the debate it is not clear whether representatives who shared the opinion that the Nama and Herero were of a "wild" and "bestial" nature did so with explicit reference to, or even implicit cognizance of, the wider debate between monogenists, who ascribed a common origin to all of humanity, and polygenists, who did not. But the figurative language of some members of the Reichstag clearly placed them among the second group. This is particularly true of Graf Ludwig zu Reventlow, a conservative spokesman on colonial policy, who saw in the Herero "blood thirsty beasts in the form of humans." Here the inversion of beasts and man is most explicit, its rhetorical power reinforced and fortified by further images documenting his deep aversions. Of these, Reventlow's appropriation of violent rape as a topos characterizing the behavior of marauding

---

12. VdR, 1903–1905, vol. 1, 60th meeting, 17.3.1904, p. 1897.
13. VdR, 1903–1905, vol. 1, 60th meeting, 17.3.1904, p. 1897.
14. VdR, 1903–1905, vol. 1, 60th meeting, 17.3.1904, p. 1897.

Africans was especially striking. Against the background of rape and sexual abuse on the part of German soldiers, he insisted that German troops simply fought as their opponents did and that the Nama and Herero were in any case worse, since young boys also participated in the collective rape perpetrated by the men. And, as he further insisted, the Africans were especially cruel, "tearing out the intestines of live women and hanging them on the next tree." Not just the men, but also the women were vicious, an example and a consequence, he opined, of male and female equality.[15]

That the Herero were especially barbarous was an assumption shared across the political spectrum, even by Social Democrats such as Georg Ledebour who criticized the German Army for "sinking down to the moral level of the Hottentots."[16] But few parliamentarians were as explicit as Reventlow in denying them—literally—their humanity. Thus Adolf Stoecker, the conservative Protestant court preacher better known for his antisemitism, insisted that "one may not judge the Herero as beasts."[17] But where explicit disavowal of the humanity of the Nama and Herero was absent, descriptive language often betrayed an implicit denial of their "specific human quality." This becomes evident in the language used to describe prisoners of war. "Fourteen hundred heads are in our hands," proclaimed Oskar Wilhelm Stübel, the director of the Colonial Department of the Foreign Office, after praising the humanity of von Trotha's latest orders.[18] The prisoners on Shark Island "died off" (*eingehen*), Dernburg told the Reichstag.[19] Then there was the range of epithets associated with the Nama and Herero as not-quite-human workers: "laboring animals," as the vice president of the Reichstag and National Liberal deputy, Hermann Paasche, called them;[20] "human material," as the colonial administrator Friedrich von Lindquist defined the Nama and Herero while pleading for their "humane and just treatment."[21]

The qualified attribution of humanity that informed these positions structured both praise and criticism of the German army's prosecution of war in Southwest Africa. That parliamentarians who denied the Herero humanity would praise the German army should not be surprising. But that criticism of the army coexisted with this qualified attribution was a more complex problem, which, in turn, raised questions about the historical place of the violent collision between peoples. Here the left-liberal dis-

---

15. VdR, 1903–1905, vol. 1, 60th meeting, 17.3.1904, p. 1897.
16. VdR, 1905–1906, vol. 1, 2d meeting, 2.12.1905, pp. 109–10.
17. VdR, 1903–1905, vol. 1, 60th meeting, 17.3.1904, p. 1903.
18. VdR, 1903–1905, vol. 6, 129th meeting, 30.1.1905, p. 4109.
19. VdR, 1907, vol. 227, 11th meeting, 6.3.1907, p. 1452.
20. VdR, 1912, vol. 284, 50th meeting, 29.4.1912, p.1520.
21. VdR, 1910–1911, vol. 262, 99th meeting, 12.12.1910, p. 3595.

course, which continually invoked humanitarian categories, proved particularly revelatory of the range of strategies German parliamentarians used to narrate the violent clash with, and near genocide of, the Herero.

Left liberals, such as Ernst Müller-Meiningen, did not criticize the colonial encounter itself, but rather addressed the conditions under which it could both satisfy German economic imperatives and universal maxims of humanity (as he understood this term). Whatever its cause, the massacre self-evidently constituted an affront to these universal maxims. Less obvious, however, was the place of these massacres in a larger historical frame. Here the world of colonial scholarship provided an ordering principle with which left-liberal parliamentarians could understand the violent collision of unequal cultures as a phenomenon that furthered progress. In his works of political geography, Friedrich Ratzel had for example argued that the dissemination of culture occurred through contact and conflict between peoples—contact that involved sometimes the annihilation, sometimes the absorption, of "lower peoples."[22] These sentiments were shared by Paul Rohrbach, though with less optimism about the suitability of black Africans to participate in "cultural raising." The most influential colonial publicist of the left-liberal milieu, Rohrbach believed that the Herero "lacked the capacity to be educated to moral independence" (68–69).[23] *Bildung* could not alter this situation, for in sub-Saharan Africa *Bildung* was "in the first instance synonymous with the education of the blacks to work." Rohrbach thus assumed black Africans to be *kulturunfähig;* and as he could not conceive of their culture, so he could not admit of their history, which, within his particular frame, also entailed a deeper question as to their humanity.[24]

Doubts and questions of this order underlay left-liberal positions, especially as left liberals attempted to discern the specific context in which, as Müller-Meiningen put it, "practical humanity" and not "sentimental cosmopolitanism" could be advanced. Following Rohrbach, that meant "education to work,"[25] for, like Rohrbach, Müller-Meiningen harbored doubts about the Herero's specifically human ability to acquire culture beyond the rudimentary work routines of a draft animal. He thus posed a question to parliament:

> Would it not be possible, much as we have reservations for wild animals, much as we have Indian reservations in North America, to build

---

22. For more detail on Ratzel and this general discourse, see Smith.
23. Rohrbach's most widely read work, *Die Kolonie,* appeared in a series edited by Martin Buber entitled *Die Gesellschaft.*
24. For a brilliant reflection on these assumptions more generally, see Gates (11).
25. VdR, 1912, vol. 284, 128th meeting, 7.3.1913, p. 4352.

reservations for the natives in the interests of the native groups whom culture does not easily penetrate?[26]

Here the language as well as the logic is important. Müller-Meiningen understood that his policy proposal was more suited for animals than for human beings; but he believed the policy to be in the interests of humanity, not of German nationalism or power politics, a point he underscored by positing an identity with other white colonizers ("as we have Indian reservations in North America"). But the idea of a reservation was also a product of failure: a failure of "cultural raising," yes; but also, and more importantly, of coexistence. For the war between the Germans and the Herero taught him that "if the blacks are to be preserved alongside the whites, then it is indispensable to sharply separate the two races from one another."[27] Embracing the idea of a reservation when it was first advanced by the government in 1905, he supported it until 1914 when the Great War broke out in Europe. In Southwest Africa, reservations were never created. But the debate around them suggested something of the measures that left liberals in Germany were willing to entertain in order "to preserve" black African peoples. As well, it revealed the pall of disappointment at the damming in of their idea of universal progress, characterized, as it was, by the elevation and subsequent homogenization of peoples. That particular conception of humanity was, in turn, informed by a liberal inability to understand nonhierarchical difference, or, as Tzvetan Todorov has put it, to imagine "the existence of a human substrate truly other, something capable of being not merely an imperfect state of oneself" (42).[28]

To the right, among National Liberals and conservatives, political positions were expressed with greater rhetorical violence and with more pronounced emphasis on the place of power in relations between white men and black Africans. As Wilhelm Lattmann, a conservative who considered his position on colonies to be progressive, put it: "a reasonable humanity must be paired with a reasonable domination [*einem vernünftigen Herrenstandpunkt*]." So that there might be no ambiguity, he anchored his "reasonable domination" in "racial-political principles" and insisted that "the black race, even when it accepts Christianity, cannot from the standpoint of race be considered to be of equal worth to the white race."[29] But it was the pairing of humanity with domination, even more than the

---

26. VdR, 1912, vol. 284, 128th meeting, 7.3.1913, p. 4365.
27. VdR, 1903–5, vol. 5, 106th meeting, p. 3391.
28. This also raises the question as to whether the rhetorical construction of the Herero and Nama as radically other (and therefore the experience of colonial rule more generally) already undermined the logical foundation of a specifically liberal ideology.
29. VdR, 1903–5, vol. 5, 106th meeting, p. 3391.

appropriation of racial theory, that was a constant among National Liberal and conservative deputies. Thus Freiherr Hartmann von Richthofen, a National Liberal deputy rather more to the left of the party, insisted that the work of "cultural raising" depended explicitly on a tangible and visible position of supremacy, white over black. "The native who is supposed to learn from the white must see him as a being who stands far and powerfully above him," von Richthofen proclaimed. From the floor, his party responded: "very true!"[30]

II

Yet the attempt to separate and then to hierarchically order blacks and whites faced an obstacle: the fact, however undesirable to the metropolitan center, of miscegenation. For miscegenation, whether consecrated by marriage or not, meant that visions of racial purity and racial hierarchy could not be maintained without confronting further issues that cut to the quick of political ideologies. For Socialists, this meant taking a stand on the desirability of racial mixing, which, from the standpoint of socialist theory, should be as welcome or unwelcome as any other kind of relation between men and women. For the government, as well as for parties to the right of the Social Democrats, the fact of miscegenation raised the fundamental issue of whether interracial relations should be consecrated by marriage, and, if not, whether the modern state could annul such marriages as had already taken place. This, in turn, placed political parties, especially the conservative parties and the Catholic Center, at a crucial juncture where it became necessary to strike a position between the ideological imperatives of modern racial theory (which proscribed miscegenation) and the sanctity of the institution of marriage.

The question of miscegenation first became an issue of parliamentary deliberation in the course of the war in Southwest Africa, a war in which Herero and Nama men were killed in disproportionate numbers while the numbers of white men, mostly German troops, swelled to roughly 10,000. This led a few conservative parliamentarians to imagine the imminent creation of "inferior creole states" and to insist that for "the white race to consider itself everywhere to be the master race . . . every sexual relation of blacks with whites in the colonies must be put under penalty of the law."[31] But the real impetus for the criminalization of interracial marriage came

---

30. VdR, 1912, vol. 284, 55th meeting, 7.5.1912, p. 1728.
31. VdR, 1905–6, vol. 3, 73d meeting, 23.3.1906, p. 2228; VdR, 1903–5, vol. 6, 164th meeting, 15.3.1905, p. 5275. For a wider and provocative discussion of the issue of miscegenation, especially focusing on the way in which gender configured the debate, see the recent dissertation by Wildenthal.

from the white settlers themselves. In Windhoek, for example, pastors of the German Protestant church decided that they would no longer allow "half-white" children in their kindergarten; school teachers and leaders of local patriotic organizations also closed ranks. Then, in 1905, the colonial government of German Southwest Africa put forth an imperial ordinance outlawing interracial marriage; in 1906, a similar ordinance followed for German East Africa and, in 1912, for Samoa (G. Braun 31–32).[32] The latter was the subject of an extended Reichstag debate, in part because the ordinance came from Berlin. The ordinance decreed that marriages between indigenous and nonindigenous peoples were no longer to be consecrated, but that interracial marriages consecrated prior to the ordinance were to be seen as legitimate. The children of such legitimate marriages were—juridically speaking—white and were to be placed on a list—a "*Mischlingsliste.*" Conversely, marriages entered into after the ordinance were to be seen as illegitimate and rendered annulled in the eyes of the law. Children of such marriages were to be deemed indigenous, which is to say black. For such children it was possible, upon application, to be considered equal to a white person, but only after proving fluency in German and displaying European *Bildung.*[33]

In this context, Wilhelm Solf, the Colonial Director, provided a remarkable defense of the new ordinance. In general terms, he argued, the issue before the house constituted a racial issue, in specific terms, a question of racial mixing. In history, so he opined, there were repugnant solutions to the question of racial mixing ("*die Mischlingsfrage*"), the most prominent of which was in the United States, where Lincoln's edict of emancipation and the ensuing Thirteenth Amendment to the U.S. Constitution served as a "warning Menetekel for all colonizing nations." Against such "misunderstood humanity," he appealed to the "instincts" of the delegates. "Gentlemen," he asked rhetorically, "you are sending your sons to the colonies: do you want them to return with black daughters-in-law?" In his mind "worse still" was the idea that "white girls might return with Hereros, Hottentots, and Bastards as husbands." To drive home his point he appealed to racial and national solidarity across lines of class division, "for with respect to the colored man even the proletarian is master." Arguing for racial egoism, he then closed by asking, "should we permit our race to become bastardized?"[34]

---

32. The ordinances for Southwest Africa and Samoa simply outlawed interracial marriage; for East Africa such marriages were the subject of special deliberation on the part of colonial administrators.

33. Braun (31–32). And, for more detail, see VdR, 1912, vol. 284, 55th meeting, 7.5.1912, pp. 1724–25.

34. VdR, 1912, vol. 284, 53d meeting, 2.5.192, p. 1648.

Here I wish not so much to analyze the speech as to focus on the response, for the positions taken for and against Solf reveal a great deal about the breadth and intensity of racial thinking across the political spectrum. First, the Social Democrats opposed such ordinances, but equivocated on whether or not "racial mixing" constituted, as Solf had argued, an issue of national importance. In a parliamentary debate in 1906, Bebel's reaction had been to ridicule talk about "mixed races."[35] But by 1912, Georg Ledebour conceded that "marriages between blacks and whites" as well as "extra-marital relations from which *Mischlinge* (half-breeds) are born" cannot be considered a "desirable condition." Why he should think interracial marriage undesirable, Ledebour did not say; rather, he engaged in an analytically safe structural critique: *Mischlinge,* he told the parliament, are the "inevitable result of your colonial policy."[36] This argument notwithstanding, it is apparent that racial thinking had, by 1912, become *salonfähig* for some Social Democrats. Ledebour even proffered the opinion that races were to be ordered hierarchically, that "physically and mentally" the Samoans stood above the peoples of Southwest Africa, and that this alleged fact had considerable consequence for one's position on interracial marriage.[37]

It is, then, a remarkable circumstance that in 1912 no one in the Reichstag raised a voice, as Bebel had done in 1906, to ridicule talk about the allegedly deleterious consequences of racial mixing. Quite evidently this particular discourse was a shared discourse. But this did not mean that all parties assented to Solf's position, for his proposal harbored a still more radical proposition: to wit, that the modern state, in the service of modern racial ideology, could undo an institution (marriage) otherwise considered, especially by conservative thinkers, to be a foundation of the social order, and, as such, sacrosanct. The most charged reactions are therefore to be found within the two groups, the Catholic Center and the conservative parties, who drew part of their legitimacy from their rootedness in religious milieus.

With qualifications, representatives of the Catholic Center had been cautious critics of *Weltpolitik,* but not of colonialism per se, especially as it furthered the cause of missionization. While sharply censuring the way von Trotha had prosecuted the war, Center leaders nevertheless remained in general agreement with colonialist positions.[38] Thus Peter Spahn concurred with the necessity of creating a reservation for "the natives" of Southwest Africa, while Matthias Erzberger thought racial mixing to be

---

35. VdR, 1906, vol. 3, 73d meeting, 23.3.1906, p. 2245.
36. VdR, 1906, vol. 3, 73d meeting, 23.3.1906, p. 2245.
37. VdR, 1912, vol. 284, 53d meeting, 2.5.1912, p. 1650.
38. This relationship has yet to be fully worked out. See, however, Gründer.

"very troubling and in the highest degree regrettable . . . not only from a national but also a moral standpoint."[39] But within the specific context of the debate on interracial marriage, Center leaders, and in particular Adolf Gröber, assumed a contrary position.

Gröber argued that he, too, was no friend of "such racial mixing," but that, unlike Solf, he derived his opposition from what he perceived to be "the considerable differences in cultural conditions." To take the opposite position, he argued, would be to assume "the standpoint of the Boers," who, according to Gröber, "did not recognize the natives as humans." Starting from this insight, Gröber then criticized the "cold-bloodedness" of recent colonial literature (presumably the work of Paul Rohrbach), especially those passages where it is suggested that indigenous peoples should not be taught to read or write European languages and, more sharply still, where it is intimated that "Negroes are not fit for Christianity." These positions, Gröber maintained, "betrayed an unwelcome brutality in German literary production." On the specific issue of marriage, he argued first in moral, then religious terms. To declare interracial marriages legally annulled would be, he thought, to "drive people to concubinage," a condition which, aside from its morally baneful consequences, would not serve German honor. But when the matter concerned two Christians, it would "in fact be simply impossible to say: Christians may not marry one another because the woman has a black or brown skin and the man a white."[40]

Gröber's oration is of interest because, even more than the Social Democratic responses, it identifies central issues concretely: first, that the modern state has arrogated to itself the right to undo a sacrament; second, that this undoing is based on a physical feature (skin color) and not on a structure of belief; and third, that the attempt is bound up with a denial of the humanity of indigenous peoples. The third point was especially marked in the juridical discussion, where scholars had argued that a legally binding marriage requires a statement of will that, however, could only be put forward by a person who is "of age" (*mündig*) and who is neither "insane" (*geisteskrank*) nor "mentally retarded" (*geistesschwach*) in the sense outlined by the Civil Code of 1897. And as it was possible for Wilhelminian Germans to think of indigenous peoples in these categories, legal scholars maintained that outlawing or annulling interracial marriages did not, in fact, challenge the binding nature of the marriage contract (G. Braun 16–18). Such arguments, while they did not hold up in

---

39. VdR, 1903–5, vol. 5, 106th meeting, pp. 3449–50; VdR, 1905–6, vol. 3, 73d meeting, 23.3.1906, p. 2232. For a detailed and nuanced treatment of Erzberger's position, see Epstein (637–62).

40. VdR, 1912, vol. 284, 55th meeting, 7.5.1912, pp. 1724–25.

court, nevertheless revealed the degree to which the colonial imagination had already prefigured a chain of reasoning that allowed the state to define whole peoples as less human, therefore less valuable, therefore as "life not worth living." And this, from one tradition of Catholic thought, was, as Gröber contended, "*unzulässig*"—inadmissible. And it was inadmissible, as the Center's Matthias Erzberger argued, because it constituted "an act of violence against inalienable human rights."[41]

The responses of conservative deputies were divided. Two Protestant pastors, Johannes Zürn of the *Deutsche Reichspartei* and Reinhard Mumm of the *Christlichsoziale Wirtschaftliche Vereinigung* addressed the issue. Zürn argued that "our Christian sensibilities" suggest that the Catholic Center should be supported, insofar as it has argued for securing interracial marriage as well as the rights of children of such marriages. But—and this "but" was decisive—"a good and healthy national race-consciousness opposes making racial mixing easier in our colonies." Zürn therefore understood that the issue involved a direct conflict between religious tradition and modern racism. Faced with the choice, he sided with the latter. "Racial mixing in the colonies," he believed, "always results in disaster," for "inevitably the children . . . develop in the direction of the bad side" and "our national consciousness [*nationales Volksbewußtsein*] is done irreparable harm."[42] By contrast, Pastor Mumm conceded that Graf Gobineau and the Bayreuth cultural circle had much to teach about race. Yet, for practical reasons, he considered outlawing interracial marriage to be an impossibility.[43]

The conservative position deserves to be analyzed more closely, for, in a way scarcely noticeable, it documents an important shift in the central assumptions of a conservative tradition. In Germany, as well as in other European countries, that tradition rested upon the ideological defense of seemingly natural institutions like the family against the encroachment of the modern, reform-minded, bureaucratic state. In this sense, as Albert O. Hirschman has shown, conservatism involved complex ways of "thinking against the future" (1–3). But in 1912 the colonial imagination involved the reverse: one thought in terms of empires, great and future struggles, and centuries. Theoretical racism, to which both Zürn and Mumm appealed, constituted a specific derivation of this way of thinking, for it was not argued that interracial marriage dissolved traditional bonds, but rather that such marriages adversely affected proximate and distant generations, tarring them, as Benedict Anderson has written, with "eternal contaminations, transmitted from the origins of time through an endless

---

41. VdR, 1912, vol. 284, 56th meeting, 8.5.1912, pp. 1741–22.
42. VdR, 1912, vol. 284, 56th meeting, 8.5.1912, p. 1732.
43. VdR, 1912, vol. 284, 56th meeting, 8.5.1912, p. 1733.

sequence of loathsome copulations: outside history" (136). And it was this quality of thinking outside history that, at least in the tradition of nineteenth-century conservatism, constituted something new, a break. And it lent to conservative racial aversions a frightening, because future-oriented, finality.

But in the colonial imagination, it was the liberals who constituted the ideological vanguard. In their arguments, both National Liberals, such as Freiherr von Richthofen, and left liberals, such as Carl Braband, appropriated the range of twisted images ordinarily associated with fin-de-siècle racist thought: the high incidence of venereal disease that allegedly accompanied miscegenation, the gendered appeals to save German women from black men, the supposed inability of Africans to achieve cultural distinction, and an obligatory admonition to heed the lessons of racial integration gone awry—as was the case, they believed, in postemancipation United States. Moreover, both Richthofen and Braband directed a considerable dose of their vituperation against Erzberger, the Catholic deputy. Richthofen, the National Liberal representative, argued that Erzberger lacked that "upon which the whole discussion in our opinion turns . . . racial feeling [*Rassengefühl*]."[44] And as if to close a century of left-liberal opposition to excesses associated with nationalism and racism (and, in particular, antisemitism), Braband now argued: "When one assumes, and rightly so, the standpoint that certain racial mixtures are harmful to the national and racial interest, then the whole range of religious considerations that our colleague Erzberger has put forward are in my opinion completely groundless."[45] Indeed, from this perspective they were. The debate then took one final turn, with the prominent Social Democrat Eduard David attempting to convince the floor that Samoan women were actually quite beautiful and, as such, "not to be thrown into the same pot with negro women."[46]

But such observations, deeply problematic in their own right, would not serve as a sufficient bulwark against the persuasive power of an ideologically driven, future-oriented racism, which, by 1912, had become part of the argumentative arsenal of the major political parties outside the Social Democratic Party and the Catholic Center.[47]

---

44. VdR, 1912, vol. 284, 56th meeting, 8.5.1912, p. 1742.
45. VdR, 1912, vol. 284, 56th meeting, 8.5.1912, p. 1744.
46. VdR, 1912, vol. 284, 56th meeting, 8.5.1912, p. 1745.
47. The vote supported the parliamentary commission's position, which was that interracial marrriages could not be rendered null and void. The final count was 202 for, 132 against, with one abstention and two invalid votes. But here we are less interested in the voting pattern, which reflected party discipline, legal objections, and practical politics, than the language of race used for and against the position of the government, as represented by Wilhelm Solf.

III

Racial thinking, it is easy to imagine, ought to be understood as a variation of xenophobia, as a last defense of the parochial and small-minded against the challenge of difference. But this way of looking at the problem, while comforting, is in certain situations ahistorical. For at the close of the nineteenth century, within the public sphere defined by parliamentary politics, people who thought in terms of race thought with the future. And the reverse was true as well: parliamentarians, such as August Bebel, who attempted to undermine the logic of racial thinking were derided as backward. Thus a conservative colonialist could, with some legitimacy, criticize Bebel by arguing that "a more backwards understanding of colonial matters than is represented by your party cannot be found"; and this, he pressed on, is "now even recognized by some in your own ranks."[48] Within the frame of the debate, there was some truth to this charge. Bebel argued for humane treatment, for universal human rights, and against the illegitimate domination of one human being over another. In short, he argued with the ideas of 1789. Catholics, as befitted them, also thought in terms not quite contemporary; they argued for the sanctity of marriage in the face of the encroachment of the modern state and against the obvious cruelty of some colonial practices. But the others thought, as Hannah Arendt once put it, "in centuries"—now in terms of cultural progress, now of Empire and coming struggles, but, in either case, with the future, and with the ideas of 1914.

One is therefore tempted to see the problem in terms of the pathology of the modern. But this too has become, in some hands, an all-too-easy analytical stance, a stance, moreover, that tends to ignore salient differences between positions. It is of course true that across the political spectrum parliamentary delegates shared the idea that black Africans ought to be the subject of "cultural raising." In turn, this idea implied notions of "the primitive" who, though contemporaneous, existed in another time and was, for this reason, perceived to be less human (Fabian 27). It is also true that the idea of "cultural raising" was predicated on cultural violence. Yet surely it is important to know whether people, politicians in this case, see the violence in their ideas (for all ideas, including those associated with multicultural tolerance, are implicated in violence). And surely it is of interest to inquire into the degree to which one's view of the world allows one to see this fact. Then there are choices. Appropriating the language of 1789 (the language of one kind of modernity), Bebel could not countenance the range of violence inherent in what was both an act of dominance

---

48. VdR, 1907, vol. 227, 11th meeting, 6.3.1907, pp. 276–77.

and, from his point of view, a project of "cultural raising." Catholics, who fundamentally agreed (also for religious reasons) with this project, perceived its violence only when it conflicted with the sanctity of religious institutions and when its cruelty all too self-evidently contrasted with notions of human rights. Conversely, liberals and conservatives thought in larger terms: progress, humanity as an abstraction, national power, race, and the struggle of races. Here too there were differences between them. Common to both, however, was the increasing willingness to accept brutality in the service of an idea and the increasing blindness to the violence done, not to nations or classes, but to humans. And this was possible, I would submit, because—increasingly—they did not see that the individual humans involved were quite as human as a white man or a white woman.

On Colonial Spaces and Bodies: Hans Grimm's *Geschichten aus Südwestafrika*

Thomas Nolden

Nation and Narration

Following yet redirecting a path that György Lukács marked out when he inserted the rise of the novel into its historical and societal context, literary scholars have spent considerable effort in the last few years mapping out the configurations in which the relationship between nation and narration can occur. One approach to this relationship has focused on the "emergence of the political 'rationality' of the nation as a form of narrative—textual strategies, metaphoric displacements, sub-texts and figurative stratagems" (Bhabha, *Nation* 2). Approaching this relationship from a different perspective, other critics analyze the "master narratives" (Lyotard) that nations have employed to portray their history as stories about their foundation, their uniqueness, and their progress. According to Timothy Brennan, "it was the *novel* that historically accompanied the rise of nations by objectifying the 'one, yet many' of national life, and by mimicking the structure of the nation, a clearly bordered jumble of languages and styles. . . . Its manner of presentation allowed people to imagine the special community that was the nation" (49). The two approaches complement each other and both take recourse in a concept of nation that emphasizes the "fictional" element in the transformation of a community of people into a nation. Nations are "inventions" (Gellner) and therefore have to be studied as creations of the imagination. Benedict Anderson's definition of the nation as an "imagined political community" (6) renders justice to the notion that the members of a nation share first of all a common reservoir of certain basic ideas about the past and present of their community, because "the members of even the smallest nation will never know most of their fellow-members, meet them, or even hear of them, yet in the minds of each lives the image of their communion" (6).

This concept of nation has enabled cultural studies to examine the images that inform this powerful construct of collective imagination called nation. The study of the process of national formation thus needs to direct its attention to the style, the symbolic patterns with which individual nations are imagined, and the roles played by illustrative symbolism, fictional representation, and cultural artifacts. Within literary scholarship, the interest in the literary coproduction of national imagination has focused on the epoch of European imperialism and on literature's complicity in the creation of a culture of imperialism. Moving the literary analysis of nineteenth-century novels from the mere description of imperialist attitudes and colonialist practices into the realm of theoretical modeling, Edward Said noted in his reading of the fictional literature of European imperialism a "far from accidental convergence between the patterns of narrative authority constitutive of the novel on the one hand, and, on the other, a complex ideological configuration underlying the tendency to imperialism" (*Culture* 70). At first glance, this evaluation seems to be just another variation and late repercussion of the initial suspicion directed toward the novel as literature's youngest genre—a suspicion still hovering over the works of even the most talented novelists of our time. Literary history has recorded the many difficulties that accompanied the emergence of the novel. In contrast to other literary genres, the novel was almost without any models in ancient literatures on which it could base its claim for aesthetic legitimacy and general approval. It had to overcome its initial reputation, tainted in the Baroque period by features that catered more to the needs of entertainment than those of religious edification. With respect to the long history of the novel and its rather slow ascendance to its status as the modern genre per se, Said's assertion that "the novel, as a cultural artifact of bourgeois society, and imperialism are unthinkable without each other" (70–71) pertains only to a rather late stage in the formation of this genre. And his statement addresses, as Said admits, primarily the novelistic production that occurred within the context of the British empire. Focusing on the colonialism that accompanied imperialism, Said emphasizes that colonialism cannot be reduced to a politics of geographical acquisition, but must be viewed as an ideological complex that comprises the very idea of Western "culture" and its esteem for a certain kind of knowledge that is complicit with domination. Said perceives a strong parallel between the strategies of domination exercised by the imperialist subject and by the narrative authority that organizes and controls fiction "premised on the recording, ordering, observing powers of the central authorizing subject" (79).

The fact that the novel flourished also in those European centers where the notion of imperial mission was less developed than in Exeter Hall does not have to be billed against Said's account as such. It might, however, challenge literary scholarship to draw a more precise and colorful picture of the many roles the European novel came to play within the course of the late nineteenth and early twentieth centuries. The absence of a "colonial" novel in German that could stand aesthetic comparison with the works of Conrad or Kipling, then, could be explained by the fact that Germany's imperial vocation and colonialist practice were weaker than, for example, Britain's. While Germany compared its colonial aspirations and policies to those fashioned by Great Britain, which had authored the book of colonialism, an author like Hans Grimm (1875–1959) sought literary orientation in the narratives of his British colleague Rudyard Kipling (Ridley; Crowhurst-Bond). However, at both the political and the literary levels, the British models proved to be of little help. Whereas the British novelist provided the aesthetic counterpart to colonial politics, the German novelist had to resign himself to a depiction of the failure of German colonialism. And yet, although this peculiar German configuration of the relationship between novel—or narration—and the imperial nation could be read almost as a reversal of the correlation manifest within the British context, the German colonial texts that were written as late as the 1920s and 1930s nonetheless display features that characterize colonial literature of the first, that is, the British generation.

The Space of Colonial Narrative

In colonial politics and discourse, the element of space and the structure of spatial relationships are among the features that define the hierarchical organization of the imagined community and that differentiate between those who are within it and those who are not, between those at its center and those at—or beyond—its margins. When "official nationalism" can be understood as an "anticipatory strategy adopted by dominant groups that are threatened with marginalization or exclusion from an emerging nationally imaged community" (Anderson 95), space also becomes the central element of the definition of colonialist imagination. The imperialist reterritorialization of the nation attempts to expand the nation's space by subjecting other cultures to a concept of space often foreign to the colonized people and land. In the metaphoric language of Hans Grimm, "a living net of orderliness" is cast on "dead land" ("Dina" 14).

With his terminological differentiation between "spatial practice," "representation of space," and "representational spaces," Henri Lefebvre presents a conceptual clarification of the functions of space and its representation. Suggesting that every society at any given point in its development produces its own relation to space, Lefebvre coins the term "spatial practice" to address the "production and reproduction, and the particular locations and spatial sets characteristic of each social formation." He holds that "spatial practice ensures continuity and some degree of cohesion. In terms of social space, and of each member of a given society's relationship to that space, this cohesion implies a guaranteed level of *competence* and a specific level of *performance*." "Representations of space" are linked to and display the "order" that regulates the spatial practice of a society by means of knowledge, signs, codes, and "'frontal' relations" (33).[1] Whereas the representation of space (as the conceptualization of space) lies within the domain of scientists, planners, engineers, and politicians, "representational spaces" created by writers, painters, and architects evolve at the borders of the coherent systems of spatial representation and thus have the freedom to "coexist, concord or interfere" with and even to "ignore" social practice (41).

Hans Grimm's "Die Geschichte vom alten Blut und von der ungeheuren Verlassenheit" (The story of old blood and of immense desolation) from his collection *Lüderitzland, Geschichten aus Südwestafrika* provides insight into the relationship and tension between the spatial practice of German colonial politics and its representation of space on the one hand and the "representational space" as presented in literary colonial narrative discourse on the other hand. The text tells the history of the territorial discovery of a region in Southwest Africa in a manner typical of Grimm's late accounts of the German colonial endeavor. The novella, which appeared in 1931, is even more removed from the short-lived era of German colonization than his monumental novel *Volk ohne Raum* (published in 1926). By 1893 the notion that the world had already been divided up among European nations other than Germany was a commonplace taught—and lamented—in textbooks used in German high schools (Partsch). Thus Grimm's novella—like his novel—has to be read historically as revisionism, politically as criticism (directed against Germany's colonial policy), and stylistically as an elegiac melodrama of German colonialism.

The novella does not commence with an introduction of the protagonists, two German brothers of aristocratic descent whose rapid mental and cultural deterioration as farmers in a deserted area of Southwest Africa is the story's focus. Instead, its very long introductory passage elaborates on the process of geographical discovery and seizure, casting the history of

---

1. For Lefebvre, "frontal relations" of production codify power relations, for example, in the form of buildings or public monuments: "Such frontal (and hence brutal) expressions of these relations do not completely crowd out their more clandestine or underground aspects; all power must have its accomplices—and its police" (33).

the African land as a story of a failed redemption through German colonialism. This opening section presents what might be called a "colonial narrative" in the sense that it is imaginative in nature and promotes an ideal of colonial expansion that German politics failed to adopt. Colonial narrative, as I understand it, displays the dominant features of the spatial practice of colonialism (discovery, military conquest, settlement, resettlement of natives, and establishment of borders, for example) by representing the space of the colonized land according to the conceptualization of space that pertains to colonialist knowledge (notions of people and nature as defined by the geography and ethnography of the time).

To this colonial narrative presented in the form of a chronicle at the beginning of the novella, Grimm juxtaposes a narrative of colonialism that captures Germany's inability to accept the challenges and fulfill the promises outlined in the colonial narrative. In this "narrative of colonialism," the spatial order promoted in the idealized and normative colonial narrative collapses and gives way to a spatial practice that neglects the hierarchies, borders, and boundaries (between the colonialist and the native) of colonialism. The colonial narrative relates to the narrative of colonialism like an idyll to a melodrama. The juxtaposition of the colonial narrative and the narrative of colonialism that characterizes the structure of the representational space of Grimm's novella—and his oeuvre in general—results in the elegiac depiction of the colonies as a lost paradisaic space:

> There is a piece of land in the Northwest of German Southwest Africa ("Deutschsüdwestafrika"); the piece of land with its mountains and its valleys, with bush and steppes and sand and watering holes has remained lonesome and strange up until today.
> First, a German missionary peeked into the secret world, but nobody seemed to live there. Then, the wagons of the Boers rattled in, searching for a way to the Kunene and searching for the promised land of milk and honey, with legendary opportunities for hunting and where a real Boer would not have to work too hard, would not have to pay taxes and would not need to obey any authority. They found hunting, and authority and taxes were absent, but there was no milk and honey, and the land was above all frightening. ("Geschichte" 77)[2]

Grimm's novella does not begin with a description of the land proper, but rather with its localization on a map whose geographical coordinates ("in

---

2. Unless otherwise noted, all translations are mine. They do not strive for an aesthetic rendition of the originals.

the Northwest of") identify the countryside as part of a national territory. At the very beginning it becomes evident that "the nomenclature of space functions as a political medium" (Russell Berman 3). The text spells the name of this territory as a composite ("Deutschsüdwestafrika"), erasing any distinction or space between the colonizing power and its colony. Only after the narrative has thus claimed the setting of the novella can it proceed to its description. Suggesting that this piece of land resisted association ("remained lonesome and strange up until today"), the narrative resists any attempt of literary composition or description—it does not appreciate the natural features of a landscape, its physical uniqueness, or even its beauty. It represents space in its most reduced and simultaneously quantified manner: as a "piece" of land that consists of basic elements that are being named in trite enumeration ("with its mountains and its valleys, with bush and steppes and sand and water holes"). The alleged objectivity of colonial representation of space favors empirical recording of quantifiable and classifiable elements over romanticizing description.

The appearance of the first missionary—his national identity carries more weight than his religious affiliation—is presented as an almost contemplative act. In a move of historical revisionism, the narrative effaces the traces of the first inhabitants (San hunters and gatherers and Nama herders) as well as the memory of the arrival of Portuguese and Dutch expeditions and navigators and the memory of the presence of the English missionaries, which all predated the German missionary's arrival in the 1840s. The tranquility of this fabricated initial discovery, stylized as an "observant" gesture in both meanings of the word, is then destroyed by the arrival of the Boers. They are characterized as anticolonialist, because they are not driven by the desire to work hard, to share the results of their labor (with a people at home), and to live within a system of law and order. To them, the northern region of Southwest Africa presents itself as a truly frightening place full of disappointments.

German colonial narrative *après la lettre* cannot simply advance colonial interests but must decompose the structure and the history of the space that it wants to claim. It also has to discount the claims of competing forces by erasing the chronology of events and by depreciating the integrity of their motives—a strategy that can be found in British and French colonial narrative as well, presenting each of these nations as "spiritually 'the whitest'" (Balibar 43). The chronicle now has prepared the stage for the arrival of the German colonialists:

> Then the Germans arrived and founded German Southwest Africa and called the Kaokoland their own as well. At the border, at well known springs, they settled the remainders of a nomadic tribe of Hot-

tentots, they had the coast checked for places to land, they gave certain legal rights to a trading company; a German appeared, motivated by his own tough will rather than by an assignment, and he spent many years climbing through the mountains and found a way through the desert and, plagued by thirst, crossed dried-up rivers to draw a powerful, unfinished map, without being paid by anyone; in his company was a Norwegian, on assignment from a trading firm, who checked where a railroad could connect Otavi with the coast. Finally, at the margin of the land, a few unsurveyed farms were sold; they remained outside of the police zone.

Then the Great War began. ("Geschichte" 77–78)

While the activities of the Boers were captured as an illusionary search ("searching . . . and searching") expressed in a series of negatives, the moves of the Germans are described according to the Caesarean formula of imperialist conquest "veni, vidi, vici." However, the decisive act of conquest proper is not narrated as one of violence and bloody subjugation as in the Roman annals. The euphemisms of legal language and the linguistic conventions of historiography allow the narrative to talk instead about the act of "founding," of "taking into possession," and of "resettlement." For the first time, the chronicle takes notice of the presence of indigenous people, who, according to the linguistic politics of colonialism, instantly become deprived of their name proper (the pejorative "Hottentots" for the Khoikhoi) and, in keeping with the spatial practice of colonialism, also become deprived of their nomadic relationship to the land.

Colonial narrative does not concern itself with the presence of the natives—they remain invisible until much later in the text. In its mythological recasting of the colony's origin, the narrative is more concerned with the introduction of an ideal protagonist/colonialist who can be juxtaposed against the representative of the colonial firms and companies as well as against the actual protagonists of the novella, who are introduced only at the end of the long opening section. The anonymous German is the adventuresome hero who in the imagination of the author could have saved German colonialism from its failure, for he is driven by his own strong volition rather than being directed by underfinanced companies or halfhearted politicians back home. With his arrival, the novella at last picks up the momentum of an adventure story, its diction becoming dynamic as the protagonist transgresses the many impediments of the country. The heroic mastery of space, expressed in action verbs, resolves in the drawing of a map. In a telling metonymic move, the map as the ultimate tool of the colonialist representation of space becomes characterized as "powerful." Indeed, the possession of a map is the prerequisite for the "transferability of geographic space" (Anderson 174) and ultimately equals the possession of power over the land. From now on, there will be a space "at the margin of the land," a border where it is not even worthwhile to survey all the farms. These margins of the map mark the space surveyed and controlled by the police, the executive force of the colonial empire. Geographic (mapped) space has thus been transformed into juridical, administrative space as the extension of a European nation, and the border now delineates "the sphere of civilization" (Noyes, "The Capture" 57). And yet, the fact that the map drawn by the German remains a fragment foreshadows at the narrative level the fractures in the colonialist's power over a country that will remain "strange." Eventually, the colonial conquest will fail just as its representation of space had been left incomplete.

With the establishment of a territory and borders, the chronicle necessarily approaches what it calls the "Great War":

> Then the Great War began.
> During the occupation of German Southwest Africa by the South Africans, a German hunter scouted through parts of the Kaokoland; he didn't want to settle for peace with the South Africans until a general peace treaty would be achieved; he was betrayed by natives, at the water, where the human being has to go, just like the animals. Later, the South Africans wrote in their newspapers that there was a piece of land in the northwest of German Southwest Africa; the piece of land with its mountains and its valleys, with bush and steppes and sand and watering holes had remained lonesome and strange up until recent days. They pretended, in their loud manner, that they had discovered and even invented this land. They copied the map of the German mountaineer without giving him any credit, they allowed some of their politicians and zoologists to go hunting, but nobody found gold and diamonds. ("Geschichte" 78)

The chronicle of colonial narrative is significant with respect both to what it records and to what it leaves unmentioned. It passes over the armed conflicts in the 1890s and ignores the revolt by the Nama of 1903 (joined by the Herero a year later), which the Germans turned into a war that killed 54,000 of the 70,000 Herero. Natives are mentioned here only in passing: they are not to be included in the annals of war. The allusion to the "betrayal" of a white man by the natives presents warfare between colonial forces as an occurrence governed by the ethical contract that binds the white people, but that is foreign to the natives who supposedly kill viciously. Thus, the natives disqualify themselves as political opponents in armed conflict. The war that the chronicle hints at is World War I, the "war at home," the importance of which for the colonial narrative lies in the displacement of the "good" colonialist by the South African occupiers. Ridiculing the story that the South Africans tell in order to create a fiction that is supposed to support their claim to the country, the narrative does not shy away from quoting itself. The distortion of historical sequence and the effacement of the presence of others (natives or competing colonialists) that characterize Grimm's novella are presented as the revisionist strategies of colonial narrative. This narrative supposes a readership too naive to recognize these strategies or to comprehend that the chronicle offered in the opening of the novella itself and the chronicle offered by the South Africans are not competing accounts, but rather two examples of the same archetype of the colonial narrative.

With the arrival of the South Africans in their ill-guided search for riches that the land does not offer, the chronicle reaches its last stage. The failure of colonization established, the narrative for the first time concerns itself with the natural setting, the landscape of the land, in a more emphatic sense. Yet, the depiction of giant mountain ranges and innumerable valleys still relates the category of space exclusively to the colonialist. The natives, the chronicle insists, do not meet the prerequisites that would allow them to be owners or masters of the land that they inhabit. Their *raison d'être* is the land's preservation and not vice versa, because it is the land that takes care of the natives the way it takes care of animals:

> And thus the land continued to remain lonesome and strange. It remained mountain ranges of incredible size whose ridges had never been touched by a white man, it remained its furrows of hundreds and thousands of valleys and small valleys which nobody knows, it remained its foot hills with rich meadows that had never been grazed by tame herds, it remained its giraffes and elephants and lions, and it appeared at some places incredibly rich in wildlife and at other places incredibly poor in wildlife, determined by the food offered by nature in a land of sun and hardship and untamed wilderness. And it guarded, sharing and following with the animals the same natural diet, its few ungoverned natives who sometimes were present, at others times gone: remainders of the Hottentots, remainders of the Ovatjimba and mostly Klip-kaffirs, shy and hidden in the mountains like baboons, when they don't want to be found, but obnoxious and importunate like mean human beings when they need something and when they find themselves in front of someone tired, sick or dependent. ("Geschichte" 78–79)

In the spatial politics of colonialism, "untamed wilderness" is not a tautology, but rather an expression of the illusion that unexplored space can retain its character once conquered and inhabited by the white intruder. The colonialist ideal of nature is not, as Peter Horn claims, "the perfect dream picture of pure, unspoiled nature" ("Die Versuchung" 335), because it does not even perceive its own spatial practice as destructive or polluting. The chronicle perpetuates the myth of an intact ecology of colonialism when it claims that the land, unchanged by the wars waged by the white man against the natives, preserves its relationship to its original inhabitants. These are part of a kind of food chain whose rationale is not the existence of the aboriginal but the preservation of the land itself. This notion of the primacy of space over its inhabitants legitimizes the colonialist claim for territorial expansion that in turn is based on the primacy of the expansionist desires of one people (the Germans) for space.

The Narrative of Colonialism

Its program of spatial Darwinism asserted, the chronicle has fulfilled its task and has prepared for the transition toward the presentation of the spatial and societal setting that has generated colonial ideology. The juxtaposition of the chronicle of Southwest Africa with the account of another colonization (that of the Mark Brandenburg) constitutes the spatial structure of the novella itself, which during the course of the narration will merge two hitherto separated settings. The main part of the novella introduces the two protagonists, members of an old aristocratic family desperately in need of its own regeneration. The owners of Großbätz in the "Neumark" (Mark Brandenburg) belong to a social class that, so the narrator insists, originally had not sympathized with the promotion of expansion overseas as the key response to the interior problems stemming from the growing social compression in Germany. Yet, the prospect of an "incredibly cheap, free, unoccupied land not spoiled by the mob" ("Geschichte" 83) reminds the conservative patriarch of the family's own origin in a colonial project (the German settlement of the territory east of the Oder in the fourteenth century): "One has to put our younger boys there, they will set out there the way our forefathers set out, and by the time we here are spent, our breed will be returning from there to our place" ("Geschichte" 84).

The remainder of the novella proves the futility of this hope and critiques the longing for racial regeneration through colonial experience as an aspiration that was conceived at a time when the prosperous and promising parts of the non-European world were already in the hands of men coming from families less spent and degenerate than the line of

Großbätz. The presentation of the young protagonists Friedrich and Sigismund as effeminate, feeble men without experience and talents makes the outcome of the novella predictable: hardly fifteen years after leaving their home in 1910, both of them fall victim to the harsh conditions of life in Southwest Africa.

The colonial narrative had strictly differentiated between the space of the colonialists and that of the natives, allowing for little overlap between these two spheres. In the narrative of colonialism, the protagonists' negligence in keeping these two spheres separated indicates the disintegration of their identity as the masters of the land. They maintain a certain geographical distance between the natives' dwellings and their own home— "to keep our distance and because of the smell" (93)—but this line of separation remains porous to their needs and desires. Friedrich and Sigismund have two native women stay in their house as domestic servants and develop within a short time a relationship of strong dependence upon them.

The sovereign perspective of the chronicle concerned with the grand course of events is gradually replaced by the perspective of a narrative of colonialism blind to essential structures and able to perceive only the narrow domestic sphere. Once the deterioration of the protagonists becomes apparent, the narrative switches to a style emulating the authoritative voice of popular ethnographic writing to condemn what it pejoratively calls the syndrome of "kaffir household" (*Kaffernwirtschaft*).

> Because of the brothers' dependency on the girls, what is called a kaffir household became a reality in Ombangonde. Features of a kaffir household are that white men stop shaving, washing and bathing regularly, that they do not change their underwear, that at night they sleep half-naked on untidy blankets and furs, that they stop being aware of the growing chaos in the home, that they avoid other white people because they are content or dull or bitter, and that any challenge to the body or to the mind appears wrong and not African to them. The presence of black wenches [*Weiber*] instead of white women [*Frauen*] in the house is a permanent feature of a kaffir household, though the black wenches are not necessarily bad, disobedient or totally lazy; a feature of a kaffir household is in most cases that the colored people lose, not their kind of loyalty, but their respect for the unattainable and untouchable white superiority of the white man who comes so close to the black being and thus loses his genuine position; or where could, at any given battlefield [*Kampfstelle*], anything be achieved without the superiority of authority? ("Geschichte" 96–97)

The climactic point here is the reference to the colonialist's position as a "battlefield" that the protagonists have opened up to intrusion. Spatial metaphors abound in this passage that judges the spatial practice of the protagonist against the standards introduced in the colonial narrative. Here, as in the colonial narrative, the category of space serves as the basic descriptor of colonial ideology, employed to present this very ideology as an objective description of allegedly natural relationships between people and their land. In this manner, the loss of order ("chaos in the home"), the refraining from social interaction with other white people ("avoidance"), the loss of one's own form of being ("coming so close to the black being") and with it the eradication of authority ("respect for the unattainable and untouchable white superiority") are symptoms described almost exclusively in language that carries strong spatial connotations, culminating in the metaphor of losing one's dominant position. The process leading to the fall of the protagonists—that is, to this deficient form of colonialism—is cast in terms of spatial movements: the lateralization of a hierarchical structure and the approximation of spheres that the spatial practice of colonialism wants to keep apart from each other. In the coordinates of the narrative, the colonialist has lost his superior, elevated position to find himself right next to—rather than above—his former subordinates. The representational space of Grimm's narrative succeeds in promoting a colonial ideology that renders the relationship between people and races as a structural and spatial order, and thus manages to disguise its racism to such a degree that even literary scholars trained under the paradigm of *Ideologiekritik* can mistake Grimm's attitude toward the African natives as one characterized by "ethnic sympathies." As late as 1989, the critic Günter Hartung stated in *Weimarer Beiträge* that in Grimm's eyes "all peoples [*Volkstum*] were given ethnic entities which had to be accepted and respected" (1667).

In the process of the destabilization of the colonial order, the attitude toward the body changes as well. The colonial narrative ascribes the responsibility for this physical decay to the "black" woman's displacement of the white woman as guarantor of order. The narrative's insistence that the black woman's shortcomings may not even be a failing of her nature or character is just another figure in the rhetoric of racism: it condemns the usurpation of the white woman's space by the female native as a violation of a most basic, categorical law—that of the spatial order of life.

It is important to note that in Grimm's colonial narrative the "black" woman does not symbolically represent what Peter Horn has called "unspoiled nature" ("Die Versuchung" 335), for the simple reason that this narrative does not operate with the image of "pure, untouched nature" in the first place. The opening of the chronicle had immediately presented the land in its geopolitical coordinates and named it according to the conventions of colonialist spatial practice. In this myth, the origin of a land is synonymous with its discovery, and the narrative's insistence that the land remained "lonesome and strange" is not meant to indicate its ability to preserve its original purity, but rather that colonialism did not succeed in incorporating it into the modern world order. Similarly, the natives of this land remain outside of the social contract that allotted every people its own space in the hierarchically structured universe of colonialism. The act of naming—a form of linguistic appropriation—that stood at the beginning of the chronicle is repeated when Friedrich and Sigismund, who had not understood the real names of their female slaves, give them names that bear the stamp of Christianity and of domestic life at home. The narrative pays as little attention to their features and their bodies as it does to the land that they inhabit. After all, the colonial narrative presented them as mere functions of space, putting them in the same category as the animals. Grimm's novellas as well as the ethnographic accounts of the time concur in the description of the female natives as "'empty' body forms" (Mamozai 282). The fears of legislators back in Germany, who had prohibited marriages between German settlers and African women, appear to have been unfounded, since the majority of male settlers were reluctant to engage in a legalized relationship with their female African subordinates. In view of the extremely small number of "mixed" couples in Southwest Africa, the resolute enforcement of this means of segregation has been called "the result of virulent and extreme racism" (Stoecker, "Position" 126). Here, Grimm's stories can be read as narrative complements to the legal prohibitions, furnishing the racist imagination of the European readership with two-dimensional images of African women devoid of any ethical depth. Not even situated in the narrow sphere where the white settler's sexual desire borders his anxiety to keep himself apart from the natives, these images are completely devoid of any erotic dimension. The female natives are irritating to the protagonists, because they represent a disruption of the colonial narrative—not as people, not as women, but as spatial entities, or bodies, transgressing the laws of the spatial order of colonialism.

Literary critics have hitherto underestimated the role and the function that space assumes in literature that promotes colonialism when they repeatedly state that in Grimm's work "space ... is a metaphor" (Ketelsen 210). Instead, space must be regarded as one of the basic categories governing the imperialist imagination. The representational space displayed in Grimm's narratives can be understood only in reference to the spatial practice and the representation of space (Lefebvre) characteristic of colonialism. Grimm's colonial narrative is programmatic in the sense that it wants to remind readers of the spatial practice of ideal colonialism by juxtaposing it to a narrative that portrays what it sees as the many deficiencies of German settlement overseas. Grimm's colonial stories furnished the German fascist imagination with the idea of a restructuring of the world that made sense even to those who imagined this reordering not primarily—or not initially—in racial terms, but rather in "natural," that is, spatial terms.

Part 2
Imperialism without Colonies

Formalism to Psychoanalysis: On the Politics of Primitivism in Carl Einstein

Andreas Michel

At the time of this writing, Carl Einstein (1885–1940) is still a largely unknown figure in American *Germanistik,* let alone in the fine arts or the history of ideas in general. A contemporary of Walter Benjamin, Einstein has received little attention although he shares many of Benjamin's intellectual pursuits as well as his fate.[1] Such unwarranted neglect is primarily due to the erratic publishing history of Einstein's writings.[2] While Benjamin's writings resurfaced in Germany in the mid-1950s, a complete, systematic collection and re-edition of Einstein's writings was not tackled until the 1980s.[3] To date, four volumes have been published, and his thought has attracted a significant number of studies over the last decade,

---

1. Einstein was born into a Jewish family. He spent most of his youth in Karlsruhe. In 1903, he moved to Berlin to study philosophy and art history. Einstein is known to have taken courses with Georg Simmel, Heinrich Wölfflin, and Alois Riehl. He established close relations to the political and expressionist journal *Aktion,* where he published before the war. During the war, he served as a soldier in Belgium. In 1928, for personal rather than political reasons, he left Berlin to settle in Paris where he befriended many of the Paris intelligentsia. In 1936, he took part in the Spanish Civil War on the side of the syndicalists. In 1940, fleeing the German forces, Einstein committed suicide in the Pyrenees.

2. Einstein's experimental "novel" *Bebuquin* is the only text that has been available intermittently since its first publication in 1912. In 1962, Ernst Nef edited a two-volume set of *Gesammelte Werke* that went quickly out of print. Sybille Penkert single-handedly started an Einstein renaissance in the late 1960s with two books that for the first time made available most of the biographical material known today as well as key texts from the Berlin archives. In 1973, she edited Einstein's *Fabrikation der Fiktionen.*

3. Medusa Verlag published volumes 1–3 between 1980 and 1985. Volume 4 was published by Fannei und Waltz Verlag in 1992 and contains a selection of previously unpublished manuscripts from the Carl-Einstein-Archiv at the *Akademie der Künste* in Berlin.

particularly in Germany but also in France.[4] Such general obscurity surrounding his work is all the more surprising given the relative prominence Einstein enjoyed as an avant-garde writer, art critic, and art historian in Berlin and Paris between the wars.[5] A friend of Georges Braque and Michel Leiris, a collaborator of George Grosz and Georges Bataille, Einstein was instrumental in making early Cubism known in Germany at a time when German artists were drawn to the emerging expressionisms of Dresden and Munich.

In 1915, Einstein published *Negerplastik* (Negro sculpture), one of the first serious Western treatments of sculpture from the African continent. A later project, *Afrikanische Plastik* (African sculpture) followed in 1921. In addition to these two programmatic writings on non-European art, Einstein published a number of essays dealing with art works from Africa and the South Sea islands that analyze them in formal and ethnographic terms. At the same time, his theoretical writings are laced with notions of the primitive in a variety of different shades of meaning, most commonly in the context of his critique of modernity. His notion of the primitive is located at the intersection of art history, ethnography, and a theory of culture (*Kulturtheorie*). Einstein's theories share this location with most discourses on the primitive at the turn of the century. This also means that figurations of the primitive are an intricate part of the politics of the times: the discourse and practice of colonialism.

The political ramifications of the representation of the non-European in Western discourses have, since the early 1980s, led to debate and a number of critical approaches to the self-complacency of more formalist studies in the humanities.[6] The present essay on Carl Einstein is a contribution to this debate. In the following pages, I shall discuss two distinct yet related figurations of the "primitive," one dating from the period before World War I, the other from the mid-1930s. In addition, my essay functions as a cautionary tale. In the present intellectual climate, it has become all too easy to prove one's political awareness through a quick indictment of what, upon first look, appears as the same old Western prejudice and is quickly labeled as such. Against such an automatic reaction, I would like to pose a critical analysis of the context within which Einstein's particular appropriation of the non-European occurs. Attention to detail, that is,

---

4. See C. Braun, Ebel, Kiefer, Kramer, Meffre, Oehm, Quast, and Sohns.

5. While *Bebuqin* was a hit among the initiated few, Einstein's pathbreaking *Die Kunst des 20. Jahrhunderts* went into three editions during his lifetime.

6. In many respects, Edward Said's *Orientalism* focused attention on a political criticism in the humanities that has since taken different directions in post-Marxism, postcolonial studies, subaltern studies, and new historicism.

involvement with the particularity of the contextual situation, will lead to a more differentiated approach to (in this case) Western depictions of non-European others.

To the extent that much of such recent work conceives of itself as a cautionary tale about the unconscious discursive consequences of Western colonialism, I present here a cautionary tale about cautionary tales. Such specular activity involves me, of course, in an abyssal structure of thought. However, this fate seems inescapable since I share a certain moral rigor with the advocates of cautionary tales. At the same time, I feel compelled to point out the problems I perceive with the particular approach to Western representations of non-European cultures that marks a book such as Marianna Torgovnick's *Gone Primitive.*

I

In *Gone Primitive: Savage Intellects, Modern Lives,* Marianna Torgovnick attempts to demonstrate how, in modernity and postmodernity, the West depends for its self-understanding upon a "generalized notion of the primitive" (22). Her desire is to point out the largely unnoticed virulence (and potential violence) of this primitivist discourse in Western culture at large. She locates its traces at the heart of academic and nonacademic constructions of non-European others, which thus help define Europe's own self-image *ex negativo.* Her study covers fields as diverse as popular culture, literature, anthropology, art history, and psychoanalysis. And she finds that, with respect to the image of the non-European, these fields exhibit a common characteristic:

> To study the primitive is . . . to enter an exotic world which is also a familiar world. That world is structured by sets of images and ideas that have slipped from their original metaphoric status to *control perceptions of primitives*—images and ideas I shall call tropes. Primitives are like children, the tropes say. Primitives are our untamed selves, our id forces—libidinous, irrational, violent, dangerous. Primitives are mystics, in tune with nature, part of its harmonies. Primitives are free. Primitives exist at the "lowest cultural levels"; we occupy the "highest," in the metaphors of stratification and hierarchy commonly used by Malinowski and others like him. The ensemble of these tropes—however miscellaneous and contradictory—forms the basic grammar and vocabulary of what I will call primitivist discourse, a discourse fundamental to the Western sense of self and Other. (8, italics added)

As suggested by the italicized phrase, Torgovnick believes that these constructions of the primitive directly and indirectly influence ("control") the way in which the West perceives non-European cultures. In her book, she is therefore concerned with the impact such depictions have upon contemporary contact between cultures today. It is in this sense that she understands her approach as a cautionary tale about intercultural representations. Her book thus exposes the political ramifications of latent primitivism in the West.

In the second section of her book, entitled "Making Primitive Objects High Art," Torgovnick pursues the virulence of such primitivist discourse at the intersection of art history and ethnography, more specifically in the writings of Roger Fry, Michel Leiris, and contemporary art historian William Rubin. Her overall agenda is to show that, despite these authors' desire to place non-European art in a positive light, their texts, informed as they are by formalist art history and academic ethnography, prove to be undermined by the kind of unconscious primitivism that she is eager to expose. While her readings represent convincing exercises in a *political* critique of primitivist discourse, there is also a more fundamental issue at work on these pages.

For Torgovnick seems not to be content with a critique of specific texts. Rather she is inclined to indict (art historical) formalism sui generis as politically suspicious and, as is important in the present context, possibly "colonialist." In the chapter on Rubin's writings on primitive art ("The Dynamics of Primitivism"), the attack on formalism takes the circuitous route of a discussion of the consequences of misreadings. The case against misreadings can, however, only be made on the basis of a rhetoric of authenticity and authority.[7] And, as I shall argue, Torgovnick marshals such an agenda to discredit the formalist enterprise as such.

She begins her argument with a quotation from Rubin's contribution to the catalog for the 1984 MOMA exhibition on *'Primitivism' in Twentieth-Century Art: Affinity of the Tribal and the Modern.* Here, in the context of (in Rubin's, as in Torgovnick's view) Western artists' erroneous interpretation (and thus misappropriation) of particular formal features of non-Western art, Rubin maintains that "it little matters, of course, if artists misinterpreted the objects in question if that misreading was of use to them" (35). This sets up Torgovnick's argument:

---

7. This latter claim is ironic given Torgovnick's express desire to question the authority of experts: "My interest is in opening the seam between 'ethnographic authority' in the figures I study and a vaguer, emotional or 'intuitive' response to the primitive often at odds with scientific or scholarly knowledge" (23). Yet, as I will show, in the present context she will replace Western with non-Western authority.

> My central purpose in discussing Rubin is to defamiliarize that "of course" and to maintain that such misreadings are consequential—psychologically and culturally, experientially and politically. Once we accept as a matter "of course" that Westerners see violence and sexuality in African masks and sculptures, it becomes all too easy to suggest that violence and sexuality are what the objects typically "must" represent, and "must" characterize the people producing them. After this the rhythms of control, domination, and exploitation develop freely. Rubin himself entertains the opening suggestions, thus triggering a dangerous dynamics. (127–28)

The context in which Rubin's comment appears, however, is not exclusively linked to the "emotive" misreading of non-European art indicted by Torgovnick. Rather, it deals with purely formalist borrowings (Giacometti, Klee) *as well as* "the modernist misreading . . . of many African figures as examples of Expressionism—as in Read's previously mentioned association of them to *angst,*" which is rejected by Rubin as a misinterpretation (35). His comment on the usefulness of misreadings for European artists follows after this and signifies that, from a formalist point of view, the spirit in which *such misinterpretation* occurred matters little when it comes to the final product. What matters for a formalist are the formal properties of the work of art.

This is, of course, exactly the point Torgovnick wants to highlight as the formalist's denial of the political dimension which, in fact, comes back to haunt Rubin. For as Torgovnick points out in the subsequent paragraph, Rubin's own writing, in an article on Picasso in the same catalog, falls back on a time-worn Western prejudice ("These 'African' faces . . . finally conjure something that transcends our sense of civilized experience, something ominous and monstrous such as Conrad's Kurtz discovered in the heart of darkness" 254). Torgovnick can thus maintain that, as a consequence of Rubin's own primitivist unconscious that went unchecked because of his merely formalist interests, the Western *misreading* of the primitive as uncivilized, emotive, and violent is perpetuated. Thus, Rubin's general comment on the usefulness of misreadings has been rendered suspicious through a recourse to a *particular* case of misreading (Rubin's own) that confirms the primitivist unconscious of Western thought.

The only question is: What exactly has been proven? No doubt, Torgovnick has proven her case. But while her case successfully demonstrates the need for political critique, its range does not extend to an indictment of misreadings in general. Not only was the verdict reached on the strength of a single example, but the particular misreading itself belongs to a specific register in the reception of primitive art, namely the "emotive" one, and thus predestines it for Torgovnick's use. There exists, however, as we will see shortly, another register of the reception of the primitive that, while formalist and a "misreading" in Torgovnick's terms, does not participate in the primitivist unconscious. From this perspective, the equation she tries to establish between formalism and bad politics (i.e., dangerous misreadings) is designed to discredit the formalist approach in general.

However, not only misreadings have consequences; all readings do. The decision to label something a reading or a misreading is a function of one's personal, political, or ideological commitment, rather than an inherent property of (correct) reading *as opposed to misreading*. Any other determination of the distinction between reading and misreading would have to legitimate itself on the basis of an implied authentic relationship to true meaning. Since Torgovnick affirms reading over misreading, there arises the question whether she is implicitly making this stronger claim for authenticity. Such a claim would, however, represent a step out of the political arena (i.e., opinions) and into a space where there is direct access to meaning. A nod in this direction may be found in the last section of her chapter on Rubin (129–37), which is presented as an alternative to traditional Western ways of appropriating non-Western works of art.

Having disqualified the formal and ethnographic approaches to non-European works of art because they inevitably slip "into their culture's emotionally charged image of the primitive," Torgovnick suggests accessing the "potentials" of "traditional African and other forms of what we call primitive art" by allowing them to "interrogate the bases of our own art" (130). Phrased in this manner, this is a worthwhile undertaking that has also been advocated by a number of critical anthropologists.[8] As such, it does not necessarily involve the category of authenticity, because this brand of "anthropology as cultural critique" may also be performed as a (mis)reading.

The implied appeal to authenticity, and thus to the circumvention of the necessity of (mis)reading (and its consequences), occurs when the aesthetic views of "traditional African carvers" represent the preferred perspective on African works of art. While Torgovnick celebrates their non-European views on beauty, form, and the social function of art, she condemns Rubin's formalist and evaluative judgments on non-European artifacts. Thus, while her major point, namely that "Western art historians need not supply any 'voice' for Africa" (136), is well taken, there lingers the suspicion that Rubin's *formalist* reading, based as it is on categories of

---

8. Here the writings of James Clifford and fellow anthropologists could be mentioned. For a programmatic treatment see Michael M. J. Fischer and George E. Marcus.

Western aesthetics, is a *misreading* of indigenous self-understanding and thus potentially complicit with "colonialist modes of thinking" (129).

It is not Torgovnick's political argument that I find wanting but rather her implied regress to authenticity (and authority). The binary opposition between Western misreading and indigenous authority leaves the politics of dissension *within* cultures as well as the theoretical problem of misreading unaccounted for. Most importantly for the purposes of this essay, such a position puts an onus on (mis)readings in general. In what follows, I argue that even intercultural misreadings, that is, readings informed by largely nonauthenticated perspectives, *can be* productive, creative, and potentially free of the negative implications associated with, in this case, primitivist discourse. Readings are always risky, and probably always "wrong," but cultural contact consists of the mutual practice of reading, not outside of power structures, but rather, and quite inevitably, in the shadow thrown by their light. While readings can always be contested, the practice of reading cannot (and I believe ought not to) be obviated by a recourse to (ever renewed forms of) authority.

II

In order to judge Einstein's formal interpretation of non-European works of art, it is imperative to place his writings in the context of his entire project. This project is, simply put, the overcoming of what he sees as the negative effects of modern European civilization. Einstein's writings emerge at the beginning of the twentieth century as a reaction to the dual processes of secularization and modernization in the West. His polemically charged political commentary in avant-garde journals like *Aktion* in the decades before and after World War I is tinged with the sense of the decline of a decadent age, and the necessity of its being overcome. Such positions were, of course, legion at the time, influenced as they were by the philosophies of Schopenhauer and Nietzsche that had such a hold over the intellectual climate of the early decades of the twentieth century. Thus, while Einstein's disparaging critiques of contemporary Wilhelminian and Weimar Germany are persistent, radical, and uncompromising, the real culprit is the epoch that has come to be described as modernity.

What he finds unsatisfactory about modernity is the loss of a common ground, a *sensus communis,* or a binding *style.* Einstein's radical rejection of contemporary society can be most accurately described as revolutionary anarchism. Neither a Marxist nor a socialist in any strict senses of those terms, his sympathies lie nevertheless with the leftist struggle against what he calls the bourgeois inventions of capitalism, democracy, and parliamentarism. Textual echoes of different critiques of alienation and functional differentiation by Marx, Nietzsche, or Simmel make clear that such modern tendencies, in Einstein's view, embody nothing but loss for both individual and community. Parliamentarism and democracy, rather than accentuating the singularity of individuals, conspire in making them disappear in an ideology of mediocrity, while capitalism atomizes social cohesiveness to such a degree that all relation is severed to a common ground that would legitimate rather than merely legalize the social bond. Thus, like most radical thinkers of his generation, Einstein's polemics against contemporary society grow into a fundamental critique of Western civilization.

Einstein's proper field of expertise is the fine arts. Though his early success comes as a writer,[9] his major achievements are in the history and philosophy of art. And it is here that Einstein wages his political struggle. He tries not only to combat what he perceives as the pernicious tendencies of "bourgeois" art as well as art history since the Renaissance, but also to identify those new developments that promise the advent of a new social formation, a new gestalt, which will substitute for the utter lack of gestalt in modernity. It is important to note that Einstein's vision for social renewal is forward-directed. The way to overcome modernity lies not in a return to tradition but in the radical espousal of aesthetic modernism, or, more specifically, in the intellectual and artistic revolt of the historical avant-gardes.[10] In this search for a radical cultural renewal Einstein turns, almost simultaneously, to Cubism and to "African" sculpture.[11]

As early as 1907, Einstein visits Braque and Picasso in Paris (Herding). What he discovers there—the early stages of Cubism—is perhaps the decisive event in his intellectual life. For in Cubism Einstein comes to see the beginnings of a revolution in art that can serve as a blueprint for a renewal in all other areas of modern culture. It is thus with immense fervor and energy that he embraces the Cubist vocabulary and militates in favor of this new style on his return to Berlin, where the Expressionist revolution is in full swing. The years before the war are of course the most celebrated

---

9. *Bebuquin* was written between 1906 and 1909, published in 1912. The complexities of this work have only recently received more extended comment. See Kramer and Sohns.

10. I am here using Peter Bürger's distinction between high modernism and avant-garde. Whereas the critical gesture of high modernism leaves the autonomous status of art in modernity intact, it is the stated desire of the historical avant-gardes to destroy this status (art as institution) and to proceed to a reintegration of art and life.

11. The term "African" sculpture, which Einstein uses in the essay, is as unfortunate as the term *Negerplastik,* for the racial and geographic generalizations they imply are equally mistaken. For one thing, *Negerplastik* includes artifacts from the South Sea islands besides those from West Africa. For another, lumping the artifacts together in this fashion makes a comment exclusively on the originators of such discourse.

years of this new movement, especially in Dresden, Berlin, and Munich. But it is clear from the beginning that Cubism and Expressionism are quite distinct. While Cubism stands primarily for a revolution in *form,* German Expressionism, at least predominantly, represents a revolutionary approach in the psychological origins of art. The qualitative differences between these avant-garde movements have important repercussions for the way in which Cubism and Expressionism received non-European art before World War I. And Einstein's *Negerplastik* ought to play a more prominent role in the contemporary assessment of this difference.

Reinhard Wegner has assembled a brief but exhaustive record of the debate surrounding the reception of non-European art in Germany during the twentieth century. As he pointed out, French art critic Jean Laude (*La peinture française et l'art nègre*) is the most outspoken proponent of the view according to which the two avant-garde movements split along intellectual and national lines when it came to the depiction of the non-European in works of art. Laude differentiates between an "analytic" and an "emotional" reception of non-European art and identifies the former with Picasso, Braque, and Gris, the latter with de Vlaminck, Derain, and German Expressionism, especially the *Brücke* artists (Wegner 7–11). Laude— who is one of the few scholars to comment on Einstein's *Negerplastik* during the decades of neglect—situates Einstein's approach to non-European art on the "French," the rational and analytic, rather than the German, emotive side of the comparison. While it is true that Einstein is an adamant critic of the rampant infatuation with the non-European at his time, his assessment of non-European art, when viewed from the perspective of his critique of modernity, is much more complex than indicated by this binary opposition. I would like to demonstrate how Einstein's formalist appropriation of non-European art makes use of both the "analytic" and, at least to a certain degree, the "emotive" interpretation of non-European art.

III

Critical of the evolutionist paradigms of his time, Einstein sets out to programmatically counteract the primitivist discourse that, as Torgovnick has shown, constructs the non-European as childlike, eternal, or ahistorical. Einstein hopes to elude these prejudices by focusing on the aesthetic properties of (what he calls) African sculptures. By this decision, Einstein first turns these artifacts into *works of art* in the Western sense, that is, into phenomena to be judged according to aesthetic criteria. Here is the opening paragraph of *Negerplastik:*

There is hardly an art form that the European approaches with more mistrust than that of Africa. To begin with, he is inclined to deny the fact that he is dealing with art here altogether. He expresses the distance that separates these forms and the continental attitude through a contempt that has created a negative terminology. This distance and the prejudices that follow from it render any aesthetic appraisal very difficult, almost to the point of making it entirely impossible; for such appraisal presupposes a rapprochement. The Negro, however, is supposedly the inferior part from the start. He can be worked on without pity and whatever he has to offer is condemned a-priori as lacking. In irresponsible fashion one fabricated vague evolutionary hypotheses on his behalf. He had to furnish some with an ill-conceived concept [*Fehlbegriff*] of primitiveness, for others he had to serve as helpless object for such decidedly false phrases as 'people of eternity' and the like. One hoped to grasp something of a beginning in the Negro, a state that would never proceed beyond the beginning stage. Opinions about the African are largely built on prejudices advanced in order to accommodate some such opportune theory. For his judgments on the Negro, the European claims a position of unconditional, almost fantastic superiority.

De facto, our non-acceptance of the Negro is simply the result of an ignorance which wrongfully indicts him. (*Werke* I: 245)

In his desire to elude the prejudices founded on evolutionist assumptions about primitive mentality prominent in the anthropological discourse at the time,[12] Einstein decides to judge African sculpture almost exclusively as a philosopher of art. In *Negerplastik,* he is therefore primarily concerned with the way in which African carvers handled the fundamental problems of sculpture—above all the sculptural representation of space.

It must, however, be added at once that, while most of *Negerplastik* is devoted to a philosophical analysis of the formal properties of African sculpture, Einstein never loses sight of the social import of this art. On the contrary, in his analysis the social function of such sculpture is closely tied to its formal characteristics. This intimate nexus between form and function is grounded in Einstein's adherence to a strong version of autonomy aesthetics. In his view, art can only function as a critique of modern civilization if it is founded upon a radical separation between itself and the his-

---

12. It is clear that Einstein must have known the writings of Herbert Spencer, E. B. Tylor, and perhaps Henry Lewis Morgan, if not directly then through the German anthropologists Leo Frobenius and Franz Boas. As early as 1883, however, Boas became critical of the tenets (and ramifications) of Spencer's ideas on social evolution and primitive mentality. On Boas's antievolutionism, see Aldona Jonaitis's "Introduction."

torical beholder. This separation is expressed through the work's formal properties. Only if it is absolute and autonomous is art able to stand apart and thus transcend the confines of history. From this perspective it is easy to see why Einstein viewed African sculpture positively: its link to the transcendent aspects of religious ritual perfectly suits his aesthetics.

While the social dimension of art is thus always presupposed, the bulk of *Negerplastik* is spent on the elaboration of the formal properties of African sculpture. In Einstein's view, the problem African sculpture addresses is the same one Cubism is concerned with, namely, to produce a sensible intuition of totality (in this case of a sculpture), something that is impossible in the three-dimensional everyday world. With respect to sculpture this means producing a formal equivalent of the different perspectives perceived by walking around the sculpture *(Bewegungs-Vorstellungen)* so that they can be seen, intuited, at once:

> It is a question of representing the parts one cannot see in their formal function, as form—the cubic, the depth quotient, as I would like to call it—via those parts that one can see; only as form, however, without inmixing of the representational [*Gegenständliche*], of mass. The parts must not be represented materially or painterly, but rather in such a way that the form through which they become plastic, and which is given naturalistically in movement, is fixed in a single instance and can be seen simultaneously. (*Werke* I: 257–58)

The different partial perspectives of the sculptural artifact come about through the various two-dimensional images that are produced on the retina. These different images are the result of different angles of visual perception. Since Einstein is interested in totality, in the immediate intuition of a whole, the question arises as to how those different angles can be unified in an artistic representation. If, in this endeavor, the artist proceeds with the idea of mass as the controlling feature, the representational result is an illusionistic depiction of space. That is to say that because of the continuity of mass that is posited rather than intuited, the artist ends up depicting an illusionistic notion of continuous space. This means that s/he gives a unified representation of an object whose intuition s/he has never had, but whose property of singular *mass* has been mathematically or theoretically deduced. In other words, rather than render perceptual experiences, the artifact ends up depicting a fact that had been posited in the first place. What is occluded "from view" is the process and materiality of actual visual experiences.

In this situation, African sculpture found an answer to the dilemma of representing three-dimensionality by turning from space as mass to space as form. In Einstein's speculative view, African artists successfully created a form that *includes* the part foreclosed to vision from any particular angle *within the part seen and depicted.* This is possible only through distortion. If measured on the scale of traditional European notions of proportion and perspective, the dominant plane of an African sculpture is distorted or unproportional *precisely because* it represents not only the seen but also the unseen parts of the sculpture. That is to say, it assimilates depth perception in its surface form:

> Every part must be plastically self-reliant and distorted [*deformiert*] in such a way that it absorbs depth, that the idea of how it would appear from the opposite side has been worked into the frontal, but three-dimensionally functional side. Every part is, then, the result of the formal representation that creates space as totality and complete identity of the singular optical angle and the intuition, and that rejects the surrogate escape that would reduce space to mass. Such sculpture will be strongly centered to one side, since, unobstructed, it now gives the cubic as totality, as resultant, while frontality merely adds up the surface. (*Werke* I: 258)

The different parts of an African sculpture are designed according to their particular necessity. Each part is proof of a distortion that is specific to itself. These parts are the result not of an integrating concept of totality established in the mind of the artist, but rather of the different depth quotients that emerge from the compromise between the seen and unseen parts given in every perspective. Such a work is at the same time radically heterogeneous and total, its parts independent from each other. The totality particular to this kind of sculpture must be seen in its formal property of the immediate grasp of space (*unmittelbares Raumsein, Werke* I: 258). And here, according to Einstein, is the real reason for the "non-European" proportions and why African sculpture has often been called primitive in the West, equated with the developmental level of children:

> Frequently one criticizes the so-called proportional distortions of African sculpture; one should realize that the optical discontinuity of space is being translated into form [*Formklärung*], into an order whose parts—since what is at stake is plasticity—are differently evaluated according to their plastic expression. Their size is precisely not what is decisive here, but rather the amount of cubic expression granted them that they must express without compromise. (*Werke* I: 258)

Thus, in African sculpture, according to Einstein, for the first time in modernity, the *form of sculpture* has been designed satisfactorily. Here three-dimensionality is designed as totality for the beholder without offering the viewer a comfortable position of entry into and domination of the work, that is, the different angles of vision have not been accommodated to the European rule of central perspective. Instead of being positioned by the sculpture, the beholders find themselves in front of a three-dimensional representation that inspires a kind of strangeness.

This then is the achievement of African sculpture: to be able to offer in an immediate presentation the entire space circumscribed by the work of art. This is what Einstein calls African realism as opposed to European realism. African realism is a realism of form rather than of mimetic presentation. The different perspectives of all possible visual acts are heterogeneously welded together in their independent, distorted ways and thus give the impression of totality. Here, then, "cubic being" is represented "as unconditioned result, since movement has been absorbed" (*Werke* I: 259).

This formalist reading of African sculpture would almost certainly be declared a misreading if one were to consult representatives of the different communities from which these artifacts are taken. In addition, this reading is driven by Einstein's own desires for a regenerative form of art that sees in the ritual dimension of African art an attractive alternative to the Western commercialization of art. Einstein's reading, in other words, functions entirely within the parameters of Western representations of the non-European. What is more, it is informed by both the "analytic and rational" discourse on primitivism (formalist art history) as well as the "emotive" reading of the non-European as other in his (potentially idealized) notion of the ritual function of art in non-Western societies.

At the same time, his reading represents a radical departure from the primitivist discourse of the times. It constitutes nothing less than a valorization of African sculpure that results in the toppling of hierarchical assumptions with regard to Western and non-Western art. For, in Einstein's view, only African sculpture has developed the pure forms of sculpture and can therefore serve as guide to European sculptors in their search for new forms. Furthermore, given Einstein's view that art represents the advance formation of societal renewal, the destruction of central perspective in African sculpture can serve as a symbol of what needs to be done in contemporary society.

In Einstein's scenario, African art thus assumes a critical function *within* the West. The formal innovations in sculpture as well as the social role of art as evidenced in non-European cultures are here seen as practices the West ought to emulate. It is no coincidence that these practices are in perfect agreement with Einstein's autonomy aesthetics. Like Simmel before and Adorno after him, Einstein championed a dialectical relationship between art's social relevance and its aesthetic autonomy. In the view of these theoreticians, artistic creations possess a special status that, while rooted in everyday reality, makes them rise above historical constraints. For Einstein, as we have seen, it is the concept of totality that guarantees art's autonomous status. Supplanting central perspective as the organizing principle of visual representation, the concept of totality introduces difference and alterity into a formerly unified canvas.

In Einstein's view, central perspective comes with a metaphysical and a political dimension, both of which he rejects. On a metaphysical level, it organizes space in a manner that accords more and more perfectly with linear, mathematical, and therefore rational calculations of distance and size. This rationalization represents for Einstein a renunciation of human in favor of logical relations. The political dimension of central perspective consists in the fact that the viewer of paintings has his or her place assigned by the painting itself. In sociopolitical terms, central perspective is therefore an authoritarian structure that leads Einstein to equate its "rule of reason" with a practice of domination reflecting the interests of the ruling class.

Against this order in visual perception, Einstein poses the new scientific knowledge in perception: the physiological processes of the human eye. Visual perception is not a question of the rational ordering of visual space but rather of a sequence of two-dimensional retinal images. This more "complex" model of human vision is explored by Cubism and, according to Einstein, by African sculpture. The end products of these artistic movements, however, paintings and sculptures, rise above any individual visual act. They present to the beholder a summary statement that transcends all individual perspectives. Thus the physiological basis of the work of art is overcome in the artistic formation of the whole into a heterogeneous totality.

This heterogeneous totality guarantees the autonomy of the work of art as well as the viewers' perspectival independence. Unlike central perspective, such a notion of totality does not favor notions of harmony, unity, and continuity. Rather, it represents an emphatic occasion to reflect upon the diversity of perspectival acts whose differences in time and space make a unified whole impossible. Only as a nonmimetic, and "formally" autonomous work, that is, one that does not organize an embodied (perspectival) vision, can art achieve this effect. Cubism and African sculpture thus represent a rupture, an epistemological break, within the regime of Western thought.

IV

There is, however, a second stage to the figuration of the primitive in Carl Einstein that needs to be addressed here. Whereas in *Negerplastik* Einstein rejected the Eurocentrist perspective of the backwardness of non-Western cultures, a discussion of his last lengthy, manifesto-like work, *Fabrikation der Fiktionen,* must qualify this judgment. In this late work, which represents a radical and reactionary indictment of the activities of the artistic intelligentsia during the first three decades of the twentieth century, Einstein's writings contain views and positions with respect to the primitive that he had clearly rejected in *Negerplastik.*

Between the writing of *Negerplastik* (1915) and *Fabrikation der Fiktionen* (mid-1930s), Einstein experiences a profound disillusionment with the political situation in Europe. The steady rise of fascist movements in Germany, Italy, and Spain seriously throw into doubt any faith in the success of leftist politics, let alone in the critical potential and regenerative power of images. Since this is where Einstein had placed his hopes for over three decades, his disillusionment is all-encompassing. He now repudiates all his prior beliefs in the sociopolitical dimensions of artistic change and views the activities of the historical avant-gardes as the futile, subjectivist, and self-centered exercises of an intellectual elite that failed to connect with any stratum of society.

The historical situation in itself, however, does not explain the surfacing of the primitivist discourse. The reasons for this development must be seen in a turn that Einstein, like a great number of intellectuals during the 1920s, made in the wake of Freud's discovery of the unconscious. During this decade, Einstein had drawn closer to the Surrealist movement, particularly its "excommunicated" renegades.[13] Like them, he had been intrigued by the notion of the unconscious as a locale from whence to launch images counter to the everyday reality of bourgeois society. During these years, Einstein supplements his formalist theory of art with a psychoanalytically inspired theory of artistic creation. Broadly speaking, this development coincides with the general historical shift from Cubism to Surrealism as the leading paradigm of artistic expression. If Cubism and African sculpture represented for Einstein the avatars of a formal revolution in visual perception, psychoanalysis supplied him with a model for artistic creativity.

---

13. Einstein left Germany in 1928 to settle in Paris. Together with Georges Bataille and Michel Leiris he published the journal *Documents—Doctrines, Archéologie. Beaux-Arts. Ethnologie* between 1929 and 1930.

Freud's psychoanalysis also exerted a strong influence on the social dimension of Einstein's thought. For Einstein was drawn to Freud's psychoanalytic reading of cultural evolution. In a number of studies from the 1910s and 1920s, Freud applies categories from individual psychology to entire social formations, establishing an evolutionary narrative of human development from the primitive to the civilized. In *Totem and Taboo*,[14] for example, Freud describes three distinct worldviews (*Weltanschauungen*) that follow upon each other: animism, religion, and science. According to this classification, the animist phase represents the most primitive stage of world views. It is characterized by the belief that thought can animate all things. One of its features is the practice (or technology) of magic. By comparing the animist belief in all-powerful thought (*Allmacht der Gedanken*) with the symptoms of a twentieth-century neurotic patient, Freud determines that both represent cases of primary narcissism. Freud thus establishes a homology between animism as a social practice and an early phase of individual psychological development. His text then proceeds to label "primitive," that is, comparable to a childlike stage, those communities that entertain animist practices.

Einstein was very much taken with the concept of animism in the late 1920s, as can be gleaned from the pages of his *Georges Braque*.[15] For Einstein, animism was tantamount to autonomous creation, where the imaginative production of meaning is valorized as against any kind of mimeticism. Thus, in a number of works that appeared prior to and simultaneously with *Fabrikation,* Einstein had used the anarchic potential of dreams and hallucinations as his main support for a theory of artistic creation.[16] In the context of this theory, animism therefore has entirely positive connotations. In the mid-1930s, however, at the time of the general disillusionment sketched previously, Einstein rejects such practices because they have been unable to serve as symbols of collective renewal. By turning his back on the avant-gardes, Einstein also rejects the premodern, non-European models for artistic creation that he had once espoused.

In this changed situation, the notion of the primitive (*die Primitive*)— not of African sculpture—now comes to be equated with political escapism and psychological regression, which, in Einstein's view, are both

---

14. I am concerned here exclusively with the third section in *Totem,* entitled "Animism etc. . . ."

15. First published in French in 1932 (now collected in German in *Werke III*), this unwieldy work is not a traditional artistic biography. Rather, it represents Einstein's most complete statement of his theory of artistic creation. Many of its ideas and themes still remain unexplored.

16. Freud, at the end of section 3 of *Totem and Taboo,* had himself suggested a comparison between the animist *Allmacht der Gedanken* and the practice of art.

figures of impotence in the face of social complexity and the necessity of political engagement. Linking antiquity and non-European cultures with animist practices and the developmental stage of children, Einstein comes dangerously close to the type of primitivist discourse he had been critical of in the first decades of the century. Although there can be no doubt that his critique is directed *exclusively* at Western artists and intellectuals (what he calls "literary latecomers" or "late primitives" in the quoted passages that follow), in the course of his diatribes he denies antiquity and non-Western cultures *ex negativo* a status of coevalness:[17]

> Oftentimes, primitives tell of their experiences in metaphoric images. Today's literary latecomers take advantage of a related technique. Primitives had not yet developed fully the consciousness of the I and of a separate identity [*abgeschlossene Person*]. They lived, perceived, and felt in groups. The modern poets—inventors of the transindividual—fled before their narcissism, their ego-neurosis, into a paradoxical, decorative language of images; they detoured into metaphorical ornamentics, in order to escape ego fixation [*Ich-Verklemmung*]. Since they were unable to fashion facts, they projected unverifiable metaphors. (*Fabrikation* 66)

It should be clear from this passage that Einstein is not interested in making any definite statements concerning non-European societies per se. Rather, as in his other writings, these societies function as a foil to understand events of his time. The indictment concerns primarily those members of the artistic intelligentsia who, through an identification with non-Western modes of art, assumed that they could reach neglected layers of the psyche from whence collective energies could be materialized. Despite this focus of Einstein's wrath, however, a level of endemic primitivism enters his discourse:

> The primitive and the child possess only a small stock of personal experiences; they have a small aspect of reality [*Wirklichkeitsfeld*] at their disposal. (They were, however, all the more vigorously pervaded by the old collective traditions [*Erbmasse*] which were a part of mythical primitive society). Late individuals often believe themselves to be able to do without practical experience, perhaps because they have a broad tradition [*Erbmasse*] at their disposal. (Narrow positive reality is then supplemented by imagination). Thus the surprise: two con-

---

17. "Coevalness" is Johannes Fabian's term for what Western discourse about the other denies to its interlocutor.

trary phases resemble each other. The early primitives feel in a collective and animistic manner. But the negatively disposed late primitives starve in the phase of separation [*Abspaltung*] since, in order to maintain their individuality, they stubbornly keep their distance. The late primitives are often escapist [*realitätsfeindlich*]; their attitude is negative. (To them everything—with the exception of their own personality—appears to be dead. Their personality is the most intense center of action. But the farther facts and things are from the subject, the more meaningless and dead they seem to them. These individualists simply exclude the double function [*Simultanfunktion*] of the collectively bound individual.) From such fear of reality grew today's archaic imaginative art. (*Fabrikation* 111)

Again, the line of attack is clear enough: modern artists are individualistic, self-centered, out of touch with contemporary sociopolitical issues that, in Einstein's view, are the necessary precondition for the rendering of collective images. Unlike artists in non-Western cultures, they are unable and unwilling to simultaneously pursue their individualism and serve the collective needs of the community. Thus their works are unable to effect social change. While Einstein here faults the artistic intelligentsia for their escape into premodern models of the social function of art, he does not distance himself sufficiently enough from the very discourse he critiques.[18] For as evidenced by the preceding quotes, in his search for a logic of social transformation, Einstein assimilated some aspects of the evolutionist paradigm that equates children and non-Western cultures. While he rejects the individualistic use the modern intelligentsia made of collective "primitive" strategies, he condemns neither such strategies per se, nor their label as "primitive." On the contrary, he summarizes all of the West's failed attempts at defining a new style under the concept of *Primitivierung*, now a pejorative term that includes in its semantic and conceptual field the psychoanalytic premises about the evolution of cultures. It is in this late work that Einstein's writings display elements of the primitivist discourse of the times.

---

18. To be sure, there are counterexamples to be found. In the following quotation, for instance, Einstein's early critique of primitivism seems to be intact: "When the occidental tradition was exhausted or seemed no longer attractive, the same people who had assumed the world monopoly on *Bildung* latched onto the primitive exotic. Now one was keen on borrowing from the last bushmen; without much thought, one fit the exotic into the old, occidental categories. Such obvious regression and geographical eclecticism were celebrated as daring discovery, although what came from a different milieu could hardly be integrated into European schemes without being destroyed" (*Fabrikation* 96–97).

V

The question that, in conclusion, imposes itself is that of the possible connection between the two positions Einstein's writings exhibit with respect to the figuration of the primitive. Can the one be explained in terms of the other, that is, can one follow Torgovnick's lead in her chapter on primitivism and art history and read Einstein's *Negerplastik* in terms of a discourse that, in the later *Fabrikation,* reinforces the discourse of primitivism? Any answer to this question presupposes a *continuity* between Einstein's *formalist* views on African sculpture and his later, *psychoanalytically* inspired, espousal of a notion of *Primitivierung*. I am suggesting that, in Einstein's case, we are not dealing with continuity, but rather with the disjuncture of two incompatible positions.

I would like to locate the seeds of this disjuncture in an essay that appeared during the revolutionary beginnings of the Weimar Republic. In 1919, in an almanac entitled *Die Gemeinschaft* (The community), Einstein published a one-page manifesto on primitive art, "Zur primitiven Kunst." This essay, which indicts European art under capitalism, is premised on a comparison between the "immediate" art of non-European peoples and the "mediateness" of the European:

> What the European world lacks in immediate art, we make up for through the surplus of art exploiters among which figure most prominently paraphrase painters and writers: indirect, second-hand humans, pensioners of tradition, in short, mediate Europeans . . .
>
> Primitive art: rejection of capitalized art tradition. European mediateness and tradition must be destroyed, the end of the formal fictions has to be acknowledged. If we blow up the ideology of capitalism, we will find underneath the only valuable remnant of the imploded [*zerkracht*] continent, the precondition of everything new: the masses who to this day are kept in a state of suffering. They are the artist. (*Werke* II: 20)

In this passage, Einstein amalgamates in characteristic fashion philosophical (immediacy vs. mediacy of experience), art historical and ethnographic (primitive), and sociopolitical (the masses) considerations. Beyond its telegram style, this manifesto-like essay constitutes the programmatic moment in Einstein's writings where the term "primitive" is for the first time used affirmatively: an (undefined) notion of *primitive art* (*not* African sculpture) is opposed to European art. Here are the seeds for Einstein's compromising position vis-à-vis primitivism in his late work. The question, however, remains as to whether this shift from African sculpture to primitive art represents a continuity or a clean break between the politics of Einstein's formalism and those of his cultural theory. Of help in exploring this question might be another point raised in Torgovnick's discussion of primitivism.

Midpoint in *Gone Primitive,* Torgovnick comes closest to furnishing a general interpretation for the West's fascination with the primitive. She sees in it the incarnation of a feeling of "transcendental homelessness." In her reading, the phrase, borrowed from Lukács's *Theory of the Novel,* refers to the desire to "go home," to return to the origin: "Whatever form the primitive's hominess takes, its strangeness salves our estrangement from ourselves and our culture" (185). With respect to Einstein, the conception of transcendental homelessness seems to possess a certain explanatory power—for just as his critique of modernity can be said to echo the sentiment Torgovnick suggests, so Einstein's desire for absolute art and a binding style can be understood along the lines of a metaphysics of homelessness.

Yet, it is here that the formalist and the psychoanalytically inspired discourse part company. *Negerplastik* is far from thematizing a return to origins. In fact, nothing is further from Einstein's early avant-gardist approach than a desire for home or belonging. Tradition, in whatever shape or form, is Einstein's explicit opponent. And, as I tried to argue, his notion of the work as a totality is one of heterogeneity, with which the notion of rest linked to the idea of hominess is completely at odds. The notion of primitive art that Einstein advocates in the 1920s, however, is based on, if not a return to, at least a strong desire for a more primitive model of social organization. In this endeavor, European (antiquity) as well as non-European models are welcome as long as they serve the transformation of what Einstein perceives as the ills of modern civilization. Thus, the argument concerning the relationship between primitivism and transcendental homelessness does indeed hold for a certain body of Einstein's later writings.

Einstein thus occupies an ambiguous position in the discourse of Western primitivism. We are confronted with two different, incommensurable Einsteins: a formalist one who, because of his valorization of African sculpture, runs counter to the predominant hierarchies regarding Western and non-Western art, and a cultural critic who, eager to find an antidote to modern civilization, is led to espouse theories of cultural evolution that place non-European societies on a lower rung of the evolutionary ladder. It seems ironic that the formalist position that Torgovnick had viewed as prone to exhibiting a primitivist unconscious is the one that, in Einstein's case, runs counter to it.

What I am suggesting then is that one should not conflate the two Einsteins. The "first" Einstein's appropriation of African sculpture in *Negerplastik,* though informed not by an ethos of authenticity but rather by a formalist reading with universalist aspirations (sculpture as such), does not reinforce ideologies of primitivism. Rather, it decisively opposes them. On a larger scale, Einstein's case suggests that formalist readings are not automatically politically reactionary and that a progressive or reactionary index ascribed to readings ought not to be grounded in an (oftentimes implicit) appeal to the authority of the originator.

Mapping the Native Body: On Africa and the Colonial Film in the Third Reich

Sabine Hake

What fuels the colonial fantasies produced by the cinema of the Third Reich? What links these stories of conquest and defeat to the larger concerns of National Socialist ideology, including the preoccupation with race and the call for territorial expansion? What assumptions about identity and the body enter into the visual representation of Germanness? And what distinguishes the images of Africa—colonialism in the cinema of the Third Reich always means Africa and refers to the period from 1884 to 1919—from other legitimizing fictions of nationhood, such as the films about ethnic Germans abroad?[1] If culture, as Homi Bhabha has argued, functions as a battleground for ideas, then one might ask what kinds of questions were at stake in films about a topic with little contemporary relevance and without strong resonances in the collective imagination (Bhabha, *The Location* 66–84). If, to invoke Bhabha again, narrative gives form to these ideas by way of its use of protagonists, times and places, established genres and stylistic means, what desires were articulated across the ideological and psychological landscape called Africa, and what anxieties were expressed through the markers of the black body and the discourses of primitivism and colonialism?

In writing this article, I have profited from critical comments by Lucy Fischer, Marsha Klotz, Mary-Beth O'Brien, and Stephen Brockmann; I have also learned a lot from the participants in the 1995 Workshop on Women and German Colonialism at CUNY Graduate Center, New York City.

1. The standard English-language literature on Nazi cinema has more or less ignored the colonial films or treats them by examining predictable themes such as non-German nationalism, the leadership principle, anti-British stereotypes, and so forth. Welch examines *Ohm Krüger* for its representation of the British (271–80). Drewniak discusses German colonialism at some length (293–99), but focuses primarily on cultural films.

With one notable exception, to be considered later, all feature films with an African theme premiered between 1938 and 1943. They included action adventures, comedies, musical fantasies, love stories, and historical dramas. The repeated shifts between conventional film genres and the openly propagandistic *Staatsauftragsfilme* (state-commissioned films) reflect the changing approaches to mass entertainment during the war years. In 1939, mainstream cinema still tried to accommodate popular tastes and relied on Hollywood perspectives on the "dark continent" both in order to express concerns about a liberated female sexuality and to indulge in fantasies of a racialized other. At that point the natives functioned as little more than extras in the renegotiation of gender roles, while the African landscape merely provided the setting for the articulation of repressed desires and unfulfilled wishes. The situation changed in 1941 when the war effort found legitimation and support in the territorial expansionism and militarization of society advocated by colonial films like *Carl Peters* and *Ohm Krüger*. But by 1943, after the devastating losses in Stalingrad, when the outcome of the war seemed no longer certain and German troops had capitulated to the British in North Africa, films about Africa again no longer foregrounded their political agenda and returned to the mixture of history, adventure, and romance familiar from Hollywood cinema. The product of such a (failed) attempt at integrating ideological positions into more traditional generic modes is *Germanin* (1943), the main film to be discussed in this essay. Several factors contributed to the transformation of Africa into a projection screen for domestic concerns: the rediscovery of colonialism as a political program and a paradigm of empire; the fascination with the "dark continent" and its primordial nature in the cultural film; the discovery of Africa as an attractive setting for adventure films; the proliferation of newsreels about German military operations in North Africa under Rommel; and, last but not least, the enlistment of the colonial imagination in seemingly unrelated discourses and contexts.[2] The proliferating images of blackness in the colonial film provide a privileged occasion for reconstructing some of these configurations and examining their contribution to the phantasmagoria of race in the cinema of the Third Reich. Unlike earlier scholars, who have

---

2. Usually shown as pre-films, cultural films with titles like *Deutsches Land in Afrika* (1938, German land in Africa) and *Deutsche Pflanzer am Kilimandscharo* (1939, German planters near Kilimanjaro) anchored the feature films that followed them as part of a continued reflection on identity and spatiality that established the reading formation necessary for their actualization as colonial and, by implication, hegemonic texts. The renewed interest in Africa also was responsible for the rerelease of cultural films about Africa from the silent period; see Georg Herzberg's review of Bengt Berg's *Sehnsucht nach Afrika* in *Film-Kurier*, 14 Jan. 1939.

focused almost exclusively on *Carl Peters* and *Ohm Krüger,* I propose to study these processes on the threshold between entertainment and propaganda: that is, the place where the boundaries between the radicalized body and the body politic appear more blurred. In the momentous shift from a political struggle over territories to an equally violent fight over the native body, I argue, the discourse of imperialism disappears into the background and, via the story of a medical discovery, gives rise to the discourses of racism, including antisemitism.

As a way of approaching these complicated issues, one might want to look at a typical, but nonetheless extraordinary, sequence from *Germanin.* For a brief moment, the natives take center stage: not as actors in their own story, but as the bodies through which other dramatic interchanges take place.[3] The occasion is a happy one. A group of natives afflicted by sleeping sickness returns to their village—cured with the help of a new vaccine, called "Germanin" by the German scientists who discovered it. Joyous cries of "They are coming! They're healed!" (in native dialect, with German subtitles) accompany their arrival. The ensuing celebration is depicted according to the conventions of the ethnographic film, from the preoccupation with native ritual and the reliance on drumming and chanting as protolinguistic discourses to the complete convergence of eroticism and exoticism under the camera's voyeuristic gaze. In the attention to female nudity and the preference for camera angles and positions that reveal bare breasts and buttocks, we can also discern similarities with the then-popular revue films. Once drums and torches are distributed, the scene is set for the community to affirm its values—and, indirectly, to celebrate German science and colonial rule. Roused by the antiphonal singing between the leader and the group, the natives begin to dance. In accordance with Western notions of "primitivism," their rhythmical movements—the shaking of heads, the raising of arms, the bending forward and backward—appear both strangely mechanical and profoundly meaningful. Forming staggered rows and concentric circles, the separate groups of male and female dancers transport themselves into a heightened state, as evidenced by the rhythmical editing and the rapid close-ups of heads and limbs. Suddenly, one overjoyed villager retrieves his German bugle and, to the shock and dismay of the others, sounds a signal that can only be understood as a call for greater German involvement in Africa. At that moment,

---

3. In the following, I refer to the colonial subjects as "blacks" or "natives," terms that—unlike others that try to disengage representation and language from the nexus of racism and oppression via recourse to a different terminology—acknowledge their position within colonial discourse and foreground the mechanisms of oppression. "Negroes" and "primitives" will only be used when the discourses supporting such terms—ethnography and anthropology, respectively—are subject to critical analysis.

the British officers who have been observing the festivities from afar appear on the scene and disperse the crowd by firing several warning shots. Questioned by the British about the origins of the bugle and the pieces of German uniforms, one man responds with a wistful reference to the years of Germany's colonial rule and his proud service in the *Schutztruppe* (colonial army). He is punished for this answer with a whipping.

What are the conditions that give rise to this scandalous representation of the natives and place them in a multilayered and constantly shifting field of meanings? Two processes can be identified for the sequence from *Germanin:* the containment of these images within certain spectatorial regimes and the appropriation of the fictions of race by other discursive formations. The images may be called excessive because they contribute little to the advancement of the narrative. Formal means such as rapid editing and extensive point-of-view shots create a visual spectacle that resists integration into an otherwise seamless realist text. Without the main protagonists, the sequence forsakes the psychological involvement so crucial for all identification processes. Instead, the framing of the sequence identifies it as an African fantasy that exists solely as a consequence of the look of the white colonizers. After all, the exhibition of the black body and the staging of tribal ritual require the colonizer and his desiring gaze. Without his presence, the natives, as natives, do not exist. Without the colonizer's desire, their actions remain incomprehensible.

Confirming the need for such perspectives, the tribal celebration appears between two scenes that introduce the two antagonists in this historical struggle over the native body. The claims to colonies in Africa are presented not by means of political or economic arguments, but via the categories of race, biology, and nature. Thus the transition from the German medical team to the healed natives is facilitated through the use of a stand-in for the natives, a chimpanzee who, during a day of mass vaccinations, steals a vial of vaccine from the German professor and hides it in a tree. Later the infected Professor Achenbach will give this last vial to his British adversary in exchange for contractual assurances of free access to Lake Victoria, the breeding ground of the tsetse fly. Just as the Germans yearn to heal the native body, the British have no scruples about sacrificing lives. Where the Germans take a protective attitude toward the indigenous population, the British are consumed by imperialist ambition; hence their aggressive behavior toward the celebrants. In this polemical juxtaposition of German idealism and British materialism, the survival and physical well-being of the natives serve as indicators of the changing balance of power in Africa. Through the spectacle of the black body, a causal relationship is established between the German commitment to humanitarian causes and the future survival of autochthonous cultures. In terms of agency, this connection finds repeated confirmation in the narrative trajectory from the native celebration where the German soul recovers its native voice to the crucial moment when the professor and his "assistant," the chimpanzee, are interrupted in their experiments by British officers. Accusing Achenbach of distributing German propaganda, they order the station closed and all medical supplies destroyed.

This kind of careful framing suggests that the representation of the natives cannot be reduced to ideological positions, but must be examined as an integral part of the visual and narrative strategies of mainstream cinema. However, the overdetermined role of race and space in Nazi ideology also requires a closer look at German colonialism as a political program and fictional construct. That such contextualization is essential for understanding the colonial as a highly unstable discourse is one of the points of departure for this essay; that this instability constitutes the very appeal of colonial representations will be its working hypothesis. Less as characters or types than as positions in an extended field of shifting signifiers, the natives provide a key not only to the visual and spectatorial regimes linking colonizers and colonized. They also shed light on the non-synchronicities that distinguish the colonial films of the Third Reich from the colonial fiction written during the relatively brief period of German colonialism and from the highly developed colonial literatures of Britain and France.[4] In acknowledgment of these complications, my reading of *Germanin* involves a double strategy: to draw attention to the importance of "blackness" as a signifier within Nazi ideology and to acknowledge its decentered position in the articulation of race and space and the triangulation of culture, nature, and civilization. By exploring the positionality of "Africa" and "blackness" in the cinema of the Third Reich, I hope to illuminate the conditions under which, and the strategies through which, these images entered into the cinematic imagination and became meaningful both as images and as signifiers of other systems of difference. I therefore focus on those moments when the spectacle of the black body arrests the narrative and makes possible the representation of other, more hidden constellations. The dynamic of presence and absence that always structures these "native" sequences sheds light on the libidinal economy of the colonial both within Nazi ideology (e.g., in relation to antisemitism) and within older theories of empire (e.g., paternalism).

In order to understand these mechanisms, we need to consider the

---

4. I am not considering adventure films where Africa functions primarily as an exotic setting. I am also not considering romantic dramas like *Kongo-Expreß* (1939, Congo express), even though it would be interesting to examine the division of labor between the renunciation of sexuality in the colonialist fictions and the conflation of Africa and (white) female sexuality in exotic fantasies clearly inspired by Hollywood.

political relevance of the colonial idea during the Third Reich and identify some of the methodological problems that emerge when reading German colonial texts as a consequence of their cultural marginality. Unlike the imperialist superpowers of the nineteenth century, the Wilhelmine Empire entered the struggle for colonies at a very late point; therein lies a major reason for the relative insignificance of its colonial literature. When, in the 1884 Conference of Berlin, Africa was divided among the colonizing nations, the Reich laid claim to the territories that, until World War I, would remain the focal point of its ambitions: German Southwest Africa, German East Africa, Cameroon, and Togo. By comparison, the colonies in New Guinea, Samoa, and Kiaochow (China) played only a minor role. Modeled after the British Chartered Companies, the so-called *Schutzgebiete* were created by means of treaties with native tribes concluded by Lüderitz in Southwest and Carl Peters in East Africa. Organizations like the *Deutsche Kolonialgesellschaft,* founded in 1887, advanced the colonial idea with arguments that either emphasized the German need for natural resources and foreign settlements or conjured up more elusive dreams of empire. Yet even after Chancellor Bismarck made colonial acquisitions an integral part of foreign policy in the age of imperialism, the German rule in Africa never gave rise to a kind of colonial discourse that captivated the national imagination through specific images, narratives, heroes, places, and symbols. Germany lost all of its colonies in World War I, and, after the Treaty of Versailles of 1919, it was largely in the spirit of nostalgic remembrance and as a consequence of various forms of displacement that the colonies remained alive in autobiographies, novels, and, later, in films.

Not surprisingly, the German literary canon offers no equivalents of a Rudyard Kipling or an E. M. Forster. While the German settlers produced an extensive body of literature, their writings never developed into the kind of hegemonic thinking that became relevant through the practice of political domination and that assumed its place within an established culture of empire. The period of German colonialism proved too short to enter into the collective imagination, and the African colonies never became German with the kind of symbolic investment that still complicates the relationships between Britain and the Commonwealth nations. As a result, just as the images of blackness in the colonial films facilitate semiotic slippage, the stories of German colonial ambition often lack narrative authority. They do not unfold against an existing horizon of expectation, nor do they command an established set of sentiments, attitudes, and beliefs. Since the loss of the colonies at the end of the war had not been preceded by a long period of unchallenged rule, the traumatic experience of disempowerment could not be undone through historical revision or be transformed through aesthetic means. The nostalgia remained a false one;

it merely served to cover up a more pervasive sense of inadequacy and a deep longing for revenge, that is, for rewriting history as the present and repeating it on other stages and with other protagonists. In colonial fictions we are confronted, then, with a production of lack, a position of absence. The narratives appeal to a discourse of power that remains predicated on the lack of power; hence the glorification of suffering and perseverance and the firm belief in a heroic future in which all memories of past humiliation will be erased.

With no new official policies in place, the calls for colonies after 1933 were framed largely in terms of revisionism; but such secondary revision, to evoke Freud, took place largely within the domain of literature and film. The firm belief in the superiority of Germany as a *Kulturnation* and the sense of shame and humiliation that had fueled right-wing polemics against the Versailles peace treaty made the colonial narrative a perfect vehicle for imaginary scenarios, scenarios in which the "dark continent" and the "black natives" came to embody specific domestic concerns and agendas. Whether these revolved around fantasies of revenge aimed at the British or culminated in the need for more *Lebensraum* in the east, the former colonies in Africa made possible these multiple inscriptions because they had never brought forth an official canon of authors and texts that would resist such appropriations. The disappearance of colonial sentiments during the Weimar years further predisposed colonial fictions to rereadings that, by the 1930s, effectively dissolved historical experience in favor of more contemporary obsessions with race and space. These processes of projection, condensation, and displacement were aided by the identification of the colonial novel with trivial literature. It marked the subject matter as a representational field with little investment in formal questions and stylistic concerns. Freed of the pressures of historical truth, the colonial assumed almost phantasmagoric qualities after the loss of the colonies; Hans Grimm's *Volk ohne Raum* (1926, Nation without space) is the best example for this kind of belatedness. The impact of loss on the imagination can be studied in all colonial literatures, but it is the very fact of a persistent marginality and a continuous association with failure and defeat that made German colonialism such a formidable subject matter for filmmakers in the Third Reich.

As the last colonial film made during the Third Reich, *Germanin* foregrounds some of these narrative strategies and hidden agendas: the racist and imperialist attitudes that enter into the construction of Africa as a contested field; the triangulation of power in the relationship of Germans, British, and natives; and the enlistment of established dichotomies like nature vs. culture, culture vs. civilization, and race vs. nation in these visual and narrative configurations. In order to achieve this kind of hypertextualization, all colonial films had to re-create the "dark continent" and its deserts, savannas, and jungles as a convincing filmic mise-en-scène, whether through exterior scenes and studio sets, typical props and costumes, or the casting of black extras. As the war continued, the construction of these exotic locations for the camera became increasingly difficult. While the exterior scenes of *Ohm Krüger* were still shot in the Grunewald studios of Tobis Filmkunst GmbH near Berlin, Bavaria Filmkunst GmbH had to move to the Prague Barrandov studios to make *Carl Peters*. A painted backdrop depicting Kilimanjaro was as close as that film got to Africa. Many of the black extras from both productions were former colonial subjects living in Germany; the comment by one extra that some films also used American prisoners of war remains unconfirmed (Opitz 77–78). That the geographical and ethnographic markers would be consistent with the semiotic field ruled by the term "Africa" proved ultimately more important than the inclusion of documentary footage or original locations. In fact, most colonial films from the period, including Hollywood films, derived much of their appeal from the fact that their African landscapes are so visibly the result of good (or bad) set design. During a time when on-location shooting became increasingly common in a variety of film genres, the representation of Africa continued to rely on artifice and make-believe.

Directed by Max Kimmich, Goebbels's brother-in-law, *Germanin* marks a point in the cinema of the Third Reich at which growing doubts about the effectiveness of overt propaganda occasioned a return to more contextualized approaches to representation.[5] Shot during the summer of 1942, this "story of a German action," to invoke the film's subtitle, abandoned the old dreams of revenge for a glorification of duty and sacrifice. The production of *Germanin* took the Ufa studio from Babelsberg to its Italian counterpart, Cinecittà near Rome. Commenting on the artistic collaboration between the two Axis powers, one critic noted: "The Italian Ministry of Popular Culture has been extremely accommodating in making enough Negroes available."[6] The male extras who appear in the sequence previously described were forced laborers from Libya, the base of the German Africa Corps before the Italian colony was occupied by British and French troops in late 1942. The female extras, according to Trenker, came from Paris and included dancers and prostitutes (402–3). However, the film's horrifying scenes of suffering and dying could not have been staged. It remains unclear whether these scenes were taken from

---

5. Film studios actively searched for suitable colonial narratives. In a book and film prize competition organized in 1941 by Ufa and the *Reichskolonialbund,* the first prize went to Fritz Spiesser's *Heimkehr: Roman eines Südafrika-Deutschen* (1943).

6. "'Germanin' entsteht im Süden," *Film-Kurier,* 26 May 1942.

contemporary documentaries or archival material and whether or not the footage came from a German production. My suspicion is that they, like much of the documentary footage used in other colonial films, were provided by the *Reichsgesundheitsamt* in Berlin and the *Institut für Schiffs- und Tropenkrankheiten* in Hamburg, which regularly financed ethnographic expeditions and conducted research on tropical illnesses.

Lacking the zealousness of *Carl Peters* and *Ohm Krüger*, *Germanin* uses the conventions of genre cinema to narrativize its ideological positions and introduce elements of adventure and romance. Anti-British sentiments are translated into the terms of the adventure film and become part of the falsifications of history that virtually constitute the historical and biographical genre during the Third Reich. To give only one example, the British assaults on the German expedition never took place; on the contrary, the real Professor Kleine and his team received much official support and assistance. In the composite figure of Professor Achenbach, the film combines the discovery of Bayer 205 (later called "Germanin") by Dressel, Heymann, and Kothe in 1916 with the 1921–23 expedition to North Rhodesia and the Belgian Congo under Friedrich Karl Kleine. The courageous game hunter, played by the famous alpinist/actor Luis Trenker, and the professor's pretty assistant are modeled on Kleine's assistants Walter Fischer and Hanna Ockelmann, who would later become the professor's wife (Eckart 69–82).[7]

The film's opening establishes a clear connection between Africa and death. Over a map of the continent followed by typical landscapes, a male voice declares: "Africa—enigmatic and immense, the mysterious dark continent threatens and seduces. Everywhere in Africa's vast expanses, behind lianas, in the unlit thicket of the jungle, death awaits." Via images of a snake and a leopard attacking natives, and of lions killing a gazelle, death is linked to the cruel laws of the jungle, the Darwinian "survival of the fittest." However, the sequence and its juxtaposition of victims and victimizers distinguishes death as the result of natural selection, a process equated with heroic struggle, from a more dishonorable death brought about by contagion and pollution, a fate suffered passively and associated with the swamp as a place of indiscriminate mixing and mingling. "But more horrifying and frightening for black people is the power of a small fly, the African tsetse whose sting transmits sleeping sickness," the voice-over declares, while the symptoms and typical course of the epidemic are shown in a series of documentary shots. Before the continent's original

---

7. The discovery of Germanin was narrativized by Hellmuth Unger in *Germanin: Geschichte einer deutschen Großtat* (Berlin: Verlag Neues Volk, 1938). On the process of adapting the historical material to the screen, see Hans Wolfgang Hillers, "'Germanin' als Formproblem."

innocence can be restored through the selfless work of the German expedition under Achenbach, before the natives are able to dance again, the black body must be displayed in various stages of sleeping sickness. In what looks like documentary footage and bears an uncanny resemblance to images from concentration camps, the natives appear as emaciated, weakened, apathetic, delirious, succumbing to death—an almost too transparent case of the return of the repressed. Maps and statistics trace the spread of the epidemic in Uganda, Cameroon, and the Belgian Congo, while the somber music and the authoritative voice of the commentator create a bellicose mood more appropriate for war newsreels than for the (fictitious) documentation of a human tragedy.

Germanin begins and ends in Africa and covers the time period from the outbreak of World War I to the years of the Weimar Republic, the despised *Systemzeit*. Illustrating the film's repeated claim that "the fight against sleeping sickness in Africa is an immortal chapter of German colonial history," the story of Professor Achenbach unfolds through the opposition of African nature and German culture, on the one hand, and German culture and British civilization, on the other. In contrast to the destructive effect of British imperialism and its liberal culture, the Germans are shown in their fight for a harmonious integration of nature and culture. After the British destroy his medical station in 1914, the professor leaves Africa and continues his search for a vaccine for sleeping sickness at the IG Farben laboratories in Leverkusen. Over stylized close-ups of factory chimneys and lab equipment, the voice-over extols the German effort to save the continent: "Through struggle and self-sacrifice, from the blood toll paid to the earth, the German spirit surged up triumphantly." The repeated emphasis on such a selfless pursuit of knowledge underscores what was then bound to appear as the ultimate injustice of the Versailles Peace Treaty. When in 1919 the African continent was divided among the enemy nations, the voice-over reminds the audience, only Germany had the power to heal—this is the scandal that drives the film's second part, the professor's triumphant return to Africa. Achenbach and his research team arrive in 1923 to test the effectiveness of the vaccine and, despite many setbacks, they triumph in the end—over the epidemic and, morally, over the British whose American-made vaccine only causes blindness. A demonstration of the German commitment to scientific endeavors and humanitarian causes, the mass healing arranged by Achenbach "proves" the Germans' superiority as colonizers. Endless streams of sick people, some on crutches, some on stretchers, converge on the medical station, with the professor-savior centrally located inside the frame. Evoking religious imagery, the scene casts Achenbach as a modern-day Christ figure. The fact that he gives the last vial of vaccine to his enemy further underscores the Christian symbolism and aligns it at once with the medical advances symbolized by the Bayer cross and the imperialist goals associated with National Socialist ideology.

Marked as the carriers of an infectious disease, the natives in *Germanin* also recall the antisemitic rhetoric of *Der ewige Jude* (1940, The Eternal Jew), which compares Jews to vermin. There is one considerable difference: the blacks are at no point associated with the kind of intentionality claimed in Nazi theories about a "Jewish world conspiracy," but suffer passively. Active behavior remains the prerogative of the white colonizers and the tsetse fly that, through attributions like "swarming," "spreading," and "polluting," takes on characteristics of the Jew via the infamous rat-metaphor from *The Eternal Jew* and thus becomes part of the larger patterns of displacement and condensation described above. Similarly, the white rats from the Bayer laboratory invite comparisons to the Nazi projects of social hygiene and racial science. While many of these hidden references materialize through comparisons and analogies, some involve a direct reversal of the attitudes, arguments, and policies leading to the Final Solution. According to the twisted logic adopted by the film, the devastation of the native body (i.e., a German protectorate) by an uncontrollable epidemic (i.e., British imperialism and the Jewish world conspiracy) justifies the persecution of the Jews. An article about the *Germanin* project acknowledged these antisemitic undercurrents when it claimed that, as a consequence of the German vaccine, "German East Africa has become almost disease-free [*seuchenfrei*]."[8] For contemporary readers, the phrase referred to the official Nazi terminology by means of which the occupied territories in Poland and elsewhere were declared "Jew-free" (*judenfrei*). Through these correspondences, Africa in *Germanin* provided the protagonists and the setting for the staging of German ambitions in Eastern Europe. Via the myth of the "dark continent," the need for territorial conquests and ethnic cleansing could be translated into seemingly natural processes of sickness and death. Likewise, through the heroic deeds of the Germans in Africa, a model was established for similarly beneficial acts of colonization in the east. Once we leave behind the fictional worlds conjured up by cinema, the relevance of Africa for articulating race and nation in relation to the Holocaust can be measured by the fact that it was, after all, a strange secret plan that implicated the continent in the persecution of the Jews: the plan of mass deportations to Madagas-

---

8. "Warum Germanin? Vom Kampf deutscher Forscher gegen den Schlaftod," *Film-Kurier,* 3 June 1942.

car. The same delusional framework, but of course without the deadly consequences, gave rise to the colonial films and their shifting field of signifiers.

Through the racial triangulations that govern all colonial narratives, the British in *Germanin* assume the narrative position of the Jews, both because they are supposedly unable or unwilling to control the tsetse and because they are caught in a complicated web of intertextual and contextual references. While the comparison between the tsetse fly and the Jew is accomplished through the established metaphors of antisemitism, the association of the British with an epidemic originates in political polemics against "the perfidious Albion" and was obviously cultivated to dehumanize the enemy in the theater of war. These racial homologies in the colonial imagination were maintained through intertextual relationships with other anti-British and antisemitic representations in films like *Aktien auf Waterloo* (1941, Stocks on Waterloo).[9] They were also fueled by rabid polemics against the Jewish influence over British foreign policy and wild speculations about the "Semitic nature" of British cosmopolitanism, liberalism, and pragmatism. Significantly, Goebbels once noted that the British were the "Jews among the Aryans" (quoted by Hoffmann 97). Defying normal logic, his statement simply collapsed a historical antagonism into racial terms subsumed under the master trope of Jewishness. The desired shift in signification was accomplished via the unspoken belief that everything constructed as different from the German character would become identical simply through the fact of its alterity.

Said's observation that "to represent Africa is to enter the battle over Africa" (Said, *Culture* 68) holds true for all colonial discourses that support existing imperialist practices. Where colonialist and imperialist goals are no longer identical, linked only through structural homologies and semiotic slippage, colonial narratives have to redefine their agenda from the perspective of defeat and renunciation. Accordingly, German films about the colonies partook not in "the battle over Africa" but in the battle over Europe. As the colonial project came to be equated not with might and glory but with selfless service, suffering for a greater cause, endless delay of gratification, and a masochistic celebration of death, representing "Africa" meant to represent Germanness and define its qualities in national and racial terms. Thus in the same way that colonialism as a narrative content must be evaluated in relation to colonialism as a political practice, fascination with the black body cannot be separated from the theories of race that, during the Third Reich, culminated in the theory and

---

9. The film was originally released as *Die Rothschilds* (1940) but withdrawn from exhibition after Britain's entry into the war.

practice of antisemitism. The identification of the natives from *Germanin* with visual spectacle draws attention to the processes by means of which questions of race, ethnicity, and nation are mapped onto the spatial topographies of Africa and linked to the territorial claims behind the colonialist project. Excluded as agents in the narrative and visually dominated in specially designated sequences, the colonized provide the battlefield on which the European antagonists meet and where the terms of racial and national identity are in fact worked out. However, the racism that informs the representation of the natives also becomes a vehicle for other forms of discrimination and oppression.[10] Consequently, these images and their visible and concealed references must be examined in the larger context of Nazi ideology and significant changes in colonial rhetoric and policy.

Against all grandiose plans for a colonial empire, British style, Goebbels's programmatic statement from 1933 confirmed the economic significance of colonies but rejected all speculation about future German settlements in Africa or elsewhere. He concluded that "colonial propaganda is no longer an urgent vital matter for our nation" (quoted by Zimmermann 170). Fascination with the exotic gave way to the vilification of the familiar—that is to say, of the Jews living in the Reich and central Europe. Imperialist ambitions shifted from the creation of satellites on other continents to an expansion of the Reich's eastern borders. As Hitler explained: "We continue where things ended six hundred years ago. We stop the endless German procession to Southern and Western Europe and turn our eyes toward the land in the east. We finally complete the colonial and economic politics of the prewar period and move on to the territorial politics of the future. But when in today's Europe we speak of new land, we can think only of Russia and the states bordering on and subordinate to it" (quoted by Zimmermann 170). While there was a revival of colonialist ideas after 1939, with Hitler railing incessantly against the "theft" of the German colonies, no concrete programs were ever formulated. However, in the realm of fiction, the German colonies in Africa assumed new significance as a substitute for the struggle for *Lebensraum* in Eastern

---

10. Recognizing the specificity of German colonialism can protect scholars of German culture from uncritically importing into German Studies notions of empire from national literatures with a long colonial tradition and a stronger high-culture investment in representing the colonial subject; it also establishes the framework within which they can profit from the theorizing of colonialism in British and American cultural studies. Of course, this raises larger methodological questions: how to apply critical frameworks developed in the British context to German colonial narratives; how to utilize concepts tested on canonical, high-culture texts on mass cultural productions; and how to theorize colonial literature from the Wilhelmine period without falling victim to the legitimizing arguments that, by insisting on those texts' relevance or quality, rely on the same dynamics of hegemony and marginality that inform colonial narratives; on this point, see Gilman (*On Blackness* 119–28).

Europe and, via this kind of displacement, also provided an outlet for antisemitic attitudes.[11]

To the same degree that the new politics of space changed the topographies of the colonial, the question of race, too, acquired new dimensions. In *Mein Kampf,* Hitler had argued that pollution by Negro blood equaled calculated attempts by the Jews to "deprive the white race of the basis for its autocratic existence by infecting it with inferior humanity" (620). After 1933, such polemical comparisons no longer fit with the pseudoscientific categories developed by Nazi racial science to prove the superiority of the Aryan race. The insistence on simplistic equations between ethnic groups on the level of image production also became increasingly unproductive given the complicated division of labor between new racial policies and military conquests, on the one hand, and a state-controlled cinema trying to combine popular entertainment and political propaganda, on the other. While antisemitism took center stage in the negotiation of differences in the political arena, blackness in the colonial film emerged as a privileged signifier for the differences between national cultures. To put it bluntly, more films were made about Africa than about the "Jewish question." The transgressive image of the native helped to define the relationship between self and other and thus made the otherness of the natives an integral part of the German quest for the self. With the more disturbing aspects of blackness suppressed from the beginning, for instance through the continual identification of a threatening sexuality with Jewishness, the specter of miscegenation rarely surfaced and the question of racial inferiority, while undoubtedly present, could be contained within the attractions of the exotic or conflated with anti-British representations. There is no doubt that it was an endemic racism in German culture and society that gave rise to, and made possible the circulation of, such a deeply compromised iconography. However, the fact that Afro-Germans and African nationals experienced discrimination during the Third Reich does not fundamentally affect the enlistment of such images as a vehicle for the staging of other racist and imperialist fantasies.

Of course, the mechanisms that in *Germanin* place the images of blackness at the intersection of two discourses, those of racism and those of nationalism, belong to the world of cinema and its all-powerful reality effects. Colonial fictions unfold through images, settings, and events that ostensibly speak for themselves; therein lies their importance as signifying systems. The visual encoding of blackness relied heavily on ethnographic

---

11. The growing attention to film as an instrument for promoting the colonial idea can be seen in "Der Film als Kolonisationsmittel," *Film-Kurier,* 15 May 1937; "Die deutsche Kolonialforderung im Film," *Lichtbild-Bühne,* 12 May 1939; and Georg C. Klaren, "Der deutsche Film und unsere Kolonien."

concepts and vacillated between the terms of ontogenesis (i.e., the Negro as child) and phylogenesis (i.e., the Negro as primitive). Of course, the romantic identification of blackness with nature, whether through its redemptive or destructive aspects, was not without its own instabilities. The language, attire, and demeanor of the natives were evoked to reflect the degree of their adaptation or resistance to the experience of colonization and to bear witness to their precarious position between cultures. The colonial film obsessively rehearsed these various stages of colonialization: the community acting in accordance with ancient ritual and tribal law; the Westernized young men who try to find an acceptable position between defiance and subordination; and the corrupt, power-hungry chieftains who sell their loyalty to the highest bidder. Precisely by visualizing the tensions between nature and culture, power and knowledge, the natives assumed their primary role as markers of difference in the colonial fantasy. But as the embodiment of race, they also became signifiers in another text.

In contrast to blacks, whose identity could be equated with their visible physical features—that is, the color of their skin—the representation of Jews in the antisemitic film from the beginning required an elaborate system of physiognomic, anthropological, and taxonomic practices. Whereas the native seemed to confirm the stability of a representation evident to itself, the Jew, despite emphatic claims to the contrary by the proponents of racial science, resisted easy categorization. That is why filmmakers for the most part refrained from such representations—unlike polemicists and caricaturists, who did not have to concern themselves with the referential qualities of the photographic image. The resultant asymmetry between the scarcity of Jewish representations and the centrality of antisemitism to Nazi ideology can be explained by looking more closely at the function of blackness as the more adaptable medium for the articulation of racial and national identities. In the cinema, images of blackness operated as a racial signifier in oppositional pairs that began with Europe vs. Africa and Germany vs. England and that extended from Germans vs. British, via the equation of British with Jewish, to Germans vs. Jews. By providing the "material" for such processes of displacement, the native body facilitated a confrontation with the British as the other colonial power and a stand-in for the Jews.

The cinema of the Third Reich turned to images of blackness and an established iconography of the exotic and the primitive in order to represent other differences through an established genre of difference. The figure of the noble savage served to redefine conceptual pairs like nature vs. culture, culture vs. civilization, masculinity vs. femininity, and race vs. nation in accordance with National Socialist ideology. As the sign that needed no explanation, blackness in the colonial films highlighted the tensions between German and British colonists and helped to juxtapose two notions of race, the idealized union of natural and social law symbolized by the natives and the decadence and corruption identified with British civilization and, through further semiotic slippage, with Jewishness. The construction of German identity depended both on the confrontation between black and white and the triangulation of these terms by means of interactions between the colonizers and the colonized, on the one hand, and the German and British colonizers, on the other. In contrast to colonial narratives where definitions of self were always predicated on the positioning of the native as the other, the relationship between the Germans and the natives was inflected by, and used in, the articulation of a more complicated relationship, that between the Germans and the British. As their shared ethnic background had to be played down in light of the alignment of Britishness with Jewishness, the traditional dichotomies of race (i.e., in terms of white vs. black) gave way to a more complicated articulation of race that drew upon such overdetermined concepts as national community and racial state. That is why Germans and natives in colonial films often seem to re-create pseudofamilial structures, with the settler or explorer assuming paternal authority. The portrayal of the natives as dependents and, where the familial model applies, as "children" was predicated on the assumption of their cultural inferiority, that is to say, their primitivism. Within this logic, any act of violence committed against the natives only served to underscore the need for the Germans to look out for the natives' welfare. Similarly, any hostile actions by the British were bound to strengthen the paternalistic relationship between, to quote National Socialist terminology, the Aryan and the Negroid races.

Having examined the representation of the natives from *Germanin* in the larger context of racial and colonial policies, as well as through their encoding in specific narrative and visual strategies, I want to use the remainder of this essay to consider the centrality of race in the colonial film by looking at the highly politicized conditions of its production and reception. The need for historical contextualization, both in the evaluation of racial stereotypes and of colonial narratives, is particularly evident in the case of *Ohm Krüger* and *Carl Peters,* two openly propagandistic films from 1941 about the colonies in Africa. Despite big budgets and aggressive advertising, both were commercial failures. The official investment in these prestige productions can be measured by their careful presentation as public events, which included extensive reporting about shooting schedules in the trade press and gala openings attended by politicians and accompanied by cultural programs. On 21 March 1941, *Carl Peters* premiered in Hamburg, the harbor of German emigration and a symbol of

German defiance against British domination in the North Atlantic. In a prescreening lecture, Hartleb from the *Reichskolonialbund* praised the contribution of this great German hero who, incidentally, had grown up in nearby Neuhaus an der Elbe. Two weeks later, on 4 April 1941, *Ohm Krüger* (Uncle Krüger) opened spectacularly at Berlin's prestigious Ufa-Palast am Zoo, with Minister Goebbels and other Nazi officials in attendance and with Hans Knappertsbusch conducting Liszt's *Les Préludes*. A *Staatsauftragsfilm* whose production costs of more than five million RM made it one of the most expensive films of the Third Reich, *Ohm Krüger* received numerous distinctions, including the prestigious designation "Film der Nation." By casting Emil Jannings and Hans Albers, arguably the most popular stars of the Nazi period, in the title roles, both films used the vacillation between star and role as a means of building up the charisma of these historical figures.[12] Moreover, in the confrontation between Jannings as Paul Krüger and Ferdinand Marian as Cecil Rhodes, *Ohm Krüger* developed further the physiognomic (i.e., antisemitic) categories from *Jud Süss* (1940, Jew Süss), with Marian as Süss Oppenheimer and Heinrich George as Duke Karl Alexander. In both cases, the Germans were played by large, massive character actors. Using intertexts in a similar manner, *Carl Peters* took advantage of the Albers persona of the fearless adventurer and was clearly modeled on the Canadian Western *Wasser für Canitoga* (1939, Water for Canitoga).

Reviews of *Ohm Krüger* praised the spectacular battle scenes and found the portrayal of the English court very convincing; the sequences that attempted "to repeat the horrors of the English concentration camps" were widely acknowledged as "accomplishments that captivated even the most discerning film viewer" (Wulf 412–13).[13] However, the film also reminded some officials of the pitfalls of ideologically overdetermined narratives. There was always the danger that audiences might object to negative stereotyping on ethical or aesthetic grounds or indulge their fascination with native culture. For instance, reports by the secret police, the *Sicherheitsdienst* (SD), noted public opposition to the overly positive portrayal of the "racially ambiguous Boers." Other scenes, including one with British missionaries handing out guns to the natives, were rejected as too

---

12. In a long speculative piece, Jannings hailed *Ohm Krüger* as the beginning of the classical German national film; see "Gedanken zu meinem Film 'Ohm Krüger,'" *Film-Kurier,* 29 Mar. 1941.

13. On the Berlin premiere, see Günter Schwark, "Meisterwerk 'Ohm Krüger' festlich uraufgeführt," *Film-Kurier,* 5 Apr. 1941. Presenting German colonialism in Africa as a model for the Nazi's imperialist ambitions in Eastern Europe, *Ohm Krüger* had one of its official premieres in Preßburg, Slovakia, in the presence of President Tiso; see the extensive report in *Film-Kurier,* 6 Oct. 1941.

tendentious. "There is the danger," concluded the SD report on *Ohm Krüger,* "that such propagandistic exaggerations may undermine the credibility of the historical film story" (Albrecht 196).

Even as historical films presumably committed to the "truth" and the preservation of history in the present, *Ohm Krüger* and *Carl Peters* rely heavily on the narrative strategies of dominant narrative cinema. In the tradition of Karl May's mythologizing of the American West, the films conjure up an imaginary Africa by means of camera work, lighting, and mise-en-scène, including the symbolic use of landscapes. The struggle of the Boers recalls hardships suffered by the pioneers, and encounters between Peters and the tribes emulate those between American soldiers and Indians. The men at the forefront of the colonial struggle, the patriarchal Boer president fighting British aggression and the fanatical German nationalist acquiring colonies for the fatherland, bear all the traits of the typical Hollywood hero. Their commitment to the nation seems to justify all violations of established law. In fact, their greatness as leaders is only heightened by the social ostracism they experience in their pursuit of the colonial idea. Translated into the conventions of narrative cinema and transformed in accordance with Nazi ideology, history dissolves into the rarefied sphere of German manifest destiny.

Directed by Herbert Selpin, a specialist in adventure films, *Carl Peters* was from the beginning perceived as a programmatic statement on "the colonial mission of the German nation that is and always will be a world-historical fact and an integral part of German life."[14] The film goes to great length to show Peters as a man ahead of his time, a man whose mission would only be completed by the Nazis in the aggressive pursuit of *Lebensraum* in Eastern Europe. With its virulent antisemitism, its relentless attacks on Social Democracy, and its mockery of parliamentarism, *Carl Peters* is very much a product of Nazi ideology, including its cult of leadership that situates the fanatical Peters in opposition to the Wilhelminian culture of corruption and compromise. The film follows Peters from his first expedition to East Africa in 1884, which resulted in sought-after contracts with several tribes, to his appointment as *Reichskommissar* in 1890. Although *Carl Peters* carefully avoids the complications of sexuality, notions of gender remain an integral part of the narratives. Sexual difference returns with a vengeance in the identification of other protagonists with the feminine. Just as the portrayal of the vain chieftain in *Ohm*

---

14. Felix Henseleit, " 'Carl Peters' in Hamburg erfolgreich uraufgeführt." On the Berlin premiere, see *Film-Kurier,* 30 Mar. 1941. Leading politicians and Africa experts commented on the colonial idea in conjunction with *Carl Peters* in *Film-Kurier,* 16 Apr. 1941; illustrating the mutual instrumentalization of fiction and reality, the same page contains an article about the advances of the Africa Corps.

Krüger aligns the native with female and infantile behavior, the German parliamentarians in *Carl Peters* are characterized as too loquacious, too hysterical, too feminine, and too "Jewish" to be real men of action. The whitewashing of the historical Peters, a sadistic psychopath known as the "man with the bloody hands" and relieved of all official duties because of his brutal treatment of the natives, shows the degree to which censored biographies and revisionist histories invariably prepare the ground for a return of the repressed. Sexuality functions as one of its conduits. Presenting Peters as the father of German colonialism, the screenwriters obviously felt the need to erase all references to his association with Frieda von Bülow, the prolific writer of colonial novels, who gives a thinly veiled autobiographical account of their relationship in *Im Lande der Verheißung* (1899, In the Promised Land). However, the film's substitution of a disturbingly close relationship between Peters and his mother for this (unfulfilled) romance only brings out the pathologies in this process of historical falsification. Authoritative and competent in his interactions with the natives and uncompromising against the British, the Peters of the film thus faces his most dangerous enemies at home and is brought down not by his own failures, but by political intrigues.

As a result, the battle over Africa in *Carl Peters* takes place on two fronts. In the colonies, Peters finds himself in competition with the British, whose colonial policies he challenges with iron determination. The German–British confrontation is mirrored in the exploitation of the black natives by Arab slave traders who operate under British protection. This doubling sets up an opposition between the innocence of the natives and the high moral principles of the Germans, on the one hand, and the greed and lust for power embodied by the British and their Arab associates, on the other. In Germany, resistance to the colonial idea and the rise of German nationalism is identified with the figure of Dr. Kayser, whom at one point Peters refers to as "the Privy Councillor from Mount Sinai." The reasons behind the conflation of antisemitic and anti-British positions are laid out by Peters in his speech accepting the position of Reich Commissioner. Turning to Dr. Kayser, he announces that he is determined to prevent that "our colonies are left in your hands and those of your ilk.... And please don't forget: I can be much more explicit." Introducing a decidedly contemporary perspective, the fictional Kayser episode was obviously added to compensate for the historical Peters's defeat on the home front and to link the old project of German colonialism to the ongoing persecution and annihilation of the Jews. As long as Germany remained its "own worst enemy"—that is to say, as long as Jews and Social Democrats controlled the government—the Reich would be divided and weak; this is the film's underlying message. Ending on such a highly suggestive note, the film found a resolution only in the new world order of National Socialism and, ultimately, the Final Solution. What remains for the fictional Peters (and his mother) is to believe in victory and, in the film's closing shot, to walk toward the Victory Column in Berlin; what remained for the film's historical audiences of 1941 was to embrace the promise and the obligation captured in the final image of "Kilimanjaro as an eternal symbol of German Africa."

One reviewer of *Carl Peters* praised "the visually very strong episodes with the natives that show the good, constructive spirit in which Carl Peters began and completed his work."[15] He was probably referring to the scene in which Peters enters a burning village and rescues its unsuspecting inhabitants from Arabs authorized by the British to traffic in "black ivory." Set free by their savior in dramatic scenes that recall antislavery imagery, the natives start drumming and announce the coming of the good Germans across the savanna. Having shown his commitment to black autonomy under German supervision, Peters from then on encounters no further hostilities. In a long, triumphant sequence, he travels up the river, and wherever he and his companions arrive, they are greeted with great friendliness. Following the obligatory treaty signing and exchange of gifts, the natives time and again raise the German flag and celebrate their new existence under the "protective rule of the illustrious German emperor."

As in *Germanin,* encounters with the natives are staged from the perspective of the white man and involve the same vacillation between feminization and infantilization. The emphasis on ritual, with the camera lingering on the black men's facial decoration, body adornment, and elaborate costume, combines the tradition of the ethnographic film with 1930s notions of the primitive as well as the perspectives of Nazi racial science. To what degree such categories present the native as a privileged image not only of childhood and innocence, but also of unrepressed sexuality, becomes evident as the celebrations continue into the night. The racial encoding of eroticism can be observed in the film's attention to women ecstatically shaking their breasts and buttocks. There is some indication (e.g., through editing) that these transgressive images might be a hallucination of the feverish Peters. Whatever the case, all images of blackness are linked to the white gaze that, quite literally, constitutes their existence as the markers of difference. Separated from all diegetic spectators and subject only to the camera's gaze, the natives and their rituals take on an uncanny resemblance to the "ornament of the masses" created by the Nazis in their public spectacles and mass events. Tracking shots along rows of armed warriors in war paint employ the same formal devices that

---

15. Henseleit, review of *Carl Peters, Film-Kurier,* 22 Mar. 1941.

characterize self-representations of the Nazi regime (e.g., low camera angles, symmetry, serialization). In such moments, Riefenstahl's fascination with the Nuba makes perfect sense. For in her photographs of black warriors she only continues the aestheticizing of military ritual and heroic masculinity begun by *Triumph des Willens* (1935, Triumph of the Will); a colonial film like *Carl Peters* reveals this hidden connection.[16]

In *Ohm Krüger,* an anti-British orientation is so pronounced that it threatens to destabilize the very system of colonial representations on which it too depends. Directed by Hans Steinhoff, the film is loosely based on motifs from Arnold Krieger's novel *Mann ohne Volk* (1934, Man without people) and a biographical novel published simultaneously, *Ohm Paul* (1941) by Joachim Barckhausen. The portrayal of Paul Krüger, president of Transvaal from 1883 to 1902, as a figure of almost biblical proportions elevates the Boer War to an existential struggle between a traditional agricultural society and an imperialist world power. The film's story culminates in the inhumane treatment of the Boers in British concentration camps, a perverse reversal that places the Boers, as the stand-ins for the Germans, in the role of the victims.[17] Within the ideological formations of the time, these scenes helped to justify the existence of German concentration camps by creating historical precedents and establishing a false logic of cause and effect. Like the Nazis, the Boers in the film explain their need for new land by appealing to natural laws and their need for ethnic survival. Whether they are cultivating the wilderness or preserving their ethnic identity, they see Africa only in terms of its value for the Boer cause. For the British, Africa remains an object of speculation, defined primarily via its economic uses but also subject to more irrational fantasies of conquest. Touching the globe, Rhodes at one point raves about the erotic promises of the dark continent: "This Africa! Must it not tempt the imagination of a man, these immense and impenetrable spaces? . . . I love this Africa as one loves a woman."

Whereas femininity in British colonial narratives often functions as a disruptive force, as a challenge to the masculinity of the colonizers, the portrayal of the chieftain in *Ohm Krüger* as dishonest, vain, and excessively fond of clothes brings into relief supposedly male traits like honesty, austerity, and determination. Such an opposition constitutes Krüger as an almost mythological patriarchal figure outside the sexual implications of

---

16. One of these scenes, which was shot near Munich, is described in "Zum ersten Male die deutsche Fahne über Ostafrika," *Film-Kurier,* 6 Nov. 1940. The Zanzibar sequences were shot on the Barrandov studio lot in Prague; see Georg Herzberg. For earlier reports on the production, compare "Aufnahmen zu 'Carl Peters,'" *Film-Kurier,* 27 Sept. 1940.

17. Exploiting such connections, the *Film-Kurier,* on 27 Nov. 1940, published the recollections of an old Boer woman who participated in the *Ohm Krüger* film as an extra.

gender; the possibility of miscegenation is excluded from the outset. The idealization of the Boer leader is made possible by the feminization of the black leader. When Krüger visits his most trustworthy ally to clear up some disagreements, he finds him in front of a mirror, dressed in a leopard's skin and a fantasy uniform jacket, admiring his own image until he recognizes the stark outlines of Krüger's black hat and white beard in the same mirror. Confronting the black man, "Ohm Paul" reminds him of their long friendship and, by questioning the other's new loyalties, uncovers the degree of his corruption. The chieftain mentions British missionaries, their Bibles and guns, and points respectfully to a portrait of his new "white mother," Queen Victoria. Assuming his responsibilities as the strict but well-meaning father, Krüger grabs the black man's lapel and shouts "you *Rabenaas*" (literally: raven-black carrion), an expletive that combines elements of contempt and affection. Responding to threats that he will be skinned alive and his skin used for drum skins, the fearful chieftain changes his mind and promises to surrender all his guns—very much like a child promising to mend his ways. It is in the context of such infantilizing and feminizing that the place of action then moves to Buckingham Palace—another female space—as the source of all past and future threats to the status quo.

In closing, I want to look at an early film that works with very different assumptions about German colonialism and thus brings into focus some of the larger issues at stake. Because of its positive portrayal of the British and its allegedly pacifist tendencies, *Die Reiter von Deutsch-Ostafrika* (1934, The horsemen of German East Africa) had to be banned in 1939. Directed by Herbert Selpin for the Terra Film-AG with a relatively unknown cast, the film was produced "under the protection of the German Colonial Association" with the explicit goal of keeping the colonial idea alive; hence its promise at the end: "One day we shall come back, sooner or later." General Paul von Lettow-Vorbeck, who had led the German troops in East Africa, and Minister of State von Neurath attended the Berlin premiere on 3 November 1934 at the Ufa-Palast am Zoo.[18] Selpin's film tells the story of German colonialist Peter Hellhoff, the owner of a coffee plantation, and his wife Gerda in the Kilimanjaro region before and during the war. The invasion of their private lives by political conflicts structures the narrative from the moment when general mobilization disrupts the couple's wedding to repeated attempts by the German settlers

---

18. On the Hamburg premiere, see *Lichtbildbühne,* 20 Oct. 1934; on the Berlin premiere, see *Lichtbildbühne,* 3 Nov. 1934. Both premieres were accompanied by colonial exhibitions in the foyer and speeches by representatives of the *Reichskolonialbund* and the *Kolonialamt.*

and their British friend to remain on friendly terms. Justified externally by the conditions of war, the atrocities committed by the British and the maneuvers of the Germans to avoid capture do not diminish the men's respect for each other. The colonial world thus invoked remains one of honor, integrity, and commitment. Just as the British continue to be treated as equals, subject to a colonial code that plays down national differences, so the natives are portrayed in a way that raises the possibility of insurrection and miscegenation. The film contains a scene in which the terms of colonial power, British style, are unmistakably defined in sexual terms, that is, via interactions between the white man and the black woman. While that moment remains marginal to ideas of German colonialism, it introduces a homology between German and British colonial narratives that is highly unusual in the context of older literary traditions and strangely disruptive with respect to the function of the colonial in National Socialist policies and filmic practices.

The sequence from *Die Reiter von Deutsch-Ostafrika* uses the absence of the white woman to stage sexual desire in a way that is almost paradigmatic in its orchestration of looks and its assumptions about race and gender.[19] From the outset, the images of dancing natives are inseparable from the three white men observing the nightly celebrations. In the absence of a paternalism that reserves all negative stereotyping for the British, the colonial gaze becomes the erotic gaze. The entire sequence is constructed around close-ups of female dancers in native costume and male drummers and dancers in Westernized clothing; these shots alternate with medium shots of the white men standing on the side. The exchange of looks focuses on one young woman, Milini, whose body becomes the channel of communication between the three friends. Still angered by a letter from his fiancée, the main protagonist exchanges glances with the beautiful dancer in a series of close-ups. These are followed by a medium shot of two of the men staring intensely at one another, with the older British friend placing his arm on the younger man's shoulder in a warning gesture; then the camera cuts to a medium shot of the dancing group and to a medium long shot of the three men in deliberately relaxed body positions. Peter's sudden announcement that Milini from now on will work in the kitchen betrays his awareness of the black woman as a sexual being. Insisting on his right to sexual fulfillment and defending the practice of concubinage common among early settlers, he maintains: "A woman belongs in the house." But

---

19. This attention to issues of race and gender may be due to the fact that the screenplay was written by a woman, Marie-Luise Droop, based on her novel *Kwa heri*. For an account of the on-location shooting by the only woman in the film crew, see Ilse Stobrawa.

his British friend, who is obviously more experienced in colonial matters, warns: "Yes, of course, but—you [he pulls his lapels], no black woman!" Even after the arrival of Peter's fiancée, Milini remains a disquieting presence, resisting Gerda's friendly gestures and showing signs of hostility during the couple's wedding reception.

On one level, the film follows existing conventions in staging the encounter between black and white in gendered terms, with Africa representing the feminine. The fetishization of the black woman as an object of desire outside any narrative constraints and her identification with a mythic femininity become necessary to the degree that the white woman acquires more masculine qualities; hence her attire (jodhpurs, riding boots) and a boyish confidence reminiscent of Weimar's New Woman. On another level, however, *Die Reiter von Deutsch-Ostafrika* undermines its own colonial agenda. By identifying the colonial project with the British, it renounces all claims to an authentic German colonial narrative. Several years later, such mistakes were no longer possible: Africa had been redefined for the purposes of a new topography of spatial claims and racial boundaries, and this early colonial film had to be suppressed.

The films discussed in this essay thrive on specific displacements and condensations and, in so doing, turn Africa into the scene of decidedly European ambitions and anxieties. Yet images of the "dark continent" also interfere with such strategies and introduce an additional set of markers grounded in colonial literature and traditions of exoticism, on the one hand, and the overdetermined discourses of racism, nationalism, and antisemitism, on the other. In these configurations, Africa becomes visible in the way it brings out the identity of the colonizers encountering themselves in the other. Tempting the intruders through its pristine landscapes and primordial sensuality, the "dark continent" invariably rejects those who lack the strength of character to resist its allure (e.g., succumbing to excessive drinking or consorting with native women). However, not to be touched by the other, to completely resist its attractions, suggests an insensitivity and soullessness that, according to this model, has to be considered incompatible with higher cultures. Accepting the challenge of difference thus becomes a proof of inner strength and that volatile ingredient of Germanness called *Seele*. Under these conditions, the encounter with the "dark continent" does not really change Germans; it merely brings out their true nature.

As my discussion has shown, the structures of the colonial imagination allow for the enlistment of the black body in other stories and for other purposes than the propagation of German colonialism. Just as racial and national stereotypes are part of a more complex system of differences, the connection between representations and what is often perceived as their unmediated relationship to reality must be problematized before their discursive function becomes available to critical analysis.[20] It is on such an essentializing of the other that its power as a signifier depends, and that function of the other should not be repeated in the terms of criticism. In colonial films from the Third Reich, racism, exoticism, nationalism, and antisemitism define the terms under which the binaries of colonial discourse—culture vs. nature, mind vs. body, male vs. female—are collapsed into an ongoing triangulation of desire. Defeated on the field of colonial politics, the Germans in their films appropriated the colonial through a double movement: the instrumentalizing of established colonial narratives in a continuation of war by other means and the pursuit of an attraction that allowed them to encounter themselves in the natives. The ideological trajectory behind this vacillation is captured in a *Film-Kurier* headline from 16 April 1942; it simply reads: "Heimat—Ostfront—Afrika" (Homeland—Eastern Front—Africa).

---

20. That is why Robert Stam and Louise Spence note: "The exclusive preoccupation with images, however, whether positive or negative, can lead both to the privileging of characterological concerns . . . and also to a kind of essentialism, as the critic reduces a complex diversity of portrayals to a limited set of reified stereotypes" (Stam and Spence 10). On this point, see the illuminating analysis by Chow (27–54).

Reading the Face of the Other: Arnold Zweig's and Hermann Struck's *Das ostjüdische Antlitz*

Leslie Morris

> Our history is in our retina. Every image returns our face. Death briefly held in check, O face of the world become ours.
> —Edmond Jabes, The Book of Shares

Das ostjüdische Antlitz (The East European Jewish countenance), published in 1919 by Arnold Zweig and Hermann Struck, explores the complexities of German-Jewish identity in the Weimar Republic by turning its gaze to the *Ostjude*. The *Antlitz* is a compilation of fifty-five lithographs of East European Jews, drawn by Hermann Struck while he and Zweig were stationed in Lithuania in World War I, accompanied by Zweig's essay offering the reader a map to help read Struck's Jewish faces. The *Antlitz* is neither a literary nor documentary text, but rather an attempt to "bear witness," as Zweig repeatedly asserts, to the East European Jewish experience. In this essay, I will explore how Zweig's and Struck's construction of the *Ostjude* both affirms and problematizes their own identities as German Jews. Looking at the *Antlitz* as a split text, I will investigate how the face of the *Ostjude* evokes the face-to-face encounter, as explored by the contemporary French Jewish philosopher Emmanuel Levinas. For Levinas, the "face-to-face with the other" signals the ethical moment in which the face "at once gives and conceals the Other" ("Time" 45). Levinas's exploration of the trope of the face, of time and timelessness, and of the ethics of looking at the Other can, I argue, help us to situate *Das ostjüdische Antlitz* within current discussions about German-Jewish identity.

The face of the *Ostjude* in *Das ostjüdische Antlitz* engages the imagination of the creators of this text. This iconography of the face of the

Ostjude does not so much promote a reciprocal encounter between German Jew and *Ostjude*—Levinas's "face-to-face"—as provide a means for Arnold Zweig and Hermann Struck to explore the paradoxes of their own identities vis-à-vis that of the *Ostjude*. Written at the height of the radical valorization of the *Ostjude* by German Jews anxious to impart to the Jew of the East all that had vanished from Western, modern Jewry, *Das ostjüdische Antlitz* evokes the world of East European Jewry as a lost and somehow more authentic Jewish life.[1] As a cultural symbol, the *Ostjude* stands at the center of the complexities of German-Jewish self-definition, and nowhere is this more evident than in the book produced by Zweig and Struck.

Jewishness and Germanness, as they are articulated in *Das ostjüdische Antlitz,* are neither unitary nor monologic. The *Antlitz* is split between narrative text and visual image, but it is also split in that it asserts both Zweig's Germanness and his Jewishness by simultaneously establishing his distance from, and fascination with, the *Ostjude*. As the visual text disrupts the narrative and the narrative struggles to assert itself over the visual, the battleground between German Jew and *Ostjude* is set. The authorship is both clearly stated and contested—Zweig and Struck assert their individual identities as German Jews and as artists, while at the same time insisting on the fragmented nature of this identity. Zweig uses the pronoun "we" to include himself as a participant in the Jewish world around him, but at the same time creates, through the German language, a critical distance from Yiddish, the language of the *Ostjude* he is describing. Struck, on the other hand, signaled his Jewish, Zionist, and artistic identities in earlier etchings by signing them with a Star of David instead of his name, thereby replacing his individual identity—his name—with a collective, political, and nationalist symbol.

In the 1919 preface[2] to *Das ostjüdische Antlitz,* Zweig and Struck foreground the act of looking as constitutive of the book: "This book speaks about the *Ostjuden* as someone who has tried to see them" (7).[3] Not only do the German Jews Zweig and Struck try to "see" the *Ostjude,* but they create a specular relationship between German Jew and *Ostjude* as they look at the *Ostjude*—their other—and ultimately see themselves. Although all but two of the fifty-five drawings are portraits of living subjects, Zweig and Struck remove the individual from the face of the *Ostjude* to present in

---

1. See Michael Brenner's new study of Jews in Weimar culture and his discussion of "the authentic *Ostjude*" in his chapter "The Invention of the Authentic Jew."

2. Zweig wrote a preface to the second edition in 1922.

3. Originally published in 1920 by Welt-Verlag, Berlin. Struck and Zweig date this foreword "Sommer 1919/Im Monat Ab 5679," insisting on the split between the Jewish and Western calendars, between Jewish and German time. All translations are mine.

narrative and visual form "das ostjüdische Antlitz."[4] Zweig and Struck do not depict the individual, but rather the collective *Ostjude*—an Everyman of the shtetl—as they navigate the complex terrain of German-Jewish identity in the Weimar Republic.[5] Accompanied by Struck's drawings, Zweig's narrative becomes a testimony to his perception of the *Ostjude* from his vantage point as a German Jew in the German army during World War I.

Zweig expressed an awareness of the split nature of German-Jewish identity throughout his life and writing career. As Jost Hermand has pointed out, despite Zweig's perhaps paradigmatic status as a representative of the liberal German-Jewish bourgeoisie, he was nonetheless always aware of the "precarious ambivalence" between his admiration of the German cultural tradition and his role as Jewish outsider to this tradition (Hermand 67).[6] *Das ostjüdische Antlitz* provides us with a text to explore the complexities of German-Jewish cultural and national identities that ensue from the ambivalence that Hermand addresses. The "iconography of the exotic," as Sander Gilman has phrased it, also provides an instance in which the German Jew occupies a colonizing position vis-à-vis the East, in which subjectivity for the German Jews Zweig and Struck is constituted by looking at their other, the *Ostjude* (*Self-Hatred* 279).

The narrative and visual texts of *Das ostjüdische Antlitz* are an extended panegyric to East European Jewry, perpetuating many of the same myths and misconceptions about the *Ostjuden* as both philosemitic and antisemitic propaganda. A central point in Zweig's essay is the notion that the *Ostjude* is more authentically religious than the Western, modern Jew. The opening passage describes the Western Jew as vanishing in the "pulp [*Brei*] of an eternal Now-time [*Jetztzeit*] of all large cities," of crumbling away with a "feeble, desperate piety" (*Antlitz* 14). In contrast, the

---

4. The question of the homogeneity or monolithic status of the *Ostjude* is explored by Shulamit Volkov, who identifies various factions of the *Ostjude* in Germany and argues that what is often seen as a cohesive group is in fact much more fragmented and heterogeneous. Volkov suggests as well that the relationship between Western Jew and *Ostjude* in Germany was one of specularity and that the identity of the Western Jew was dependent, in part, on the realization that the *Ostjuden* were future *Westjuden*.

5. "Antlitz" is a somewhat archaic word, with a resonance similar to the English "countenance." The centrality of "the face" to this volume is exhibited as well in the publishing history of the text. Zweig objected to the publisher's choice of portrait for the cover of the first edition in 1920 and insisted that a second edition appear the following year, with a different cover and an entirely different order of lithographs accompanying the text. This is the edition that is available today.

6. Hermand cites this ambivalence as the reason for Zweig's "greatness" and also for his complexity, maintaining that this complexity prevented Zweig from having a one-dimensional worldview.

Ostjude preserves the age-old traditions and, unlike his Western brother, does not "crumble" or deteriorate in the *Brei* of modernity:

> The old Jewish man of the East, however, preserved his face. This face looks out at us from the stories of Mendele: guileless and dreamy and exhibiting a purity that only becomes possible through renouncing the high price of worldly activities and the happiness of such worldly activity. (*Antlitz* 14)

The *Ostjude* in this opening chapter is "preserved," not crumbling. The face that looks out at us is not caught in the decline that constitutes urban Jewish life as Zweig formulates it in his description of the Western Jew, but is suspended in the annals of Yiddish literature, notably in the pages of the Yiddish writer Mendele Mochher Sforim.[7] But not only is this "guileless and dreamy" face evoked as the embodiment of the *Ostjude* in a quintessentially Yiddish text, the face of the *Ostjude* "looks out at us" as well. Zweig's gaze falls on a Jew who is both "other" and also, in looking back at Zweig (and, ultimately, the reader/spectator), part of them (or us). These moments when the German Jew observes the *Ostjude* and is then forced to turn back and reexamine himself constitute the specularity central to the *Antlitz*.

The specularity in the act of looking is central as well to the work of Emmanuel Levinas. Levinas identifies the moment of looking at the face of the other as a moment of self-interrogation, for the self in Levinas's work is defined by its multiplicity and by its status as nonimage (Handelman 208–12). In a gesture of a perhaps Levinasian self-interrogation, the 1919 preface includes a citation from the Jewish "brothers and sisters" in the Lithuanian town in which Zweig and Struck were stationed. Here Zweig and Struck state that they will "bear witness" for the *Ostjuden*—addressed here as "euch"—and conclude on a high note, one that nonetheless ensures their narrative and discursive distance from "them," the *Ostjuden* whom they are trying to see: "Still: the testimony of a person does not fade. So we will bear witness for you and leave it to those who know to tell where only one of us is speaking and where we are both speaking" (*Antlitz* 9). With this reminder of the slippery task of bearing witness—the reader is both "der Wissende" but also incapable of really knowing who is speaking—the narrative begins.

The narrative structure of the book suggests a concept of regeneration

---

7. Along with Sholem Aleichem and Y. L. Peretz, Mendele Mochher Sforim ("Mendele the Bookseller") is considered one of the most important Yiddish writers at the end of the nineteenth century and beginning of the twentieth. Perhaps significantly for Zweig, all three "patriarchs" of Yiddish literature died during the war years.

and time that Levinas explores in his writing. Not only does Levinas's "face to face" configuration exist within time and history, but "the condition of time lies in the relationship between humans, or in history" ("Time" 45). As the book moves from the first chapter on *der Greis* (old man) to the final chapter on *der Knabe* (the boy), Zweig creates a reverse timeline that highlights the future life of European Jewry. The first chapter consists of eleven lithographs of faces of older male *Ostjuden*. In this chapter, Zweig situates the *Ostjude,* here in the metonymic figure of the *Greis,* as the embodiment of the last of the line, as inescapably epigonal, and as the convergence of the past struggling to move into the future. The figure of the *Greis* in Zweig's text is the emblem of an ancient culture preserved for one final lingering moment: he is, in Zweig's words, "the experienced and tested son of a long-lived people . . . the sense of reality of a long-lived person, which appears to be embodied in him, a son of the earth" (21).

Reading Zweig's portrayal of the East European Jewish face through the lens of Levinas's face-to-face encounter, it becomes clear that the voice linking Zweig and Levinas is that of Martin Buber. Levinas acknowledges his debt to Buber in a number of essays, including "Martin Buber's Thought and Contemporary Judaism," in which he praises Buber for having drawn the world's attention to living Judaism (*Outside* 8). Levinas praises the "poetic" quality in Buber's reliance on Hasidic myth while giving a passing nod to critics such as Gershom Sholem who saw this reliance as "imprecise" and "hagiographic" (*Outside* 8–10). As an extended revery or homage to Buber's portrayal of the "living Judaism" of Hasidic Jewry evoked in his Hasidic tales, the *Antlitz* seeks to breathe a similar sort of life into the lost world of the *Ostjude.*[8] The stylized and mythological picture of the *Ostjude* that Zweig evokes in his narrative and that Struck captures with the pictures is consonant with the emergence of interest in Jewish mysticism seen first in Buber's Hasidic tales and later popularized in Weimar literature. For the German and German-Jewish reader in the early 1920s, the caftan-clad *Ostjude* who stood as the antithesis of the enlightened and assimilated bourgeois German Jew symbolized either the dark side of the assimilated German Jew or else, in later years, the possibility for a new kind of socialist vision. The *Ostjude,* in this vision, stood for the rebirth of Jewry from the demoralized and decadent position of modern, Western Jewry.

As participants in the *Ostjudenkult* of the early 1920s, both Zweig and Struck create even more idealized portraits of the *Ostjude.* Drawing from Buber's tales of Hasidic life, they seek to create a "true" picture of East

---

8. Michael Brenner suggests that Zweig's *Ostjuden* are like living characters out of Buber's tales.

Jewish life during the war. As Steven Aschheim has observed, Zweig and Struck craft an image of the *Ostjude* who, "with his slow tempo, his different rhythms, was a reminder of the integrated whole, of the unbroken relationship between the person and the work he performed" (202). This unbrokenness and unity are set in opposition to the alienation and degeneration of the urban, bourgeois, assimilated German Jew. If Judaism is to move forward out of the morass it finds itself in, then all hope for the future lies with the East European Jew.

In the opening chapter, Zweig is concerned primarily with regeneration and time. The *Ostjude* embodies the perpetuity of tradition that also characterizes Jewish practice. This preoccupation with tradition is also expressed in the unbrokenness between the person and his tasks that Aschheim observes. As Zweig explains:

> Studying, studying that lasts an entire life time, studying, which the unremitting/incessant giving up of the whole body and all of human power to the point of teaching, studying imparts to the simple Jew this inexhaustibility of being . . . there is no mastery here, for the difficulty of the task of the Talmud is endless. There are scholars who make progress and advanced scholars, beginners and experienced, but no one who is initiated, no one who has attained completion or perfection, no just ones [*Gerechten*]. (*Antlitz* 27)

As the text moves forward from the figure of the *Greis* to the "Knabe Israel" of the last chapter, it also underscores the centrality of the relationship between time and timelessness in Jewish life and practice. The first drawing is a profile of an old Jewish man that Zweig captures in the following way: "He turns his eye from me and looks out into the distance that is nothing but time" (*Antlitz* 13). In this passage and, indeed, throughout the text, there is an insistence that the *Ostjude* occupies a perpetual "Nowtime," yet one that is nonetheless teetering on the edge of destruction. As a result, Zweig's celebration of East European Jewish life and the *Ostjude* is also inescapably nostalgic and elegaic. This interplay between past and future is crucial to the logic of the text, for the narrative moves backward as it later focuses on Jewish youth and ends with an impassioned plea for the "Knabe Israel" to step into the role of judge of man. Struck's drawings that accompany this chapter capture the arduousness and travail—the becoming—that Zweig characterizes as the essence of the life of the *Ostjude*.

Zweig's notion of time in his construction of Jewish generations is echoed in Levinas's exploration of temporality and regeneration ("fecundity") in *Totality and Infinity*. Levinas theorizes the child as an "everrecommencing being," as an ontological category that lives on into the future as an "absolute future" (267). For Levinas, "fecundity" is not the passing on of selfhood and identity from father to son, but rather part of a process in which the ego is made multiple and ever-changing. In his essay "Time and the Other," he further elaborates his concept of alterity as it relates to fecundity: "Paternity is the relationship with a stranger who, entirely while being Other, is myself, the relationship of the ego with a myself who is none the less a stranger to me" ("Time" 52).[9]

Zweig's text suggests a similar process of re-generation of time and regeneration, or multiplication of the self, like that which Levinas terms "fecundity." The very generic quality of the countenances Struck draws and Zweig narrates—the ultimate facelessness and timelessness—can be read as the sort of multiplication or regeneration that Levinas describes. That Zweig places a picture of the *Greis* at the beginning also suggests this sort of fecundity—the self is split and multiplied as it moves backward through the generations. Zweig's placement of the *Greis* at the start of his book and the face of the "Knabe Israel" at the end suggests Levinas's conception of an absolute future, a movement into the future that also encompasses the present and the past.[10]

Zweig's ruminations on the future of East European Jewry continue in the following chapters with detailed descriptions of Struck's etchings of Jews engaged in prayer and study. The opening lithograph in the second chapter depicts a Beit-Ha-Midrash, or house of prayer,[11] while the remaining fourteen lithographs show Jewish men engaged primarily in religious practice, with a few lithographs depicting the *Ostjude* at work. The third chapter opens with a picture of a house in the Jewish quarter of a Lithuanian town in order to explore East European Jewish family life. The remaining lithographs in this chapter, which are all of women, stress the importance of domestic life and the consonance between appearance and task. The hermetic and insular world of the shtetl that these *Ostjuden* inhabit is emphasized in three different lithographs of an old woman peering from the "shell of her large scarf/shawl" like a "turtle" (*Antlitz* 90).

However, the very unity of the closed community of the East European Jew that Zweig and Struck portray also evokes the *Ostjude* as static and ahistorical. If the opening chapter establishes the *Greis* as the embod-

---

9. This idea is also explored in Julia Kristeva's *Strangers to Ourselves*.

10. This conception of the relation between history and the future is also found in the work of Walter Benjamin. See, for example, the figure of the Angel of History in "Theses on the Philosophy of History" in *Illuminations*. Handelman adds to this "Benjamin's idea of a disjunctive messianic instant which disrupts the flow of historicist time" (Handelman 203).

11. This is one of two pictures in the entire *Antlitz* that is not of a face. The other is the first picture of chapter 3, which depicts a house in the Jewish quarter of a Lithuanian town.

iment of the *Ostjude*, later chapters suggest the Jewish mother as the other half of this equation: "Jewish woman, with a child in her arms, reveals the most closed figure of the East. Only the old man, the Torah scroll in his arms or holding the book with both hands, is her equal" (109). Struck's drawings and Zweig's narrative craft a vision of the *Ostjude*, both the *Greis* and the Jewish woman, as the hope of the future of Jewry. The hermetic quality, the "most closed figure of the East" that Zweig attempts to capture in his description of the *Ostjude* at prayer, underscores the affinity between the *Ostjude* and the Orient:

> But if you have ever been allowed to be in an Islamic mosque during a service, you would recognize aspects of the Oriental in the Jew . . . the praying *Ostjude* in his utmost rapture is more similar to the dervish than to any modern Jew. The devotion of the modern Jew is the exact opposite of this Oriental Jew: the modern Jew exhibits a Western gesture of self-absorption as he quietly opens himself to receive heavenly peace. This is the exact opposite of the motorized, dynamically charged essence—spurred like the arrow from the bowstring—of the Jew at prayer. (*Antlitz* 46–47)

Zweig describes the *Ostjude* as a kind of davening[12] dervish in contrast to the contemplative, inward praying of the Western, modern Jew. Zweig does not use the terms *Ostjude* and *Jude* interchangeably, but instead highlights that the *Jude* is the modern Jew, an individual, Western European subject living in current, changing time, the opposite of his construction of the *Ostjude*. This *Ostjude* is Zweig's orientalized, essentialized, and ahistoricized other, the dervish who exhibits "utmost rapture."

In the final chapter of the *Antlitz,* however, in an exploration of the theme of Jewish youth, Zweig develops his encounter with a kind of utopian Socialism and liberal politics. Influenced by the work of Gustav Landauer and by Martin Buber's messianic Judaism, Zweig had also turned to East European Jewry as the hope of the future and the site of a viable form of socialism. A text that even more unambiguously illustrates the interplay between past and future as it suggests the political viability of the *Ostjude* for a socialist vision is Zweig's 1929 volume *Herkunft und Zukunft: Zwei Essays zum Schicksal eines Volkes,* which contains the written text of *Das ostjüdische Antlitz* (1919) and *Das neue Kanaan* (1924). Although the volume is dedicated to Struck, it does not display any of his lithographs. Instead, scattered throughout the *Antlitz* section are drawings

---

12. "Daven" is the Hebrew for "to pray." It signifies a sort of bodily connection to the act of prayer.

by Max Liebermann, Marc Chagall, Joseph Budko, Lionel Reisz, and A. Kosloff, and four photographs of Palestine in the *Neues Kanaan* section.[13] In the afterword to the volume, written nine years after the *Antlitz,* Zweig recognizes that his perspective has shifted during those years: "*Das ostjüdische Antlitz* describes a world that is lost, even from its very interior" (Zweig, *Herkunft* 228). In bringing together the two essays, the one on East European Jews and the other on Palestine, Zweig hopes *Herkunft und Zukunft* will serve either as a call to action (*Weckruf*) or as commemoration.

Before the war, Zweig's Jewish identity was primarily articulated through his affiliation with Buber's cultural Zionism. In 1916 Buber published Zweig's *Die jüdische Bewegung* and also founded the magazine *Der Jude* to which Zweig contributed a number of essays. In the course of his exposure to the culture of the *Ostjude* during the war and under the influence of Gustav Landauer and Buber, Zweig's vision of Zionism grew increasingly more socialist. His various attempts to valorize and reify the world of the *Ostjude* were an expression of this development.

What is striking about the valorization of the *Ostjude* found in the text of *Das ostjüdische Antlitz,* however, is the absence of a narrating "I." As they slip unself-consciously into the shul and the house of the *Ostjude* they are portraying, both Zweig and Struck attempt to lose the awareness of themselves as outsiders to this world. The stylized pictures—the fact that they are generic "countenances"—and the accompanying narrative with its rhapsody on the authenticity of Jewishness as found in the *Ostjude,* subsume the subjectivity of the artist and writer to the "stille Größe" (silent grandeur) of the world they are trying to capture. The grandeur of this world, for Zweig, consisted in its status as both a "versunkene Welt" (a world gone under) and also as a "Volksgemeinschaft" (a close community); in both cases the *Ostjude* embodies a premodern and unfragmented wholeness.[14] Into neither the irretrievable, lost world nor the hermetic and close-knit East European Jewish community, as Zweig defines the world of the *Ostjude,* is it possible for his "I" to find entrance.

---

13. The interplay between the visual and narrative texts in *Herkunft und Zukunft* is strikingly different from the originals. Rather than serving as extensive commentary on Struck's lithographs, Zweig's text becomes the main one, with the few drawings serving as a different kind of commentary. Furthermore, the style of images in the later volume is more varied. For instance, Max Liebermann's "Betender Jude" is a simple ink sketch, whereas the portrait by Lionel Reisz, "Bildnis," is more in the style of Hermann Struck. The two works by Chagall, "Lesender Jude" and "Jüdischer Friedhof," represent an even greater departure from the stylistic techniques of Struck.

14. For a discussion of the nineteenth-century perception of the "oneness" of the *Ostjude* in contrast to the materialism of the Western Jew, in particular Heine's response to the *Ostjuden* he encountered, see Aschheim 186–87.

The narrative possibilities chosen and rejected by Zweig's text are particularly illuminated by other texts about *Ostjuden* written in the same period. If Zweig's text precludes the articulation of the "I," Alfred Döblin's representation of the *Ostjude* in his *Reise in Polen* (*Journey to Poland,* 1926) underscores the presence of a narrative voice. Here the German Jew travels into the land of the *Ostjude* first and foremost as a writer, but also as a tourist, anthropologist, and above all as a Western (German) Jew, intent on finding Jews that he cannot find in Germany. In contrast to Döblin's larger project of revolutionizing the German novel and creating the "epic" novel, which would have at its core the dissolution of the "I" as a narrative principle, *Reise in Polen* articulates an "I" throughout. The first section of chapter 1 begins, however, with a stuttering, wavering narrative voice: "I—am not here. I—am not in the train," and ends with Döblin's description of his first sight of Jews in Warsaw:

> All at once, a lone man with a bearded face comes toward me through the crowd: he wears a black, ragged gabardine, a black visored cap on his head, and top boots on his legs. And right behind him, talking loudly, in words that I recognize as German, another one, likewise in black gaberdine, a big man, with a broad red face, red fuzz on his cheeks, over his lips . . . I feel a jolt in my heart. They vanish in the throng. People pay them no heed. They are Jews. I am stunned, no, frightened. (7)

The sight of the Jews here is also accompanied by the language—Yiddish—that is both familiar ("words that I recognize as German") and foreign. In an essay written eleven years after his trip to Poland, Döblin again underlines the idea of the *Ostjude* as the authentic, visible Jew: "East European Jews can be Jews, but Western Jews cannot be Jews."[15] Like Zweig's experience in Bialystok and Kovno, Döblin's journey into the land of the *Ostjude* is automatically an examination of the relationship between German Jew and *Ostjude* as he muses on the sights—and sounds—of *Ostjuden* in the Warsaw train station.

Whereas Zweig and Struck aim to "bear witness" to the *Ostjude,* the Austrian Joseph Roth's intention in *Juden auf Wanderschaft* (Wandering Jews, 1927), on the other hand, is to report ("Bericht erstatten") on what he acknowledges can only be a fraction of East European Jewish experience. As such, the representation of the *Ostjude* in Roth's book avoids the monolithic grand sweep that Zweig unwittingly perpetuates, and prohibits

---

15. Döblin, *Flucht und Sammlung des Judenvolkes: Aufsätze und Erzählungen* (Amsterdam: 1935). Cited in Heid (39).

the kind of demarcation between *Ostjude* and German Jew that Döblin and Zweig construct. Roth interrogates the category of *Westjude,* declaring "almost all Jews were once western Jews, before they came to Poland and Russia. And all Jews were once *Ostjuden,* before some of them became Western Jews. And half of all Jews who today speak disparagingly of the East had grandfathers from Tarnopol" (20). Roth admired Döblin's account of the Polish Jews and praised his insight and lack of condescension in describing the *Ostjuden* whom Döblin encountered in Poland. In contrast to Döblin, however, Roth's book describes the *Ostjude* in the West, in the East, and in the Western ghettos of Vienna, Berlin, and Paris, but it is neither a travel document nor a novel. Roth's book is less a self-interrogation of his own Jewish and Austrian identity than it is a document about the various experiences of East European Jews.

Perhaps the most striking contrast to *Das ostjüdische Antlitz* is another text from the Weimar period in which the German Jew observes and narrates the *Ostjude.* In *Mein Weg als Deutscher und Jude* (1922, *My Life as German and Jew,* 1933), Jakob Wassermann chronicles a journey not into the land of the *Ostjude,* but rather through his split identities as Jew and as German. The futility of trying to reconcile German-Jewish relations and Wassermann's self-proclaimed inability to fully "see" the *Ostjude* is tied, ultimately, to his rejection of Zionism. In a passage in which he explains his aversion to Jewish nationalism, Wassermann writes:

> When I saw a Polish or Galician Jew I would speak to him, try to peer into his soul, to learn how he thought and lived, and I might be moved or amazed, or filled with pity and sadness; but I could feel no sense of brotherhood or even of kinship. He was totally alien to me, alien in every utterance, every breath, and when he failed to arouse my sympathy for him as an individual human being he even repelled me. (196–97)

Wassermann attempts to see the face—the individuality—of the *Ostjude* but can, in the end, only see an alien being, a situation he attempts to explain: "Does not our dissension derive from the fact that you are a Jewish Jew while I am a German Jew? Are these not two distinct species, almost two distinct races, or at least two distinct modes of life and thought?" (197). At the same time, Wassermann articulates the anguish he, as a German Jew, feels in embodying both Germanness and Jewishness:

> German Jew—you must place full emphasis on both words. You must understand them as the final product of a lengthy evolutionary process. His twofold love and his struggle on two fronts drive him

close to the brink of despair. The German and the Jew: I once dreamt an allegorical dream, but am not sure that I can make it clear. I placed the surfaces of two mirrors together; and I felt as if the human images contained and preserved in the two mirrors would have to fight one another tooth and nail. (220–21)

In Wassermann's dream, the battle site contained within the German Jew suggests a specularity that is similar—the act of gazing at the other ultimately forces a reexamination of the self—to the face-to-face encounter in Zweig's text. Unlike Wassermann, Zweig articulates the split not within the category of German Jew, but rather between German Jew and *Ostjude*.

In presenting a panoply of faces, all of which converge to become "Das ostjüdische Antlitz," and while undertaking the task of trying to "see" the *Ostjude* and at the same time of speaking for him, Zweig and Struck participate in the larger questions of Jewish language, silence, and the trope of the face as they are explored first by Franz Rosenzweig and later by Emmanuel Levinas. In *The Star of Redemption,* written in 1917 on the Baltic front and published in 1921, Rosenzweig articulated the relationship that Levinas later draws on as he explores the relation between the face and subjectivity.

Precisely this ultimate and most fundamental spontaneity is denied the Jew because he addresses God in a language different from the one he uses to speak to his brother. As a result he cannot speak to his brother at all. He communicates with him by a glance rather than in words, and nothing is more essentially Jewish in the deepest sense than a profound distrust of the power of the word and a fervent belief in the power of silence . . . So far as his language is concerned, the Jew feels always he is in a foreign land, and knows that the home of his language is in the region of the holy language, a region everyday speech can never invade. (quoted in Rosenzweig 298)

According to Rosenzweig, the glance between Jewish "brothers" is what constitutes Jewish language and communication, but it is also the glance at the "face" that ultimately, for Rosenzweig, creates communion among people (Handelman 209). The split between sacred (Hebrew) and quotidian (Yiddish) language in daily Jewish life leads to a lacuna of communication, although Rosenzweig constantly stresses the importance of the gaze: "One thing is necessary, of course, but only one: that men have a countenance at all, that they see each other" (quoted in Handelman 210).

The relevance of Levinas and Rosenzweig for a reading of *Das ostjüdische Antlitz* lies in this relationship between Jewish faces and Jewish voices. Zweig and Struck problematize both seeing and speaking in the *Antlitz,* and yet there exists a lacuna of ethics, in Levinas's sense, in the decidedly one-way glance of Zweig's and Struck's work. The imperative that Rosenzweig articulates in the gaze between brothers is consonant with the ethical imperative found in Levinas's "face to face" encounter.[16] The question of ethics and the interplay between seeing and speaking the other are also of central concern in Levinas's later work, where he shifts his emphasis from the "face" (and sight) to that of language.[17]

The question of "Jewish" language, which Gilman describes as damaged, broken language, is central for understanding the context in which Zweig writes about the *Ostjude* in Weimar Germany. The absence of the unassimilated Jewish voice, of Yiddish, in Zweig's text, and the insistence instead on portraying the face of the *Ostjude* with the language of the *Westjude,* points to Zweig's ultimate position as German Jew in the writing of the text of the *Ostjude.* Gilman's insights are useful for illuminating this point:

> What remains is that the "sight" of the Jew—the registration of the external signs of Jewishness—is a "truer" indicator of the nature of the Jew . . . than is the mutable sign of the Jews' language, a language which is corrupted as well as corrupting by the world in which the Jew in the diaspora lives. (*Body* 64)

In describing the "brokenness" and "corruption" of Jewish language, Gilman also asserts that the Jew's gaze "becomes the functional equivalent of the damaged language of the Jew" (*Body* 68). But where, in Gilman's model, can we fit the Jewish–Jewish gaze that Zweig and Struck state as their intention in the preface to the 1919 edition? The relationship between seeing and speaking the other, in this case the *Ostjude,* is evident in Zweig's

---

16. See Susan Handelman's excellent discussion on Rosenzweig and Levinas. She suggests that the recurrent use of the face in Levinas's philosophical writings may be an attempt, in the wake of Derridean deconstruction that she feels has eclipsed the question of ethics, to "retain the sense of human ethical immediacy in signification" (227). Handelman points out that although Derrida borrows the idea of the "trace" from Levinas, for Derrida the trace is ultimately of a text and not of the other (231). For Levinas, on the other hand, the concept of the trace is vital to his theorizing of alterity and "ethical" subjectivity.

17. Susan Handelman argues that "Levinas, like Rosenzweig, is 'translating'—simultaneously both philosophizing a biblical figure and Judaizing philosophy. . . 'Before the face' becomes the inversion of an autonomous reason of-and-for-itself into a for-the-other, i.e., ethics" (Handelman 211–12). Here Handelman cites James Ponet's work on the Hebrew derivation of "panim" as coming from the root "paneh," to turn, and argues against the strict interpretation of the derivation of "face" in Levinas's work.

and Struck's narrative and visual texts, but Zweig's construction of the *Ostjude* is complicated by his ambivalent relationship to the languages of the *Ostjude:* the religious Hebrew language and the vernacular Yiddish. At the beginning of the second chapter, for example, Zweig describes the *Ostjude,* in another essentializing gesture, as "at one" with his physical surroundings, again using the example of the small prayer room in contrast to the synagogue:

> But not even in this environment is it evident how the Jew and the room in which he prays belong in reality to each other. In the small "Beit-Ha-Midrash," the "Bessmedresch," which is no larger than a room—and of which there are many in every city, hidden in small streets, in the top floors of houses or behind several courtyards—above all this is revealed. (*Antlitz* 47)

The first use of the word for synagogue, "Beit-Ha-Midrash,"[18] is the transliterated Hebrew; the second, "Bessmedresch," is Yiddish. That Zweig includes the Yiddish "Bessmedresch" in quotation marks suggests both his affinity with and his distance from the language of the people he is describing. Here, just for a moment, the voice of the *Ostjude*—the distinctly Jewish voice, the Yiddish voice—enters the text. Is this a sort of linguistic slumming on Zweig's part? Perhaps it is also a denaturalization of the language used in the text, calling the reader's attention to the terms of its representation and pulling the reader away from any attempt to see it as a transparent version of reality. The inclusion of the "Bessmedresch" in quotation marks underscores the complex and paradoxical dialogue between Germanness and Jewishness that is enacted within Zweig's voice.[19]

But if the non-Jew and the European, modern Jew are presented as the active subjects capable of agency, the *Ostjude* is passive, ahistoricized, and essentialized. Zweig's text raises the question of what it means for the Jewish-German writer to turn his gaze on the other, who is at the same time recognized as a kind of "Ur-Jew" and therefore inescapably akin to him. Zweig's and Struck's stated agenda is to "speak of the *Ostjuden* as someone who has tried truly to see them." The split text of *Das ostjüdische Antlitz* suggests that these two German soldiers/Jewish intellectuals are in fact attempting to depathologize (in Gilman's sense of the word) and thereby reconstitute themselves as Jewish subjects by presenting the *Ostjude*—their other—as the "real," authentic Jew, and themselves as full

---

18. The literal translation for this Hebrew word is "house of study."

19. See Michael Brenner's detailed discussion of the emergence of Berlin in the 1920s as a center of Hebrew and Yiddish culture.

subjects. Thus the attempt at a face-to-face encounter in *Das ostjüdische Antlitz* remains one-sided. The countenance of the *Ostjude* derives not so much from "reality" as from images engraved in the imagination of the German Jews Arnold Zweig and Hermann Struck.

Blacks, Germans, and the Politics of Imperial Imagination, 1920–60

Tina Campt, Pascal Grosse, and Yara-Colette Lemke-Muniz de Faria

From the end of the nineteenth to the middle of the twentieth century, imperialist politics repeatedly redefined relations between Africans and Europeans in Africa. At the same time, a new dynamic between African colonies and European metropolitan centers also brought Africans to Europe and, with them, a new set of problems for defining the relationship between Europeans and people of African descent. Europeans were faced with the dilemma of specifying a place for blacks *as blacks* within their social structure. Of course, biologism as a dominant political discourse ensured that racial categories largely determined the social position of the colonized. "Race" served as a criterion that defined all individuals culturally and therefore socially on the basis of supposed biological "difference." Nevertheless, racial politics did not provide a universal explanation for all social relations. Rather it offered a basis for manifold action. The presence of colonial subjects in Europe remained essentially a colonial question: despite political conditions that differed from those in the colonies, how could colonial domination be maintained in Europe?

As an expansionist power in Africa, Germany was not immune to these general political and social developments. Although the presence of Africans in Germany did not necessarily constitute a novelty (Debrunner; P. Martin), different groups of blacks arriving after 1885 challenged the stereotypes about Africans that had taken root in the German imagination over several centuries. Yet, because of repeated attempts undertaken in the course of the twentieth century to adjust the lives of blacks to conform with preexisting ideas, a strange symbiosis of fiction and truth developed

---

We thank Jeffrey Schneider for his helpful comments, criticism, and translation of large parts of the German manuscript.

in Germany, where reality often began to imitate imagination. The social construction of blacks imbued them with symbolic significance. At the same time, it offered the potential for conflict, since the individual lives of blacks did not always correspond to the symbolic meaning attributed to them. This constellation opened up two fundamental possibilities for both the German state and German society: either to reject their imagined interpretations of blacks, thereby avoiding conflict, or to continue believing that the lives of blacks in Germany could be molded on the basis of the "anthropological cabinet" of the eighteenth and nineteenth centuries. The coexistence of these contradictory strategies informs the fundamental ambivalence toward blacks in Germany in the twentieth century.

The dynamics of imperialist politics endowed blacks with a series of specific functions in German society. Though guided by utilitarian intentions, various heterogeneous political interest groups drew on imperialist images to attribute diverse meanings to all Africans *as blacks*. A recognition of the social context and purpose of specific groups of blacks in Germany opens up a more historically grounded understanding of the discourse on race that differs from traditional explanations. In our exploration of images of blacks within German society, unlike Sander Gilman's (*On Blackness without Blacks,* 1982), our essay investigates a history of "blackness *with* blacks." In so doing, we analyze not only a complex social construction of blackness, but also the intricate negotiation between imagination and imperialism that underlies German colonial and racial policy.[1]

Like all European colonial powers, Germany experienced the migration of colonial subjects to its metropolitan centers. Thus African migrants to Germany (primarily from Togo and Cameroon) comprise one of the three groups at the center of our study. Arriving between 1885 and 1918, they became a symbol of Germany's imperial greatness as a much more tangible claim to *Weltpolitik* than any ethnological museum. Yet, their presence in Germany was desirable only as long as it could be controlled for colonial purposes. Thus, even after the loss of Germany's colonies after World War I made them technically stateless foreigners, their lives in Germany remained bound to German colonial politics. Considered a living bridge to the lost colonies, the Africans were expected to serve as future ambassadors of Germany after the eventual restoration of the former colonial possessions. Thus, in the interwar period, the German state assigned the Africans a niche that exemplified a politics of "colonialism without colonies."

---

1. For a sociohistorical analysis of blacks in Germany, see the recent or forthcoming dissertations of Pascal Grosse and Yara-Colette Lemke-Muniz de Faria, as well as Tina Campt.

If the presence of former colonial subjects fueled the hopes of German society even after the loss of its colonies, two other groups—namely, black occupation soldiers after World Wars I and II—provoked more traumatic responses. Since the occupation by black troops followed Germany's defeat in wars that were guided by expansionist motives and—particularly in World War II—based on notions of racial superiority, German society experienced this presence all the more acutely. Black soldiers intensified the trauma of defeat because they inverted the established colonial relationship of domination between "whites and blacks" on German soil.

The first of these two groups, French colonial troops deployed by the French government as part of the occupation of the Rhineland following World War I, was a variant of colonial migration that affected Germany only indirectly, but all the more effectively.² The German campaign against the "Black Horror on the Rhine" (*Schwarze Schmach am Rhein*)³ stylized the colonial troops as marauding hordes that raped women and desecrated German culture. However, this war of propaganda was not only an expression of injured German pride after the war. It portrayed the "brotherhood in arms" between white and "black" Frenchmen not only as specifically anti-German, but as a dangerous form of racial equality that could lay the foundation for anticolonial emancipation efforts.

The deployment of African-American soldiers during and after World War II provoked reactions that were no less complex. Yet rather than concentrating on the soldiers themselves, the German public focused primarily on the children they fathered with German women. While these children were defined as a social as well as a "racial problem," they also served as a political instrument in connection with the recent Holocaust. Their tolerated presence in Germany supposedly documented the fact that Germans had learned from the errors of National Socialism and relinquished racial imperialism grounded in *Blut und Boden* (blood and soil) ideology. The inheritors of this Nazi legacy used black children to make the world aware that Germany had overcome its past.

Rather than exploring Germany's mystified nineteenth-century images of the African continent, we examine their ambivalent conse-

---

2. The systematic deployment of African soldiers in European armies was one of the specific forces behind colonial migration as well as one function of Blacks in European society.

3. The term "Black Horror" is most often attributed to the English journalist Edmund D. Morel, a former activist for the rights of indigenous African colonial peoples. Morel's article "The Black Plague," published in 1920, marked the beginning of an international outcry regarding the alleged sexual misconduct of black troops in Germany. "Schwarze Schmach" is, of course, not a literal translation of Black Horror—it connotes more of a moral revulsion (that is, "black disgrace").

quences in the twentieth century after the German defeat of 1918. Rarely is the period of German history from 1920 to 1960 linked to the politics of overseas imperialism. Thus in tracing a continuous imperialist imaginary after the loss of Germany's overseas possessions, we illuminate an essentially postcolonial phenomenon. The very possibility of grouping together these three heterogeneous groups of "Blacks" under one heading is itself a product of European imperialism of the last century, which developed the category of "race" into a universal instrument of domination (Arendt). Despite their differences, former German colonial subjects, French colonial troops, and the children of African-American soldiers all had a specific relationship to imperialist politics in Germany. Understanding those relationships not only reveals the complex dynamic of German imperialism, but also contributes to a more differentiated approach to the history of Africans in Germany.

The "Black Horror on the Rhine" as an Act of German Displacement

In this first section, our point of departure is Germany's initial confrontation with a substantial black presence within its own borders—an incident that Gilman describes as "the first major confrontation between the German image of blackness and the reality of the black" (*On Blackness* xii). Here we are referring to the use of African colonial troops by the French in the occupation of the Rhine and Saarland following World War I. It is in relation to this incident that we will begin our exploration of the interaction between the constitution of the "fiction" of blacks in Germany and the reality of their presence. Rather than establish a simple dichotomy, we will probe the tensions of this interaction as a dynamic of mutual implication that serves as one of the central structuring mechanisms of an imperialist imagination.

The presence of between 14,000 and 40,000 African colonial troops of occupation in Germany and the at least 600 to 800 children born of their liaisons with German women were a concrete fact to which German society responded in a variety of ways: meetings of various types of public interest groups both in Europe and North America, proclamations and resolutions by workers and women's organizations, as well as discussions among high-level diplomats, politicians, and military officials. Many of these public responses are documented in the campaign waged against the presence of these black troops and their offspring in German newspapers and periodicals shortly after their arrival. The significance of this campaign lies in its value as a record of the public discourse on the so-called Black Horror on the Rhine. It evidences the transformation, within this debate, of these black soldiers and their offspring into a phenomenon only remotely related to the reality of their presence—namely, the metamorphosis of African occupation troops into the "Black Horror" and the subsequent emergence of the figure of the "Rhineland bastard." These tropes would serve as instruments of displacement in the immediate post–World War I period. The process of racialization, catalyzed in the antiblack discourse of the campaign against the black troops, provided an important vehicle for the perpetuation of an imperialist imagination.

The domestic confrontation between Germans and a substantial group of blacks occurred in the context of Germany's defeat and the loss of its "Great Power" status on several different levels: as a military, diplomatic, and, particularly, colonial power. It came about during a period of domestic crisis and political instability. Until the 1919 occupation of the Rhineland by the French following World War I, contact between Germans and blacks had for the most part been restricted to Germany's colonial holdings on the African continent, except for a few instances of black immigration to Germany (P. Martin; Gilman; Opitz, Oguntoye, and Schultz).

In the summer of 1920 the number of black soldiers among the French occupation forces was estimated by German officials to be between 30,000 and 40,000; Allied officials cited much lower figures, ranging from 14,000 to 25,000 (Lebzelter 37). These troops were drawn from France's colonial holdings in Algeria, Morocco, Tunesia, Madagascar, and Senegal. The post–World War I occupation of Germany—that is, the *military* occupation—lasted from 1919 to 1930. It is unclear exactly how long the black troops remained in Germany. Their presence, though, can be documented at least until the end of 1924, while official German complaints against them continued through 1925. Black occupation troops became the focus of international attention in April 1920 when French forces occupied the demilitarized Ruhr territory after the outbreak of civil unrest. During the taking of Frankfurt, French Moroccan soldiers fired on civilians, causing a number of casualties. In response to these events, numerous articles, pamphlets, and treatises were published protesting the use of Africans as a force of occupation in Europe.

Historians have offered divergent explanations of the goal and/or intent of the propaganda campaign against blacks (Nelson; Marks; Reinders). The dominant interpretation emphasizes foreign policy issues, asserting that the campaign was a conscious tactic aimed at discrediting France and eventually forcing the revision of the Treaty of Versailles. Other interpretations focus on racism as the primary motivation, asserting a teleological link to National Socialism. Departing from these analyses, Gisela Lebzelter provocatively argues that the discourse of this campaign expresses a form of "escape into myth" specific to post–World War I Germany. She interprets the campaign as an attempt to compensate for post–World War I German national anxieties, such as wavering social values, insecurity resulting from political and military defeat, and the breakdown of traditional institutions. Building on Lebzelter's thesis, our analysis of the articles of the propaganda campaign shows that not only the black troops, but also their children served as an important form of *Gegenwartsbewältigung* (coming to terms with the present) for the displacement of German post–World War I anxieties. Here the concept of "defeat" is crucial, for it circumscribed the context within which Germans articulated their perceptions of the black troops and their Afro-German children.

Germany's defeat in World War I was experienced not only with a sense of loss and humiliation. In the protest campaign against the black colonial troops, these troops explicitly represented German defeat:

> What offends European sensibility in the use of black troops, is not their blackness, but rather the fact that savages are being used to oversee a cultured people. Whether these savages are totally black or dark brown or yellow makes no difference. The reputation of the European culture is in danger. That is what is at stake. And precisely those peoples, those such as England and France who are dependent upon the dominance they exercise over colored peoples, should consider that with the degradation of Germany in the eyes of the colored, they degrade the white race and with this, endanger their own reputation. ("Die farbigen Truppen im Rheinland," *Die Leipziger Tageszeitung*)[4]

The language of this excerpt reveals a strategic deployment of the issue of skin color. Skin color is rejected as playing a role in the protests against the black troops, while at the same time, race/racial inferiority (the "savagery" of blacks as a race) is emphasized as the primary danger presented by the use of these troops in the occupation. The newspaper articles demonstrate that the threat that serves as the implicit and explicit subtext of this campaign is the perceived threat of racial equality embodied by the black occupation force. Germans feared that the lost war would result in racial equality in a variety of areas, not just in the military, but, to an extent, in German society itself.

In the military, the use of black colonial troops by other European countries effectively set blacks on an equal level with whites. France's use of blacks as equals to whites in the occupation presented Germany with a

---

4. The newspaper articles discussed in section I were obtained from the Bundesarchiv Potsdam, Germany, in the files of the Reich Commission for the Occupied Rhineland Zones (Reichskommissar für die besetzten rheinischen Gebiete) and translated by Tina Campt.

superficial form of racial parity that it had never before encountered—neither in the colonies, in the military, nor in German society more generally.

Perhaps more significantly, racial parity was also perceived to be a threat to German society itself, in the form of a sexual threat. On the one hand, the white German woman is presented as the channel for this threat. In several articles she is portrayed as both whore and victim (thus both an active and passive participant) of black male sexuality, which in turn was demonized as infectious, instinctual, uncivilized, and most notably, insatiable and uncontrollable. On the other hand, it was the access of blacks to white European women that represented another form of racial parity; that is, a sexual equality between black and white men in relation to (or perhaps in the possession of) white women. This was perceived as a threat to the German man:

> The Negro, who inhabits Africa and parts of the rest of the world in countless millions and generally occupies a lower rung on the evolutionary ladder, is not only brought to Europe, not only used in battle in a white country; he is also systematically trained to desire that which was formerly unreachable for him—the white woman! He is urged and driven to besmirch defenseless women and girls with his tuberculous and syphilitic stench, wrench them into his stinking apish arms and abuse them in the most unthinkable ways! He is taught that . . . he can do anything his animal instincts even remotely demand, without the slightest restraint, nay: supported by the "victors!" ("Die Schwarze Schmach," *Hamburger Nachrichten,* 30 July 1921)

Ultimately racial parity posed the most significant threat to white German men by calling into question their masculinity. This is also true in the military, where *Wehrhaftigkeit* (the capability for military service) had long constituted a major component of masculinity. Racial parity, it was feared, would deprive the white man of his "masculine" superiority:

> The "Black Horror" is not only a disgrace for Germany. It is much more. It represents the desecration of white culture in general. At the same time, it means the beginning of the end of the predominance of the white man. ("Völker Europas . . . !" *Grenzland Korrespondent,* 24 Apr. 1922)

The discourse on the black troops in the 1919–23 newpaper campaign confirms Lebzelter's reading of it as an attempt to recuperate Germany's pre–World War I "Great Power" status. This involved the displacement and/or projection of the fears attached to the changes occurring in postwar

German society onto another "surface." The black occupation troops offered such a surface, and the threat of racial parity served as a catalyst in this process. But the ultimate result of the displacement of German national anxieties onto the black troops was the *racialization* of the postwar situation. In the process, Germany's prewar imperialist status could be recuperated by affirming a position of racial superiority in relation to blacks, specifically, the black troops. This racialization was achieved by generalizing and exaggerating the "problem" of a black presence in Germany to a crisis that threatened all Europeans and the white race in general. The process of racialization is also a part of the dynamic in the imperialist imaginary that strategically transformed the presence of black occupation forces in Germany into the fiction of an all-encompassing racial threat. Here fiction and reality merged for political reasons—the much hoped for revision of the post–World War I settlement along racial lines. For the most dubious effect of the racialization of the postwar German occupation was the way in which it succeeded in constructing the black troops as a common "enemy" to all white nations, creating a point of identification between Germany and its former World War I adversaries. This in turn would lead to a closing of ranks among all whites.

The fear of interracial sex played a particularly important role in this racialization. In fact, here racialization and the threat of racial parity went beyond the discursive level. The Afro-German children of these black occupation troops were a living embodiment of the fears expressed in the newspaper campaign as the most serious consequence of this "uncontained black sexual menace"—miscegenation. These children bore the burden of perpetual identification with the post–World War I occupation, German defeat, and subsequent loss of its international and imperial status. Miscegenation and biracial children were perceived to be the ultimate threat to the "purity of the German race." Elaborating on Lebzelter's thesis, one can assert that not only the black troops, but also the Afro-German children were an important "surface" onto which Germany's defeat and the consequent loss of its "Great Power" status were projected. Black German children served a similar function of *Gegenwartsbewältigung* in displacing German national anxieties in the immediate post–World War I period.

In the 1919–23 German newspaper campaign, black German children were portrayed as the embodiment of postwar German defeat and humiliation on at least two levels. On a surface level, the issue of black German children was used as a shock tactic; its goal was to evoke outrage and repulsion and create a sense of endangerment. The message behind this strategy was that the presence of black troops would have long-term consequences for Germany, or more explicitly, for the "German race." One blatant example of this is an incident involving one of the most prominent spokespersons in the campaign against the black troops, the American journalist and former German Embassy employee Ray Beveridge. During her speech at a protest rally in Munich in February 1921, Beveridge presented two "little martyrs" of the occupation to the audience: an undernourished and underdeveloped white German child, said to be the victim of the Allied "hunger blockade," and a black German child as "living and unfortunate witnesses of the Black Horror and white disgrace" (*Münchener Neuste Nachrichten,* 24 Feb. 1921). As part of this scare tactic, the children of black soldiers were also depicted as the carriers of the infectious diseases of their fathers. In this way these children were seen as a threat to the health of the German body politic. This charge echoes similar accusations made against the black soldiers, who were accused of being afflicted not only with syphilis, but a whole catalog of illnesses including malaria, dysentery, leprosy, venereal diseases, typhus, cholera, tuberculosis, trachoma, and sleeping sickness (Marks 301).

These black German children were seen to constitute an even greater threat than their fathers. As German citizens whose residence was in no way temporary, the children presented a more far-reaching "problem." The articles of this period describe this problem as the *Mulattisierung* (mulattoization) of the German race—a process with ominous implications: "one need not wonder if, in a few years, there are more half-breeds than whites walking around; if the sacred German motherhood has become a myth and the German woman, a black whore" (*Fränkischer Kurier Nürnberg,* 24 Nov. 1920).

The perceived danger of "mulattoization" is best articulated in an article of 26 April 1922 that appeared in the *Grenzland Korrespondent.* Here the author speculates on the consequences of black progeny for Germany by applying Mendel's theory of heredity:

> If we calculate according to the so-called Mendel Laws, which maintain that the human genealogical line takes 300 years to cleanse itself of a single mixture with alien blood, the German race will be polluted for centuries to come by such a multiple and manifold mixture resulting from colored occupation. But not only the German race, the entire white race. For all traits of both parents will be passed on. Every trait need not develop into externally recognizable characteristics in every offspring... A young couple marries from one such family, pure white "since time immemorial." They look forward to their child. But what arrives is a dreadful mixed-breed child. These kinds of late-occurring bastards are usually worse than those resulting from the first conscious act of racial mixture. Woe to the white race should

the densely populated Rhineland in the heart of pure white Europe fall to "mulattoization!"

Long after the occupation is over, the traits and skin-color of these peculiar creatures, loathed by east and west, will cry out for revenge against those responsible for this crime committed in the name of victory.

The process of racialization that originally focused on the black troops culminated in their children. It is part of a continuum we will be tracing in the following sections—one that revolves around the dynamic interaction of fiction with reality. This continuum constitutes the imperialist imagination more generally through its strategic construction of the reality of blacks in twentieth-century Germany.

The "Solution" to the Native Question in Germany, 1920–40

In 1936, Friedrich von Lindequist, the former governor of German Southwest Africa and Executive Director (*Staatssekretär*) of the Colonial Office (*Reichskolonialamt*), used the phrase "the native question in Germany" (RKA 6382, 74ff.)[5] to characterize a situation that had not been foreseen in the social structure of National Socialist Germany: the presence of Africans from the former German colonies.[6] Bringing this population group into accord with Nazi racial policy—that is, "biologically" isolating them and their children from the "German *Volkskörper*"—posed a central problem for the administration. Yet, unlike the children of French colonial

---

5. All quotations discussed in section II originate from the Potsdam division of the Bundesarchiv holdings for the Colonial Office (*Reichskolonialamt*, hereafter cited as RKA); the German Colonial Society (*Deutsche Kolonialgesellschaft*, hereafter DKG); or the Racial Policy Office (*Rassenpolitisches Amt*, hereafter RPA). Translations are by Jeffrey Schneider.

6. The Africans, for the most part from Togo and Cameroon, came to Germany primarily as servants, shipmates, craftsmen's apprentices, and members of *Völkerschauen* (human exhibitions). Arriving between 1885 and 1918, they remained for long intervals of time, sometimes permanently. Because no official statistics were collected, it remains unclear exactly how many Africans resided in Germany through the end of World War I. Approximately 500 Africans and their descendants can be identified by name from the records of the Central Colonial Administration (*Kolonialzentralverwaltung*). Since the Africans listed in these records were exceptional cases requiring intervention, the number of Africans in imperial Germany was certainly much higher. The same is true for the number of Africans during the 1920s and 1930s. At the end of the 1930s, for instance, the inquiries conducted by the Racial Policy Office of the Nazi Party and the German Society for the Study of Indigenous Peoples (*Deutsche Gesellschaft für Eingeborenenkunde*) listed only about 80 "Coloreds," though other evidence indicates that there were significantly more.

soldiers in the Rhineland, Africans from the former German colonies were explicitly excluded from the sterilization programs conducted in the early phase of National Socialism (Pommerin 63f.). As the loss of Germany's colonies at the end of World War I made them stateless foreigners, it was in fact considered up until 1935 whether they should be expelled from Germany.

Such measures, however, were never carried out because they conflicted with German colonial interests. Because they believed that the recovery of the African colonial possessions was imminent, German authorities considered the Africans living in Germany an ideal instrument for establishing colonial rule. In 1934, the leading colonial bureaucrat in the Foreign Office formulated one of the guiding principles for their treatment, one that remained in effect until 1940:

> The general mood of the population on the race question has frequently exposed the Negroes to personal offenses and slights...That this situation breeds ill-feelings among the Negroes is obvious. These ill-feelings are especially unpleasant for us, as they are not confined to the Negroes living here. Because of the relationships that they naturally have to Africa, they also have an effect there... If the question of a German colonial mandate in Africa should suddenly become urgent, these circumstances can have extremely unpleasant repercussions for Germany... Thus, if possible, we should try to eliminate the reasons for the ill-feeling of the Negroes living here. (RKA 7540, 9)

The "solution to the native problem in Germany" necessitated a compromise between Nazi racial policy and colonial policy. German officials, though, believed that the problem was merely temporary in light of the final goal: the refounding of a colonial empire in Africa under the banner of racial segregation (N'dumbe).

The treatment of the Africans living in Germany was certainly not the only issue in the interwar period in which colonial and racial politics collided. Nevertheless, the conflict between the different factions in German government and society that decisively fashioned policy in both these areas makes the treatment of Africans significant. If colonial and racial policies conflicted with each other in the time between the world wars, it was not on the level of their final objectives, but on the level of priorities in the practical realization of those policies.

Forming a colonial racial policy had proved to be a fundamental problem already during the *Kaiserreich*. Since the turn of the century, the German colonial administration had endeavored to enforce a racially organized society in nearly all areas of colonial life.[7] Doubtless, the goal of racial segregation offered, on a superficial level, the most effective means for structuring colonial relationships. It is less clear, however, which political interests and social dynamics advanced a colonial racial policy within Germany. Although historians disagree about details, it is clear that colonial racial policies provided an ideological screen onto which racial standards were projected, even if they did not in fact correspond to social realities. Thus, the gap between projection and lived reality required repeated readjustments by the state in the arena of practical politics. Yet instead of realizing that colonial relations could not easily be regulated along racial lines, influential political groups and the German imperial government intensified their attempts to do so, producing a spiral of colonial racial politics that met their own standards less and less.

Although Germany forfeited its colonies at the end of World War I, the dynamic of colonial and racial politics lost none of its tension after 1918. Rather than destroying the previously mentioned spiral, the loss of the colonies augmented it with a further construction: the memory of Germany's colonial past. German colonialism became a politics in waiting—waiting to retrieve its former colonial possessions. The diplomatic defeat at Versailles helped to channel the wartime ambition to expand the German colonial empire in Africa into a highly ideological and symbolic force during the 1920s and early 1930s. With no prospects for immediate success, colonial politics now proved far more capable of creating consensus across party lines than before 1914.

In contrast, the colonial goals pursued by the National Socialists after 1933 remain cryptic and controversial. Though historians have disputed the extent to which Nazi colonial politics signaled a genuine interest in the colonial domination of Africa (N'dumbe) or served first and foremost as a diplomatic instrument of continental expansion in Europe (Hildebrand, Pogge von Strandmann), colonialist spokesmen from the Kaiserreich wielded political influence in the Nazi regime up to World War II. This constellation created a mixture of prewar imperialism with the radicality of Nazi expansionist and racial politics. The treatment of Africans in Nazi Germany was caught up in this political constellation.

The early phase of National Socialism only intensified the conflict that had existed since the loss of World War I and the deployment of French colonial troops in the Rhineland. On the one hand, the Rhineland propagandists pursued an unprecedented smear campaign against all blacks. It consistently exploited stereotypical figures from before World

---

7. The most obvious example is the question of "colonial interracial marriages" and "colonial miscegenation" after 1900. See Schulte-Althoff and Wildenthal.

War I to polemicize against the French occupation. On the other hand, the German colonial administration in Germany recruited Africans for their own propagandistic purposes. Since Germany had lost its colonies because of Allied charges that Germans had failed to treat their colonial population in a "civilized" manner (Digre), Africans in Germany served to convince the international public that the opposite was true. Thus, under the administration's direction they appeared shortly after the war in protest demonstrations against the Treaty of Versailles. Their petitions to authorities underlining their positive ties to Germany were also published in revisionist publications (Poeschel 243ff.). All colonial interest groups self-righteously rejected the Allied reproaches against Germany's "native politics." The myth of the "lie of colonial guilt" (*Kolonialschuldlüge*) had been born, and Africans were to serve as state witnesses.

The Rhineland defamation campaign against all blacks, however, ran counter to the strategy of the colonial revisionists. First, the smear campaign confirmed the international community's impression that Germans harbored strong sentiments against all colonial subjects. Second, Africans from the German colonies understood the propaganda against blacks in the Rhineland as directed against themselves. For that reason, in 1922 the colonial administration deemed it necessary to exhort those responsible for the Rhineland campaign to differentiate among the population groups currently residing in Germany. Distinguishing between "German Negroes" (*deutsche Neger*), "real Negroes" (*wirkliche Neger*), and "colored tribes" (*farbige Stämme*) was important, they argued, since

> frequently and often erroneously the real Negroes have been blamed for those horrible deeds committed by members of other colored tribes and . . . it is to be hoped that German Negroes, whose faithful affection has generally been highly esteemed, are not influenced in their attitude towards Germany by propaganda resting on such an ignorance of the facts. (DKG, 1077/1, 193)

A generalized condemnation of blacks, it was believed, would include that group which German diplomacy considered useful for the recovery of the colonies. As "German Negroes" the Africans from the German colonies should therefore be given a privileged status different from "real Negroes" and "colored tribes." Such distinctions allowed for a rhetorical compromise between the current demands of colonial politics and the racial propaganda of the Rhineland campaign.

The continued presence of Africans in Germany in the 1920s and early 1930s presented the authorities with an additional dilemma. Since the Africans were unemployed after the war, they were in need of social welfare. Under these circumstances, the colonial administration strove to return them to their homelands. Nevertheless, to prevent possible diplomatic incidents with the new colonial rulers in Togo and Cameroon, France and Great Britain, it regularly supported the Africans financially, whether they were repatriated or remained in Germany. In contrast to the government, the "German Society for the Study of Indigenous Peoples" (*Deutsche Gesellschaft für Eingeborenenkunde*) saw in the Africans an opportunity to prepare a revision of the Versailles treaty through a "policy of compliance" (*Erfüllungspolitik*). In the tradition of the antislavery movement, the society espoused, between 1925 and 1940, the goal of insuring that Africans in Germany received welfare assistance. However, the philanthropic claim of their sponsorship was merely a strategic public relations move. Their assistance was supposed to show the world that Allied reproaches directed at Germany's colonial performance were incorrect.

While the "solution to the German native question" during the Weimar Republic was intended to find a socially tolerable way to use Africans as an instrument of colonial revision, racial isolation was the goal after 1933. National Socialism now sought to reconcile its policy toward Africans in Germany with the racial principles of the state. Even if racial legislation, including the Nuremberg laws of 1935, was to be applied to the Africans and their children, the relevant ministries[8] and Nazi party organizations[9] endeavored to create a social framework for Africans that would both physically isolate them from the German population and make them useful for colonial ambitions. The result was a conflict within the Nazi party between a traditional colonial racial politics, as represented by the veterans in the Colonial Department of the Foreign Office, and the rigid racial politics of the administrators of the Racial Policy Office of the Nazi Party (*Rassenpolitisches Amt der NSDAP*) and the Department for Germany in the Foreign Office (*Abteilung Deutschland des Auswärtigen Amts*).

The compromise negotiated to this end made use of an older tradition, the *Völkerschau*—exhibitions of indigenous people that by this time had already fallen out of fashion elsewhere (Greenhalgh, 82ff.). In the course of 1935, bureaucrats and party officials drafted the concept for a "mobile Negro village" (*ambulantes Negerdorf*) that would offer the Africans the "chance to earn their livelihood through the sale of their

---

8. The Colonial Department of the Foreign Office (*Kolonialabteilung des Auswärtigen Amts*), the Department for Germany of the Foreign Office (*Abteilung Deutschland des Auswärtigen Amts*), the Propaganda Ministry (*Reichsministerium für Volksaufklärung und Propaganda*), and the German Labor Front (*Deutsche Arbeitsfront*).

9. The Colonial Policy Office of the Nazi Party (*Kolonialpolitisches Amt der NSDAP*) and the Racial Policy Office of the Nazi Party (*Rassenpolitisches Amt*).

crafts, through presentations, songs, dances, through basketweaving and other work that corresponded to their customs and practices" (RKA 6382, 3f.). The plan envisioned having this "Negro village" perform at exhibitions, fairs, and marksman festivals throughout Germany. On a primary level, the *Völkerschau* was designed as a means of implementing racial policy. The planners believed that concentrating the African population in one group would facilitate their control and "in this way, more easily prevent racial crimes" (RKA 7562, 123). The manager of the enterprise was directed "to ensure that the members of the Negro show do not engage in sexual activity with whites" (RKA 6382, 38f.). Under the name of the "German Africa Show" (*Deutsche Afrika-Schau*) the *Völkerschau* project was carried out from 1936 until its demise in 1940. Responsibility for the show was assigned to the Ministry of Propaganda in 1937, placing the "German Africa Show" in the service of colonial public relations.

Despite these efforts, the show was not an unqualified success and was discontinued in May 1940. The official reason for discontinuing the show given by the party chancellery (*Parteikanzelei der NSDAP*) invoked the rhetoric of "the native question in Germany" as it had been formulated during the Rhineland occupation: "it is not feasible, on the one hand, to make propaganda against the Black Horror in France in the press, in radio, and in film and, on the other, put Africans on stage in Germany" (RKA 6383, 369ff.). In mid-1940, though, such an explanation was merely a pretense. For with the string of victories in western and northern Europe, the administrative preparations for taking over the colonies were coming to a head. By this time, in the logic of the National Socialist colonial policy, the only "solution to the German native question" was the return of the Africans to their homelands. In 1940, successes in the war made the show unnecessary and removed the long-standing dilemma of reconciling racial and colonial policy. By the beginning of 1943, however, the course of the war in eastern Europe prematurely ended the colonial program, dashing the nineteenth-century dream of a "German India in Africa" forever.

Though indeed an amateurish enterprise, the reasons for the show's lack of success and ultimate demise are rooted in the complex and often uncontrollable interplay between colonial and racial goals. Although the plan envisioned gradually incorporating all Africans residing in Germany in this enterprise, the show never comprised more than about thirty Africans at any given time. The show actually worked against its own racial policy, intensifying a conflict it was supposed to prevent. Traveling all over the country, it made Africans public persons in direct contact with their German audiences. Thus, beyond posing a racial threat according to National Socialist racial politics, the Africans were also a living reminder of the German colonial past—a role they were intended to fulfill in public. As authentic proof of the former colonial era, they appealed to the collective memory and their presence was ascribed a symbolic content. The show's staging takes this primary mission into account through ethnographic touches:

> In the first part, a slide show was held on the acquisition, organization and the economic significance of our earlier colonies ... In the second part of the show, after a short pause, the natives demonstrated their earlier African customs and practices: a javelin dance under the direction of the chief, a short address by the same in his mother tongue, a fetish conjuration by a medicine man and, subsequently, a native dance from Cameroon performed by a Camerooner. After this dance, the natives were presented one by one with a brief description of their individual contributions to Germany ... After that an East African danced a native dance, followed by a fire dance by the medicine man and a prayer dance by the natives. At the conclusion, all Africans performed a war dance. (RKA 6383, 440)

The conception of the show was based on a mixture of entertainment and instruction. From the very beginning, the slide show created a visual reference to the German colonial past and future, personified on stage by the Africans. Listing their individual contributions not only legitimated their presence in Germany, but presented the Africans as Germany's enduring "material" connection to Africa. Africa itself, fused into an undifferentiated geographical unity on stage, also became the object of exotic longing. The promoters reproduced for the general public their own idea of the Africans as the bridge between Africa and Germany, imagination and reality, past and future, just as they had done in word and writing since the end of World War I.

The participation of "experienced Africa researchers" like Leo Frobenius provided the show with a measure of authenticity. Yet, the biographies of the African actors contradicted the postulated authentic depiction of "African life." Most had spent several decades in Germany—some were even born there—and the representation of "African life" on stage had little connection with their private lives. Of course, the stage offered the public the stereotypes they wanted to see. But stereotyping was only one of the show's deeper racial policy goals. Even more important, the show publicly undid the successful adjustment of the Africans to European life. Their past in Germany and their process of acculturation were thrown into question and removed from memory. Thus, the staged regression not only gave the German audience "proper" feelings of superiority over and against a "foreign race," but also successfully removed Africans from the social realm to the symbolic.

This twofold isolation of Africans—their physical isolation from the German people and their positioning in the symbolic real—anticipated future Nazi colonial-racial policy. In 1939, the Racial Policy Office issued "racial policy statements for the German colonial program" that made racial segregation and the strict avoidance of any acculturation to a European model the cornerstone of Nazi colonialism:

> We refuse to uproot the Native by educating him in European forms of civilization.... [We] refuse ... to snatch the Native from his home and bring him to Europe. Instead, we allow the Coloreds their full right to their homes, and, as their protectors, we demand ... from them only that which their own understanding allows them to grasp. (RPA, T 81 Roll R 9, Serial 27, 17126)

The "segregated development of the races" (*arteigene Entwicklung der Rassen*) under German hegemony precludes any reciprocal cultural relationship. In this way, the German Africa Show symbolically anticipated National Socialist colonialism.

Measured against its own ideological projections, the German Africa Show proved a failure. As a colonial official critically observed in 1939, "the effects for colonial propaganda made by the appearance of Natives in such a show ... is extremely limited ... Not the artistic performances, but rather skin color is the main attraction for the public" (RKA 7562, 128). Instead of facilitating colonial propaganda, the racial dimension subverted it. In 1939 von Lindequist summarized the show's paradoxical effects:

> We have had predominantly bad experiences ... with exotic exhibitions in Germany ... The social isolation of the Natives and their supervision was frequently insufficient and led to intimate relations with German girls and women. (RKA 6385, 42ff.)

These remarks by one of the leading colonial spokesmen reveals how the *Völkerschau*'s compromise between racial and colonial policies did not agree with the ideas of those in power. It never successfully functioned as a means of racial control. Though a special police ordinance for Africans from the colonies was considered in 1938, it was never implemented. Nevertheless, the show fulfilled an important function by anticipating the expected establishment of "German Africa" itself. For it mirrors the mental state of the bureaucrats who looked to replace the historically mature reality of the Africans in Germany with a "symbolic universe" (Berger and Luckmann).

Reaching its peak in the last years of the interwar period, this colonial imaginary both reproduced and magnified its own contradictions. Even at the start of World War II, it continued to draw on its original pre-1914 dynamic impetus—the German Empire's desire to be a *Weltmacht*. Since World War I, however, each compromise intended to synthesize racial and colonial policies only produced new conflicts that, in turn, had to be responded to with improvised strategies. Africans remained trapped in the tension between remembering and forgetting resulting from Germany's defeat. Under state supervision, they triggered the collective memory as they were forced to negate their own life history. The monolithic goal of a racially pure German world power in Europe and overseas—the only solution to this improvisational system—was effectively doomed by German military defeat. The dynamic of remembering and forgetting would be redefined in the wake of the Holocaust.

"Brown Babies" 1945–60—Instrument of "Reeducation" or Symbol of Democracy?

This third and final section examines the implications of the discourse on the Afro-German children of a second force of occupation in Germany. Against the background of Germany's defeat in World War II, the collapse of the Nazi regime, and the Holocaust, the mixed-race children of African-American occupation soldiers and German women were the object of intense public debate. According to the records of the Federal Office of Statistics (*Statistisches Bundesamt*), an estimated 68,000 illegitimate children of Allied occupation soldiers and German women were born between 1945 and 1955. Approximately 4,800 of these children were black German children of African-American soldiers. Although their number was comparatively small, these children represented the largest group of German-born blacks until that time.

As we will show in this section, the functionalization of these children carries over aspects of both the post–World War I discourse on the African colonial troops and National Socialists' use of black immigrants in Germany into the post–World War II period. More importantly, it also illustrates the extent to which an imaginary construction of this black population shaped and determined the lives and futures of these children, and how it was employed to accomplish concrete domestic and foreign policy goals. In our analysis of these discussions, as they evolved in the course of the 1950s, we will focus on various institutions: the media and the schools as well as state and private social welfare agencies.

A milestone in the history of this generation of Afro-Germans is the year 1952. In this year the 1946 age group (the year with most Afro-German births) entered the public school system and hence German public life. The impending enrollment of these children in German schools prompted the Bundestag to take up the issue of mixed-race children in German society, or what was then referred to as the *Mischlingsfrage*. Based on their racial background and their supposed "difference" from other children, a debate ensued as to whether Afro-German children would be "better off in the homelands of their fathers."[10] But in the course of this debate the members of the Bundestag distanced themselves from this proposal for a collective resettlement. One of the reasons given for the cool response to the proposed relocation of the Afro-German children derived from the experiences of German missionaries in North Africa. They reported that the "conflict in the lives of half-castes among Europeans and Negroes could not be denied." For, as they stated, "the half-castes were despised by both Europeans and blacks" (VDB/SB). Representative Rehling elaborated that it was for this reason that the missionaries discouraged "handing over" these Afro-German children to the United States. In her view, the *Mischlingsfrage* would continue to be a "domestic problem." Under pressure because of the children's pending entry into the public school system, the representatives concluded that the attention of the German public would have to be turned to this "issue" (VDB/SB).

At the center of the ensuing discussions within state agencies, among pedagogical experts (for example, in public and private youth welfare organizations), as well as in the media (Frankenstein, Simons), was an expressed concern for the integration of the children into German society. But the extensive and multifaceted discussions did not articulate the *Mischlingsfrage* as a question of the welfare of Afro-German children in Germany. On the contrary, the discourse revolved around Germany's National Socialist past. The fate of the Afro-German population was set in direct relation to Germany's recent history. As Klaus Eyferth, Ursula Brandt, and Wolfgang Hawel state in their 1960 study, "Colored Children in Germany: On the Situation of Mixed-Race Children and the Task of Their Integration":

> Whether Germany succeeds in achieving total equality and social integration of these colored children is an issue of undeniable political

---

10. All references to the *Bundestag* debate on the situation of African-German children in this section are quoted from the offical transcripts of the *Bundestag* deliberations, "Verhandlungen des Deutschen Bundestages, Stenographische Berichte, 1. Legislaturperiode, Sitzung am 12.3.1952, Punkt 10 der Tagesordung." Band 10/198, 8507 (hereafter VDB/SB).

importance. With the failure of humanism and basic common sense in the frenzy of Nazi racism, we cannot again allow ourselves to betray our self-defined laws and ideals (neither vis-à-vis ourselves or other peoples) by denying members of our community their rightful place only because they carry the traits of another race. We would then have to question our own political maturity and the validity of our most basic humanitarian and Christian principles. For in the eyes of others, they would lose all credibility. (109)

In many ways, the statements of Eyferth et al. exemplify the German discussions of these children's integration. The political implications of their integration served as the decisive factor in determining both German responses and the more concrete measures implemented. Germany's political maturity—that is, its progress toward democracy—would, in the future, be measured by its treatment of the black German children. As Representative Rehling unequivocally declared in the Bundestag debate, Afro-German children offered "an opportunity to work off some of the guilt that the burden of Nazi racism has left on the German people" (VDB/SB).

German calls for a smooth integration of Afro-German children into West German society were rooted, on the one hand, in the moral debt it supposedly owed these children as a legacy of National Socialist racial politics. Yet on the other hand, the concern expressed for the children's integration must also be seen in relation to Germany's postwar diplomatic interests. The Federal Republic was committed to proving to itself and, more importantly, to the rest of the world that it was able to bury Nazi racial ideology. The integration of Afro-German children was a means toward this political end.

In his 1991 book *Im Anfang war Auschwitz: Antisemitismus und Philosemitismus im deutschen Nachkrieg,* Frank Stern argues that the public rejection of antisemitism and emphasis on a pro-Jewish public policy in postwar Germany became increasingly identified as a prerequisite to becoming a democratic state. Stern maintains that Allied efforts to implant democracy into Germany following World War II, together with Germany's own desire to make amends for the crimes of the Holocaust, unintentionally led to a functionalization of the Jewish people and their persecution under National Socialism. This tendency was reflected not only in Germany's postwar policy toward the Jews, but also in its attitudes toward and treatment of the post-1945 generation of Afro-Germans.

The analogy between the situation of Jews in Germany before 1945 and that of black German children after 1945 was articulated both within and outside of Germany, but in each case with different intentions and implications. For instance, serious doubt was expressed in the American press as to whether these children had any possibility of a secure future in Germany. The explicit and recurring point of reference for such a critique was NS racial policy and the Holocaust:

> How are the Germans, associating the color of the children as they grow older with the hated era of occupation, going to react to the new population element? There will perhaps be no more than 10,000 of these children and adults all told. There were 700,000 Jews. What might some future Hitler do to rid the nation of this dark minority which belies the claim of the purity of the German people? Would this minority be exterminated? The German people have demonstrated that they are capable of such an act. ("Brown Babies in Germany," *Pittsburgh Courier*, 7 May 1949)

Germany was quite conscious of the explosive potential of this analogy as it was formulated by the victorious powers abroad. In pamphlets, films, and periodicals as well as at pedagogical conferences, in schools, and at parents' meetings, the German public and, in particular, professionals in the fields of pedagogy and psychology were introduced to the situation of purportedly "disadvantaged" Afro-German children. But the implicit goal of this initiative was quite different from its explicitly articulated aim of preparing the German public for the encounter with its newest ethnic minority. In the discourse of this initiative, this new group of racial others was presented as the instrument of a postwar racial enlightenment of the German people, the goal of which was the elimination of racism, prejudice, and antisemitism (Frankenstein; Simons).

The German education system was given primary responsibility for accomplishing the social integration and equalizing the status of Afro-German children. As Social Democratic representative Nadig asserted in the previously mentioned Bundestag debate, teachers had "the major task of preventing the resurgence of older strains of racial hatred by taking a stand on this issue." To prepare educators for this task, guidelines for the treatment of Afro-German children were established, based on a series of directives issued by the German Ministry of Culture in February 1952 and the recommendations of two pedagogical conferences on the equal treatment of Afro-German children.[11]

Yet, despite such extensive preparatory measures, in the years that

---

11. "Erlaß des Kultusministers von Nordrhein-Westfalen an die Regierungspräsidenten" on "die Behandlung von Negerkindern, die Ostern zum erstenmal in die Schule aufgenommen werden." In "Schulaufnahme von Negerkindern," 120. Minutes of the conferences of the "Verein Christlich-Jüdischer Zusammenarbeit" or "World Brotherhood Association": "Mischlinge und Schule" and "Das Schicksal der Mischlingskinder in Deutschland."

followed it was not the teachers, but the Afro-German children themselves who came to take on the role of educators. This inversion of the classic pedagogical situation occurred in the context of a transformation of the discourse on Afro-German children throughout the 1950s. On the one hand, toward the end of the 1950s educators began to regard German society itself, rather than Afro-German children, as the "problem" hindering their integration. One important example of this development is Eyferth et al.'s previously mentioned study (parts of which were originally published as early as 1958) and its assertion that the German public was "not yet free of racial prejudice," as it still believed in the "superiority of its own race" (109). By 1960, educators seemed to agree that the solution to racism lay in a "long-term, strategic process of education." But at the same time, this process of education was formulated as one in which Afro-German children served the function of educators or even "therapists" of the German nation; they were to fulfill the task of "healing Germany's racial malady" ("Rassenstolz") and "educating her to tolerance and justice" (Hurka 17).

> The colored children in Germany have a great educational task to fulfill. The problem of these mixed-race children and their education is for us a problem of educating and influencing adults. These children are needed to heal the German people of its racial malady. Each individual child confronts its environment with the unavoidable necessity of taking a stand on the race problem and the fate of mankind. (Mann 53)

German racial enlightenment was supposed to proceed along the following lines: a confrontation with black German children in schools, orphanages, playgrounds, and so forth would force Germans to deal with racism and their National Socialist past. For that reason the suggestion of separate classes and orphanages for Afro-German children (made in a 1952 survey printed in the *Frankfurter Rundschau*) was resoundingly rejected.[12]

The decisive turn in the postwar discourse on Afro-German children came around 1957, when the generation entered adolescence. In addition

---

12. Despite government opposition to the segregation of these children, there existed numerous private initiatives that implemented segregationist approaches to the education and upbringing of Afro-German children. These initiatives expressed the philosophy that because of their skin color, Afro-German children would be the objects of constant ridicule and discrimination in their contact with the outside world. Isolated because of their "difference" from those around them, these children were viewed as having no possibility of developing into confident, emotionally healthy individuals. The most comprehensive of these projects was the "Albert-Schweitzer Home for Mixed-Race Children" (*Albert-Schweitzer-Kinderheim für Mischlingskinder*) that operated from 1955 to 1959 in Hessen.

to the shift in pedagogical perspective, the year also witnessed a thematic shift. The discussions now focused on planning the children's lives as adults. Of particular concern were their prospects for vocational training and their integration into the German work force. Again, black Germans were to demonstrate to the world that "racial prejudice in Germany was a thing of the past" (Nissan 231).

The pedagogical concern expressed for the children's integration both in the school debates of the early 1950s and in the vocational planning debates was based on the biological objectification of their racial heritage. Integration was no longer the ultimate goal, but rather the segregation of white from black Germans. This tendency is most revealingly articulated through the particular emphasis placed on the necessity and utility of intensive language training for Afro-German children. The implicit argument was that extensive language capabilities would be especially important for children of African descent in their later professional lives, in the countries they would eventually (and necessarily) choose as their future homes:

> In order to give particular consideration to the individual and societal particularities of these cases regarding their choice of occupation, my recommendation would be training as skilled workers. For this occupation makes half-castes not only a competitive work force in their own economies; it also offers them a good foundation in the event of their future emigration. Moreover, half-castes are especially suited for work in tropical or subtropical regions as a consequence of the physical traits inherited from their fathers. Aside from these commercial considerations, a humanitarian purpose would also be served by such a deployment of these individuals. For in regions with predominantly colored or mixed populations, they would feel their "difference" much less, though we cannot forget that because of their upbringing and childhood environment they would perceive themselves primarily as Germans and Europeans. (Kursawe 338–39)

In the discussions on the future prospects of these children, their eventual voluntary emigration was a consistent element—an idea that directly contradicts calls for their integration. These children's "difference" and what was referred to as their father's "hereditary physical traits" were explicitly emphasized in discussions of the children's future vocational training. At the same time, precisely those so-called traits that until that time were seen as disadvantageous were now postulated as potentially advantageous. Afro-Germans' alleged unsuitability to the German climate was now reformulated by one pro-integrationist as meaning that in an "appropriate climate" Afro-Germans would be able to live "among their own." Moreover, with the "training as skilled workers" that they received in Germany, they would possess the optimal qualifications for a secure future in their new (read "true") "tropical or subtropical homeland." These children are no longer considered to be instruments of racial reeducation of Germans—now they are exported to serve Germany's economic and diplomatic interests. This functionalization of the black German children represents the primary element of continuity in the 1950s discourse.

The late 1950s discussions about the Afro-German children of African-American soldiers can also be seen to perpetuate the construction of blacks as a bridge between Africa and Germany. The "German Africa Shows" of the Third Reich presented African immigrants as fictive representations of Germany's colonial past. In the 1950s, when West Germany wanted to take advantage of the economic and political possibilities that relations with African nations offered, a new scenario was invented; in it, a young generation of Afro-Germans would serve as commercial mediators between blacks and whites, that is, between Africa and Germany. German economic interests and those of Afro-Germans were constituted as identical.

For "humane and commercial" reasons, the voluntary emigration of Afro-German youths was portrayed as the most "appropriate" solution. It was presented as being in the interests of Afro-Germans and, at the same time, important for German society. As a "valuable work force," Afro-Germans were given a special role in the German economic and commercial landscape. As Eberhardt Schneckenburger wrote in 1957, "For the more talented of them, their choice of occupation will be seen in relation to the increasing economic and political importance of colored peoples," since "current developments were necessarily leading to the expansion of contact with these peoples" (8–9).

Yet this vision of Germany's postwar future overlooked or ignored not only the social and cultural background of the Afro-German youths (that is, as *Germans*), but also their own wishes and aspirations for the future. The prevalence of the biologist argumentation that, based on their physical characteristics, Afro-Germans were practically predestined to fulfill a bridge function, serves as a disturbing confirmation of Eyferth et al.'s assessment that Germany was at the time unable to "conduct itself in a manner free of racial prejudice" (109). Despite the authors' concluding appeal to members of the German community "not to deny them [Afro-German children] their rightful place simply because they carry the traits of another race" (109), the exact opposite took place. The strategic instrumentalization of Afro-German children renders Germany's expressed intentions for their integration highly questionable.

The mere existence of this relatively small group of black German children provoked the initiation of premature welfare efforts and prompted extensive planning for their future, solely on the basis of their race. As a consequence of the circumstances of their birth shortly after the collapse of National Socialism and their skin color, they came to serve a strategic political function: as proof of Germany's rejection of NS racial politics and as a measure of the antiracist posture of the Federal Republic in the immediate postwar period—in effect, they functioned as a counterweight to the antisemitism of the Third Reich.

Conclusion

In this essay we have attempted to chart three moments in a continuum called the German imperialist imagination. Our exploration has focused less on imperialism than on the imagination's ability to engender concrete political goals, as well as strategic imperialist aspirations, within the domestic boundaries of German society. Our project has located a politics of the imagination in public discourse on and, to some extent, in the social policy directed toward Germany's black populations in the Weimar Republic, the Third Reich, and the immediate postwar Federal Republic. In each of these contexts this politics took the form of a tension between fictive images of blacks and their social reality. At the same time, our analysis has emphasized the internal contradictions within these fictions.

While fiction and reality are often postulated as discrete phenomena, our analysis of the historical sources has proven the untenability of such a clear distinction. For in each of the cases investigated here, the "reality" of blacks in Germany has been necessarily shaped and defined by their representation. It was this dynamic of mutual implication that propelled the politics beyond colonial containment and territorial expansion back to the domestic realm and fueled the functionalization of blacks at multiple levels—discursively, ideologically, politically, and materially.

In closing, we must emphasize that the patterns we have traced here can be considered partial at best. For they constitute only the first step in the larger historiographical project of reconstructing the history of blacks in Germany and of Germans of African descent, a history that would examine the construction of race within its equally significant social, political, and ideological investments.

Part 3
Imperial Fantasies after 1945

Of Seeing and Otherness: Leni Riefenstahl's African Photographs

Lisa Gates

Leni Riefenstahl left for Africa in 1956, armed with a Leica camera and a vision of the continent culled from the pages of Hemingway's novel *The Green Hills of Africa.* She read the book in one night, she writes in her autobiography, inspired by the following passage: "All I wanted to do now was to get back to Africa. We had not left it, yet, but when I would wake in the night, I would lie, listening, homesick for it already" (72). It is Hemingway's notion of homesickness that attracted Riefenstahl to Africa. It is an interesting way of describing homesickness, as it conveys not only the depth of longing, but suggests a longing for something that is not there. Certainly, in 1956, Riefenstahl experienced this kind of homesickness—postwar Germany no longer wanted her. The artistically and critically successful films she had produced during the Third Reich—*Triumph of the Will* and *Olympia*—were internationally boycotted. Rumors circulated in the press, some true, others false, about the extent of her involvement with Hitler and her knowledge of the extermination of Jews, Gypsies, and other "undesirables." Her name was tainted, and not only was her earlier film work ignored—save for excerpts from *Triumph of the Will* used in anti-Nazi films—but her film career was in jeopardy. What studio or financier would back the most famous artist of the Third Reich? But Africa, a continent where Riefenstahl was largely unknown, represented a new beginning, as it had for so many European settlers before her.

Of the countries she visited, Riefenstahl was most intrigued by the Sudan, to which she would journey several times over the next twenty-five years. From these travels she published pictorial pieces in German and British magazines and three books of photographs, two of which, *The Last of the Nuba* and *The People of Kau,* I discuss in this essay. These glossy coffee-table books are intended, in Riefenstahl's words, to document two disappearing cultures, the Mesakin Nuba and the Southeastern Nuba (*Last of the Nuba* 4). What kind of document this is, however, is a matter of debate. For some, the photographer and amateur ethnographer Riefenstahl produced work of significant anthropological value; for others, her books serve as further evidence of her fascist sensibilities. Some charge ethnography with deception; other accept it as truth. In this essay, I suggest that the true function of popular ethnography lies somewhere in between. By comparing Riefenstahl's texts and photographs to representations of the same peoples by another amateur ethnographer, Oskar Luz, I discuss how she uses discourse and imagery borrowed from a Western notion of exoticism in order to construct, unwittingly, a story of the Western self. More than the story of a vanishing African people, her books are the story of a vanishing European power, of a classical humanism that no longer has a place in the postmodern, postcolonial world. Popular ethnography, be it in the form of Riefenstahl's articulate, elegant, and sensual photographs or Luz's prosaic, pornographic writings, resurrects on a metaphoric plane the long-standing battle between the European and native. It creates a space for continued imperialism, a kind of metaphorical domination that attempts to exert another form of control over the African. This is the real translation of popular ethnographic discourse, a notion of otherness that allows the Western speaker simultaneously to applaud and insult, to sexualize and degrade, to present and represent—a form of speech that retains a metaphorical power after political power has been restored to its rightful owner. Ultimately, what is most disturbing about Riefenstahl's photography is not so much her nostalgic vision of Africa, but its success in the commercial market: it suggests that Riefenstahl's ethnography—that fantasy of a black, exotic other—remains, to the Western mind, preferable to the realities of the African, African-American, and Afro-German existence.

The story of the Nuba books actually began before Riefenstahl opened her camera case, even before she joined the Luz expedition in 1962. It began with a photograph of a Mesakin Nuba wrestler in *Stern* magazine, which Riefenstahl discovered on her first trip to Africa and which, as she writes in her autobiography, inspired her search for the Nuba. Of the moment of departure in 1962, she writes:

> At last, I was sitting in the plane, leaving everything behind me, as though a great load were slipping from me and I was starting a new part of my life. I didn't just yearn to see Africa, I was magically drawn by a very specific Africa—the dark, mysterious and still barely

explored continent. All this was very impressively conveyed in a photo with which I couldn't part and which shows a black athlete carried on the shoulders of a friend ... the black man's body looked like a sculpture made by Rodin or Michelangelo and the caption read: "The Nuba of Kordofan." There was no other information. (462)

From Riefenstahl's description of this one simple but powerful photograph we gain insight into far richer territory: her preconceptions of both the African and of herself, the artist. Africa may represent a new beginning for Riefenstahl's career, but after reading this passage, one wonders whether the same holds true for Africa. From her metaphors to the object of her search, Riefenstahl's journey is about repetition and renewal, not invention. Her journey to Africa begins with the resurrection of one of the oldest and least original imperialist tropes: the oppressed European, searching for freedom in a "dark" and "unexplored" land. And like the explorers and opportunists who preceded her, Riefenstahl is searching for something very precious, an unusual kind of treasure: the hidden repository of the classical humanist aesthetic, the heirs to the bodies of ancient Greece, Olympia, and Nuremberg.

Like most successful explorers, Riefenstahl uses the tricks of the trade—in this case, glass beads, aspirin, vitamins—to get what she came for: extraordinary photographs of extraordinary bodies. Both of the books discussed in this essay, *The Last of the Nuba* and *The People of Kau*, were commercial and artistic successes and restored Riefenstahl's reputation as a great artist in a way that denazification alone could not accomplish. But it was precisely this commercial success and the aesthetic continuity between Aryan soldiers, Olympian athletes, and Nuba warriors that also got Riefenstahl into trouble. In a 1975 article for the *New York Review of Books,* Susan Sontag argues that Riefenstahl's glossy photographs are nothing more than a seductive reprise of the fascist aesthetic she perfected in her films. The charge of aesthetic continuity is certainly a valid one, but it needs to be examined not only within the context of Riefenstahl's art, but also within the context of popular ethnography, the site where Western notions of the primitive and the exotic are formed. That these are *black* bodies on display has significant implications for Sontag's charges of fascism and suggests a need to move beyond the Third Reich to consider Riefenstahl's aesthetics within the wider context of popular ethnography.

When thinking about popular ethnography, it is important to differentiate it from the scientific category of ethnography. In the most literal sense, ethnography means the graphic representation of a people, and it is still used in this descriptive sense by the anthropological community today. Popular ethnography can be viewed as ethnography's commercial cousin. While the ethnographic text is presented as third-person, scientific discourse, popular ethnographic writing is dominated by first-person narration and subjective impressions.[1] Popular ethnography is not scholarly, but often passes as scientifically credible because of its nominal tie to the ethnographic text. It is perhaps best embodied in magazines such as the American *National Geographic* and the German *Geo*. Unlike their scholarly counterparts, these publications turn a profit and enjoy a wide audience, proffering the *Reader's Digest* equivalent of anthropology to the average Western household. Where anthropology is scientific and academic, popular ethnography is mainstream and accessible, open to any interested party with a camera. Where anthropology produces dry, carefully organized and delineated studies, popular ethnography presents a compelling visual narrative. Though Riefenstahl's books are a cut above most popular ethnographic fare, they are still meant for the armchair traveler, those educated and interested citizens of the world who want to appreciate the beauty of Africa, but who don't necessarily want to endure the physical hardships of travel. Popular ethnography is a category that seems progressive because it introduces the non-Western world to a Western audience and purports to be accurate in its representation—after all, isn't the camera the best mimetic tool available?

In the case of Riefenstahl's Nuba books, the fact that the author, the ethnographer, is first and foremost an artist and aesthete should already make us nervous. Her body of work, from the Weimar film *The Blue Light* to the Nazi spectacle *Triumph of the Will* to the independently produced *Olympia,* clearly outlines her specific and limited notions of physical and natural beauty. In *The Blue Light,* it is the dramatic landscape, colored with unusual filters, that is the star of the film. In *Triumph of the Will* and *Olympia,* it is the formal patterns of pageantry and the young, healthy male bodies that are repeatedly and excessively valorized. Indeed, Riefenstahl speaks candidly about her aesthetic sensibilities:

> I can simply say that I feel spontaneously attracted by everything that is beautiful. Yes: beauty, harmony. And perhaps this care for composition, this aspiration to form is in effect something very German. But I don't know these things myself, exactly. It comes from the unconscious. . . . What is purely realistic, slice of life, what is average, quotidian doesn't interest me. I am fascinated by what is beautiful,

---

1. There are many anthropologists working today, like Clifford Geertz and James Clifford, who reject the possibility of absolute objectivity in their work. There remains, however, a belief in the value of the ethnographer's cultural alienation as the distance necessary to produce a more accurate, more "objective" ethnographic text.

strong, healthy, by what is living. I seek harmony. When harmony is produced, I am happy. (Interview)

This aesthetic bias should in many ways discredit Riefenstahl's work as an ethnographer. Certainly it does distinguish her from mainstream popular ethnography, such as *National Geographic,* or ethnographers in general who claim to possess an open mind and unbiased camera. By recognizing Riefenstahl as an amateur ethnographer with strongly defined aesthetic tastes and as an artist working with ethnographic material, we can already anticipate certain patterns in her photography. We assume that the healthy young body, especially the male body, will be the focus of her work, and that the differently abled, differently aged, and differently primitive will not appear. But is this bias the basis of a fascist aesthetic, as Sontag suggests, or just standard popular ethnographic procedure?

To explore this question, I turn to the photographs of the Nuba. In these two books, two stereotypes in particular emerge, those of the noble savage and his alter ego, the ignoble savage. The first, the noble savage, is embodied by the Mesakin Nuba featured in Riefenstahl's first book, *The Last of the Nuba.* The Mesakin, according to Riefenstahl, inhabit a primitive utopia. They live in total isolation from the outside world, even from neighboring Nuba tribes. But as much as this isolation cuts them off from the potential benefits of modernity—such as an escape from poverty—it also keeps them free from the evils of the outside world: crime, alienation, and broken communities. The Mesakin, as Riefenstahl sees them in 1962, are every explorer's fantasy, a people living outside modern times. It is here, inside the mountain walls of this African Eden, that Riefenstahl finds her noble savage. On the second page of *The Last of the Nuba,* for example, there is a photograph of a young man playing a crude handmade lyre. It is late afternoon, judging from the lighting, for much of the man is lost in shadow, and the strings he plays are visible only as shadows across his palm. Where there is not shadow, the sun turns the rock and the wood of the lyre a warm brownish-yellow and catches on the metal of his nose-ring. The photograph itself, with its mix of shadow and sun, is beautiful, and its subject, the nude "primitive" with musical instrument, embodies Schiller's notion of the naive.[2] What Riefenstahl has discovered here in the Sudan is another ancient Greece, a community where all men participate in and contribute to cultural life. This totalizing idealization is, to be sure, a distortion, but, at first glance, the discovery that the aesthetic ideals of classi-

---

2. According to Schiller's definition, the naive is characterized by a harmonious, unmediated connection to the natural world. See his essay "On the Naive and Sentimental in Literature" (1795).

cal humanism are alive and well in Africa may seem a redemptive gesture. After all, it is not just that the African—the black, uncivilized man—is beautiful, according to Riefenstahl, but ironically, he now possesses that ideal community that we Westerners have lost long ago. Riefenstahl's stylization of the Nuba becomes a measure of his sameness, rather than his difference. The message for the Western reader is a hopeful one of brotherhood, in which the European and African are united in the larger community of classical forms.

The Mesakin's alter-ego, the ignoble savage, is the subject of Riefenstahl's second book, *The People of Kau*. Riefenstahl "discovers" these people in a dream after her bittersweet 1974 return to the Mesakin. With her newly published book in hand, she is horrified to discover that "her" gentle Mesakin no longer resemble those in the photographs she took a decade earlier. Forced by a drought to seek work outside the villages, the Mesakin have been "corrupted," or more accurately, integrated, into modern, postcolonial society. Now they wear clothes and, like Adam and Eve in a post-Edenic world, are ashamed of their nakedness. But fortunately for Riefenstahl, the English title of her book was something of a misnomer: the Mesakin Nuba weren't really "the last"; the violent, knife-fighting Nuba of her dream still exist. These southeastern Nuba, called the Kau by Riefenstahl, stand a better chance of resisting "corruption" by modernity in part because of the isolation of their villages, in part because of their "wild" and "passionate" nature—all that is opposite to the peaceful Mesakin, Riefenstahl writes. The pinnacle of cultural expression in this society and the centerpiece of *The People of Kau* is the wrestling match, the ritual in which the men decorate their faces and bodies, wrap bracelet-like knives around their wrists, and fight to near death. The fights are extremely bloody. And, for Riefenstahl, they are exciting. She shows us fifty-four pages of photographs, many of them close-ups of the warrior circling, striking, and clutching his opponent in a bloody embrace. Because of the Nubas' black skin and painted faces, the deep red blood looks especially striking. But these are, after all, images of violence: of heads being slashed open, of men severely and sometimes mortally wounded. Listen, for example, to Riefenstahl's description of a wrestling match: "The first bout begins. The men start by fighting with staves, but these are hurled aside within seconds and the fight continues with wrist-blades. Two fighters of equal strength confront one another. There is graceful and balletic alternation of attack and defense, lunge and parry." Here the individual fighters are subsumed into archetypal forms of struggle that are immediately cast in Western terms, as if a slightly dangerous waltz were being performed. She continues: "Any blow is legitimate, whatever part of the body it lands on, but the most common target is the head. Head-blows connect with an audible crack that evokes a kind of ecstasy from the winner's supporters. . . . Excitement mounts steadily as the bouts become more and more savage" (*The People* 222–23).

The aesthetics of this description, the link established between the sounds of violence and ecstasy, closely approximate the tenets of fascist aesthetics outlined by Sontag:

> Though the Nuba are black, not Aryan, Riefenstahl's portrait of them evokes some of the larger themes of Nazi ideology: the contrast between the clean and the impure, the incorruptible and the defiled, the physical and the mental, the joyful and the critical . . . What is distinctive about the fascist version of the old idea of the Noble Savage is its contempt for all that is reflective, critical and pluralistic. In Riefenstahl's casebook of primitive virtue, it is hardly—as in Lévi-Strauss—the intricacy and subtlety of primitive myth, social organization of thinking that is being extolled. (88–89)

Certainly Sontag's great finds in *The Nuba*—"the pairs move together, heaving and straining, huge muscles bulging" (133)—pale in comparison to the spectacle of violence in *The People of Kau*. But are the two stereotypical images of the savage reconstructed by Riefenstahl necessarily fascist? Certainly Nazi ideology has a well-established tradition of crossing historical boundaries, of freely borrowing iconography and redefining it to fit its own purposes. But would fascism—a word that Sontag exchanges freely with Nazism—cross racial boundaries this freely? Logically, the fascist celebration of the primitive would invoke a blond-haired, blue-eyed fantasy of the Germanic *Volk,* not the black Nuba of the Sudan. Sontag's dismissal of this point is alarmingly casual, for it is of critical importance that these bodies are black and not Aryan. If Riefenstahl's images of the Nuba are fascist, how can we account for the aesthetic idealization of an "inferior" race? To accept this contradiction, I argue, would entail a watered-down version of fascism, devoid of the historical specificity that is an integral part of Sontag's critique. It is ultimately more interesting, I suggest, to move from charges of fascist aesthetic—is she or isn't she a Nazi?—to a discussion of the aesthetics of racial representation in popular ethnography. In shifting the frame of the debate, many of Sontag's important observations, such as the use of stereotype and the eroticization of the body, do not get lost in the shuffle, but turn out to be typical modes of race representation for the white Western audience. Does this mean that popular ethnography is fascist? Not necessarily, but it does mean that fascism and popular ethnography share in the eroticization of power and domination—no real surprise, as they are both incarnations of a Western will to power.

Another ethnographic account of the Mesakin was published in a 1966 edition of *National Geographic* by Horst and Oskar Luz, a father and son team who led the expedition Riefenstahl joined. Entitled "Proud Primitives, The Nuba People," the article is dramatically different from Riefenstahl's book. Her stylized portraits of the male body and almost literary prose belong in the camp of the high-brow; Luz's rendition is clearly the middle-, even low-brow cousin, offering sensationalized portraits of primitive hardship and female bodies. What this coincidental pairing of Luz and Riefenstahl illustrates is not only the wide variety of distorted representations of the other that exist. More importantly, it suggests that the discursive stylizations of race that Sontag identifies as fascist are not uniquely Riefenstahl's, but part of the larger discourse of popular ethnography.

The first scene recounted by both Riefenstahl and Luz is, appropriately, the first encounter with the other. Here, it occurs in the form of a young, naked Mesakin woman who stands on an outcropping of rock and twirls a switch. As the German photographers approach in their Landrover, she jumps back into the bushes. These are the facts. Riefenstahl describes the scene as follows:

> We travelled for almost a week before we reached Kadguli. . . . our hopes had come to nothing. All the same we did not want to give up the search yet. The tracks so far had become difficult enough, but from now on, they became even more unpleasant. Our vehicles forced their way through the long grass. Piles of stones and immensely old trees gave the landscape a romantic character. The mountains seemed to be getting further and further away; the valley became narrower, and the track more and more stony. But then for the first time we saw round houses on the hills, clinging to the rocks like birds' nests—they could only be Nuba houses. We went on further towards the hillside, where we could see a long-legged, young woman swinging a switch. She had no clothes on, and the only adornment on her black body was a string of red pearls. We kept still. She looked at us in terror, and then, with a single leap, disappeared into the bush. (10)

This encounter provides a good example of Riefenstahl's literary and aesthetically minded style of ethnographic discourse. The journey itself is carefully inscribed in another classic imperialist trope—the hunt—only now, of course, it is the camera that is used to shoot. The hunters/photographers forge ahead through a bleak and difficult terrain, with moments of aesthetic relief in the scattering of trees and stones. Finally, they see the "signs," "tracks"—houses that are then recast as bird nests—and then, the object of their journey, the Mesakin. It is ultimately the drama, the language of the hunt, that is of greatest interest to Riefenstahl; even the body of the Mesakin woman receives relatively little attention and becomes important only insofar as she represents the object of the hunt, the animal. In keeping with the metaphor, the woman is terrified and leaps into the bush, forcing the reader to ask whether this is really a young woman or a frightened gazelle that has been caught in the headlights.

Luz's account, however, offers very different reasons for stopping so suddenly:

> As we skirted a steep knoll one morning and Mesakin huts came into view, Horst jumped on the brakes. . . . Shouts came from the bus following close behind us: "Are you crazy? We almost rammed you!"
>
> Horst just stared. I followed his gaze to a graceful young girl standing in the breeze on the rock outcropping. Unencumbered except for bead strings around her neck and waist, she was a black nymph on a pedestal. But she moved. Her torso made writhing sinuous motions and her arm swept an arc above her head. . . .
>
> It was not hard to persuade the boys to stop. (679)

Here we have the opposite of Riefenstahl's version, both with respect to narrative focus and style. The description of the landscape, the drama of the hunt are both elided, and a sexualized black female body is placed at center stage. Yet another discursive continuity between postcolonial present and colonial past is posited here, only here it centers on the seductive powers of the black woman that so intrigued nineteenth-century anthropologists.[3] The style too is markedly different from Riefenstahl's: where Riefenstahl sees gazelles, Luz sees gazelles in heat. Where Riefenstahl sees the romanticized image of the exotic, Luz sees an animal sexuality.

This sexualization of the non-Western female body is not unique to the Luz article, but has long been standard editorial practice in *National Geographic*. Founded in 1888, the magazine was intended to show the beauty of exotic locales to the American public, but was most famous for its pictures of bare-breasted native women. Like Riefenstahl's use of the classical male form, these photographs were intended to demonstrate the

---

3. See Sander Gilman's work on nineteenth-century theories of the African woman's heightened sexuality (see *Difference and Pathology; Sexuality*).

sameness of us and them, that under the costume and skin color, there was an anatomy that tied us together. Of course, it was specifically the female anatomy, and for many readers, the magazine thus acquired another function, that of soft-core pornography. As Samuel Delany writes of his own voyeurism in the 1950s, it was precisely "the closure of the scientific discourse around them that legitimated the wholly extra-discursive, furtive, privatized and silent use of their verbal and pictorial images for sex, usually masturbatory, though the didactic purpose was always larger" (49). While this pornographic function has since been superseded by magazines such as *Playboy* and *Penthouse,* the message to the predominantly white readership in the segregated 1950s was that if a young man felt the need to sow his proverbial wild oats, he should plant them in black soil (50).

In Luz's article, the sexualization of the female body is historically updated and used to address a slightly different power imbalance: the postcolonial order, a place where Western domination has at least nominally been overturned. In another photograph, Luz shows us Mesakin women carrying large baskets on their heads and follows with a close-up of the woman's head after she takes the basket off. There on the top is a round bump from the weight. The caption reads:

> Goddesses in ebony, women carry basketloads of millet weighing as much as 75 pounds. They step through the unharvested field on their way to drying racks two miles distant. The expedition tested the Nuba under the stress of heavy work. Results show that these human work horses endure burdens and heat that would fell a European. (682)

This test, it turns out, is even somewhat scientifically executed: one of the expedition members measured the pulse rates of the working Nuba men and women by running electrodes from their earlobes to a recording instrument. There is probably a grain of truth in Luz's "scientific" observation: it is hot when the expedition visits, and its members are not used to such heat. The Mesakin, as we learn from Riefenstahl, work around the heat: they rise before dawn to work in the fields and take a siesta during midday. This fact, however, is omitted in Luz's article. Instead, he opts for a racial explanation, one that careens from exoticism to racism in four short sentences, and even invokes "science" as a legitimating factor. The women are simultaneously "goddesses in ebony" and "work horses," able to perform hard labor in extreme heat. Contained within this sexualized description, however, is an implicit justification of slavery. Given Luz's observation, it is no wonder that Africans and not a European people were kidnapped and imported to the Americas. They, after all, not only possess a physical constitution better suited to hot climates but even manage to look good in the fields. In the postcolonial 1960s, in the face of civil rights and black power, this style of popular ethnography resurrects a kind of plantation erotics and makes a nostalgic appeal to a time when white dominance was more secure.

If the representation of the female body reflects a Western desire for control and dominance, what about the function of the male body in ethnographic discourse? Surprisingly, the imagery presented in Luz's article is strikingly similar to the fascist aesthetic outlined by Sontag. How these male bodies are valorized, however, is quite different for the two photographers. For Luz, the exaggerated musculature of the male Mesakin becomes a measure of his primitiveness. For Riefenstahl, in the following passage especially, the idealized male form of the Mesakin becomes the ticket for admission into her hall of beauty:

> A thousand, perhaps two thousand, people were moving about in the light of the setting sun on an open space thickly surrounded by trees. With their strange body-paint and fantastic adornment they looked like beings from another planet. Hundreds of spear-points danced against the red glow of the setting sun. In the middle of the crowd, larger and smaller circles had formed, inside which pairs of wrestlers were facing each other, making feints at each other or fighting or dancing, with the winner carried out of the ring shoulder-high, just as I had seen it in Rodger's picture. I was stunned, and did not know what to photograph first. Everything I saw was so unusual, so curious, and so immensely fascinating. It was not only what one saw which was so intensely exciting, but what one heard as well: there was a ceaseless drumming, and above that the high-pitched trilling of the women and the shouts of the men. Soon I found myself in the midst of them, hands were stretched out to me, faces laughed into mine, and I saw that I was among good people. (*The Last* 11)

Once again, Riefenstahl's hunt is successful; she does indeed find the bodies promised in the *Stern* photograph. But rather than merely observe, she involves herself in the ceremony and attempts to move from the position of outsider, of Western observer, to participant. Her description, her reconstruction of the event from different sensory impressions, the aural as well as the visual, is all part of a syncretic impulse, an attempt to bridge the distance between self and other, German and African. But even in the midst of this utopic moment of communion, Riefenstahl's reliance on a clichéd discourse of exoticism suggests an underlying distance, one that thwarts her good intentions.

Now read Luz's account of the same event:

> While the last stragglers were still arriving, the teeming mass of dusky bodies already was falling back here and there to form open circles of fighting rings. Greased with butter and sesame oil, the bodies of the girls and women glistened in the afternoon light ... When spectators pressed too close to their barrel-chested heroes, wardens drove them back by beating the ground at their feet with long handled leather paddles, like oversized fly swatters. A wrestler dances into the ring, looks challengingly around, assumes a frightening stance, elbows on his knees—and waits. Whoever accepts the summons enters the ring ... Now the two men take measure of each other, crouching, wary, flexing bulging biceps. To awe the opponent, they whirl with springy steps, shake arms and shoulders, limber up and ripple their muscles. (698)

Clearly there are significant differences between Luz's and Riefenstahl's recordings of the same ceremony. Luz writes exclusively in the "neutral" third person, making no attempt to identify himself or join in the festivities. As in the earlier example, his interest is reserved for the "action" and avoids any attention to the setting. The most interesting difference, however, again centers on the type of racial discourse used by the authors: Riefenstahl's colorful extraterrestrials are replaced here by "teeming masses." Riefenstahl works with a more literary and imaginative racial discourse, one of gazelles and aliens, and avoids the sensationalism of Luz's greased women and displays of brute male strength. But how different are these models? There is one overriding, pivotal similarity in the language of Riefenstahl and Luz—the use of military metaphors to describe the "primitive" male. This mindless glorification of male physical strength, after all, is the crux of Sontag's objection to Riefenstahl's work. And yet, Luz does the same thing; instead of "the pairs move together heaving and straining, huge muscles bulging," we have "barrel-chested heroes" and "flexing bulging biceps." In essence, we have the same aesthetic of the male African body, a correspondence that does not so much link Luz to fascism as it links Riefenstahl to popular ethnography. It is precisely this idealization of brute male strength that serves as the preferred aesthetic representation of the "primitive" male in popular ethnography. Ultimately, it does not matter if that body is inflated to cartoon-like proportions or rendered in fine classical form, as both representations are highly subjective and distorting. This similarity between Luz and Riefenstahl also suggests that neither the aesthete nor the neutral reporter/photographer is successful in documenting otherness. What they successfully construct in its stead is a reflection of their own desire, personal, cultural, or a combination of the two. In Luz's case, the caricature of the Mesakin wrestler represents a backlash against African independence. It takes precisely that element that the West fears most—African strength—and defuses the threat by confining it within a cartoon, the battle between half-Neanderthal beings. The message is simple: African power, because of its primitive nature, poses no real threat to the Western world.

In the particular case of Riefenstahl, however, the representation of the male body is structured by a conviction underlying all her work: a belief in essentialism and its representability through the harmonious, classical ideal of the male body. In *Triumph of the Will* and *Olympia,* Riefenstahl's camera works to construct the essence of both Nazis and athletes, by idealizing the male, not the female, form. Think of the famous diving sequence in *Olympia,* for example, in which the various divers converge to become simply the athlete's body, defying the laws of gravity in supernatural motion. The women's diving sequence, in contrast, is presented as fairly straightforward reportage. And in *Triumph of the Will,* Riefenstahl's camera reproduces the Nazis' self-aggrandized image: the lofty leader with the well-organized masses of men following in his wake. Women do appear, but only on the sidelines, as the camera pans along the parade spectators. This same aesthetic project and bias is imposed on the Nuba people. Here Riefenstahl photographs the ceremonies, the nudity, their skin color, the art of the Nuba men—only those stereotypical markers of difference from the West. We see nothing of their diurnal existence, the long months spent working the fields, how they live and how they die. What we do see is a carefully crafted vision that posits culturally constructed notions of difference in classical forms, deeply reminiscent of *Olympia* and Winckelmann.[4] At some level, this image of the black African does much to establish commonality between the Western viewer and non-Western culture. But these photographs do not simply imitate *National Geographic*'s quest to illustrate the non-Western world as a friendly, happy place much like our own; rather they serve as space in which Riefenstahl can reenact her own cultural unconscious, an act that is no longer possible in postwar Germany.

In many ways this discovery of the classical body on African soil represents a search not only for artistic renewal, but also for continuity. It is no accident that Riefenstahl casts much of her narrative and impressions in the language of dreams.This dreamworld of Africa becomes a place of refuge from postcolonial struggles and postwar politics, a place where

---

4. See, for example, Winckelmann's *Reflections* (1755) and the prologue to *Olympia,* featuring the dissolve from a Greek statue to a modern discus-thrower.

Riefenstahl's artistic and cultural imagination still has free reign, and where the construction of native culture and the resurrection of a deeply problematic notion of cultural nationalism go unquestioned. These photographs represent, Riefenstahl insists, the dying breath of native culture; by the time the reader can purchase her book, these worlds as she presents them no longer exist. These images do indeed, as the Marxist critic John Berger might say, mark absence, but it is a very personal loss that is recounted.

What Riefenstahl mourns in these photograph collections is ostensibly the loss of authenticity, the corruption of a pure culture by the modern Western world. Ironically, that process had started long before Riefenstahl entered the village, and long before the race for colonies began in preceding centuries. What she really mourns is the loss of her personal vision of otherness and essence, one that is drawn from eighteenth-century ideals of national culture, when Herder's *Sprachgeist,* the spirit of a language, was an unproblematic concept.[5] Now, as more and more Africans wear Western clothing and speak the language of the West, not only has their traditional culture changed, but their experience as Africans can be heard by the West without the assistance of interpreters and ethnographers. Certainly this was even the case for much of the Sudan in 1956, the year of Riefenstahl's first visit, and the year of the Sudan's independence from England. Instead of chronicling this rapidly changing world, however, she constructs a fantasy of primitive life, one that is all the more seductive because of the intensely beautiful color and scenery that she captures with her Leica. There is finally only one photograph in the collection that suggests the truth of the Nuba experience (43), the only one in which Riefenstahl herself appears. It is late afternoon and Riefenstahl walks along a cliff. She looks hurried, as if she needs to reach a certain point in the landscape before the light changes. Behind her walks a Nuba man, tall, dark, and beautifully shaped. He is naked, save for Riefenstahl's luggage that he carries on his shoulder. And, not surprisingly, they are holding hands. This image, to me, conveys the centrality of Riefenstahl's relationship to the Nuba. As an artist, she claims to feel a deep respect and friendship for these people who for centuries, in her mind, have fully possessed a sense of cultural identity. And yet, in the photograph, it is Riefenstahl who walks ahead, who pulls this beautifully sculpted man along the path. Though it is his territory, she is the one who determines where they go. He is the one who carries the literal and metaphoric baggage of her vision.

---

5. For further discussion of the impact of Herder's belief in essential cultural identities on developing notions of race, see Anthony Appiah.

White Ladies and Dark Continents in Ingeborg Bachmann's *Todesarten*

Sara Lennox

"[Austria] is different from all other little countries today because it was an empire and it's possible to learn something from its history. And because the lack of activity into which one is forced there enormously sharpens one's view of the big situation and of today's empires," Ingeborg Bachmann remarked in a 1971 interview (*Sätze* 106). The postcolonial theory developed over the past decade helps to explain how the central European setting of Bachmann's texts and the figures that inhabit it may be inflected and configured by "the big situation and today's empires." For over a decade, postcolonial scholars have argued that European history cannot be detached from the history of imperialist practices for which Europe has been responsible; as Anne McClintock puts it, "Imperialism is not something that happened elsewhere—a disagreeable fact of history external to Western identity. Rather, imperialism and the invention of race were fundamental aspects of Western industrial modernity" (5). As postcolonial theorists and a range of scholars investigating the construction of "whiteness" have recently begun to demonstrate, the racial formations of the imperial world were constitutive of white European identities in the metropole as well as in the colonies, "race" thus helping to define the most intimate domains of modern life, including gender relations, the sexual politics of the private sphere, and sexuality itself. Reading Bachmann's uncompleted novel cycle *Todesarten* (Ways of death) through the lens offered by postcolonial theory can show how imperialist discourses and racial fantasies that accompany them help to constitute the female figures on which those novels focus.

As my title suggests, this essay will investigate how Bachmann represents the relationship of imperialism to the construction of the white female psyche in the *Todesarten*. "White Lady" (in English) is a phrase Bachmann associates with Eka Kottwitz, one of the figures in a *Todesarten* fragment (a point I will explore in greater detail later); "Dark Continent" (in English) is the term Freud used in *The Question of Lay Analysis* to describe "the sexual life of adult women." Freud's use of this image, the term Victorians applied to an Africa to which their own imperialist activities would bring light (Brantlinger), reveals, Mary Ann Doane has argued, the imperial underpinnings of Freud's theory:

> The force of the category of race in the constitution of otherness within psychoanalysis should not be underestimated. When Freud needs a trope for the unknowability of female sexuality, the dark continent is close at hand. Psychoanalysis can, from this point of view, be seen as a quite elaborate form of ethnography—as a writing of the ethnicity of the white psyche. Repression becomes the prerequisite for the construction of a white culture which stipulates that female sexuality act as the trace within of what has been excluded. (211)

From very early on, similar imperial imagery also shaped Bachmann's writing. Her poem "Liebe: Dunkler Erdteil" (Love: Dark Continent, 1957) represents the Dark Continent as a lush and exotic realm of sexuality beyond the repressive boundaries established by Europeans, with black masculinity—"the black king"—figured as the agent of an erotic power before which the poem's "you" prostrates herself and at whose mercy she conceives herself to be: "But there you always fall upon your knees, for he chooses and rejects you without grounds" (Filkins 295). Bachmann's poem might be regarded as a rather conventional European projection of orientalizing motifs onto a non-European geography, and such a reading would not be wrong. But, by brushing this poem somewhat against the grain (to use Walter Benjamin's phrase), it is possible to advance a more interesting reading that treats this poem as a representation of the degree to which racialized and imperial fantasies are constituent elements of the European female psyche. Bachmann's later treatment of the intersections of imperialism and female identity, I want to propose here, also oscillates between those two positions, sometimes projecting familiar European fantasies onto a non-European backdrop, at other times achieving a more profound interrogation of the imperial fundaments of central European femininity. By examining the literal encounters of Bachmann's protagonists with (inhabitants of) the Dark Continent in two uncompleted *Todesarten, Der Fall Franza* (The Franza case) and the Eka Kottwitz fragment, I want to show how discourses of race and empire underwrite her female figures' identities. Virtually alone among postwar women writing in German, I want to argue, Bachmann attempts to explore the racialized foundations of central European fantasies, yet by continuing to project white fantasies onto non-European figures she herself does not entirely escape the racist structures her work attempts to challenge.

In an often-quoted introduction to *Der Fall Franza,* Bachmann provided instructions on how to read her book: "The real settings, the interior ones, laboriously covered over by the external ones, take place somewhere else" (*Projekt* 2: 78). In the 1980s, the feminist scholars who rediscovered Bachmann's writing regarded *Der Fall Franza* as an exploration of the location and function of femininity within discourse that provided the key to understanding Bachmann's entire oeuvre: as Sigrid Weigel put it in her introduction to the 1984 *text + kritik* volume that became a landmark of feminist Bachmann criticism, "in [her texts] it is a question of a structural relationship between fascism, patriarchy, ethno- and logocentrism and the central role of language/writing for a context within which the 'feminine' as the embodiment of repressed otherness is subjected to the most varied ways of death" (5). In this reading, Bachmann's tale of Franza's flight from her tyrannical Viennese husband into the North African desert in the company of her beloved brother Martin is an investigation of the mechanisms via which an oppressive Western order denies women and other "others" a voice. This analysis mainly elides gender and race, viewing them as equally the product of a single system of subordination, and "the whites" against whom Franza inveighs are conceived to stand synecdochically for domination *tout court*. As Weigel puts it: "The whites thus stand for the insight that the history of colonization and the history of patriarchy have different victims but a single perpetrator" (82). That is clearly Franza's own view of her situation, for she compares her husband's brutal treatment of her to the colonial exploitation of native peoples and their indigenous treasures. Other evidence in the novel, however, suggests that Franza's position should not be equated with Bachmann's own. For 1990s feminists, of course, forced by protests of women of color to acknowledge white women's racial privilege, readings that fail to disaggregate race and gender have become impossible. In its various unfinished versions, I want to show, Bachmann's fragment can be read as a contradictory text that at some points concurs with Franza's own conflation of gender and race, but in other instances holds Franza's treatment of race and empire up for examination. In neither case, I want to emphasize, is Bachmann's unfinished novel *about* North Africa, but about how a European woman (whether Franza or Bachmann herself) represents her orientalist encounter with it.

Bachmann's various accounts of her own trip to Egypt and the Sudan in spring 1964, which she initially wished to integrate into her Büchner

Prize speech, then intended as a separate novel, the *Wüstenbuch* (Desert book), and finally used as the basis for the North African sections of *Franza,* are all structured around a recurring leitmotif: "The whites are coming, I am of inferior race" ("Die Weißen kommen, ich bin von niedriger Rasse") (*Projekt* 1: 180). As she revealed in a draft introduction to *Franza,* these phrases are borrowed from Rimbaud (*Projekt* 2: 73), more specifically *Une saison en enfer,* where Rimbaud maintains "Je suis de race inférieure" (I am of inferior race, 95), and, somewhat later, "Les blancs débarquent. Le canon! Il faut se soumettre au baptême, s'habiller, travailler" (The whites are debarking. The cannon/canon! It is necessary to submit oneself to baptism, to get dressed, to work, 98). As Christopher Miller observes, though Rimbaud later traveled to Africa (where he became a gunrunner and possibly a slave trader), here his critique of "whites" and identification with Africans ("Je suis une bête, un nègre" [I am a beast, a Negro, 97]) is merely a vehicle for advancing a critique of contemporary French civilization by drawing on Africanist motifs: "His artificial Africanness consists of an image that persists in European discourse, that of the free reign of desire, of removal from the mediation of language and the rule of repression" (152). Dirk Göttsche has maintained that the structure of *Franza* reflects "Rimbaud's conceptual world. Rationality, masculinity, and European culture are associated with the principle of the objectivizing domination of nature and humanity, while the magical, the feminine, and the Egyptian (colored [*sic*]) culture are associated with a subordinate but utopian counter-principle" (149–50). In the final version of *Franza,* Bachmann expands Rimbaud's remarks into a forceful denunciation of the hegemonic force of European cultural imperialism that, the editors of the critical edition observe, recalls the analysis of colonialism in Fanon's *Black Skin, White Masks* (*Projekt* 2: 476):

> The whites are coming. The whites are landing. And if they are forced back, then they'll come again, no revolution or resolution or law of currency exchange can help, they'll come again with their spirit when they can no longer come any other way. And they will be resurrected in a brown or a black brain, it will still be the whites, even then. They will continue to possess the world via this detour . . . (*Projekt* 2: 438–39)

But despite the affinities of Bachmann's statement to the analysis of one of the most renowned critics of Western imperialism, one might nonetheless maintain that for Bachmann, as for Rimbaud, these racialized images represent their own European instrumentalization of the language of empire;

colonialist metaphors serve the primary function of providing a vivid trope for the all-pervasive force of a European rationality from which they endeavor to disengage themselves by aligning themselves with that which Europe designates as its other. As Miller puts it, "The gesture of reaching out to the most unknown part of the world and bringing it back as language . . . ultimately brings Europe face to face with nothing but itself, with the problems its own discourse imposes" (5).

The earliest versions of *Der Fall Franza,* drafts for Bachmann's Büchner Prize speech and her *Wüstenbuch,* were written in the first person and to some extent still retain autobiographical elements ("they [her male Arab acquaintances and, as emerges later, her lovers] call me, with short peremptory syllables, always by my surname, while I only know their first names, bakma, how are you. I say, I am fine. I really am" [*Projekt* 1: 239]). Those drafts already revolve around European problems to which North Africa is conceived to offer alternatives and answers (and already cite Rimbaud as the antecedent to Bachmann's own approach). The ends to which, at least at an early stage of the text's composition, Bachmann wished to turn the journey are evident in her initial plan for the account of her own trip to Egypt and the Sudan in spring 1964; as the editors of the critical edition point out, she first intended to contrast the "sickness" of "unloved Berlin," where she spent a fellowship year in 1963–64 as she attempted to recover from the devastating effects of the dissolution of her relationship with Max Frisch, and the "healing" she had experienced in the North African desert. In the novel's final version, Franza remains convinced that the desert will be a site of healing for her because, like Rimbaud, she takes it to be a location where "the whites," that is, the forms of European thought of which she conceives herself to be a victim, hold no sway. One can thus locate this text within a long line of narratives in which the Orient is conceived to correspond or respond to the traveler's own interior needs. For the "belated travelers" of the late nineteenth century, as Ali Behdad observes, the trip to the Orient was a voyage of "romantic self-discovery" (21), a "solitary quest for elsewhere" that was "a response to the onset of modernity in Europe" (16).

It is then possible to read Franza's journey to North Africa as what Behdad has identified as the contradictory discourse of "belated Orientalism." That discourse, as Behdad describes it, often

> vacillates between an insatiable search for a counterexperience in the Orient and the melancholic discovery of its impossibility . . . On the one hand, these texts identify themselves differentially against . . . the truth claims of official Orientalism by expressing an unease with

classification and 'objectivity.' On the other, they find it impossible to avoid the 'baggage' of Orientalist knowledge that has mediated the desire to produce another discourse on the Orient. (15)

Franza's experience of the Orient is often explicitly shown as mediated by her European guidebooks, citations from which dot the text as recognizably foreign bodies. Though Franza appears to be entirely disinterested in the guidebooks, her response to Egypt takes the form of a romantic repudiation of everything the guidebooks recommend, a defiantly dichotomous reaction still negatively determined by the terms of the prescriptions it rejects. Franza fervently insists that, as she travels deeper into North Africa, she has left behind the entire canon of Western knowledge and eluded European power: "The whites. They were finally no longer here" (*Projekt* 2: 255). She also warns herself that white cultural hegemony is not so easy to evade: "I will come into my own here. But the alibi of the whites is strong. Don't forget that" (*Projekt* 2: 277). But exactly this representation of North Africa as a site of Oriental otherness that can rescue Franza from Europe reveals itself to be a product of romantic white fantasies that are themselves constructed by and mediated through the orientalist texts of earlier travelers.

How Franza's (or Bachmann's?) white female fantasies about the Orient might be connected to the dark continent of white female sexuality is most clearly revealed in various accounts of an "orgy" (*Projekt* 2: 271) in the *Wüstenbuch* that survive in the novel's final draft only in veiled allusions to the "embraces on the Nile" (*Projekt* 2: 328) and the suggestion that Martin has slept with two Arab acquaintances. As Said has remarked, "the Orient seems still to suggest not only fecundity but sexual promise (and threat), untiring sensuality, unlimited desire, deep generative energies" (188). To Oriental travelers, the association between the Orient and the freedom of licentious sex meant that "the Orient was a place where one could look for sexual experience unobtainable in Europe. Virtually no European writer who wrote on or travelled to the Orient in the period after 1800 exempted himself or herself from this quest" (Said, *Orientalism* 190). The first-person narrator of the *Wüstenbuch* conceives her erotic encounter with Salah, Mahmed, and Abdu, always framed by the Rimbaudian refrain, "The whites are coming. I am of inferior race," to extract her from whiteness altogether—"Three bodies that intertwine, the single satisfaction, the killing of the other race" (*Projekt* 1: 257). She also represents (à la Eldridge Cleaver) the transgressive sexual act as a gendered act of revenge against domination by white *men:* "The white man is inferior. And he's afraid that I'll say it out loud. I killed him in our bed, he will never forgive his inferiority. He needs the police against it, law, arrogance, he needs violence, because he can't prevail in his bed" (*Projekt* 1: 283). As in "Love: The Dark Continent" (or in Bachmann's radio play *Der gute Gott von Manhattan* [*The Good God of Manhattan*]), here eroticism also extracts the lovers from the ruling order and aligns them with the quintessential otherness for which the Orient stands. As the journey to North Africa made it possible for Franza to dismiss bacteria-induced illnesses, so similarly the "I" of the *Wüstenbuch* imagines that venereal disease is of no concern to nonwhites: "The venereal diseases of the whites, I understand very well that no one knows them here" (*Projekt* 1: 240). Sex with her three Egyptian friends cures her of the "sexual illness" of white femininity: "I thought of it as an act of revenge, and it was not a revenge, but the repudiation of ridiculous notions. From now on the venereal diseases of the whites will only make me laugh" (*Projekt* 1: 272). Bachmann's effort to combat white culture reproduces several of its core racial and sexual preconceptions: that the Orient is a site of licentious and wanton sexuality; that men of color are particularly potent and gifted lovers who, in competition with white men, lust especially after white women; that sexuality is outside of culture, thus associated with "others" also thought to be exterior to civilization; and that through her sexual relationship with a man of color a white woman can declare herself "disloyal to civilization" and place herself outside its bounds. Paradoxically, one might maintain, Bachmann's attempt to escape whiteness proves how very white she is.

Yet a question might be asked of this novel fragment similar to the one asked of a novel that represents a much more viciously racist white consciousness, Conrad's *Heart of Darkness:* is this a racist novel or a novel about racism? Frequently Bachmann's texts offers hints that readers should regard Franza's own judgments with some skepticism. In one of the last drafts of the novel Bachmann clearly pokes fun at Franza's romantic notion that she is destined to become a heroic martyr whose (distinctly masochistic) sacrifices could save the Third World (surely a liberal and female variant of the Victorian conviction that European efforts would bring light to the Dark Continent):

> ... perhaps she could do something, but it had to be something real, later Africa or Asia, under the hardest conditions, with sacrifice, with heroism, sacrifice definitely had to be part of it, and it should be grand, lots of effort, but glorious for her, with an early death, she would jump in after someone who was drowning, dash into a burning house and throw a child out the window into the blanket waiting to catch it and then burn to death, bandage a wounded man and then be shot by mistake in North Africa. (*Projekt* 2: 233–34)

Franza's declaration that she has escaped the whites is somewhat undercut by the ubiquitous bottles of Coca-Cola she drinks along her journey; as the title of Reinhold Wagnleitner's study of U.S. influence in Austria after 1945, *Coca-Colonization and the Cold War,* suggests, Coca-Cola can readily serve as a powerful and easily recognizable symbol of Western cultural imperialism. In the North Africa destined to save her from the whites, she encounters acts of brutality that do not fit her dichotomous model of evil Europe and pristine Orient: a woman bound by the hair at the Cairo train station, and a camel slaughtered at a wedding feast, both figures with whom she identifies (again appropriating non-European experiences as her own), so inexplicable in their otherness that her European categories leave her at a loss to interpret them. One of the most striking indications that Franza's appropriation of North Africa might be regarded as Bachmann's attempt to represent white female fantasies about the Orient is her mystical experience on a Red Sea beach, convinced that she has seen God and her father when she is in fact confronted with a dead tree trunk. Her response, "The Arabian desert is surrounded by broken conceptions of God" (*Projekt* 2: 288), is, the editors of the critical edition point out (*Projekt* 2: 486–87), quite possibly borrowed from *The Seven Pillars of Wisdom,* written by one of the greatest romantic orientalists, T. E. Lawrence ("Lawrence of Arabia"). It is possible then, that when Bachmann comments on a travel party of elderly American women, "all over sixty and equipped with sticks and huge hats . . . recalling an age gone by, grand travelers who were served ceremoniously, recalling Nile steamers that traveled all the way to the granite quarries and to Elephantine" (*Projekt* 2: 268), she means that description of the Western woman traveler on her grand tour of the Orient also to apply, *mutatis mutandis,* to Franza, who is, in fact, in an earlier version of this same passage called a "Lady," in English, by an Egyptian soldier in Luxor (*Projekt* 2: 103), underlining the fact that in the context of Egypt she, too, is a White Lady.

One might then maintain that Franza's travel accounts, like those of many women travelers to the Orient who preceded her, consist of the fantasies she projects onto North Africa, those fantasies thus comprising "the interior settings" disguised as a travel narrative about real geographical sites. Perhaps one could even read Franza herself as the Dark Continent, her travel to North Africa thus conceived to be a journey into the unknown territory of her own psyche. Bachmann's description of Franza's fascination with the monuments of Egyptian antiquity might then be conceived as an elaboration of Freud's own imperial metaphor in his *Aetiology of Hysteria,* where he compares his own task to that of "an explorer arriv[ing] in a little-known region where his interest is aroused by an expanse of ruins with half-effaced and unreadable inscriptions." After questioning the region's "perhaps semi-barbaric peoples" and excavating the site, the explorer may decipher and translate the inscriptions: "Saxa loquantur!" (The stones speak! 191–92)—a passage that recalls Franza's geologist brother's effort to find a geological explanation for his sister's illness. On the other hand, even if it should be possible to read this contradictory text as an investigation of race and empire, it is not so clear that Bachmann's metaphorizing of the imperial traveler—that is, using the journey to a real non-European country as a vehicle for exploring the state of the European psyche—could not itself be regarded in some complex ways as an imperial gesture. One might then direct a critique against Bachmann's use of North Africa similar to that which Susan Shapiro leveled at Jean-François Lyotard's treatment of "the jews":

> "The jews" becomes a way for the European subject both to critique the (logo) center and identity with/as the margins of the West without changing its terms. It maintains the logic of the West by reducing otherness to a symbol of the limits of the West, its limit-text. . . . While it is clear that "the jews" is a constructed trope, the constructedness of the *real Jews* is effaced or forgotten. . . . [T]here is no space left in the West for the intervention of actual Jews in their multiple and conflicting identities. (190)

It is very possible that the "sickness" from which Franza is suffering is that of whiteness, or white femininity, itself ("She hadn't come to Luxor," writes Bachmann, "but rather to a point in her sickness, not through the desert, but rather through a sickness" [*Projekt* 2: 269])—but that is not a malady from which Bachmann was entirely immune herself. And, furthermore, even should this have been the reading of her novel that Bachmann intended, over a decade of scholarship focused on *Franza* shows that such an interpretation was not evident to most readers. Perhaps it was for such reasons that Bachmann finally abandoned this novel fragment altogether; as she wrote to her editor in 1966: "the manuscript seems to me like a helpless allusion to something that still needs to be written" (*Projekt* 2: 397).

In later *Todesarten* texts Bachmann developed more successful strategies for representing the encounter of the White Lady and the Dark Continent. Where *Der Fall Franza* had directly thematized the clash of race and gender categories, later texts merely *display* a female psyche constituted by historically specific discourses of race and gender. Her figures are so entirely the products of history that they are unable to advance a critique of their own circumstances beyond that which prevailing discourses would allow. One might even maintain that in certain respects White Ladies in Bachmann's later *Todesarten* texts accede to a definition of themselves as the Dark Continent: that is, they accept the racial preconceptions that define white female sexuality as unexplored terrain, a riddle, an enigma, that white men wish to colonize but whose heart of darkness neither they nor women (who in these texts remain mysteries to themselves) can fully plumb. Though White Ladies cannot be represented as the direct agents of imperialism, they are clearly implicated in its racial logic, as being as captive to racial fantasies and projections as white men (though implementing them in gender-specific ways). One key component of their racial identity is thus their utter obliviousness to their own racial determinants. As well, *contra* scholars who attempt to exempt Germans and Austrians from Orientalism because Germany and Austria had no direct national interests in the Middle East, the vantage point from which Bachmann views imperialism emphasizes the imbrication of all Europeans, not just those with an explicitly colonial past, in the imperial/neocolonial and racial order of the West. Such a reading of Bachmann's investigation of imperialism makes it possible to read her haughty rejoinder to criticisms of *Malina* as something more than a feeble justification for that novel's apparent lack of attention to politics: "And when, for example, I say not a word about the Vietnam War in this book *Malina,* not a word about all sorts of catastrophic conditions in our society, then I know how to say something in another way—or I hope that I know how to say it" (*Sätze* 90–91). What Bachmann's texts quite deliberately portray, one might maintain, are the imperialist fundaments of the kind of consciousness that made U.S. intervention into Vietnam possible and also enabled Western European support for that military engagement.

A key incident in Bachmann's Eka Kottwitz/Aga Rottwitz fragment, added to that unfinished novel in 1968–69, moves the violent encounter of race and gender to the center stage of the *Todesarten.* An African student accompanies Countess Kottwitz, a brilliant political journalist and the novel's protagonist, home after a lecture and makes violent love to her. Though the countess, hitherto quite uninterested in lovemaking ("over thirty, she still . . . had . . . not a clue what an orgasm was" [*Projekt* 1: 419]), experiences the sexual encounter as a bestial assault, she finds it has left her sexually awakened and "completely transformed" (*Projekt* 1: 427). Though the African declares his love for her, Countess Kottwitz, "who was no Lady Chatterly" (*Projekt* 1: 426), refuses to acknowledge her newly aroused passion for him. Instead, she proclaims she is now finally able to love her current boyfriend Jung. When Jung leaves her for another woman, Eka throws herself from a window and is permanently paralyzed. The scene immediately preceding the sexual encounter offers a clue to how Bachmann wanted her story to be read: sitting in a bar in the Hamburg hotel Vier Jahreszeiten, Countess Kottwitz orders a drink called a "White Lady."

One might read this passage as a vivid illustration of the white female fantasy Fanon describes in *Black Skin, White Masks:* "A Negro is raping me." In general, as Mary Ann Doane points out, Fanon views sexuality as a major arena for the articulation of racism. His analysis of this racialized fantasy is founded upon Helene Deutsch's and Marie Bonaparte's definitions of adult female sexuality as fundamentally masochistic. That conception of femininity finds support in many passages in Bachmann's writing: the "I" of *Malina* muses, for instance, "[N]o normal man with normal instincts [has] the obvious idea that a normal woman would like to be quite normally raped" (*Projekt* 3.1: 614). Following Freud, Fanon maintains that normal adult female sexuality requires the renunciation of aggression and the acceptance of properly female passive sexual aims. In a racist society, Fanon maintains, "the Negro becomes the predestined depository of this aggressiveness. If we go farther into the labyrinth, we discover that when a woman lives the fantasy to be raped by a Negro, it is in some way the fulfillment of a private dream, of an inner wish. Accomplishing the phenomenon of turning against self, it is the woman who rapes herself" (175). Doane's gloss on this passage is useful: "Fanon finds that the fantasy of being raped by a Negro constitutes the assimilation by the woman of a cultural treasurehouse of images concerning blackness and their incorporation within what is a basic structure of femininity" (221). Though Bachmann might have formulated Fanon's explanation somewhat differently, his is an analysis with which she might not fundamentally have disagreed. From "Love: The Dark Continent" and *The Good God of Manhattan* through *Malina,* Bachmann's female figures seek out powerful men who hurt them to whom they can submit themselves, and their sexual pleasure is greater if they can also conceive themselves to be contravening social taboos. To the White Lady, rape by a "Negro" meets these criteria optimally.

What makes the portrait of this White Lady far more compelling than those of Bachmann's other figures who achieve a transgressive sexual satisfaction is the careful delineation of how precisely the features of Countess Kottwitz's character that make "rape" by a "Negro" especially exciting to her also prevent her from acknowledging this relationship as one that finally meets her sexual needs. Jung is represented as an indifferent lover who fails entirely to respond to Eka's awkward attempts to arouse him:

> Jung had kissed her a few times, in the early days, that was the single form of affection that occurred to him, otherwise he fell upon her occasionally, and Eka didn't admit to herself that it was unbearable for her, that she expected something else, she just didn't know what, and sometimes she was overcome by silly notions, she threw herself

on him like <a> child and hugged him and pressed herself against him in the desperate hope that something would occur to him. Jung either shoved her away with a laugh <or> called her a silly teenager, while Eka's face got grayer and grayer and more and more strained and had nothing at all in common with that of a teenager. (*Projekt* 1: 420)

The encounter with the African takes place as a consequence of mutual sexual attraction, as Bachmann underlines in a passage that charmingly reproduces the confusion of swelling sexual passion: "then he took her by the hand, and she saw his beautiful black hand, her beautiful white hand, both beautiful hands, slim, too long, hands too long, hands too much" (*Projekt* 1: 424). But as this enormously erudite woman has no idea where the student's African homeland might be located ("He was from Somaliland, and Eka admitted to herself that she didn't exactly know, for once not exactly, though she knew everything exactly" [*Projekt* 1: 424]), so the only terms Eka can find to describe their passion derive from a racist vocabulary that defines their erotic exchange as violent and barbaric: "In the next moment the Somali student had torn her from the armchair, perhaps not exactly torn, but taken" (*Projekt* 1: 426); "in this situation that just seemed grotesque to her" (*Projekt* 1: 425); "it's bestial, I'm dying, I'm dying" (*Projekt* 1: 425); "After he raped her once more he left" (*Projekt* 1: 427); "I was no longer a human being, I was an animal" (*Projekt* 1: 429). She can experience sexual pleasure with the African because the intensity of the sexual act disrupts her white interpretive schema: "it was simply the end of all her preconceptions" (*Projekt* 1: 425) and it unsettles her ego boundaries: "her ego [Ich] was eradicated" (*Projekt* 1: 430). But once she reestablishes her psychic boundaries ("in the process of restoring her ego" ["dabei, ihr Ich wiederherzustellen"] [*Projekt* 1: 425]), she is convinced that she loves only Jung, a white man. In their commentary to this passage, the editors of the critical edition point to its affinities to the utopian "orgy" of the *Wüstenbuch,* a connection supported by a later version of this passage in which her "rapist" is called "Abdu," also the name of one of the trio of Egyptian lovers. But what makes this fragment different from Bachmann's other utopian evocations of erotic transport is Eka's incapacity to transcend the cultural limitations that prevent her from embracing a sexual relationship proscribed by the culture of which she is part.

Of course, there is a way out for the White Lady, as Bachmann underlines via her allusion to D. H. Lawrence's novel: to satisfy her sexual needs, Eka could follow the example of Connie Chatterly, jettison her miserable affair with Jung, and cast her lot with the Somali student. In a paper called "Do White Ladies Get the Blues? Nancy Cunard and Desire," Sabine Bröck has shown that other twentieth-century White Ladies, like Lady

Nancy Cunard, heir to the Cunard steamship line fortune and patron of the Harlem Renaissance, made the decision to flaunt racial and sexual taboos. Yet not just racism, but also her aristocratic fastidiousness make that impossible for Eka, in whom even bad taste in furniture occasions a physical reaction, and this student dares to call her "Liebchen" and wants to sleep with her after they have made love: "sleep with her, now that was really the last straw" ("mit ihr schlafen, das war nun wirklich die Höhe") (*Projekt* 1: 427). As Biddy Martin and Chandra Mohanty put it in a quite different context: "Change has to do with the transgression of boundaries, those boundaries so carefully, so tenaciously, so invisibly drawn around white identity" (203). Unable to transcend the definitions that constitute her, Eka instead constructs a story that allows her to remain who she is and affirm her sexuality, too: "I don't love this Negro, I love Jung" (*Projekt* 1: 428). But, as the editors of *Pleasure and Danger: The Politics of Sexuality* emphasize, the myth of the black rapist is a sexual story that white men tell each other to justify their violence towards black men *and* their control over black and white women (Snitow et al. 328). By opting for that myth, Eka makes the choice to reinsert herself back into a racist social order that also subordinates women. After Jung leaves her, even that narrative construction is no longer available to her, and there is no way for her both to remain a White Lady and to affirm her sexuality; she is paralyzed by her absence of choices. So she leaps from the window, destroying the body that has betrayed her, and henceforth is also really, not just metaphorically, paralyzed, confined for life to a wheelchair. In one of the introductions to *Der Fall Franza,* Bachmann called her female figures' implication in categories of their social order "thinking . . . that leads to dying" ("das [Denken] . . . das zum Sterben führt") (*Projekt* 2: 78). Like the other *Todesarten,* the Eka Kottwitz fragment reveals the self-destructive consequences of women's compliance with the dictates of the society that has called them into being.

What conception of the formation of female subjectivity underlies the Eka Kottwitz fragment? While criticizing Fanon's flattening of the complex concepts of sexual difference, desire, and sexuality, Gwen Bergner has recently argued that one of his major accomplishments in *Black Skin, White Masks* is adding race to psychoanalysis's explanation of the projection of subjectivity: "Fanon transposes psychoanalysis—a theory of subject formation based on sexual difference—to a register where it accounts for race as one of the fundamental differences that constitute subjectivity" (76). One might argue that that is also Bachmann's achievement in this text, that that is how she represents "history within the subject" ("die Geschichte im Ich" [*Werke* 4: 230]). In pursuit of her project of developing a *"situated psychoanalysis*—a culturally contextualized psychoanalysis that is simultaneously a psychoanalytically informed history" (72), Anne McClintock proposes that Julia Kristeva's notion of "abjection" helps to explain the function of racist exclusions in modern industrial societies. Following Freud, Kristeva also maintains that civilization is founded on the repudiation of those elements society considers impure: "The abject is everything that the subject seeks to expunge in order to become social; it is also a symptom of the failure of this ambition . . . the expelled abject haunts the subject as its inner constitutive boundary; that which is repudiated forms the self's internal limit. The abject is 'something rejected from which one does not part'" (McClintock 71). This conception of abjection might help explain both the disruptive allure of sex with the Somali student for Eka and the urgency of her denial that she is aroused by him; the abject, Kristeva argues, "simultaneously beseeches and pulverizes the subject" (5). If the rejection of blackness and of an active female sexuality is the guarantee of the stability of Eka's white female psyche, acknowledging the repressed and threatening otherness they represent could cause the whole racial-sexual edifice to come tumbling down. Yet, though it is quite easy to advance a psychoanalytic explanation for the psychology of Eka and other *Todesarten* figures, it may also be important to stress the limitations of such a Freudian model. As Ann Laura Stoler has recently pointed out, much postcolonial analysis is based on "the premise that colonial power relations can be accounted for and explained as a sublimated expression of repressed desires in the West, of desires that resurface in moralizing missions, myths of the 'wild woman,' in a romance with the rural 'primitive,' or in other more violent, virile, substitute form" (167–68); yet it is exactly this "repressive hypothesis" that Foucauldian analysis has drawn into question. Though Bachmann clearly understands (female) desire as molded by social forces, much of her work seems also premised on the assumption that "desire is a basic biological drive, restricted and repressed by a 'civilization' that forces our sublimation of it" (171), to use Stoler's formulation. Foucault would of course argue that desire was not repressed by or opposed to a (racialized) order of civilization, but produced by it. The question that might then arise is to what degree notions of a natural and primordial desire that civilization needs to channel and regulate might relate to or even derive from imperial strategies developed to control unruly oversexed natives (or white women, for that matter—a speculation that the application of the Dark Continent motif to white female sexuality would support). As Stoler puts it, "The nineteenth-century discourse on bourgeois sexuality may better be understood as a recuperation of a protracted discourse on race, for the discourse of sexuality contains many of the latter's most salient elements. That discourse on sexuality was binary and contrastive, in its nineteenth-century variant always pitting that middle-class respectable sexuality as a defense against an internal and external other that was at once essentially different but uncomfortably the same" (193). If there is merit to this argument, it might be possible to maintain that Bachmann's attempt to grapple with the racialized fundaments of female sexuality, by portraying a female figure whose repressed (or abject-ed) desire is loosed by her sexual encounter with a black man, might still remain captive to precisely the discourses of race, gender, and sexuality that her texts want to interrogate.

As well, one might again ask whether in this text Bachmann also contributes in a less complicated way to the perpetuation of racist stereotypes. Though the complex narrative stance of this fragment makes it difficult to determine to what degree Eka's responses determine the representation of the sexual encounter, to what degree a (somewhat) more impartial narrator is speaking, the sexual act seems to be portrayed as violent, brutal, and lacking in reciprocity, the Somali student oblivious to Eka's protests and cries of pain: "she noticed that he didn't notice at all, not because he was a sadist to whom her tears, her despair gave pleasure, but rather because she was no one at all for him, not a person, merely an object" (*Projekt* 1: 425). The student himself is represented as a noble savage possessed of a wholeness unavailable to Europeans: "he was so at one with himself, with his body, with his will, that he simply didn't hear this Eka, this blind woman, any longer," and his sexual potency is nothing short of prodigious: "then he lay down, after two hours, and said to her . . . I'm very tired today, please forgive me" (*Projekt* 1: 426). Finally, the student is not treated as a subject in his own right; except in the very last draft, he has no name and, though a student of political science in his fifth semester, is unable to express himself in German: "Eka . . . didn't understand for a moment how somebody could speak German so badly and could study here nonetheless" (*Projekt* 1: 423). This text, one might thus argue, is not an account of the complexities and misunderstandings of cross-cultural encounters, but instead uses rather conventional representations of a black figure to talk about the problems of white women. As Leslie Adelson inquired, faced with a not entirely dissimilar treatment of black men in a text by a white German woman writer: "If the story is not about the relationship to blacks as persons, and it is not, then why use them as a symbol?" (*Making Bodies* 52). Though it is always difficult to determine to what degree the perspectives of Bachmann's figures and her own coincide, it appears that other portraits of black figures in her texts (leaving aside the embarrassing racist gaffe of her 1956 poem "Harlem": "The black city rolls its white eyes" [*Werke* 1: 113]) suffer from similar problems. In a passage omitted from the final version of *Malina* the "I" seeks the sexual services of an otherwise mute black man during a transatlantic crossing: "[O]n the ship to America there was an arrogant young Negro at the bar, looking for work, dismissed from a French band, with a miserable vocabulary, he always came in the night, during the day we greeted each other fleetingly, he acted as if he didn't know me, I also scarcely looked at him" (*Projekt* 3.2: 719). "Again and Again: Black and White," an unpublished poem in the *Nachlaß*, recalls the racial fantasies of "Love: The Dark Continent." The poetic "I" imagines that her skin has absorbed the color of her black lover and fancies "that my young blackness derives from your old / from your age-old native blackness." "You call me," the poem concludes, "like the Queen of Zambezi" (Ms. 454). Though Bachmann is clearly attempting to mobilize racial images for antiracist purposes, her appropriation of them to address the needs of white women seems to retain white women at the center with the resources of the rest of the world at their disposal—a practice that suggests that Bachmann herself is not altogether exempt from the criticism she directs at her figures. One might thus make the same point about Bachmann that Adelson has made of Anne Duden's portrait of violent black GIs in *The Opening of the Mouth:* "As to whether *Opening* explodes a racist premise or reproduces it, I can only answer, yes, it does both" (*Making Bodies* 54).

A 1966 essay by Christa Wolf, still one of the most profound assessments of Bachmann's writing, might, though written in a much different context, provide some explanation for why Bachmann was not always able to overcome the limitations of her own white European standpoint. "She has never been in a position," writes Wolf, "to search for affiliation with a progressive historical movement. She tends rather—or at any rate lets some of her characters tend—to step out of society, to track down, in despairing isolation, the conditions that her society dictates to the individual, to seek out the price that naked existence demands and that is paid a million times over." The solution to the problems Bachmann addresses can not, Wolf argues, be solved by an author or texts alone, but depends instead on "changes in society that would give his profession a new foundation and himself a new responsibility" (*Reader* 94). A decade and a half later, as the emergence of postcolonial peoples and their writing increasingly compelled Westerners to ponder their own complicity in imperialist postures and practices, Wolf asked in her third *Cassandra* lecture: "The literature of the West (I read) is the white man's reflection of himself. So should it be supplemented by the white woman's reflection on herself? And nothing more?" (*Cassandra* 225). Virtually alone among postwar German-language writers—as Wolf noted in the *Cassandra* lectures—Bachmann moved in the direction of the "something more" that Wolf was seeking, reflecting on the White Lady *in order to* raise questions about the racialization of the white psyche. Precisely her own implication in the conditions she described permitted her to extrapolate from Austria's imperial past to examine the dissolution of other empires, and the persistence of imperial attitudes, in the present. By probing the racialized foundations of white female identity, exploring discontents of the white female psyche that are also her own, Bachmann is thus able to show why merely appropriating the racial prerogatives of the white man will not suffice to meet the needs of the White Lady.

Imagining Migrants' Literature: Intercultural Alterity in Jeannette Lander's *Jahrhundert der Herren*

Leslie A. Adelson

There is no question that since the 1980s the category of "migrants' literature in Germany" has functioned both as a marketing strategy and as a burgeoning academic field.[1] Whereas so-called migrants' literature could prove to be a site of investigation crucial for rethinking the premises of *Germanistik* and even German Studies in an increasingly multicultural arena, however, this transformative intellectual potential has been neither widely recognized nor pursued. There is, to be sure, in the broader field of cultural studies[2] much discussion about the alleged fixity or fluidity of ethnic identities (often conflated with cultural identities) as well as nationalist categories of analysis. According to Edward Said, for example, "No one today is purely one thing" (*Culture* 336). In an antiessentialist look at the growing interest in international literatures and literary studies, Homi K. Bhabha seeks to locate culture in a kind of "third," "in-between," "hybrid" space—a space characterized by the "transnational and translational" forces that shape imagined communities (Bhabha, *The Location;*

---

1. I would like to thank John Sarefield and Cassandra Bonse, who provided valuable assistance in securing research materials for this project. All translations provided for passages from the Lander novel and from critical literature are my own. See Adelson ("Migrants' Literature") for an overview of some of the pivotal developments in the arena of migrants' literature in Germany and references to scholarly explorations of them. Fritz J. Raddatz's recent call for critical studies of German literature by nonnative authors (whom he considers to be "deutsche Schriftsteller") recognizes a lacuna in German scholarship while it remains oblivious to discussions of and publications on this topic outside Germany. Any number of dissertations currently under way in the United States, Germany, England, and abroad may easily shift our understanding of "migrants' literature in Germany" in unpredictable ways in the not too distant future.

2. See Bathrick for an introduction to this field and useful references for further study.

Rutherford "Interview").[3] While Bhabha may at times be faulted for obscuring necessary distinctions between "migration" and "metaphor"— or, as Elisabeth Bronfen has noted, for fusing "political reality and rhetorical gesture" (74)[4]—he does address a crucial alteration in the profile of contemporary literatures. "Where, once, the transmission of national traditions was the major theme of a world literature, perhaps we can now suggest that transnational histories of migrants, the colonized, or political refugees—these border and frontier conditions—may be the terrains of world literature" (12). Yet, the question still remains: what does it mean to speak of cultural "identities" in the context of transnational histories that "migrate" in both political and imaginary terms? Writing on "Cultural Identity and Diaspora" with reference to new Caribbean cinema, Stuart Hall has this to say: "Identity is not as transparent or unproblematic as we think. Perhaps instead of thinking of identity as an already accomplished fact, which the new cultural practices then represent, we should think, instead, of identity as a 'production,' which is never complete, always in process, and always constituted within, not outside, representation. This view problematises the very authority and authenticity to which the term, 'cultural identity,' lays claim" (222).[5]

Precisely this call to problematize the authority and authenticity of the alleged "origins" of identity has gone largely unheeded by scholarship on migrants' literature in Germany.[6] Too frequently this scholarship has sought to address the relationship between an author's biographical experience (viewed especially in terms of ethnic origins) and his/her textual production by reducing the latter to the former. In this manner literary texts are seen simply as so much testimony to a reified encounter between Alien

---

3. In a related vein see also Rey Chow's arguments against the geographical determinism and cultural essentialism that have influenced, from her perspective, much of East Asian studies. Bhabha's reference to "imagined communities" is clearly derived from Benedict Anderson's seminal work of that title.

4. Bronfen actually accuses both Bhabha and Said of this. It is indeed not always clear how Bhabha's focus on "the 'foreignness' of cultural translation" (Bhabha, *The Location* 227) differs from his concern with generic characteristics of linguistic signs. Bronfen's discussion of exile as a "third space" (71) between a lost culture and an acquired one is, on the other hand, too rigid in its distinctions between exile and migration to be useful here.

5. Hall speaks of cultural identity as always contextualized or "positioned" (222), by which he means produced in a particular context and hence nonessentialist. One could of course argue that this claim holds for cultural identities in general, not simply those formed in diaspora. For a more extensive theoretical discussion of the related concept of "positionality," especially as it pertains to women's studies, German Studies, and multiculturalism, see Adelson (*Making Bodies*).

6. Although a few individual scholars have challenged this impasse, my purpose here is to address a persistent, overriding trend in the field.

X and an equally hypostatized land of immigration. Is it possible, we must ask, to account for some kind of relationship between authorial experience and literary text without this methodologically positivist reduction? If we cease to understand an author's experience as confined to the origins of a fixed ethnicity, then we can shift our focus from the production of authentic testimony (qua literary text) to the negotiation of cultural meanings (through sites and processes of interpretation). While this does not provide a fixed formula for understanding the relationship between given authors and their texts, it does promise greater insight into the fundamentally dynamic processes of cultural production.

This dynamism informs national cultures as well, and not simply those that we might deem international or transnational.[7] One could even argue that if we took the implied "multi" in "culturalism" seriously, we would not need the tautological phrase, "multiculturalism." More and more this term is used to conjure a rigid sense of multiple but separate cultures, each understood as clearly defined, demarcated, and fixed. Without suggesting that recognition of this tautology is sufficient to render culturalist concerns for the "political right of autonomy" (Rutherford, "A Place" 10) obsolete, I would nonetheless submit that a scholarship of migrants' literature in Germany that fails to scrutinize the production of complex cultural meanings in shifting historical contexts is one that will remain inconsequential and peripheral to international cultural studies and future-oriented German Studies as well.

Continued insistence on a methodological positivism that conflates or even equates ethnicity and textuality cannot even pretend to address the historical legacy of German colonialist fantasies, nor can it render German Studies interesting to scholars concerned with the "larger" cultural legacies of British and French colonial practices. When contemporary migrants' literature in Germany is cast simply as an encounter with ethnic "otherness," a politically progressive interest in today's "others" yields only a methodologically regressive preoccupation with ethnicity that does little to illuminate or challenge the function of colonialist fantasies in any historical period, past or present. Although the textual analysis to follow here seeks to break with an established approach to migrants' literature in Germany, it would on the other hand be ludicrous to claim that Lander's novel is representative either of contemporary migrants' literature or of a

---

7. Bhabha addresses this explicitly when he claims, "there is no 'in itself' and 'for itself' within cultures because they are always subject to intrinsic forms of translation" (*The Location* 210). I am reluctant to rely solely on Bhabha, however, since he tends to privilege linguistic processes without fully accounting for their material effects. On broader issues of materiality, embodiment, and semiotics see Adelson (*Making Bodies*).

German colonialist imagination. Rather, this essay explores the very particular textual and historical functions of the types of colonialist mappings within which *Jahrhundert der Herren* (Century of the masters) unfolds. This concerns in turn a paradigmatic shift in the cultural significance of contemporary German literatures.

The dynamic hybridity of cultural production, to which reference was made previously, comes into even sharper view when we attend to the phenomenon of intercultural alterity, a kind of cultural "difference" that transgresses the alleged parameters of two or more given cultures. This would seem to be the case whenever non-German, migrant authors write literature in German. Yet, intercultural alterity should not be equated with an exchange between two or more *stable* cultures, but with a shifting relationship between inherently *unstable* (albeit historically concretized) phenomena. What this means is that scholars must account not only for the production of cultural meaning, but also for the slippage to which such meaning falls prey. Under what circumstances do certain cultural meanings fall away? Do prior meanings disappear altogether or do they continue to cast a shadow onto those that displace them? How are such palimpsests to be read? When and why does such residual cultural "matter" become politically invested in ways that demand to be read against a familiar grain?

Intercultural alterity is not simply about shifting cultural paradigms, however, for it also concerns the alterity of historical experience. This means, for one thing, that the historical experience of one person or group can at best be appropriated (not reproduced) for others. This means, in turn, that cultural responses to historical events and structures entail imaginary constructs of selected histories as they relate to selected, present-day issues in perhaps altogether different experiential contexts.[8] While attention to the social effect of imaginary constructs plays a pivotal role in contemporary cultural studies, one can see that reading the palimpsests of historical imagination has become a focus in more particular scholarly arenas as well. Benedict Anderson's seminal work on the *Imagined Communities* of nationalism could be mentioned in this regard, as could studies of myth reception (Moddelmog; Blumenberg). Leo Spitzer's brilliant exploration of three centuries of cross-cultural, cross-generational lives of assimilation and marginality in Africa, Europe, and South America similarly stresses the importance (albeit not an exclusive one) of imaginary factors that shape human perception of historical events

---

8. See Adelson (*Making Bodies* 1–36) for a general discussion of this issue as it relates to contemporary German Studies and pages 22–27 for a summary of Agnes Heller's theses in *A Theory of History* (1982), to which my own work is indebted.

(*Lives*).[9] In the realm of contemporary Holocaust studies one likewise notes the increasing urgency with which scholars seek to address the forces and presence of historical imagination as it affects our understanding of the memory, representation, and truth of the Holocaust. *Probing the Limits of Representation,* edited by Saul Friedlander, and *Representing the Holocaust,* recently published by Dominick LaCapra, spring to mind in this connection, as do any number of essays by Dan Diner on the subject or Frank Stern's studies of conflicting memories in postwar Germany. For Michael Geyer and Miriam Hansen, writing on what they call the "memory movement of the last twenty years" (184), the Third Reich "has become an imaginative construct" (177). "Since the Third Reich is handed down as imagination rather than as actual experience," they contend with an eye to the present, "remembering the Holocaust has shifted from being an issue of motivation (the willingness to remember) to an issue of representation (how to construct the presence of the past)" (177). This does not render the Third Reich any less real, it should be noted. At the same time, its contemporary reality cannot be construed in the same way in which it was considered real in the 1930s and 1940s.

In light of these musings I would like to probe some of the intersections of transnational and intercultural alterities at work in Jeannette Lander's most recent novel, *Jahrhundert der Herren.* This text thematizes experiences of migration as well as the slippage of imagination that occurs when a cultural myth or legend is displaced from one historical, cultural context to another. Set in Shri Lanka[10] during the civil wars of the early 1980s, Lander's novel revolves around a non-Jewish German woman who has fled a marriage to a highly successful businessman who had falsely accused her of infidelity and withdrawn all affection for her. Escaping to Shri Lanka with her infant daughter, she renames herself (from Ilse to Juliane Brabant) and works diligently to establish her economic independence as a producer of fine textiles. In the process she must encounter and negotiate various Shri Lankan forms of alterity, most of which she recognizes as modes of difference that she is ill-equipped to grasp. The ostensible cultural point of orientation for Juliane Brabant lies outside her own immediate experience (in either Germany or Shri Lanka), for the explicit comparison here is to a Christian heroine of early medieval legend, Genoveva of Brabant, whose husband's aide falsely charges her with adultery, thereby effecting a chain of rupture, banishment, and eventual restitution.

In Lander's case it is evident that the author's life, works, and recep-

---

9. Interested readers may also wish to consult "Invisible Baggage," Spitzer's account of the role of imagination in creating a displaced "Austrian" world for Jewish refugees in Bolivia during the Third Reich.

10. The government changed the official spelling in 1991 (Oberst 128).

tion have been profoundly affected by cultural alterity and migration. Herself a Jewish-American immigrant to Germany in the early 1960s, Jeannette Lander is perhaps best known for her Suhrkamp/Insel novels of the 1970s, which challenged many conventions of the so-called German-Jewish question by foregrounding and historicizing multivalent difference (see Adelson, "There's No Place"; *Making Bodies* 87–124; Lorenz 254–61). What I would like to highlight here, however, is not any supposedly "authenticating" experience of migration and alterity for a given author, but the structural and cultural paradigms of alterity at work in the novel at hand. *Jahrhundert* addresses very specific historical conflicts that are seemingly very distant from German concerns. In dealing with experiences of migration and complicating simplistic notions of alterity (German/Jewish or German/Shri Lankan) by drawing on cultural myth, it appropriates imaginative constructs from one historical period in order to infuse them with new cultural meaning in another. The dynamic production of historical and cultural alterity can be traced here in ways that should unsettle some of the positivist, essentialist assumptions that continue to inform much of the scholarship on migrants' literature in Germany. Finally, by discussing this novel in the context of "migrants' literature" in Germany, I mean to suggest that rigid academic distinctions between a "Jewish" thematic (confined to the legacy of the Holocaust) and a "migrant" thematic (restricted to the experience of "guestworkers") serve only to reinforce the reification of historical experience in cultural terms.[11]

The cultural map informing the protagonist's perspective in *Jahrhundert der Herren* is displaced onto a geographical landscape far removed from the Federal Republic of Germany. In three senses the issue of cultural transference is rendered here centrifugally as opposed to centripetally. First, Shri Lanka becomes the immediate but not the central grid on which displaced cultural meanings are explored. Second, the Genoveva of Brabant legend is invoked explicitly only once in the entire novel. Third, this particular medieval legend could hardly be considered central to German (or European) culture. Among German authors, Ludwig Tieck and Friedrich Hebbel have been the most famous of the few to adapt this legend for literary purposes.[12] It might be worthwhile to consider Lander's novel in terms of the postcolonial literatures that Bhabha associates with "the demography of the new internationalism" (Bhabha, *The Location*

---

11. I am speaking here of what I consider to be structural pitfalls in the field of postwar German Studies, not necessarily views explicitly articulated by particular scholars.

12. Tieck's play, published in 1800, is entitled *Leben und Tod der heiligen Genoveva.* The 1843 play by Hebbel is called, simply, *Genoveva,* even though it directs more attention to the majordomo who desires Genoveva in her husband's absence and then falsely accuses her of adultery when she spurns his advances.

5).¹³ Although Bhabha's focus is clearly on narratives of displacement, exile, and diaspora that speak on behalf of indigenous persons and communities so affected, Lander's novel in no way pretends to speak for the Tamils persecuted by the Sinhalese since the country was granted independence in 1948 or for any of the island's inhabitants subjugated by British colonialism. And yet the colonial legacy provides a vital backdrop and counterpoint for the novel's exploration of the transferability of European culture (via the Brabant legend). In its theme, locale, and structure, *Jahrhundert der Herren* poses postcolonial challenges to contemporary German Studies. Because the text does not address the historical legacy of German colonialism, these questions pertain primarily to cultural theory at a juncture when transnational categories have become at least as important as national ones. This realization ties in as well to the question as to whether a Jewish-American author can write a novel in German that takes place entirely in Shri Lanka and still have it read as German literature.¹⁴ The way in which *Jahrhundert der Herren* must be read as German literature is one that both defies nationalist definitions of culture and nonetheless attends to the historical particularity of cultural meanings that can either sustain or challenge a nation's imaginative concept of itself.

The only explicit reference to the medieval legend that seems to provide the cultural point of departure for Juliane Brabant's tale comes at roughly the middle of the novel. The protagonist has been doggedly pursuing her goal of economic independence in Shri Lanka from her estranged husband back in Germany, even as increasing signs of violence associated with island politics strike closer and closer to her home on a former tea plantation. The constant sound of government recruits practicing with their firearms in the valley below Greystones, the "master's house" (*Herrenhaus* 37) that she has inherited from her brother, the hanging of a Tamil servant's brother by parties unknown, and the murderous mining of train tracks by one militant group or another are enough to heighten her fears for herself and her household, but not to dissuade her from traveling to various cities to cultivate her business interests. On one such trip to the interior she and her entourage are surprised on a mountain road at night by three ruffians who commandeer the vehicle, with no explanation, for their transportation needs. Fearing the worst but surviving unharmed, Juliane awakens the next morning, thinks of the physical safety that she

---

13. Speaking of the "transnational and translational sense of the hybridity of imagined communities," Bhabha even remarks on the fact that Shri Lankan theater today "represents the deadly conflict between the Tamils and the Singhalese through allegorical references to State brutality in South Africa or Latin America" (*The Location* 5).

14. Similar problems plagued the reception of Lander's earlier work, which frequently transgressed conventional national and cultural boundaries (see Adelson, *Making Bodies*).

once associated with Germany, and cries (162–63). Later that morning she and her party drive through the same stretch of mountain forest where they had been terrorized the night before. This is where the first-person narrator introduces the Genoveva legend by name. "Hidden in the forest, the Genoveva of a legend lived with her child, hiding in the forest from a husband who had falsely accused her. He, too, was called Brabant. From the milk of a doe Genoveva sustained herself and her child" (164). In this instance the saving grace of the European forest of legend is linked to the distant sense of safety previously associated with Germany, both far removed from the civil wars of Shri Lanka.[15] In this case, the contemporary—but at this moment for the protagonist, imagined—place of Germany is tied to the expanded (transnational or *pre*-national) cultural space of Christian medieval Europe. The invocation of this expanded cultural signifier in turn raises important questions about the relationship that the narrative posits between the text's many generalized, dichotomous references to "Europe" and "Asia," on the one hand, and the negotiation of particular, localized experiences in Germany or Shri Lanka, on the other. The function of signifying names and particularizing places in this novel should be seen in this light.

Although the woman of this medieval legend is mentioned only once by her personal name (Genoveva), the legend is implicitly invoked throughout the novel by virtue of a geographical reference to the medieval duchy of Brabant, territory now affiliated with parts of the Netherlands and Belgium. This geographical reference, however, is mediated through the name of the husband in this text: Alexander Brabant. Whereas *re*-naming herself and her child serves a significant purpose for the protagonist (it gives them new lives in both bureaucratic and symbolic terms), it is curious that she retains her married name of Brabant, as if to say that this place-name is one that she cannot shed. Even her choice of new first names for herself and her child reflects two options, one determined genealogically and one expressing affinity. (She renames herself after her mother's mother, and her daughter's new name is that of the protagonist's favorite childhood friend.) Since the Brabant legend revolves around the fate of a woman falsely accused of infidelity and thereby serves as a kind of cultural mirror for Juliane's own plight, the geographical name reference (Brabant) already points to the issue of cultural transference. Does the legend

---

15. Although the novel provides no dates, the events depicted probably fall in the early years of the 1980s—after the founding of the Tamil Tigers (in the late 1970s), after the beginning of the Mahaveli water project, and before the shift toward even more widespread radicalized violence that followed the presidential election in 1982 and the general election in 1983. July and August of 1983 were especially gruesome months. See J. Spencer, Piyadasa, Venkatachalam, Oberst, Otis and Carr, and Moore.

transfer from one historical context to another? Can Juliane Brabant transfer to another place and culture? These two questions are related.

On one level, the text posits the transferability of the Genoveva legend based on the gender coding of women's subordination to patriarchal rule and whim.[16] To be sure, this redirects the dramatic focus away from the Christian themes of innocence, martyrdom, and redemption that Tieck and Hebbel had pursued to a focus on women's emancipation. The wronged wife in *Jahrhundert der Herren* does not desire the restoration of her husband's goodwill. On the contrary, she wishes only to free herself from his domination and influence and ultimately conspires to have him murdered by Tamil terrorists so that he will be unable to undermine her livelihood in Shri Lanka or take their daughter away from her. She grows to see her marriage as "a parasitic life form" (140), and in one of the few dialogic exchanges she has with indigenous women, Juliane Brabant imagines that she has a "sister" in the wife of the resthouse manager in Badulla, "the same as me, as different as we were in all else" ("meinesgleichen, so verschieden wir auch in allem waren" [98]). This "sisterly" bond that the protagonist feels is predicated on the other woman's fears that her husband will abandon her and her secret plans to ensure her economic survival in that eventuality.[17] In a scathing review of the novel, Eva-Elisabeth Fischer goes so far as to charge that Shri Lanka serves only as "exotic background for a not especially original theme: How does a woman become a human being responsible for her own actions in patriarchal society?"

Fischer is right to ask about the meaning of Shri Lanka for this European tale of one woman's liberation from the patriarchal yoke of her marriage, but the critic's conclusion is premature. The literary narrative itself insistently provokes that question by repeatedly positioning the protagonist in historical, cultural, and economic terms vis-à-vis Europe, Germany, and Shri Lanka. The image we are given of Ilse Brabant in Germany is that of a dutiful, charming wife of a successful corporate executive. With all the leisure time that her husband's activities afford her, she weaves and dreams. As soon as she disembarks from the airplane in Shri Lanka, land of her anticipated emancipation, she begins to shed her one-dimensional role of "wife." Yet she also grows conscious of what will prove to be an even more resilient bond with the man whose murder she later arranges: "Suddenly large, suddenly white, suddenly Western, European, in the wrong place" ("Plötzlich groß, plötzlich weiß, plötzlich westlich,

---

16. For a summary of the Genoveva legend see the entry under that name in the *Brockhaus Enzyklopädie* (109–10).

17. Juliane's sense of sisterhood is subsequently unbalanced by the other woman's direct request for Juliane's assistance, which Juliane withholds.

europäisch, fehl am Ort" [10]). From the beginning of her encounter with Shri Lanka, then, Juliane is additionally marked by the island's history of colonialism, in which she had not thought she had a part. Despite the occasional moment when she feels "relieved of her strangeness" ("der Fremdheit enthoben" [68–69]), she is more often than not characterized as a foreign element in a world that also seems strange and foreign to her. Juliane's perceptions of the foreignness that separates her from the Shri Lankans are customarily filtered through the reflective consciousness of the narrator concerning her own epistemological failures. "With no inkling of this place" (13), she at first plans to understand (33) and later realizes that she only thinks she understands the world around her when she in fact has no solid sense of orientation at all: "At times one thinks one recognizes an order, but one that resists orientation and leaves behind the impression of coincidence instead. One is confused and irritated" (66). As time progresses, she learns more and understands less. Unable to recognize the smiles of Supaya, the servant who is with her almost constantly (182), she is also shocked to find that her cook has been slaughtered during one of her absences, his rotting remains scattered around the kitchen floor. "What do you smell, what do you hear, what do you see? What don't you see even though it's there? Do you hear what you think you hear?" (189).[18] When a man comes to her offering his services as a chauffeur in exchange for being able to drive his own car and have his family live with him at Greystones, Juliane ponders her own ignorance: "I don't know the people of Shri Lanka. Their relationship to each other. Their way of dealing with each other. What, for them, is self-understood, not having to be mentioned. But above all, what goes undiscussed, unspoken. What boils up inside them, ferments on in secret" ("Ich kenne mich in den Menschen Sri Lankas nicht aus. In ihren Beziehungen untereinander. In ihrer Art, miteinander umzugehen. Was für sie selbstredend ist, nicht erwähnt werden muß. Vor allem aber, was nicht besprochen wird, nicht ausgesprochen. Was innen brodelt, geheimgehalten weiter gärt" [219]). Attending a Hindu festival toward the end of the novel, Juliane recognizes that she has remained on the periphery (despite all the business relationships that she has set into motion). All the things that she makes happen in Shri Lanka are not enough to diminish what she now perceives to be a "strangeness in one's very being [*Wesensfremdheit*]" that exceeds any supposed cultural, linguistic, or racial difference (254).

This is a puzzling claim. What "Wesen" could be meant here if the

---

18. These reflections are prompted by both the human and natural cultures on the island.

narrator's consciousness has been refining a sense of Juliane's historical and cultural positionality, not any alleged "essence" of European, German, or Shri Lankan being? If the protagonist's weaving entails "the manifestation of the secret pattern of her innermost structure" ("das Sichtbarwerden des geheimen Musters [ihrer] innersten Struktur" [140]), what underlying patterns can we discern in the novel's deep structure? Juliane Brabant wants to free herself from the domination that she experienced as an economically privileged West German wife of the late twentieth century. Although one might be tempted to posit a preliminary symbolic link between her subordination as a woman and the conventional gender coding of colonized peoples as "feminized," it cannot be said that Juliane feels a kinship with the indigenous peoples of Shri Lanka (or they with her). Acutely conscious of her epistemological blind spots vis-à-vis the Tamils of Shri Lanka in particular, the protagonist also reproduces some of the most tired European stereotypes about "Asia" and "Asians." Virtually every first observation that Juliane makes concerning a Shri Lankan native entails some information about the darkness or lightness of his/her skin. "Asia is a part of the earth that is foreign to my very core, asylum for holiness-bestowing poverty" ("Asien ist ein mir im Wesen fremder Erdteil, das Asyl seligmachender Armut" [16]). "I wish I could rid myself of the feeling that the men of this island are repulsive" (61). "Asia is duration. Asia has time" ("Asien ist Dauer. Asien hat Zeit" [119]). While Juliane is personally inclined to reject the arrogance of presumed cultural superiority, she is historically positioned to make choices that are already ensnared in complicated webs of past histories and ongoing cultural paradigms. There are no absolutely "free" choices here. The "emancipated" woman's obnoxiously worldly lawyer from Antwerp, whom she has just accused of being able to use commercial means to commit genocide without a moment's hesitation, responds by telling her that she must decide on whose side she stands. It is significant that he calls her at this point by the name that she had rejected upon her arrival in Shri Lanka: "dear Ilse" (208). In a sense this name calls her back to a culturally and economically positioned part of her own history that she had thought she could shed when she left European territory. The question that the Belgian lawyer tells her she must eventually face is one that had occurred to Juliane in an earlier episode. In a secret encounter with a Tamil separatist, whose initials—not coincidentally—are also J. B., Juliane listens to his pained tales of injustice, murder, and torture inflicted upon the island's Tamil population by the government and independent forces and wonders: "Where do I stand then? Where do I stand with my daughter, my possessions, my plans, my livelihood, yes, even my life when it comes to his civil war?" (108).

In many ways, where Juliane stands has been at least circumscribed, if not prescribed, by the circumstances of her arrival in Shri Lanka. Identified simply as a "wife" in Europe, the protagonist becomes a property holder, a mistress of Tamil servants, and an operator of a textile business on the island. Her view from Greystones is "far [*weit*]" and "domineering [*beherrschend*]" (37); there she is "Herrin" and "Besitzerin" (38), female forms of *master* and *owner*. Even though she inherited the estate from her deceased brother, who was not a businessman but an ornithologist and a deserter in World War II, Greystones is a former tea plantation, which links it to one of the major colonial economies of British Ceylon (Venkatachalam 2; Otis and Carr 204), and the brother's devotion to natural science links him to Alexander, whose distrust of Juliane derives, not from an aide's false accusations as in the medieval legend, but from the scientific assessment of Alexander's infertility by his surgeon. Juliane herself shares this blind faith in Western medicine when she initially scorns a local doctor's Ayurvedic treatment for her dangerously infected mosquito bite (89–90). The woman who seeks to rid herself of her husband's domineering influence finds in fact that she becomes more and more like him as her business pursuits bear fruit: "I am living like a man: giving orders, making assessments and decisions, taking risks. I had no idea that I was capable of this" (141). Despite this likening of Juliane to a generic "man" and the novel's frequent implied allusions to Genoveva of Brabant (every time the name "Brabant" is mentioned)—which would seem to reinforce the generically "patriarchal" dimensions of the modern narrative—these generalizing gestures are deceptive. The "century of the masters" is clearly cast in more specific historical terms characteristic of the British colonial rule over Ceylon, and Juliane easily adapts many of the postures, attitudes, and habits associated with white European colonials. When she calls herself "daughter" of the masters (121), she recognizes that her life story is conditioned in part by this history of colonialism and its legacy. The question still remains, of course, whether she is predestined to be fully complicitous in the legacy of colonialism or whether her lawyer's question to her (about which side she will ultimately stand on) is open and not simply rhetorical.

When the narrator returns again and again to Alexander Brabant as her interlocutor (the familiar "du" to whom the narrative is addressed), this is indicative of a dialogue that she chooses to continue to cultivate as much as it has chosen her. Alexander is clearly not a British colonial, but as a leading negotiator for an EC economic delegation sent to clinch a multimillion-dollar business deal with Shri Lankan officials, he stands to profit from the postcolonial relations on the island, which perpetuate the subordination of Tamils via noncolonial means.[19] Juliane actively makes herself complicitous in a similar way: "I am an instrument of the masters, I thought, but I knew no way out. I didn't want to know one. I didn't want to get out" (280). Her complicity is not confined, however, to economic exploitation. When her business arrangement with the powerful Buddhist clergy allows her enterprise to become a reality, she agrees to its terms, one of which stipulates that only Sinhalese sales clerks will be hired for her showcase store in Colombo, although Tamil schoolgirls do the actual weaving.[20] (Appropriately enough, she has named her store *spider*.) In an even more chilling vein, Juliane chooses to send a mildly retarded Tamil youth on a perilous errand, knowing full well that he could be kidnapped, tortured, or killed en route. This boy in fact disappears from narrative view under circumstances that can only be presumed to be violent. For this Juliane feels guilty: "So I heap guilt upon guilt. There is no degree of guilt. Lies, half lies, murder. It's no excuse to have been born into the century of the masters" (234). Given that the narrator had thought these same words when a local woman asks for assistance that Juliane knows she will not provide (102–3), we are left with a sense of both cyclical repetition and violent intensification.

Juliane, of course, makes herself most directly complicitous in murder when she convinces the Tamil separatist J. B. to assassinate her husband—an attack that will serve her purposes as well as those of the Tamil militants. At this juncture she realizes, "I felt completely at one with my time, with my heritage" (318). Fully conscious that she is calculatedly exploiting a violent postcolonial situation to achieve a highly personal objective, she is marked as different from the other J. B. and very much like the husband whose life she causes to end. This apparent focus on the protagonist's cultural and historical positioning is at odds, however, with the narrative's simultaneous appeal to generalizations and repetitions. When Juliane learns that her Tamil servant's brother has been found hanged on the town lamppost, her response is a generalized one: "The world is full of murder" ("Die Welt ist voller Morden" [75]).[21] After she has secured the promise of help for her

---

19. Otis and Carr point out that Shri Lanka's formal democracy effectively ensures the dominance of the Sinhalese majority over the relatively very small Tamil minority.

20. Scholars generally seem to regard the modern Buddhist clergy of Shri Lanka as major proponents and benefactors of Sinhalese nationalism (see J. Spencer 2).

21. I am grateful to Susanne Zantop for alerting me to the fact that this is a line from a World War I song called "Wildgänse rauschen durch die Nacht" (Wild geese rustle through the night). This intertextual allusion provides an additional example of the novel's structural invocation of dehistoricizing generalizations. As will be shown, this structural feature is only one element of the puzzle that Lander constructs for her readers.

business venture from the Buddhist clergy, she yearns for the "sleep of innocence," for "life is guilt" (171). The recurrent theme of generalized guilt and violence echoes through the occasional verbatim repetition of sentences or sentence clusters. We have already seen one example of this (the passages pertaining to guilt on pages 102–3 and 234). Another such cluster of repetition involves the novel's conclusion, which mirrors its beginning in an almost liturgical invocation of the cyclical routines of the Shri Lankan garden, Juliane's plantation residence, and Supaya bringing Madame's tea (9, 319). Immediately preceding this narrative repetition at the novel's end is the narrator's assertion "that injustice will be avenged. It doesn't matter when or how" (319). Her interlocutive focus on her murdered husband thus evokes an image of karmic cycles of wrongdoing and retribution.

In a text so rich in descriptive detail—with a narrator who draws our attention repeatedly, not only to what she observes, but also to what she becomes conscious of knowing—these structural tensions between generalizations and repetitions, on the one hand, and on specificity and innovation, on the other, merit some scrutiny. Are we to conclude, as one reviewer has done, that this is a novel about the demise of ethics, about a European protagonist who merely accepts her own contradictions in relation to an Asian land (Jacobs)? To be sure, Ilse Brabant is a wronged woman who becomes Juliane Brabant, committing several transgressions in the process, murder among them. One could read the novel's appropriation of the Genoveva legend not only as an inversion from subordination to liberation, but also as an inversion from innocence to guilt. What becomes then of the issues of historical and cultural transferability in this postcolonial text?

The politicized notion of cyclical violent conflicts has at times been invoked in order to characterize the recent civil wars in Shri Lanka as a contemporary manifestation of an ancient, precolonial animosity between Tamils and Sinhalese. This dehistoricizing view has been rejected by scholars whose studies reveal that the ethnic categories and tensions of the postcolonial era do not predate colonialism but were instead called into being by British colonialist categories and hierarchies of "race."[22] Although it

---

22. See Rogers; Stirrat; J. Spencer 7–9; and Elizabeth Nissan and R. L. Stirrat. Uyangoda associates the contemporary racialized view of Sinhalese Buddhist nationalism with European Orientalist scholarship, which may have "inspired the twentieth-century Sri Lankan scholars also to claim *Aryan* status for the Sinhala language" (41). Ironically (as Uyangoda also points out), these Orientalizing categories of scholarship and related colonialist categories of administration ultimately fostered a Sinhalese "sense of prestige and superiority over the colonial ruler" and Tamils alike (41). Obeyesekere provides an insightful account of how nineteenth-century Western scholarly versions of Shri Lankan Buddhism infused a "missionary lexicon" of superior and inferior cultures into local Buddhist teachings, which were subsequently used to articulate both anticolonialist and antiminority (anti-Tamil) positions.

does not delve into the nuances of scholarly debate, Lander's text nonetheless rejects the theme of ancient "natural" conflict by focusing on the divergent positioning of Tamil and Sinhalese subalterns under British colonialism (40, 105–7). This historicizing gesture has its counterpart in the specific positioning of Juliane Brabant's epistemological horizons. Can this persona transfer to another place and culture? we asked earlier. Characterized by much of the text as generally "white," "European," and "Western," this figure would seem on the one hand easily transferable by virtue of the especially widespread legacy of European colonialisms and cultures. Yet, we know too much about Juliane's blind spots and the stumbling blocks that they represent to her quest for a life-style fundamentally different from her previous one. Although benefiting from certain privileges of class and culture, she is clearly hampered by what she presumes to know and what she realizes she does not understand. On another level, however, the protagonist is positioned as both more and less than simply "white," "European," and "Western." This is revealed in her pivotal first encounter with Harry Silberzweig, the sole Jewish character in the entire novel. Introducing himself to this fellow German (at a formal Christmas party given by a government official) as a free-lance business consultant, Harry performs "a subservient bow like an eager Hitler Youth, clicking his heels in exaggerated fashion. His eyes revealed the sad sarcasm of this gesture only to someone who was able to combine Harry's last name, his age, and the recent history of Germany, where Harry came from. But in Shri Lanka there was hardly anyone who could make these connections" ("übertrieben Hacken klickend, einen Diener wie ein eifriger Hitler-Junge. Seine Augen verrieten nur dem den traurigen Sarkasmus dieser Geste, der seinen Familiennamen, sein Alter und die jüngere Geschichte Deutschlands, woher er stammte, kombinieren konnte. Aber das konnte in Sri Lanka kaum einer" [138]). Here it is once again, at least partly, a name that signifies a history attached to a place. Juliane—whose own name signifies a legend attached to a place, which we try to "read" in this novel—distinguishes herself in this circle by recognizing a particular meaning evoked by the signs that Harry presents to her. This marks not only Harry (as a German-Jewish survivor of the Holocaust) but also Juliane, for her epistemological field of recognition links her to a historical-cultural arena in which these particular signs have acquired a weighty significance. Her ability to read certain historical signs roots her in a cultural field in which politicized meaning accrues to that history. While this is something that she never achieves in Shri Lanka, it would be misleading to assume that her encounter with Harry confirms her essential "Germanness." Harry himself is a moveable sign (he has been working in Southeast Asia for twenty years), and what he "signifies" is not a constant. This is evidenced by the fact that no one else at the sizable holiday party "reads" him the way that Juliane does. Given that the Third Reich, the Holocaust, and their legacies (in real as well as in symbolic terms) were and continue to be transnational phenomena, we could say that Harry Silberzweig functions in this episode to signify the "transnational and translational" (Bhabha, *The Location*) quality of historical alterity, which becomes cultural "matter" in this German, postcolonial narrative.

Whether the legend of Genoveva of Brabant transfers from one historical context to another was the related question that we had asked. We have already seen that the Christian theme of innocence and redemption is thwarted by Juliane's attempts to free herself from her dependence on Alexander, attempts that serve only to ensnare her in an even more complex web of complicity and accountability. In another dimension, consciousness of which is not reflected in Lander's narrative, the geographical space onto which the narrator seeks to displace the Brabant legend is already occupied by a Hindu legend of a mythical wife's fidelity, cruelly tried and tested by the demon ruler of the kingdom of Lanka (today the island known as Shri Lanka [Grimal 215]). This is the stuff of the *Ramayana,* together with the *Mahabharata* said to be "the most influential epic of India" (Eliade 213) and "a kind of a family bible for millions of Hindus" (Klostermaier 85). The Sanskrit epic poem, which has known countless written and oral adaptations, relates the tale of Lord Rama, his faithful wife Sita, and the demon Ravana, who kidnaps Sita in an unsuccessful attempt to dishonor and discredit her. As Supriya Nair has noted, Mahatma Gandhi invoked this popular Hindu myth to promote passive resistance against the British colonials in India. For Gandhi India was Sita, "kidnapped" by the British colonial demon Ravana (Nair). This legendary account of a wife's fidelity challenged on mythical ground thus *might* have played a more central role than Genoveva of Brabant for this German novel set in postcolonial Shri Lanka. Instead, Lander's literary exploration of the transferability of a medieval Christian legend to a contemporary setting outside the territory of Europe but within its field of cultural influence probes the parameters of what it means to speak of "German" or "European" culture at a time when strictly nationalist categories of cultural analysis are less and less useful. By no means does this negate the relevance of particularized historical analysis or of imaginary constructs that continue to draw on nationalist paradigms. But it should complicate our analytical categories and render us distrustful of those that purport to address "migrant" German culture without forcing us to scrutinize very carefully the all-too-static assumptions that keep us going nowhere.

Christoph Hein's *Horns Ende:* Gypsy Essences and German Community

Sara Friedrichsmeyer

> To write, in order to describe, to describe, in order to be able to continue working, in order to be able to hope. . . . The naming, the writing is not yet the action transforming the world, but it is the precondition for all change.
>
> —Christoph Hein

I

According to several recent studies, Gypsies[1] are the most despised and distrusted minority in a united Germany.[2] Other studies provide evidence that the prejudices with which Germans have associated them have been remarkably uniform since the fifteenth century, when their presence was first documented in German-speaking lands.[3] To be sure, the German example is not unique; similar responses have been registered over time

---

1. Fonseca reports on the increasingly popular reaction among the people themselves to the word "Gypsies," a designation she uses throughout her study. "Roma" is also a favorite all-encompassing name (228), but because Germans use the word to refer to one Gypsy group (i.e., "Roma and Sinti"), I will use the designation "Gypsy."
2. See, for example, Friedrich and Schubarth; I thank Patricia Herminghouse for providing me with this study. For an overview of German responses, see Margalit (8); I thank Katharina von Ankum for providing me with this article. See also Romani Rose's work. For an overview of European reaction to the Gypsies in today's Europe see "Alle hassen die Zigeuner." Ariane Barth's report on the tensions caused by Gypsies in Hamburg is less neutral.
3. See Fraser for a recent, brief history of the Gypsies in German-speaking countries (84–91). For more detailed discussions see Arnold; Gronemeyer; Mode and Wölffling.

throughout the Western world. In the late twentieth century, Gypsies are perhaps the last people whose depiction remains unswayed even by considerations of political correctness. The images with which they have long been associated continue to be perpetuated in a way no longer acceptable regarding other minority cultures. The highly spiced "Zigeuner Chips" sold in German markets, for example, rely for their popularity at least to some degree on preconceived notions as does the herbal tea called "Gypsy Cold Cure" available in this country, with its claims to near-magical and natural healing. Describing Finnish festivities surrounding Midsummer's Eve, the writer of a recent *New York Times* article relies on another stereotype when promising that "[v]isitors can have their fortunes told by a real Gypsy" ("Helsinki"). Known at least in the Western world predominantly through fixed images, they are, as Isabel Fonseca confirms in her 1995 *Bury Me Standing: The Gypsies and Their Journey,* among the least understood people on earth.

Since the late eighteenth century, German and indeed Western representations of Gypsies have been intricately linked with the Enlightenment goal of controlling and transforming the earth. For the developing middle class that accepted this mandate, the challenge was understood largely in terms of economic growth and the development of nations. Linked to another European discourse that ranked civilizations according to certain developmental stages, this thinking favored people who had accepted the values we associate with modernity, such as reason, property, individual development, and historical progress. Thus civilizations or cultures have not been characterized merely in terms of their variety, but instead within a hierarchy reflecting Western notions of development. It is a form of ranking based on the perceived ability of a culture to overcome a "natural" state and enter history as a "developed" culture, a progression never attributed to Gypsy groups. Indeed, as Katie Trumpener has argued, they are usually represented as out of time and without history.

Although it is only recently that self-identified Gypsies have begun to speak of the clash between their indigenous cultures and German ambitions,[4] German-speaking peoples have a long tradition of speaking for them or about them, usually within the framework of an attraction/repulsion complex. This complex has found expression not only in the popular imagination; as in a variety of other national literatures, Gypsies in German literature have come to be equated with either a dangerous challenge to the bourgeois order or a welcome relief from its strictures. For writers concerned with promoting the development of bourgeois society, Gypsies

---

4. Romani Rose is perhaps the best known, but others writing in German are also emerging, among them Mariella Mehr and Ceija Stojka. See "They Couldn't Take Our Thoughts" for a recent English-language interview with Stojka.

have been imagined as an anarchic, threatening presence, remote from all social and historical processes. Alternately, writers intent on challenging a middle-class existence have often used Gypsies to depict a more organic, carefree, and autonomous way of life.[5] Through such representations, Gypsies are reduced to metaphor, to textual strategy, or to emotional effect.

Because they have not been colonized in a traditional sense—discussions involving Gypsy groups do not focus on territorial expansion, for example, or on the acquisition of an overseas empire, and they have very little to do with the spread of market capitalism—the various Gypsy groups are not included in examinations of postcoloniality or imperialism.[6] Yet the long history of their troubled presence and representation in Western culture speaks for including them in the discourse of "the unequal and uneven forces of cultural representation involved in the contest for political and social authority within the modern world order" that Homi K. Bhabha defines as postcolonial criticism ("Postcolonial Criticism" 437). For concerned critics, Christoph Hein's 1985 novel *Horns Ende* can afford a means of initiating the discussion.

Hein has frequently aligned himself with Enlightenment goals, referring to himself in 1992, for example, as "an Enlightenment moralist" ("ein aufklärerischer Moralist," *Chronist* 11). As the epigraph to this article underscores, he is convinced of the writer's responsibility to work through literature to urge readers to engagement with the social world. And in many ways *Horns Ende* is commensurate with that self-definition. It begins with a recollection: "In that year the Gypsies arrived late . . . and everyone hoped they had chosen another city" (6). "Everyone" refers to the villagers in the fictional GDR village that is the setting for the novel, and memories of their presence, ranging from the almost benign to the vitriolic, form one of the main thematic lines through which Hein demonstrates and condemns the deeply embedded intolerance of the village population.[7] By choosing reactions to Gypsies as a measure of intolerance, Hein is not merely acknowledging a long-standing Western prejudice, but one of

---

5. Thomas Mann's dismissal of the "gypsies in a green wagon" in *Tonio Kröger* is among the best known examples of the former; Nikolaus Lenau's 1838 poem "Die drei Zigeuner" illustrates the latter approach. See Trumpener and Djurić for other examples of their appearance in German literature. See also my von Arnim article.

6. See Williams and Chrisman on the lack of consensus in current definitions of colonialism and imperialism.

7. Most critics understand the inclusion of the Gypsies as Hein's challenge to life in the village. Bulmahn speaks of their "alternative modes of behavior" (258); McKnight sees them as a "crystallization of counter-imaging [*Gegenbildlichkeit*]" (424); Lindner speaks of their value in having preserved "a kind of inner autonomy" (160); Preußer sees them as part of Hein's "critique of civilization" (138); and Hammer has suggested that they represent "a kind of catalyzing function [*Katalysatoren-Funktion*]" (*Chronist* 11).

which he claims personal knowledge. The images with which he portrayed them, he has remarked, were drawn from his childhood experiences about the summer presence of a migratory group of Gypsies in his own GDR village (*Chronist* 31). Given Hein's frequent articulations about his adherence to Enlightenment principles, it is fair to speak here of authorial intent, and Hein's warning is against bigotry in general, not only that directed against Gypsies or those of other ethnic groups; the villagers are also taken to task for their intolerance toward the title character, another German. Nor is the prejudice Hein attacks just an East German phenomenon. As a broadly intended "message" against intolerance, *Horns Ende* is surely effective on one level.

Yet on another level, Hein works against that "message," at least regarding attitudes toward other ethnic groups. In making his point, he falls victim to a kind of stereotyping that perpetuates, if not intolerance, then certainly exclusionary thinking of the kind usually associated with a postcolonial perspective. For in addition to urging his readers to discard their negative images of Gypsies, he also constructs an idealized image of "Gypsiness" to serve as an example to his readers of a positive human community, a model for their own "imagined community," to use Benedict Anderson's well-known phrase.[8] In this positive projection, their alleged rootlessness has been recast to appear as a response to gentle and natural rhythm; the clannishness for which they have been so often criticized, as community solidarity. Although the differences are now weighted as positive, the novel still assumes that members of different cultural groups, here Gypsies and Germans, are markedly distinct. It is important to recognize that for Hein, as for others implicated in this kind of thinking, the view of the Gypsies upon which the idealization is based is just as much a product of Western fantasies as are the more frequent negative portrayals. It has very little to do with the reality, the diversity, and the enormous complexity of Gypsy life.[9]

By discussing *Horns Ende* in this context, I mean less to criticize Hein than to demonstrate that even conscious and engaged contemporary writers can still be susceptible to wholesale notions of Gypsy alterity. The assumptions of cultural homogeneity that underlie the novel reflect a mindset that Said has referred to as the "us" versus "them" mentality that has become a "hallmark of imperialist cultures" (*Culture* xxv).

---

8. Critics generally accept Hein's idealization of the Gypsies without recognizing its essentializing nature. McKnight, for example, comments that Kruschkatz's contact with the Gypsies "brought him into contact with humanity [*mit der Menschlichkeit*]" ("Mosaik" 425).

9. If evidence is still needed refuting claims to a homogeneous Gypsy culture, see, for example, Margalit on Sinti condescension toward Roma (28–29).

II

Formally, Hein's novel is complex. Each of the eight chapters is introduced by a prologue in which an unnamed figure—identified by most critics as Horn—urges another unidentified person to search for the "true" facts of his death some thirty years earlier.[10] In thirty-nine monologues interspersed throughout the eight chapters, five inhabitants of the village where Horn spent his final years take up the task, some more willingly than others. But about the museum director Horn and the problems with the Party that led to his suicide, we learn only sporadically and then in fragments.[11] Hein structures the monologues so that the five speakers display little evidence of common purpose. Their recollections instead show agreement only in their common hostility toward outsiders; the suspicion and hostility they harbor toward Horn is just as pronounced as their antagonism to the Gypsies. Although their recollections are ostensibly intended to ascertain the truth about Horn's life and death, what emerges from their embarkations into memory has less to do with factual information about Horn's life than with revelations about village life and about the speakers' less-than-fulfilled existences. Spodeck, the village physician, corrupted by his father's money, despises his life, his family, and his patients. Mayor Kruschkatz, trapped in the village after his earlier hopes of using his position there as a stepping-stone to higher office elsewhere had evaporated, lives friendless and alone (20). The most pathetic figure in the book, Gertrude Fischlinger, the shopkeeper with her swollen and aching legs, is unable to communicate with her son Paul and is the victim of psychological and sexual abuse by her now absent husband. Marlene Gohl, a victim of a different kind, is one of the mentally ill whom the Nazis and their village sympathizers had intended for extermination, alive only because her mother chose to die in her place. Regarded now by the villagers as hopelessly mad, she is lovingly tended by her father. The one child among the speakers, Thomas, tells a story of maturation as a process of increasing disillusionment.

As every speaker remarks over the course of the novel, the summer when Horn died was also the Gypsies' last summer in Bad Guldenberg.

---

10. Hein himself admits that he intended these introductory dialogues to be ambiguous (Jachimczak 59). Most critics consider Horn's partner to be Thomas.

11. Having been expelled from the Party in Leipzig for reasons never made clear to the reader, he had come to Bad Guldenberg in the early 1950s to work as curator of the local museum. Again, and for reasons apparently no more substantial, he was in 1957 denounced for espousing what one speaker calls the ideology "of a fruitless, exhausted humanism" [*eines fruchtlosen erschöpften Humanismus*] (86). Hein has pointed to some similarities between his title figure Horn and a Leipzig historian who committed suicide in the 1950s (Jachimczak 59).

Although one speaker dismisses the tendency of the villagers to associate the two occurrences (22), Hein has structured the novel so that the nexus cannot be ignored. Not only does the text begin with the Gypsies' arrival during May in 1957, the year of Horn's death (6), but it ends with their final exit from the village that same September, shortly after his suicide. The linkage underscores Hein's point that Horn and the Gypsies are the unintegrated outsiders.[12] Because Hein provides no omniscient narrator to synthesize their various versions, no "truth" about Horn's death is ascertained; nor does he develop a narrative voice to define the Gypsies. We learn about them only through the personal histories of the townspeople.

Except for Marlene, whose exaggeratedly romanticized views the reader is expected to filter through an awareness of her mental illness, the speakers regard both Hein and the Gypsies as disturbing presences in their midst, as intruders. Although the degree of contempt elicited by their outsider status does vary, it remains a consideration for all the speakers. In the case of Horn this is explained by his being, as Kruschkatz phrased it, "unsuited for a life among human beings" (61). The speakers have a similar exclusionary response to the Gypsies, and when they weave references to these visitors into their constructions of the past, it is with distaste and usually in the most blatant of clichés. As they remember village life, Hein shows them responding to the Gypsy presence with all the unexamined stereotypes of centuries of censure. The visitors are remembered as dirty (138), as thieves (10), as being good with knives (12), and as eating cats to keep their bones "supple" (13). The women are referred to as witches (11), as marked by eroticism (71), and as not bearing, but stealing children (100). One speaker dismisses them all as being "like children who don't want to grow up" (182).

The five speakers remember that the Gypsies live differently, dress differently, and speak a strange language. Thomas describes their living quarters as smelling "of food, sweat, and alcohol" and the women as having "dark fuzz above their lips" (66). Dr. Spodeck dismisses the visitors as "this far-traveled misery" ("dieses weitgereiste Elend," 9), a "dark-skinned clan with its colorful rags and gray curly hair" (8). Although Kruschkatz finds himself as mayor occasionally in the position of defending them, they remain for him "a heap of misery that disturbed the village with its dirty poverty and its unintelligible guttural sounds" (138). Gertrude Fischlinger introduces an additional moral condemnation with her protests of trying not to believe "the terrible stories" people tell about the chief and three Gypsy women (155–56). Many hold the summer visitors responsible for

---

12. Actually, Marlene is not integrated, but her presence is grudgingly accepted; her father likewise remains outside the web of community activity.

the demise of tourism, hence for economic decline, in Bad Guldenberg (135). Others insist they undermine the drive toward socialism; by renting their horses for the summer to the farmers for field work, the Gypsies are, according to this version, deluding the farmers into thinking they can function without government help (136–37).

This is, however, by no means an anti-Gypsy novel. To be sure, the negative stereotypes are all there, but placed as they are in the mouths of characters who become increasingly unsympathetic with each new registering of prejudice, the stereotypes are meant to be discredited.[13] To ensure that his readers respond appropriately, Hein also intervenes directly to combat certain persistent negative images, for example that of Gypsies as supporting themselves through stealing. We hear Thomas repeating his friend Paul's condemnation of the visitors for this alleged crime, but that complaint is undercut by Gertrude Fischlinger's chilling recollections of her own son's habitual thievery. At other times, stereotypes expressed by one character are neutralized by another. Thomas, for example, is told by his friend Elska that Gypsy girls are dirty (71), but this disclosure takes place only after the reader has been presented with a disturbing portrayal of Elska's own primitive and particularly unhygienic living conditions (66).

Despite the title, the novel then is only ostensibly about Horn. Hein is interested in much more than in the retelling of the life and suicide of a colorless museum director in an obscure GDR village of the 1950s. But neither is it about a migrant group of Gypsies taking up summer residence on the village meadow. Instead, Hein develops the villagers' aversion to both Horn and the Gypsy contingent as a way of pointing to the bigotry, the entrenched antipathy for difference that has long defined his own society, and, even more importantly, the detrimental effect it has had on that society. As the aggregate of their recollections demonstrates, the villagers have failed to shape a livable community. The failure of Mayor Kruschkatz's actions to create anything resembling a workable community is underscored by his painful admission that the "settlement of crazy people" has taken from him everything he ever valued (131). And through the eyes of the boy Thomas, we are granted insight into the life of his father, one of the pillars of village life, whose reputation as an upstanding citizen and model of respectability was enhanced by his Sunday walks with his family in the carefully tended *Kurpark* and by his punctual departure every morning for work as the village druggist (108). Through Thomas is filtered his father's distrust of not just the Gypsies, but of any "new faces" (31) in the village.

---

13. There are gradations of difference in these characters; Hein, for example, has indicated his intention of showing a positive human dimension in Kruschkatz (Jachimczak 63), although to this reader it is barely discernible.

Hein bursts this bubble of respectability and along with it the pretense of shared community values when Thomas, home alone one day, discovers his father's carefully hidden collection of pornography (104). Another incident indicts his mother as well: Thomas recalls her summer pastime of greedily picking such an abundance of berries for preserving that jar after jar must be fed to the chickens the following spring (52). Even the shopkeeper Gertrude Fischlinger, less despicable than the other adult speakers, is not an ideal community member. Though her experiences as a shopkeeper over many years have taught her not to connect Gypsies with stealing (126–27), she does not speak for them. Rather, she directs her energies at deflecting the criticism of the other villagers who do not approve of their presence in her shop. The picture that emerges from the recollections is thus of petty, mostly cheerless, and sometimes even bitter people in a village that is anything but a community. The particularly venal Dr. Spodeck, engaged in writing a history of the village, is entirely credible when he describes his saga as a "history of human nastiness" (113–14).

III

But Hein intends his novel as far more than a portrayal of intolerance and its results. He has called *Horns Ende* a "novel about history, about understanding history, and also about writing history" (Jachimczak 62), and numerous critics have focused their investigations accordingly.[14] But he has also made it clear that history's appeal lies for him in its application to the present (*Als Kind* 147).[15] And the present for Hein in 1985 meant socialism and the ongoing attempts to create a viable socialist society.[16] Thus the memories he gives his characters help position Hein in the long and contentious debate about the period after 1945 as a continuity of or a break with the past. The villagers are all implicated to some extent in the Nazi evils through Marlene's history, since one of them had denounced her to Nazi authorities (156–57). By linking the villagers' loathing for out-

---

14. Some of Hein's most important essays on history are collected in *Als Kind habe ich Stalin gesehen*. A number of critics have written on the novel's inferences for reading and writing history (cf. B. Fischer; McKnight; Lehmann; M. Braun; Löffler).

15. For readers, that present is also shared by Gypsies. Romani organizations are still in the 1990s fighting for official recognition of the Nazi persecution itself and for the same war crimes reparations long extended to members of other affected groups. The struggles in Berlin over whom to include in the Holocaust Museum are also pertinent here.

16. *Horns Ende* is in fact the second work in a trilogy on controversial, even taboo, historical periods or events in the GDR. The first of the three, his 1983 *Der fremde Freund* (published in West Germany as *Drachenblut*), had as its background the 17 June uprising of 1953. *Der Tangospieler* (1989), the third of the series, dealt even more openly with its setting of the "Prager Frühling" of 1968.

siders and their antipathy toward difference to their earlier support for Nazi policies, Hein pointedly reminds his readers that though the political structures have changed, people have not. Elsewhere Hein has articulated what *Horns Ende* implies: "There was a caesura and there is continuity" (Jachimczak 61). There was no *Stunde Null,* neither in the West nor in the East (Hammer, "Versuch" 35).

Hein's emphasis on the continuity of history implies that GDR life in the 1950s was not the incipient utopia that socialist realism presented in its official histories of the period. Socialism had indeed not triumphed in the Bad Guldenberg of the 1950s, nor, in Hein's view, has it made much progress since. The villagers' recollections reveal their lack of community spirit in the past and, as their isolated, alienated existences and the monologic form of their remembering suggest, they have learned nothing about meaningful communication or about shaping workable communities in the intervening years. They remain as intolerant in the 1980s as they were in earlier decades. The bold and perceptive critique of GDR society enhanced Hein's reputation considerably, especially in the West.[17]

Shortly after the *Wende,* Hein emphasized his continuing concern about intolerance in the context of the *Vergangenheitsbewältigung* that had also been his focus in the novel: "The past that we do not confront will not only not disappear, but it threatens to return" (*Als Kind* 136). And, as in *Horns Ende,* the repeat of the past he specifically fears still comes in the form of intolerance for minority groups: "The new Jews have already been identified, and in my country too they are the foreigners" (*Als Kind* 136). In the best Enlightenment tradition, his writing—fictional as well as essayistic—can be seen as rooted in a belief that his readers are educable, that once convinced of their flaws they will strive to overcome them, and that writers have a role in creating an awareness of their imperfections.

Although Hein does not intend that his villagers be judged evil—their discriminatory tendencies are relativized by repeated references to the truly malevolent Bachofen (cf. 134–35)—he takes care to expose their inhumanity, in part by denying them a normative voice. None of them comes close to being a model; their abysmal histories contain no germ of hope for the future. But neither does he allow Horn to become the moral center, although by contrast to the other villagers and because of his past, Horn is a relatively sympathetic character. Through various recollections of Horn's inability to relate to others, gleaned especially from the overlap-

---

17. Its reception resembles that of much GDR literature: the more critically it viewed the GDR, the more positively it was reviewed in the West, and vice versa. For the troubled publication history of the novel see McKnight (*Understanding* 74–78); see also Sevin (182–85).

ping accounts of Gertrude Fischlinger and Thomas, the reader is never allowed to see in Horn a model for humanity.

Rather, Hein presents the Gypsies as a norm for his readers. Hein has carefully orchestrated the villagers' monologues so that from the various overlapping and conflicting accounts there emerges a view of Gypsy solidarity that contrasts soundly with the lack of social bonding, with the unfeeling and exploitative relations that prevail among the villagers. Clearly Hein cannot be faulted for perpetuating negative stereotypes of the Gypsies. Nor does he commit some of the more egregious errors documented by postcolonial critics; there is, for example, no paternalistic gesturing toward bringing the Gypsies under the umbrella of Western culture. Nevertheless, although not as pernicious as negative stereotyping, Hein's evocation of a peaceful, migratory group living unimpeded by national laws or political forces or economics, and moving in rhythm with its own timeless desires, is also harmfully prescriptive. Without exploring the reasons for or the ramifications of the solidarity of the particular group in Bad Guldenberg, he accepts the equation of their life-style with positive human community. If based on tribalism or common victimhood, however, their solidarity is not necessarily a productive contrast to village life. On the other hand, perhaps there are more positive reasons for Gypsy forms of community that, if explored, could have made the association less reductive.

His positive projection also denies the centuries of persecution and exile that have been the social force behind their nomadic life. To be sure, their life-style is connected to a lack of homeland, but that Gypsies have no homeland is not necessarily the result of choice. And even after the persecutions of the Gypsies during the Third Reich, Hein does nothing to combat the identification in the popular imagination of Gypsy life with an idealized nomadic existence; nothing in the novel challenges their representation as a carefree and defiant alternative to a more humanized, more civilized Western culture. Hein's single-minded focus on his German villagers and on the improvement of his own German society leads him to another strange and particularly unfortunate lapse: rather than Gypsies, it is Germans, the Gohls, who in the novel are the victims of the Nazis.[18] Because he is interested in the Gypsies only as they can be used to reflect a positive norm for his German audience, he brackets out their diversity, the complexity of their sociohistorical experience, and their own troubled history; an ironic contrast—and surely unintended—in a work struggling to find meaning in history.

---

18. For pertinent works on the treatment of the Gypsies during the Third Reich, see Fonseca's bibliography (312–14); for a German account see Hohmann.

Despite his sympathy for the Gypsies and his good intentions, by setting up the solidarity of the Gypsy group as a contrast to life in Bad Guldenberg—by using an undifferentiated ethnic group as a metaphor for some presumed way of life—Hein perpetuates what Said refers to as "invented essences" ("Criticism" 40), operating as if, to paraphrase Said, there were a Platonic idea of "Gypsiness" that guarantees those values with which Hein associates it in the novel to be pure and unchanging. This conviction that everyone is principally and irreducibly a member of some race or category that will forever remain unassimilated is the basis of what Said defines as the "epistemology of imperialism" ("Criticism" 40). To be sure, literature works by association and image, but the novel unintentionally exemplifies the dangers that can accrue when a literary image of an entire group of people is based on reductive thinking. This novel promotes the notion of a deep gorge between "natural" cultures existing outside of political history and those nations moving purposefully through history toward self-realization. Further, this hierarchy of cultures that the novel supports forces a similar rift between the individuals within the cultures—here between Gypsies and Germans—all of whom are consigned by the rhetoric to membership in a homogeneous culture anchored only in the imagination.

The history of German literature abounds with outsiders who function as mirrors to an ossified collective before staging their own disappearance, and the pattern is repeated here. Horn commits suicide, and, with the departure of the Gypsies in the same year, the village is once more free of their unwelcome presence. Although the inhabitants of Bad Guldenberg are unable within the fictional work to learn from their history,[19] their unhappy example is intended to help Hein's readers to forge their own cultural destiny, to learn from the villagers' errors, and to form livable German communities.

IV

In one of his most quoted and intentionally provocative essays, the 1982 "Öffentlich arbeiten," Hein voices the same concerns about a still-developing German cultural identity that are given fictional form in *Horns Ende* (34–38). Socialism, he fears, is endangered by the lack of a public sphere for *Kultur,* a term he then goes on to define as "the total intellectual [*geistige*] work of a people [*eines Volkes*]" (36).[20] In this 1982 essay Hein

---

19. Some critics believe that such a renewal takes place within the novel (cf. Bulmahn).
20. See Bathrick for a discussion of the enormous importance in the GDR of what he calls the "culture question" (*Powers* 42).

was arguing—understandably—against censorship and was one of the first to do so in the context of a deficient public sphere; his definition, however, of what is endangered by that absence is instructive for the present discussion. As in the novel, this essay too is premised on a belief in the homogeneity of cultures and in a static notion of cultural identity, bracketing out all the evidence that cultures are themselves differentiated and extremely heterogeneous, and that any notion of a *Volk* must surely exist only in the imagination.

The essay provides additional background for understanding Hein's monocultural concerns in the still-unwritten *Horns Ende*. As readers quickly recognize, the "Erinnere Dich" with which each of the novel's chapters begins is a reference firmly rooted in Western intellectual history, in the need to know the self.[21] But it is not only an individual search for self-knowledge that Hein urges in the novel; he is even more concerned with a collective or cultural identity. In "Öffentlich arbeiten," Hein not only articulates the importance of cultural identity, but points to ways for developing and maintaining it. Cultural identity, he asserts, is possible only through a critical examination of, even engagement with, other cultures: "That which is your own can only be developed by means of what is foreign. Peter needs Paul, Marx says, . . . to know himself. . . . Our culture must shape and prove itself through [a critical examination of] other cultures" (35–36).

Hein studied philosophy in Leipzig, and when he insists, as here in this essay, that "the foreign" is necessary for understanding and developing "that which is your own," he is allying himself with the conventional categories of the Idealist tradition according to which the self can know itself only by knowing that which it presumes or imagines to be separate from it. Recent critics have demonstrated the problems with this model for individual self-knowledge,[22] and there are other, equally disturbing considerations when the subject/object paradigm for knowing is applied to cultures. As this novel so explicitly demonstrates, the model, by calling for rigid and artificial distinctions between peoples, can result in what is tantamount to the reification of one entire people in the service of the identity construction of another.

Both *Horns Ende* and "Öffentlich arbeiten" raise important epistemological questions, not just because Hein is one more well-meaning writer who ends up perpetuating myths about a group she or he has no

---

21. As Hammer points out, the reference is to one of Socrates's lines in Plato's dialogue *Hipparchos* ("Christoph Hein" 1360).

22. On the problems with Enlightenment traditions of identity creation see, for example, Young.

intention of demeaning. If a subject can gain knowledge or identity, whether individual or cultural, only by objectifying something presumed to be outside itself, then the construction of a mirror, an "other," is appropriate and even efficacious. If the Idealist model alone offers the possibility for developing a communal or national cultural identity, then Hein's objectification of the Gypsies—or any other writer's objectification of some other group—is not only justified, but indeed requisite. As exemplified by what happens with his Gypsies, however, any cultural identity that Hein and his German readers construct for themselves is manifestly at the expense of the Gypsies. Buttressed by the language and paradigms of Idealist philosophy, Hein has perpetuated in the novel a politics of exclusion, setting up insurmountable boundaries between cultures and the individuals relegated to each rather than working toward their elimination.

There is some textual evidence in *Horns Ende* that Hein intuited the strictures of his reliance on the subject/object model. In the affectionate friendship that the artist Gohl has for many years maintained with the Gypsy chief, stereotypes and essences have been transcended. With this friendship Hein seems to infer that a different kind of personal interaction is possible from that practiced in Bad Guldenberg. Although their friendship is remembered somewhat differently by the various speakers, there is some consensus that the friendship is not reliant on a shared language, one of the traditional markers of national and cultural identity. Although hardly a major strand of action, the friendship does indicate that Hein was on some level questioning his understanding of cultural identity. There is no indication that the two friends relate as self versus other. In the brief allusions to their friendship provided us, there is as little xenophilia as xenophobia. Far from valorizing difference, theirs is instead a kind of human interaction based on unquestioning acceptance and some generosity of spirit, one that has rejected the concept of "difference" altogether. Difference has in fact ceased to exist as a category for critical analysis.

True to his concept of himself as a "reporter, a chronicler" (*Als Kind* 203), Hein has throughout his career insisted that he is no more intelligent than his readers and that he can "only say something about the path that we have taken" (*Texte* 52). Wisely, he has never promised his readers answers and instead has only volunteered his help in understanding their common past. Yet in *Horns Ende* he is also, with this friendship between the artist Gohl and the Gypsy chief, ever so tentatively, and in a way he is still not able or willing to define, offering an intriguing hint about positive human community, and about what will be required to overcome the "us" versus "them" mentality that remains a constituent element in the postcolonial imagination.

Ethnic Drag and National Identity: Multicultural Crises, Crossings, and Interventions

Katrin Sieg

> *What is past is not dead; it is not even past. We cut ourselves off from it; we pretend to be strangers.*
> —Christa Wolf, Patterns of Childhood

I

In 1988, the French playwright Bernard-Marie Koltès attempted to stop a production of his play *Le Retour au Désert* (Return to the desert), directed by Alexander Lang at the Thalia Theater in Hamburg, because Lang had cast white German actors in the roles of a black African and an Arab. At a panel discussion later that year, a number of prominent German theater scholars and critics accused Koltès of censorship and insisted on directorial authority and autonomy over what they interpreted as the "biological correctness" of Koltès's casting recommendations. Lang claimed that casting actors of color would have jeopardized "the homogeneity of the ensemble."[1] The remark highlights a slippage between cultural and racial homogeneity that is constitutive of postwar discourses on national identity in West Germany. While race and ethnicity were taboo terms in the postfascist German states, the notion of culture as discrete, bounded, and proper to a specific nation reveals the term as a stand-in for "race," resisting contemporary conceptualizations of cultural and national identity as

---

1. "I would have found it difficult to push the production too far toward naturalism and cast black actors in these roles; the homogeneity of the ensemble would have been eroded" (*MordsWeiber* 68).

heterogeneous, hybrid, and in process. A presumed discordance of acting styles, along with another critic's assertion that Germans had to play these roles because Germany's lack of colonies had resulted in a scarcity of actors of color, thus served to exclude people of color from a theatrical production about ethnic tensions in postcolonial France.[2] Moreover, Lang's dramaturge went on to explain that the Arab character, whom Koltès had suggested should be played by a Turkish actor, was deliberately encoded as a turbaned Oriental, so as to avoid being interpreted as a *Gastarbeiter* by German spectators. The assembled critics unanimously applauded the postmodern, German production that had underscored the play's universal themes such as "sibling rivalry and the master–servant dyad" and avoided a realistic (and therefore banal) portrayal of postcolonial problems. Casting an actor of color, they contended, would have closed down the universal interpretive dimensions that a white actor in brownface and exotic costume ostensibly opened up. With this argument, the theatrical avant-garde displaced political concerns and social accountability onto questions of style—boring realism versus sophisticated postmodernism. One might then see their evaluations as a measure of the bourgeois theater's alienation from material concerns and political commitments, and hence the social irrelevance of that particular institution. While the theater artists' insistence on artistic autonomy disavowed the representational weight of ethnic markers in the context of a multicultural society, their remarks on orientalist signifiers suggest that the sociopolitical meanings of race are operative even when the representational referent of the masquerade is deliberately obscured. In other words, the presence of ethnic and cultural minorities in Germany, as well as the centrality of racially configured struggles in that country's history, have created interpretive frames within which ethnic impersonation, no matter how fanciful and fantastic, attaches to political meanings.[3]

I consider that panel discussion to be a key text about the German state theater's approach to multicultural representation; it demonstrates in exemplary fashion the discursive compound I propose to examine here. The thinly veiled xenophobia (contained in the notion of a "homogeneous ensemble"), historical "forgetting" (of German colonialism and its

---

2. Michael Merschmeier: "[T]he staging of these plays will be more difficult for us than in France. Because West German society is less multicultural than French society. This is an effect of the lack of former colonies" (*MordsWeiber* 69).

3. In the same discussion, Klaus Pierwoß mentions that plays about the social problems encountered by migrants in Germany were performed by white Germans in brownface as well (*MordsWeiber* 70).

legacy),[4] and disavowal of a social referent (the Turkish migrant) are the components at work in cross-racial impersonation, or what I will call "ethnic drag." By that I mean the impersonation of ethnic others by a subject that stages and conceals its dominance. This performative practice enacts the terms of multiculturalism in the form of a series of displacements. It both excludes the material bodies of cultural others, and subsumes the markers of difference (turban, skin color) under "universal meanings" whose aesthetic and metaphysical dimensions can be adequately expressed only by "German" bodies. Practiced across artistic genres and social sites, this performative tradition has gathered considerable representational weight, extending from the journalistic investigations of Günter Wallraff and Gerhard Kromschröder, to television series, and to the mass-cultural spectacle of the annual Karl May festival.[5] Ethnic drag has created a representational field on which race and national identity have been paradigmatically articulated in postwar West Germany. Cultural intercourse is performed to the exclusion of social and political encounters and change.[6] This dynamic calls attention to the way in which "multiculturalism" has come to accommodate, rather than challenge, the patterns of exclusion and ghettoization that characterize the lives of ethnic minorities in Germany. In the 1990s, the political implications of this divergence have become especially poignant.

My discussion of ethnic drag will begin by raising methodological questions and then proceed through readings of what I consider exemplary texts that are clustered around the beginning and the end of the "old" Federal Republic. The dramatic adaptations of Karl May's Wild West stories (beginning in 1952) and R. W. Fassbinder's film *Katzelmacher* (1968) provide mass cultural and avant-garde uses of drag that I will examine in the context of postwar refigurations of nationality. Working in—as much as against—the same genre as Fassbinder's Critical Volksstück, Kerstin Specht's play *Lila* (1990) offers a complex critique of unification that eschews neat East–West, male–female schematic accounts of that epochal event. The piece also marks an impasse in the leftist/feminist critique of

---

4. The forced sterilization of the black German descendants of German colonists in Africa during the Third Reich, for instance, suggests that the alleged scarcity of actors of color is a result of racism, rather than proving a lack of racism. See Opitz et al., *Showing Our Colors: Afro-German Women Speak Out*.

5. Gerhard Kromschröder's book *Als ich ein Türke war* preceded Wallraff's by two years. For a fairly recent example of ethnic drag on television, see *Motzki,* a series that revolved around competing claims to "German" identity after reunification. These claims are embodied by a West Berlin *Kleinbürger,* his East German cousin, and their neighbor, a Turkish grocer who was played by a white, East German actor.

6. Hazel Carby makes a similar argument (193).

drag and its colonizing gesture. Finally, Emine Sevgi Özdamar's comedy *Keloglan in Alamania* (1991) provides examples of reverse appropriation, rewriting such high cultural master texts of drag as Puccini's *Madama Butterfly* from a minoritarian perspective.

II

> *Despite their billings as images of reality, these Negroes of fiction are counterfeits. They are projected aspects of an internal symbolic process through which, like a primitive tribesman dancing himself into the group frenzy necessary for battle, the white American prepares himself emotionally to perform a social role.*
>
> —Ralph Ellison

For a theater scholar, ethnic drag poses the choice of two concepts and performative traditions with somewhat different methodological implications: the notion of blackface and the history of minstrelsy in the United States offer interpretive tools for describing and understanding similar practices in German popular culture. One recent study, Eric Lott's *Love and Theft* (1993), has provided a sophisticated account of the ways in which minstrel shows in early-nineteenth-century America contributed to the class- and gender-inflected articulation of whiteness, specifically the formation of a white working class. Lott's central thesis posits a dynamic of erotic fascination and material expropriation, love and theft, as being inscribed in the practice of blackface. The term is particularly useful in the way it enables a reading of theatrical stereotypes and plots alongside historical and political processes and struggles; in that respect it promises to be instructive despite national differences.

The concept of blackface could serve to inaugurate an understanding of ethnic impersonation in German culture that is attentive to the class, racial, and sexual politics within which it plays and that it helps produce. The political meanings of blackface, the implications of its practitioners' conceit to speak for and about black people in a thoroughly racialized culture, have long been acknowledged in the United States, as evidenced by the naming of segregation laws after the minstrel stock figure Jim Crow. That awareness has created its own interpretive pressures, obliging Lott to contest the assumption that minstrelsy is nothing but a transparent reflection of white supremacy. In contrast, ethnic impersonation has never been problematized in Germany. The concept of blackface allows me to throw into relief the material power relations that this practice both embodies and disavows.

Despite these analytical benefits, I have decided against using "blackface" as a guiding term; to an American readership, it carries very specific historical meanings that do not apply to the German context. To be sure, there is no direct analogy to the minstrel show with its derisive lampooning of an other that was excluded from the audience, but nevertheless not so far away. Lott's claim that "the minstrel show worked for a hundred years to facilitate safely an exchange of energies between two otherwise rigidly bounded and policed cultures, a shape-shifting middle term in racial conflict" (6) is specific to nineteenth-century America. Lang's turbaned Oriental or May's Indians are dramatic stock characters that revel in their ostensible lack of referentiality. Nor are impersonations of, say, Turks as institutionalized and of comparable cultural centrality as American minstrelsy figures.[7]

The other concept of impersonation available to the theater historian and critic is that of drag; analogously to blackface, drag tells us little about actual or historical women, and much about the figuration of femininity in the patriarchal imaginary. In *Feminism and Theatre,* for instance, Sue-Ellen Case considered men's impersonation of women in Greek as well as Renaissance theater and concluded that this practice enacts the exclusion of women from cultural production and their circulation as aesthetic objects in a way that inscribes their confinement to the domestic sphere and their legal status as property in homosocial societies. However, Case later developed another notion of drag that focused on the counterhegemonic, subcultural uses of the term. In "Towards a Butch–Femme Aesthetic," she shifted the ground of gender impersonation away from the dominant stage where men dressed as women perform for other men, and where the referential frame is understood to be bi-gendered and heterosexual. Instead, her attention to lesbian butch–femme performances opened up a reading of drag that destabilizes the ontological underpinnings of gender, where the codes of masculinity and femininity enter into the play of seduction and manage to evade the discipline and punishment of the realist regime. While this notion of drag is not generally available to dominant cultural practices, I find it productive in relation to minority literature in Germany, specifically to the play by Özdamar that I will discuss.

Rather than providing a "shape-shifting middle ground" between two

---

7. Moreover, the German stories themselves, their tone, and the roles they assign to racial others all differ from the minstrelsy model. Rather than caricaturing the cultural traditions of racial others communing among themselves, German impersonations dramatize interracial encounters, as in the case of the Karl May festival. The exception to that general observation is the impersonation practiced in German club culture. The so-called Western Alliance, an umbrella organization for clubs devoting themselves to frontier culture (impersonating cowboys as well as Indians) comprises 140 clubs. There are also clubs that emulate African tribal cultures. I have discussed the Indian clubs in "Wigwams on the Rhine."

antagonistic races, ethnic drag in mainstream German culture describes a triangulated communicative structure, a theater of identity in which the brown–white relationship pivots on an absent third party. In the following section, I want to argue that the first appearance of this trope reveals that third party to bear the contours of the Jew. The Indian here serves as a stand-in that allows the other genocide to go unnamed, a factor that is crucial to the production of meaning in and of ethnic drag.

III

> *Karl May's childish and criminal fantasia has actually—though obliquely—influenced the history of the world.*
> —Klaus Mann, 1936

Picture this scene: a blond, blue-eyed man in leather shirt and leggings tied to a post, surrounded by howling, tomahawk-swinging Indians. Their chief raises his hand—a hushed silence falls; all eyes are riveted on the two figures facing each other. Cutting the white man's ties, his majestic counterpart, face covered by a thick layer of brown make-up, initiates the following exchange:

"Be my friend!"
"I already am."
"My brother."
"With pleasure."

The frenzied applause, the whistling and cheering that follows the ritual oath of blood brotherhood is only surpassed at the final curtain call, when a full ten-minute ovation greets Indian chief Winnetou who, again and again, rides across the stage, his hands raised in a greeting that includes the entire audience in the red–white brotherhood.[8] In the course of the Karl May festival during the summer of 1971, that bond came to encompass 120,000 spectators swooning with the passionate, romantic affect of interracial encounters.[9] No doubt we are in the presence of catharsis, but what are the exact contours of the subject that is thus purged of pity and fear?

The containment strategies devised by these melodramatic tales reveal

---

8. This scene is described by Dietmar Grieser (100–101).

9. Statistics on spectators in *Der Wilde Westen* (48–49). The festival does not shy away from interracial sex and reproduction either. The stage adaptation of May's story *Half-Breed*, produced in 1986, casts the title figure as a biracial hero who "promises to use his biracial heritage to work as a mediator between the races and bring about peace" (*Der Wilde Westen* 80).

a great deal about postwar Germany's phantasmatic self-representation and explain the eminent adaptability of Karl May's works, seemingly so removed from historical truth or social reality. Karl May's vision of a peaceful coexistence between white and red races was predicated on the supremacy of a national subject configured in the universalist terms of religion (Christian piety), rather than ethnicity. May's pietist Old Shatterhand, in his very commitment to peaceful solutions, gentle persuasiveness, and Christian mercy, creates ever new and more opportunities for his stubborn foes to attack him after he has pardoned them. And, because of their ultimately savage nature, he never succeeds at converting the Indians to Christian virtues, proving their extermination to be a tragic, yet just, by-product of evolution. May's undiminished popularity may be due to the way he cleverly cloaked a social Darwinist narrative in religious rhetoric. Yet the failed conversions (with the exception of Winnetou himself) that drive his plots reveal the disavowed biologist underpinnings of national identity, which is increasingly unable, and unwilling, to assimilate any others. Moreover, the author averted accusations of imperialism by attributing the negative qualities associated with aggression and conquest exclusively to the Yankees.

Such an emplotment of a national subject appears to have been well-suited to the Federal Republic's project of proving its humility and loyalty to Western democratic and diplomatic principles, and foreswearing a representation of German identity marred by the recent history of militarism, imperialist aggression, and racial chauvinism. The postwar stagings of the Winnetou saga equally rehearse the displacement and disavowal of German nationalism's racial underpinnings. That dramatic move paralleled the return to a status quo ante in West Germany's philosemitic political culture, a supposedly innocent time before the racist aberration of the Third Reich and the Holocaust. The Wild West scenario enacted in Bad Segeberg, in which Old Shatterhand and his German companions journey west to aid American Indians embattled by greedy Yankees, refigures the imperialist fantasy underwriting the blood brotherhood into a potent *Wiedergutmachungsfantasie* (fantasy of restitution).

This disavowal of historical liabilities worked quite literally. The open air theater in Bad Segeberg, built around a small mountain that forms the ragged backdrop for Karl May's Westerns, was constructed by the Reichsarbeitsdienst in 1937 to serve as the region's *Thingplatz*.[10] Here, National Socialist speechmakers depicted a savage other bereft of any

---

10. National Socialist administration designated these communal gathering places as stages for the *Thingspiel,* as well as for political rallies. Henning Eichberg translates the *Thingspiel* as "sacramental play" and notes that it was "a new dramatic genre which received a great deal of attention and was institutionalized by the Nazis between 1933–37, but was then forgotten very quickly" (134).

nobility; when Winnetou first rode across the stage at Bad Segeberg in 1952, his futile battle against his people's genocide must have created ghostly historical echoes in the ears of those local workers who built the stage designed to propagate the strengthening of the Aryan race and the eradication of European Jewry. The symbolics of blocking racial narratives of struggle, survival, and supremacy across the surface of a mountain, which Leni Riefenstahl's films perfected in the 1930s, seem to have remained unchanged since then. Contemporary stagings alternate horizontal mass choreographies of Prussian battle formations with a vertical trajectory of racial/religious ascent.[11]

The interracial encounter is ghosted by a third party, whose absence nevertheless organizes the meaning of drag: Germany's ethnic minorities; and in the early postwar years those were mainly represented by the so-called displaced persons, survivors of the Holocaust. The depth of the silence about the Holocaust and the inadequacy of the philosemitic gesture to confront and work through the antisemitic atrocities of the Third Reich, as well as the political exigencies of West Germany's assimilation into Western treaties and power blocks, delineate the historical and critical matrix within which drag repeatedly figured and rehearsed race and its disavowal in West German national identity. Frank Stern views 1952 as the watershed year in which West Germany's "partial sovereignty, economic, political, and military integration into the West were directly intertwined with *Wiedergutmachung*" ("Reflections" 160). From then on, philosemitism was confirmed as a political style, designating at once the instrumentalization of antifascist and post–antisemitic sentiments for a democratic foreign policy and acceptance into international alliances, reflecting all the while the profound silence about the Holocaust. Nineteen fifty-two is also the year in which the Karl May festival opened. At that historical moment, and within that particular constellation of political and psychic pressures, the festival offered scenarios of racial struggle and catharsis that validated German supremacy, sublating it into a "universal," Christian superiority, and eliding the immediate historical referent and victim of racial chauvinism.[12] At a time when representations of German–Jewish relations—past or present—were lacking and taboo, the ambiguity of the antisemitic/philosemitic attitude was played out across the body of the Indian. The dread of an other perceived as both assimilating and unassimilable, an

---

11. For a more elaborate reading of the Karl May festival, see my article "Wigwams on the Rhine."

12. May's casting of "Germanness" in terms of Christian virtues, patriotic sentiments, a sense of *Gemütlichkeit,* and local customs constituted a characteristically Romantic compound of values that encoded and sustained antisemitic attitudes, a mixture of sentiments that the Jewish publisher and philosopher Saul Ascher criticized and attacked.

other figured as the polar opposite of (Christian) civilization and therefore of inferior status in the evolutionary scheme, and the apotheosis of interracial love and understanding fantasized as an antidote to genocide after the fact—these complex and contradictory textual operations and performative affects register the semitic contours of the displacement conducted at the Karl May festival.

The silence about the Holocaust and its survivors underwrites the practice of drag, yet the precision of that elision renders it legible as a fantasy of restitution. I am not saying Winnetou is a Jew in disguise, but that the taboo created a psychic need and interpretive matrix that rehearsed both the continuities and discontinuities of racial articulations with German nationality in the postwar years. The cathartic moment of blood brotherhood, which includes all spectators, purges racial hatred as well as grief about it. Winnetou's unbroken pride, his admiration for the "good" whites (= Germans), and his refusal to hold them responsible for the atrocities of the "bad" whites (= Yankees) register postwar Germans' fantasies of absolution and restitution: to be forgiven for the horrors perpetrated and to render them undone, a contradiction attesting to the processes of denial at work in postwar German culture. The peculiar distance between historical reality (the genocide of native Americans in the 1860s) and the fiction of interracial love (May's Winnetou saga written in the 1890s) are eerily repeated at the Bad Segeberg festival. Just as Klaus Mann earlier charged that Karl May had made Hitler possible, *Winnetou* functioned after the war and the Holocaust—at least phantasmatically—to undo them.

IV

> *Whenever I think of the Indian, I remember the Turk.*
>
> —Karl May

The apotheosis of interracial love staged within the Aristotelian paradigm of catharsis served to gloss over the historical break dividing fascist imperium and Western democracy. The critique of unacknowledged fascist continuities that emerged in the 1960s also addressed itself to the theatrical vehicle that executed and dissimulated that ideological sleight of hand. Rather than inviting audience empathy with a doomed other in ethnic clothes, the two texts I want to discuss in the following section highlight "race" as a set of traits and codes that are ascribed to and mapped onto an other's body, rather than being depicted as biologically or psychologically inherent in it. Rainer Werner Fassbinder's film *Katzelmacher*, in which the author himself played the role of the Greek guestworker Jorgos, dramatizes the visual encoding and social enforcement of values and bodily properties that are then claimed to be natural and innate. The film insists that the subjects of race are the Germans, rather than the migrants with whom they come in contact; in the 1960s, that reversal had profound political implications for addressing the "problem" of race in Germany.

What one sees then in this representation of race is its production by the community. Nevertheless, there remains the troublesome issue that a "white" German still reads as "blank" in this film, as seemingly unracialized—an operation that hinges on assumptions of universality versus racial particularity. Kerstin Specht's play *Lila* (1990) likewise borrows from the conventions of the Critical Volksstück. It chronicles the story of a Philippine mail-order bride now married to a villager in the former West Germany, using the Philippina to mark a perspective from which the gendered and racial logic of reunification and the reconfiguration of a national subject could be accomplished. Like Fassbinder's Greek, the title figure in *Lila* remains completely unelaborated; she functions as a catalyst rather than an agent.

Moreover, the genre within which both texts fall has its ambiguities written into it already. Although it offers some critical potential, its uses for a critique of race and nationality are limited. The Critical Volksstück is the one genre that has historically been used to stage encounters with an other—racial, class, or sexual. The best-known authors of this genre that first emerged in the 1920s were Ödön von Horvàth and Marieluise Fleißer; from the beginning, it stood as an alternative model of political theater to the didacticism of the epic stage represented by Brecht. Rather than dramatizing the dialectic movement of a revolutionary subject for intellectual inspection, the Critical Volksstück accelerated and heated up the pressures of contradiction within the closed communities it depicted into dense images and metaphors that would implode the social body rather than staging its progression toward enlightenment.[13] The dramatic personnel's experience of oppression is wholly mediated by mass culture and thus always leads to brutal (self-) destruction that leaves the system of oppression unchallenged. Its rejection of closure constitutes both the genre's radical potential and the root of its appropriation by the very culture industry it purports to indict. Critics have pointed to the Critical Volksstück's sexual politics of brutality and noted how it is easily and frequently coopted into a titillating sexism. Likewise, the genre's methodical heating up of existing social tensions allowed for the staging of racism, unmitigated by

---

13. For further discussion of the politics of the Critical Volksstück, see Susan Cocalis and my chapter on Marieluise Fleißer in *Exiles, Eccentrics, Activists*.

humanist or philosemitic agendas. Because of the contradictions built into this anti-genre, the play's intensification of brutal and alienated social conditions might be interpreted as an exhortation to radical change—or as a tragic tale evoking pity and fear for the victim of violence. Jorgos may thus be viewed as an unfortunate, but half-deserving victim—after all, he exhibits a nationalist chauvinism not unlike his tormentors' when it comes to meeting a Turkish laborer as a new addition to the village. In short, the play might be read as a racist text rather than a critique of racism.

Fassbinder adapted the play *Katzelmacher,* which he dedicated to Marieluise Fleißer, into a film. In 1968, Fassbinder, then head of the antitheater in Munich, himself played the Greek migrant Jorgos who is recruited to work in a small town in Bavaria, becomes sexually involved with one of the local girls, and is beaten up by a pack of young men.

Jorgos's function in the film is to highlight economic and social shifts in postwar Germany; he serves as a catalyst, rather than performing a role that is itself socially, psychologically, or sexually elaborated. We know nothing of the character's motivations for taking this job, the work itself, his past, or his desires. His body provides little more than a blank screen on which communal tensions and antagonisms are played out. Interestingly, Fassbinder chose not to represent Jorgos's ethnicity visually (such as makeup, hairstyle, costume), but exclusively through his linguistic habits. Jorgos speaks poor, broken German. The process of racial ascription is made visible by leaving the position of the other blank, as it were, by not providing the ethnic signifiers readers suspect, speculate about, and perceive. What one sees instead in this representation of ethnic relations is the structural function of difference for the formation of national community in its racial articulation.

The outsider is portrayed at once as ordinary (like the other Germans) and unknowable. He functions like a mirror, reflecting nothing but the social order. At the same time, his subjectivity remains unrepresentable and opaque. The villagers' unceasing speculations about Jorgos's strength, his sexuality, and his political convictions, which they endeavor to read off of his body, endow that body with a sort of hyperpresence and designate it as a hieroglyph. To decipher it means to find the key to his identity, which is assumed to be "already there" and waiting to be unlocked.

The presence of the foreigner exacerbates internal struggles and contradictions around class and gender within the community that escalate in the village men's attack on Jorgos. The physical brutality provides no catharsis or resolution, however. Instead, the final scenes in the film underline the racialization of class as well as sexual relations; the prospect of hiring another guestworker, and thus integrating foreign labor into German economic structures, parallels Jorgos's insertion into the sexual dynamic of the village.

The impact of the economic miracle on the village's class structure can be felt, on the one hand, in the downward mobility of the unskilled and underemployed German males now in competition with poor southern Europeans. On the other, national economic growth has made upward mobility possible for women and enabled their entrance into the work force. Significantly, it is a woman who doubles the number of her employees, her profit margins, and her chances for economic and social advancement by hiring Jorgos. At the end of the film, she announces her decision to hire another guestworker, a Turk, illustrating the tremendous profit Germans gained from foreign labor. Typical for the Critical Volksstück, *Katzelmacher* brings economic and sexual struggles into contiguity. Sex is depicted as a transaction through which economic and social status are negotiated. When gender roles and material privileges cease to coincide, the clash takes the form of misogynistic as well as racist violence. The affluent Elisabeth's dinner table and the village bar she frequents with her two male employees become arenas of male aggression. The German men's macho posturing and their sexual jealousy of the mythically potent Jorgos highlight the production of (white, German) masculinity at a time of gender reorganization and crisis. In other words, Fassbinder's drag performance grafts the ascribed potency of a racialized, southern European sexuality onto a masculinity that is portrayed as jeopardized and failing due to female competition and professionalization during a period of economic growth. Ethnic drag in *Katzelmacher* drives a dynamic of homoerotic fascination for the southern European male body and cultural/sexual expropriation in the formation of working-class, heterosexual masculinity.

Fassbinder's film illustrates the dilemma faced by a new generation of critical theater artists in the 1960s, namely that language in late capitalism sutures the subject into ideology rather than enabling a critique of it. Elisabeth, Jorgos's articulate and masterfully exploitative employer, is a case in point. The incoherent, nearly speechless Jorgos, then, inhabits at once the most materially oppressed position within this community and the one that is least interpolated into dominant ideology. By virtue of his silence, Jorgos's position can be appropriated for a critical, even utopian agenda. Ethnic drag in *Katzelmacher* marks race as a privileged discursive site for launching a critique of language and ideology; an enterprise, however, that can only be accomplished by evacuating cultural specificity. While Alexander Lang and various theater critics want to subsume race under "universal values," Fassbinder harnesses ethnicity to a postmarxist critique of class.[14]

Feminist theory has analyzed the vexed problem of speaking and being spoken for in enormous detail. Moreover, feminist scholars have paid a great deal of attention to a visual economy in which the lushness and beauty of proliferating images mystifies rather than transparently reflects women's social existence. Perhaps this is why much recent theater by women refrains from perpetrating the same figuration of exclusion and hyperrepresentation when it comes to speaking about ethnic and cultural differences. Many feminist playwrights have grappled with the vicissitudes of a multicultural society.[15] In their plays, the traditions that Koltès's critics had furiously defended now appear less self-evident, more of a liability. In plays like Jelinek's *Stecken, Stab und Stangl* (1996), the masked figures remain silent, as if trying not to become guilty of speaking for an other. These ghostings of drag allow feminist playwrights to navigate between the desire to put their own social and educational privileges at the service of oppressed minorities[16] and the knowledge that such representations, too, commit an elision: aesthetic representation can indict the system (theatrical and political) that produces speechless subjects, but remains stuck in this deconstructive gesture.

Silence on Germany's very literary stage (*Sprechtheater*) signals a crisis of agency. Had Fassbinder's theater mobilized an antiracist critique, contemporary masquerade seems to revolve around its own complicity, guilt, and paralysis. Kerstin Specht's play *Lila* (1990), like Fassbinder's film, cannot supply the figure of the other with subjectivity, but presents it instead as a blank space around which nationalist discourses generate, accelerate, and finally implode their binary codes. This text also illustrates how the conjunction of deconstructive paralysis and the urgent desire for political agency can flip back into a notion of universal humanism that erases rather than includes marginalized voices.

---

14. Arlene Teraoka discusses a similar rhetorical gesture in relation to Günter Wallraff's *Ganz Unten* ("Talking Turk").

15. Some examples are Elfriede Müller's *Goldener Oktober*, Bettina Flessner's *Asyl*, Anna Langhoff's *Transit Heimat*, and Elfriede Jelinek's *Stecken, Stab und Stangl*. See also Helga Kraft's last chapter.

16. In an interview about her play *Stecken, Stab und Stangl*, which deals with the recent murder of four Roma men in Austria, playwright Elfriede Jelinek explained: "I wished to put at the disposal of this oppressed minority which lives under unbelievable conditions, whose children are automatically sent to special ed classes, who don't get any opportunity for an education, to put at the disposal of these people everything, the best of what I have artistically created: To speak for those who are without language or whose language we don't understand, that was very important to me."

The play is titled after a young Philippina who marries a German man in the region of Oberfranken, near the former border to East Germany. The title figure remains unelaborated and silent; her position, however, is appropriated for a critical perspective from which the transformation of sexual, ethnic, and economic conditions following reunification appears in sharp contrast. It is also the position from which the possibility of resistance is considered most emphatically.

The play's division into two parts underscores the profound changes reunification has brought. The first part of the play contrasts two seemingly incompatible attitudes toward racial heterogeneity: while some villagers revile Siegfried's bride Lila and equate foreign origin with a disease threatening to infect the healthy social body, others half-enviously, half-admiringly note the material and sexual advantages Siegfried will reap from his marriage, the infusion of "fresh blood" into the family, and Lila's perceived submissiveness. The Philippine woman represents to the villagers the epochal changes brought on by the opening of the borders and the subsequent, dizzying rearrangement of the German map. While their previously peripheral location had translated into economic atrophy and social backwardness, their now central location suddenly catapults them into modernity, confronting them with international travel and trade, different gender systems, and economic competition with technologically advanced as well as third world nations. Siegfried's mother balks at these changes, preferring the familiar horrors of tradition that award her a modicum of authority to the unfamiliar ones she fears from Lila. To the Mother, tolerance and integration into the family and the village are predicated on Lila's unconditional surrender to a rigid regime of local German customs, including the sexual division of labor. The compound of "German" culture and female subservience is exemplified and epitomized by a scene in which the Mother teaches Lila to cook potato dumplings. She rebukes her daughter, who points out that Siegfried, a cook by profession, could probably prepare his own food, and instructs Lila:

> Remember how it goes? Now you boil them. *She pours boiling water over the dumpling dough. Steam shoots up. Lila jumps back in fear.* And now make dump-lings, litt-le balls. *She quickly forms a dumpling.* Now it's your turn! *She takes Lila's hands and submerges them in the hot dough. Lila shrinks back, weeping.* Oh Lordy, what a wuss. Oh Lordy. Gotta get used to this. A bit of heat, you won't die from it. (*Lila* 15)[17]

---

17. The dialogue is written in a stylized regional dialect: "Merkst du dir des, wies geht? Jetzt mußt du sie abbrühen. *Sie schüttet kochendes Wasser über den Kartoffelteig. Es dampft. Lila weicht erschreckt zurück.* Und jetzt Bäl-le machen, Klös-se. *Sie formt einen Kloß, so schnell, daß man kaum zusehen kann.* Jetzt du! *Sie nimmt Lilas Hände und taucht sie in den*

The Mother's sadism is directed against Lila's ignorance of German culture and rules, yet her own attitude toward those rules is increasingly ambivalent. The Mother had derived her social status from her parental authority, from her ability to perform hard work, as well as from her willingness to subordinate her own wishes to her father's ideas about feminine propriety. Lila's clothes and hairstyle, her premarital sexual activity, and her leisure (she goes dancing and lounges in the sun) throw into crisis the Mother's lifelong agreement to defer gratification, articulated through the discourses of motherhood and the Protestant work ethic. The marriage renders futile her own sacrifices and hopes for securing social status and respect for Siegfried: "He could have been mayor. With the right wife he could have been anything" (19). Where Jorgos had posed serious competition to male German laborers because he could undersell them, Lila's hypersexualized appearance signals Siegfried's aspirations to bourgeois status, shifting social codes upon entering late capitalism, and the changing parameters of femininity. The epochal conflict figured through the antagonism between the Mother and Lila escalates in a series of violent acts and leads to the Mother's descent into a mad rage, the burning down of the parents' house, and the death of Siegfried's sister in the fire.

Specht's decision to embody the contradictions of late capitalism in an old woman and a postcolonial woman of color is not without irony. Aside from the Critical Volkstück's central tenet, that those most oppressed within an ideological system nevertheless have strong subjective investments in it, the playwright also calls attention to the ways in which interrelated, but not analogous, hierarchical systems can produce critical junctures that enable as well as obviate possibilities for intervention. Listening to Lila sing, the Mother remembers her own father's refusal to let her play the guitar, because "this won't do for a girl" (24), and for a moment her bitterness creates a connection between them, based on the injustice the Mother experienced and a momentary identification with Lila as that which the older woman could have been. When the Mother realizes, however, that her daughter is showing Lila affection and threatens to slip out of the Mother's control, she furiously reasserts her authority by calling Lila an Asian whore. Race works here to reinstall hierarchy where gender identification and solidarity would have thrown the Mother's lifelong dedication to protecting men's interests into question. However, while gender enables a tentative connection between the two women across cultural and class differences, it also works as a relay that regulates access to the new regime of capitalist femininity. While race figures as the

---

heißen Kloßteig. Lila fährt schreiend zurück, weint. Ach gottla, ist des ein Zeichela. Ach Gottla. An sowas muß man sich gewöhn. A bißla heiß, da stirbt me net."

harbinger of the new—calling up the dread of cultural contamination and moral corruption, the loss of social cohesion in the context of increased class and geographical mobility, and also the allure of commodity culture, upward mobility, sexual permissiveness, and an elaborate leisure industry—patriarchy is shown to operate as a bridge between economic/ideological systems, a bridge, however, that not everyone gets to cross. Patriarchy functions as a conduit that stabilizes an otherwise disruptive shift in modes of economic and ideological production, providing continuity across a historic break while also acting as a discourse in which epochal contradictions are most violently played out.

Of the play's four female characters, only two survive the first act. The second act opens in an utterly changed landscape. The ragged, derelict Father guards the field of ashes where his house once stood against the wave of modernization and prosperity that has swept over the village. Its location in the Berlin hinterland has offered profitable opportunities for many, and a supermarket chain is interested in buying up the Father's land. The male villagers are shown to have profited from reunification in various ways: the local rifle club can afford a trip to the Munich Oktoberfest, a realtor is showing off his newly buffed and surgically improved body as well as his expensive leisure equipment, and another man boasts about his affluence since renting out rooms to Berlin tourists. Economically and socially, the play seems to celebrate the arrival of modernity by indicating a linear progression from poverty and stagnation toward affluence, leisure, and instant gratification. A look at gender relations in this paradise belies this pretty picture. Gender is dramatized as the battlefield on which class and racial conflicts are fought and on which the epochal antagonisms are inscribed most violently. One rifle club member refers to his "daily war with the old woman" (36), a friend tells the Father of one woman setting fire to her husband when he cheated on her, and Lila physically attacks Siegfried. Moreover, after the first part focused on relationships among women, their disappearance from the second part of the play—with the exception of one woman's brief visit and Lila's silent presence at the end—is all the more noticeable. The field of ashes that the Father watches over serves as a memorial for his dead daughter, and through his binoculars he can see the sanitarium where the mad Mother is first kept and then taken away to be buried. When Siegfried returns with Lila and their son, he asks his Father to sell the land so that he can send the boy to a boarding school and treat Lila to a vacation—"you know how women are," he winks at his father (48). In a singular, insurgent act, Lila kills Siegfried. She refuses to be spoken for or to justify Siegfried's ruthlessness and greed. The odd threesome that camps out on the burn site—the derelict Father, Lila, and her son—seems to mark the refuse of modernization, those who will not or cannot participate in capitalism's promise of wealth and fulfillment.

Contrary to those feminist critiques that posited discourses of race and gender as analogous, and therefore assumed a solidarity between women and people of color, Specht's play, by making women pay the price for the German population's upward mobility, affluence, and first world status, accounts for the ways in which patriarchal structures sustain racial and class inequities. Specht uses Lila as a catalyst to set internal contradictions in motion but, aside from her one unexplained act of violent protest, Lila is not accorded subjectivity or agency. The end of the play slips into a somewhat sentimental, melodramatic pose, with the saintly Father and insurgent Philippina drowning in the din of technological progress.[18]

Specht's play, written in 1989–90, contributed early on to the differentiation of a feminist critique of reunification that, in pointing out that women were the "losers of the *Wende,*" eschewed the ways in which women in a "multicultural" Germany are divided along multiple axes. Specht rejects the notion that either the East/West dichotomy or gender differences are the main social fault lines in unified Germany.

Although *Lila* is remarkable for its critique of generic and political models, the Critical Volksstück, due to its built-in dualism, cannot dramatize encounters beyond the community versus outsider scenario, nor can it convey the experience of the outsider.[19] *Lila,* too, remains caught in the representational dilemma of displacing a subaltern position whenever it is depicted—the problematic conflation of *vertreten* and *darstellen* that Gayatri Spivak discusses in her seminal essay "Can the Subaltern Speak?" In having Lila react violently against Siegfried's speaking for her, Specht points to the limits of her own critical project. Yet her inability to represent race without ventriloquizing a subaltern voice produces a peculiar, secondary displacement: since Lila cannot speak, that prerogative falls to the Father whose ruminations close the play, a figure curiously outside of the discursive matrix the play maps and apparently untouched by the historical forces to which the playwright otherwise pays such meticulous attention. In his disinterested love for Lila, his belief in a harmonious future encompassing many cultures, and his respect for a past everyone else wants to forget, his voice seems to come from outside of ideology or his-

---

18. The Father's final monologue is drowned out by the sound of "traffic noises" and "the approach of mowing machines" (50).

19. One recent play by Anna Langhoff tried to go beyond these limitations by staging the interactions within a group of Eastern Europeans thrown together in a German refugee shelter. Although the play manages to decenter "German," it merely multiplies the problem of speaking for, rather than with, others.

tory but is tinged with the overtones of the Christian martyr.[20] The Father approximates the universalist, humanist subject who is empowered to articulate a critique of race, class, and gender in a manner that renders Lila, a disquietingly unpredictable, confoundingly unruly, and alarmingly violent other, obsolete.

The only production of the play at the time of this writing took place in 1990 at the Nuremberg Municipal Theater. It cast an actor of color in the role of Lila. The production visually coded the displacement of an ethnically marked outsider-position from Lila to the Father, by having him appear "naked, his body covered with color as brown as the soil" (38) on the field of ashes, as one reviewer described the scene. The reappearance of the figure of the exceptional German, typical of the fantasy of restitution that Ruth Klüger analyzed in postwar German literature about the Holocaust, is surprising in a feminist text that assigns him the mission of providing a way out of the imperialist impasse. Yet the very imperialism that is being combated comes back to haunt this production through the ethnic coding (or coating) of the Father.

V

> *The Empire Strikes Back. Good bye.*
> —Emine Sevgi Özdamar, Karagöz in Alamania

Is ethnic drag so ensconced in theatrical systems of meaning as to be seemingly impervious to leftist and feminist deconstructions? *Keloglan in Alamania* (1990), a play by Emine Sevgi Özdamar, offers a reverse appropriation of ethnic drag from a minoritarian perspective and agenda. It appropriates colonialist figures and props from European high culture and puts them to work for a cast of Turkish migrants. The text, which takes seriously the questions of ethnic difference and authenticity, manages to reveal the disavowed racial inscription in German nationality and to mark the desire for representation as well as its impossibility under present conditions.

Emine Sevgi Özdamar, better known for her prose works, such as *Mutterzunge,* a collection of short stories published in 1993, and the novel *Das Leben ist eine Karawanserei* (1992), for which she received the Bachmann Prize, has close and long-term ties to the theater as well. Trained at the acting conservatory in Istanbul, she worked as a stage and film actor, as well as a dramaturge and director. Her unpublished, little-known, and rarely performed plays *Karagöz in Alamania* (1982) and *Keloglan in Ala-*

---

20. Reviewer Manuel Brug calls him a "hermit doing penance" (37).

mania (1991) accord center stage to the experiences of Turkish migrants in Germany. Özdamar invents a dramatic hybrid that crosses the tropes and conventions of Turkish puppet theater with the political strategies of epic theater, a tradition with which she became familiar during her work as a dramaturge and assistant director to Benno Besson at the *Volksbühne* in East Berlin in the 1970s. Analogous to the often segregated experiences of male and female migrants, the plays trace the gendered axis that divides immigration procedures, residency requirements, education, work, and the home. While the earlier play, with its many untranslated Turkish passages, seems to address itself mainly to migrant audiences, *Keloglan* uses the device of a narrator/translator, the cat Tekir, to make the play accessible to people with no knowledge of Turkish. Moreover, it concerns itself with questions of citizenship vis-à-vis cultural multiplicity at a time when the former was being revised (the new, more restrictive *Ausländergesetz* took effect on 1 January 1990) and the latter redefined radically in the context of reunification. *Keloglan in Alamania* is a comedy; its pungent humor owes much to a sense of political emergency, yet it eschews confrontations along neatly defined national lines. Instead, the play not only strives to elicit solidarity with the political plight of migrants, but also sketches the outline of a coalition politics that crosses national and gender lines for a radical critique of present legal and cultural practices. Since *Keloglan* is only available as an unpublished manuscript from the Verlag der Autoren, a more detailed description is warranted.

When the curtain opens, the audience witnesses a rehearsal of Puccini's opera *Madama Butterfly* that soon ends when a break is announced and the actors leave to get something to eat. The cat Tekir then enters and launches into a comic monologue that serves as exposition for another plot and dramatic personnel, seemingly unrelated to the opera rehearsal. Tekir sums up the trials and tribulations of the youth Keloglan, who must either find work or a wife before midnight, when he turns eighteen, in order to avoid being deported. Keloglan is spurred on by his aging mother Kelkari, a former singer who now works as a cleaning woman. She confides to the audience her plan of buying a German bride for her son, and the main portion of the play chronicles their combined efforts to obtain residency and work permits for the unhappy Keloglan. With much slapstick action and many comic plot twisters, the two not only fail to make any progress toward their goal, but see their hopes and dreams recede further and further into the distance. Their fate seems sealed when robbers steal Kelkari's concert piano, her hiding place for the bridemoney. Without a job, a bride, or money, Keloglan falls into a deep sleep of exhaustion and despair. At this point, the author herself intervenes in the plot to force a reversal.

Taking recourse to the fantastic devices of the stage rather than abiding by the rules of verisimilitude, the playwright sends in a German fairy-tale forest replete with Little Red Riding Hood and the Wolf, as well as two Shakespearean elves. The elves, in midsummer night fashion, put a spell on Keloglan and Little Red Riding Hood who, upon waking up, fall in love with each other, and the happy ending is just around the corner when Kelkari retrieves her possessions and her money. She pays Red Riding Hood 5,000 DM to marry Keloglan, and the troupe lines up for the wedding chorus from—what else?—Smetana's opera *The Bartered Bride*. As the clock strikes midnight, the stage manager hands the happy couple telegrams from the Minister of Labor and the Chancellor, a gift of 100 DM, as well as the coveted residency permit, and the curtain falls.

Situated as an intermezzo to a high cultural performance, *Keloglan* calls up *Butterfly* as the supreme imperialist fantasy—the "oriental" woman dying of love for a white, Western man. Keloglan and Kelkari insert themselves into this drama, transposing it into a burlesque register and rewriting its ending. Against claims of Germany's lack, or brevity, of colonial domination, the racist myths and tropes of colonialism are shown to persist in transnational, high cultural, operatic and theatrical forms. This opera encapsulates the racist myths and figures of colonialism, which continue to exert their high cultural and hence highly subsidized powers of seduction. Rather than offering one more deconstruction of dominant discourses and evacuating racialized subject positions, however, *Keloglan* summons this apparatus for its own purposes, putting Puccini, Smetana, and Shakespeare to work for its cast of Turkish migrants.

When Kelkari first enters dressed in Butterfly costume and wig, she pushes a giant floor polisher across the stage while singing a Puccini aria. Her appearance immediately sets up a complex reference system of theatrical and social codes that rejects any simple binary relationship between "real" Turk and fictional character. As Kelkari tells her story, her oriental costume comes to signify not only the ethnicity others ascribe to her—the romanticized image of the young, tragic Asian woman—and that in a sense she always wears for the hegemonic spectator. Her tattered wig also measures Kelkari's social descent from opera diva to cleaning woman since coming to West Germany. Floor polishing and operatic singing inscribe competing yet related ethnic gestures on the same body, gestures that resonate within the disjunctive discursive field of "multiculturalism"—denoting both cultural diversity and commodification, and a racially stratified class and legal system. Kelkari is held to Butterfly's promises and deemed unworthy to partake in the economic transaction of performance at the same time. The opera, after all, is not only a place where the symbolics of race are negotiated, but also a social institution offering economic security and enormous social prestige to its employees.

By inserting a laboring, migrant body under the orientalist mask, Özdamar performs a kind of minstrel mimicry: she intervenes in the economics of exploitation that follow from the commodification of marginal subjects and claims the financial and legal profits on behalf of them.[21] However, the superimposition of two ethnic embodiments also risks collapsing the one into the other, insinuating the "realness" of Butterfly from which, Koltès's detractors argued, she can only be saved by casting a white actor in that role. Unlike Alexander Lang (or Fassbinder or Jelinek and others), Özdamar takes up the challenge of a "real" Turkish body—one that resides in a certain place or else is denied residency, that cannot eat out of fear, that threatens to hurl itself out of a window—to stage its political determinants. Yet ethnicity never comes to rest on these bodies but continues to circulate, strip, masquerade again, and change clothes one more time. In this play, a Turkish woman dresses up in "oriental" costume and wig, a wolf masquerades as a pug-dog, and a Turkish boy impersonates first a German man and then an oriental woman. Rather than attaching to bodies, Turkishness is figured through the play's references to cultural and narrative traditions and motifs—hybrid as they are in their imbrication with epic theater—and its irreverent parodying of German fairy tales and folk songs.

Despite the palpable, physical effects of ethnicity on bodies that are forced to signify, it is important to note that under her Butterfly wig Kelkari is bald, as is Keloglan. Wigs and moustaches, primary ethnic signifiers, foreground race as constructed on the body, not an essential trait inherent in it. They also underscore the performative competence of their wearers, who use them to gain access to certain roles and spaces. Moreover, subjects are shown to have, within limits, a choice of props.

Kelkari and Keloglan have opted for two distinct migrant roles, determined by gender and generational differences. Kelkari, a first-generation migrant, plays to the expectations already in place; her strategy is that of hypermarginalization, which has afforded her a modicum of economic security, at the price of her artistic aspirations as well as upward mobility. By taking the oriental mask as her form of appearance, she has consented to be commodified in the only form that accords her value.

Keloglan, on the other hand, strives for a different standard and cul-

---

21. Since *Keloglan* has rarely been performed, however, this effort might be seen to have failed— according to market rules, then, the reappropriation of commodified identities by the people who are still held to those identities has been denied. Like Keloglan, this play is refused entry into the domain of production; it's a closet drama.

tural identity: having grown up in Germany, he likes to break-dance and play with his toy robot, and he prides himself on his dj skills, mixing and matching Elvis with the Rolling Stones, the Beatles with Nina Hagen, and Grönemeyer with Pink Floyd. Identifying with the seemingly race-neutral ideals of German youth culture, and in hopes of economic security and legal recognition, Keloglan then chooses to *pass as* German: he dons a blond wig and bleached moustache and walks off to look for work.[22]

In view of the legal exhortation to assimilate to German norms, and Keloglan's competence to approximate and impersonate them, it is important to understand his failure; it provides crucial insights into the contradiction built into naturalization procedures. The law prescribes assimilation, on the one hand, and delimits it as an invasion of the constitutionally protected sphere of property, on the other.

What happens? The blond Keloglan runs into two youths in the street who masquerade as a head of lettuce and a bottle of salad dressing respectively, and who tell him that there is an opening for a carrot-impersonator. When Keloglan calls the employer and asks for work, he describes himself as a "blond Turk" whereupon the employer hangs up. The youths who report the job opening to him (mis)read the blond Keloglan as German; they are duped, attesting to Keloglan's success as a passer. To the audience who witnesses their reaction, ethnicity is thrown into relief as performative: the spectator *sees* "Germanness" *as a racialized performance* that bestows an identity and concomitant economic and legal privileges on a subject that she knows is not German. She can see the outlines of the visual regime of race that informs the dupes' perceptions; in other words, the pass does not rely on the stupidity and readerly incompetence of the duped youths. What is thrown into sharp relief is the indeterminacy of racialized identities themselves, and their failure to line up with nationality. Not every German is blond or white, nor every white person a German. Only through the pass can Özdamar make "race" show as the disavowed underpinning of national identity.

If Keloglan's impersonation is successful with the youths, why does Özdamar have him sabotage his pass to the employer by announcing himself as a blond Turk, that is, as someone who looks like, but is not, German? Özdamar weighs the supposedly liberating insight into the arbitrariness of ethnic signifiers against the stability of institutions and apparatuses that have the power to call up ethnic discourses and punish any transgressions. It is the horrendous material investment of identitarian fictions that necessitates the ever-tightening policing of ethnic differences devoid of any

---

22. Moreover, the need for this identification is written into the *Ausländergesetz*, which asks the foreign national for proof of an affinity and familiarity with German culture and values before granting naturalization.

biological certainty. The employer embodies these institutions. When Keloglan announces his transgression to her (she could not have detected it on her own), she denies him access.

In the Blondoglan scene, in which Keloglan both passes and fails, Özdamar demands access to protected identitarian positions and contests the forms of appearance under which alone this is currently possible. In other words, Keloglan should be able to impersonate a carrot without having to don the blond wig first. The evacuation of identity championed by Judith Butler and other performativity theorists marks the starting point, not the end, of Özdamar's politics. She poses the question of identity not in terms of knowledge and truth—as an epistemological problem—but in terms of material investments: as a problem of property, appropriation, and agency.

How is one to claim the protection of property—of one's own body, its labor and products, of a high-priced identity—under a law that constitutes legitimate, "natural" subjects by protecting them against "unnatural," not-naturalized ones? When Keloglan as Blondoglan claims the right "to property in his own person"—which John Locke had formulated as the first natural right of "every man" from which all others follow—"his own person" is made to refer back to the category of unnatural, invasive, threatening, and worthless subjects that "every man" must be protected against. He cannot claim a property right to his own person, because he himself is what the property of others must be protected against. That means that any not-naturalized subject's claim to property (which the pass constitutes) will constitute fraud. Hence the irreversibility of ethnic drag—its sign system remains legible only in one direction: colored signs on white ground.

Following his unsuccessful pass, the play's plot traces the gradual loss of Keloglan's means to perform within the coordinates of ethnicity and gender: his wig, his moustache, and his pants. When robbers break into his house and cannot find any valuables, they force Keloglan to defecate in a pot, since orientalist lore has it that "there is gold in every oriental household," and they are bent on extracting it from its last possible hiding place (21). Özdamar challenges the notion that masquerade plays with surfaces only; like gender, ethnicity reaches into the subject's physical and psychic depths. If the Freudian subject learns his basic lessons via the erotics of ownership and the possession of a private body through that which that body excretes—experiencing it as property that must be expended in the assurance that it will always be replenished—Keloglan is shown to own neither his body nor its products; by definition he cannot qualify as subject. At that point, Keloglan dons the Butterfly mask—the wig and costume Kelkari had left behind in her pursuit of a bride.

Butterfly and her colonial inscription, then, is revealed as the default setting for the tragic feminized colonial pining for her Western despoiler. At that moment, Keloglan—locked into the Butterfly position—seems clearly headed for tragedy. The outcome of his predicament, were this a realist play, is briefly indicated by a documentary film clip of protesting foreigners being deported. Yet the author herself intervenes in this trajectory:

> *Sounds of a type-writer and the author's voice:*
> The writer of this play could not find a timely solution to the problems of the foreign youth Keloglan. Therefore she let him fall asleep. In reality, he would have woken up in the morning and gone home, he would perhaps have had a cup of tea, the police would have come to get him, and he would have had to leave the country on the first plane. But here . . . ? (24)

Breaking with the realist regime, the characters are no longer caught in the pathos that weighs them down through the convention of ethnic drag, be it as May's tragic Winnetou, Puccini's suicidal Butterfly, or Specht's insurgent Lila. Drawing on the comic conventions of Turkish puppet theater, Kelkari and Keloglan's plight is presented with much eye-winking and silliness. The irony of the ending, in which Kelkari presents Little Red Riding Hood as the "bartered bride" to the happy Keloglan, forestalls a reading that would affirm either Kelkari's or Keloglan's strategies for rights to their own body, its integrity, and its labor; it carefully notes the mnemonic blindspots, the autoerotic vanity, and the colonialist entitlement on which the Western subject operates and that are written into constitutional law and residency applications. It also insists that the migrant subject cannot *not* claim full representation under that law. Özdamar brackets the biological truth of Turkish ethnicity and instead casts it as a *commitment* neither Kelkari nor Keloglan can afford to make under the present circumstances. The Turkishness in which the play's German personnel so firmly believe (from the robbers to the employer, all the way up to the chancellor) is marked as an impossible identity, one that under the present terms cannot even be imagined, much less practiced, figured only as that which is effaced by the double negative of Blondoglan and Butterfly.

VI

Ethnic drag in postwar German theater orchestrates power relations within discourses of nation and "race." The diverse uses and appropriations of ethnic drag for hegemonic as well as counterhegemonic endeavors, which this essay has tracked, attest to its centrality within German theater and performance. Given the often deliberately fanciful, nonreferential character of the masquerade, the usefulness of reading images of minoritarian subjects in an effort to glean information about minority cultures in Germany seems dubious. Rather, I have emphasized the *performative* dimension of ethnic drag, that is, the strategies through which theater and performance make spectators take up certain positions and actions within a national matrix. These strategies include spectatorial address, the complex process by which race is simultaneously evoked and disavowed in German discourses of nationality, and the effects of intercultural "exchange" in the absence of social and political equality—considerations that resonate forcefully within contemporary debates about citizenship, migration, and multiculturalism.

Inspired by feminist and queer accounts of drag, the masquerade of ethnic subjects offers a privileged vantage point into the processes by which a German subject fleshes out its cultural, racial, and historical contours. Feminist theory has celebrated drag as a practice that foregrounds powerful and historically weighty sociosemiotic systems as constructed rather than essential and thereby immutable, and also as a way to playfully reinterpret them. Ethnic drag, as well, provides valuable insights into nation and "race" as performative rather than organic. It also illustrates, however, the risks of deconstructing these terms. Emine Özdamar's play, while marking the colonial overdeterminations of migrant subjects and situating them entirely within the realm of artifice, suggests that a rhetoric of authenticity might still be used effectively to compel subjects to act.

Let me mention in closing that during recent years the German state theaters have slowly altered the casting practices that Koltès's critics still vehemently defended and that provided the point of departure for this essay; many ensembles now include actors of color. The shifts in the configuration of "race" and nation that this has effected are fascinating. The power relations that ethnic drag rehearses, however, will take more than casting policies to undo.

Epilogue: "Land of Truth—Enchanting Name!" Kant's Journey at Home

Willi Goetschel

Discussions of colonialism often seem to turn their topic into a question of morality. A modus of moralizing from the academic pulpit about the ills of the world, speculations about the tacit or expressed—but in any case illicit—desire of European colonialism presume that there is such a thing as a not-always-already-colonized territory, people, or body politic. Such criticism certainly can be powerful and convincing, if expressed by the "beneficiaries" of such civilizing engagement—or enterprise. The matter seems, however, a bit more problematic for the European or North American who feels called upon to succor the "natives."

Such moralizing threatens to exploit the colonial situation once more by deriving pleasure from posing masochistically (yet still authoritatively) as universal culprit. The hermeneutic circle of such a reversal ultimately asserts its hold one more time over its subjects. However, this hermeneutic circle must be broken if colonization is to be abandoned altogether. If voices that take a critical stand with regard to the colonial politics of Europe are as old as colonialism itself, there are several reasons why they have mainly gone unheeded. Most importantly, it needs to be noted that while governments have always appreciated the ornamental function and ideological reassurance of intellectual support of their politics, thinkers have been received with disinterest or hostility proportional to the critique they dared to utter. At least as long as the battle over the justifications for colonialism rages, it seems as if the debate about colonialism is bound to boil down to the simple question of the right morality, or, for that matter, the right of morality.

Kant's *Critique of Pure Reason* (1781) adds a new dimension to this debate when it exposes the paradigm of critical thinking itself as predicated upon the model of colonization. Instead of condemning or justifying this model, however, Kant exposes colonization as what necessarily takes place where knowledge is produced. Colonization of space and time, in one of the innovative insights of his *Critique,* is the precondition for the possibility of knowledge. The radical rejection of colonial politics that Kant consistently and resolutely articulates, especially in *On Perpetual Peace* (1795–96) and the *Metaphysics of Morals* (1797), is thus a result of his consistent awareness of the problematic, one could say "critical," import of colonialism. A close look at the passage in the *Critique of Pure Reason* central to our concern allows us to appreciate the key role of Kant's miniature narrative there about the Island of Truth as a constitutive element for his project of critical philosophy.

In order to appreciate the critical implications of this passage, a preliminary reflection on the role of narrative in Kant and its role within the context of the project of the critique of reason altogether is required.

Kant's Narratives

Kant built the theoretical architecture of his critiques on several foundational narratives. The groundwork as well as the operation of his critical thinking are connected to the role and function of these narratives. It may be helpful to keep in mind that, for Kant, grounding is not a constitutive concept but a metaphor whose cognitive status is tenuous and dependent on performance. In a passage that presents in its innocuous wording a rather crucial point for the conceptual framework of the *Critique of Judgment,* Kant notes that, among others, words like "ground," "foundation," and "base" operate as metaphors. They transfer the reflection about an object of intuition onto an entirely different concept to which an intuition may never correspond. Thus for Kant the project of grounding in itself implies a metaphorical slippage whose epistemic validity remains problematic. Symbolic hypotoposis or metaphors represent indirect second-order representations of concepts. Kant's critical conception of the functioning of the symbol thus points to an understanding of the metaphor as a function that, in analogy to the schematism, associates a concept with an intuition; except with the distinction that its symbolic use does so with concepts of reason rather than with concepts of understanding and therefore with concepts that do not have corresponding intuition a priori. The symbol thus rests solely on the function of reflective judgment. While schemata perform the connection between intuitions and concepts in a determinate way, the analogies of metaphors carry out a double move. First, they apply a concept to the sensible intuition, and then they apply the mere rule of reflection on an intuition to an entirely different object

(*Critique of Judgment* para. 59). As Kant formulates it, "our language [is] replete with such indirect exhibitions according to an analogy, where the expression does not contain the actual schema for the concept but contains merely a symbol for our reflection" (para. 59). Language, one could say, is, as a result, in its crucial functions a product of reflective, which in this context means aesthetic, judgment.

As a consequence, the *Critique of Judgment*'s self-referential turn to reflect its own preconditions for its grounds highlights the critical project's larger theoretical framework. The third *Critique* poses the question concerning the conditions of its own possibility. Its response is, not surprisingly, a stipulation that redefines the critical enterprise as one that is eminently self-constitutive. The grounds for its grounds, so to speak, is the faculty of judgment, which, in turn, is the theoretical description of grounding functions: that is, as aesthetic judgment. For Kant the problem of the impossibility of grounding his critique in a direct, straightforward manner represents a ubiquitous challenge, since he recognizes that any attempt at laying foundations or grounding requires, and presupposes, the symbolic use of metaphors. In this way, one could say, Kant also ungrounds his critique. The narrative moments in Kant address precisely this problem.

From the early essayistic and precritical writings (that is, the writings prior to the *Critique of Pure Reason*) to the creation of a new philosophical genre, the *Kritik,* crucial moments in the formation of Kant's philosophy are marked by the use of narratives. They serve in the precritical writings as points of departure for his philosophy.[1] In a critical move against traditional metaphysics they attempt to bring their presuppositions into the open. They point at the empirical and contingent nature of the formation of knowledge at a specific place and moment in time. As these narratives initiate the critical discourse, however, they assume constitutive importance. In this shifting to a constitutive function, the necessary and critically intended use of narratives displays its significance for Kant's endeavor. Now, Kant's goal is to seek an expository mode that transcends narrative justification. His critical point, after all, is that, unlike theory, narrative is based on contingency.

In the precritical phase the heuristic function of what might be called a theoretical narrative, that is, a narrative designed both to make possible and to reflect upon a theoretical intervention, serves as the Archimedean lever with which Kant is able to heave all metaphysics off of its foundations. In the *Critiques,* however, when Kant proceeds to design a purely

---

1. For a detailed discussion of the so-called precritical essays and the literary nature of the *Critique of Pure Reason* see Goetschel.

theoretical architecture for the formation of knowledge, these narratives become integrated into the course of the presentation of the argument. This is done in such a way that their specific narrative quality seems to become part of the theoretical argument itself.

Assimilated to the theoretical formation of the first *Critique,* they appear as part and parcel of a homogeneous discourse, emptied of its contingent contents. What was the critical lever for Kant's initial search for the new medium of his critique turns into a theoretical doctrine in the process of the realization of the *Critique.*

There are four narratives that play a central role in this process. In the *Critique of Pure Reason* we find them interwoven into the arguments and surfacing at crucial junctures and transitions. They are (1) the cosmological, (2) the autobiographical, (3) the colonial, and (4) the world-historical narratives. Yet they are not master narratives in that they authoritatively present the result of a philosophical investigation that has reached its end. Rather, they represent partial accounts that only taken together reflect upon the *Critique*'s argumentatively open and dynamic structure. Together, they create a text that seeks to replace its narrative traces with an argument free of any narrative residues. Relegated to what on the surface may appear as a merely ornamental function, these narrative moments attest to the aporia of conceiving discursive truth free of any narrative minimal structure.

In *Universal Natural History and Theory of the Heavens* (1755), with which Kant had planned to introduce himself to the public as a promising writer,[2] he presents a narrative that is to constitute the grounds on which the "I" stands. To conceive the platform necessary for any epistemological subject, some kind of cosmology is required to ground that subject's possibility somewhere in space and time. Kant provides such a platform in the form of the travelogue, an occasionally quite extravagant, fanciful, and fantastic description of an imaginary journey through outer space that assumes at times even science fiction–like qualities. The *Universal History* includes a visit to the moon and to the sun complete with the discussion of their possible inhabitants as well as the population of other planets.

This serves to establish a narrative about the constitution of the universe in order to constitute the "I" of the author of this discourse. This constitutive move can best be illustrated with a quote from this essay. Kant's almost demiurgic enthusiasm becomes epistemological when, during the course of his argument, he shifts his ground from "Give me only

---

2. Shortly after publication of this first major writing by Kant the publisher went bankrupt and his inventory was sealed. Only a few copies of Kant's *Universal Natural History and Theory of the Heavens* were distributed.

matter, I will build you a world with it" to the supplemented version: "Give me matter, I will build you a world with it! that means, give me matter, and I will show you how a world shall arise" (*WW* I: 235f.). The Archimedean point is transposed here into an epistemological argument, but this transition to the epistemological level retains the fundamental constitutive function. The formation of the universe and its planet Earth becomes, thus, literally a ground for the Kantian discourse. And its ground can only be laid by a narrative. Kant seems to recognize this when he gives his essay the title *Universal Natural History and Theory of the Heavens.* The formation of the discourse of the "I" cannot be abstracted from this kind of grounding. In a critical move against the problematic Cartesian self-constitution of the Ego by way of tautology, Kant's cosmogony suggests that the concept of the "I" cannot be thought without a narrative frame of cosmological reference. It alone, the argument implies, provides the precondition for the discourse of an "I." The motive of the *Universal Natural History and Theory of the Heavens* consists in precisely establishing this condition.

Thus the stage for the "I" is prepared, and it is not until this moment that the autobiographical narrative becomes possible. Experience, perceptions, observations, and sentiments are introduced in fragmentary form to illustrate the theoretical discourse by means of examples and applications. But, more importantly, these fragmentary autobiographical narratives serve to define the parameters of the theoretical discourse. This practice denotes an experimental method that attempts to develop a foundation of knowledge from its own basis, the philosophical self-experience of its author. This can only be brought into theoretical discourse by way of telling a story, in however abbreviated form it eventually may appear. A look at the *Observations on the Sentiment of the Beautiful and Sublime* (1764), the *Essay on the Diseases of the Head* (1764), and the *Dreams of a Spirit-Seer* (1766), as well as other precritical essays provides ample evidence. For our purpose it may suffice to note the pervasive presence of such autobiographical traces in Kant's precritical essays (see Goetschel). They function as crucial moments for the constitution of his discourse. It is their task to introduce a working notion of the "I" that is vague enough to secure the experimental character of the essays yet strong enough to make the experimental discourse possible in the first place. The fragmentary autobiographical narrative thus serves in the precritical essays to establish the framework for conceiving the epistemological subject.

When in the *Critique of Pure Reason* the new concepts of space and time are introduced as forms of pure intuitions, they might appear as empty abstractions of a formal thought process. It is significant, however, that the first chapter of the *Critique* introduces the Transcendental Aesthetics that establishes the concepts of space and time as necessary preliminaries to the Transcendental Deduction. The cosmological narrative resurfaces here, at this stage of the *Critique,* in a highly condensed version. It is boiled down to an implicit reference to a narrative that is no longer told, but tacitly presupposed and incorporated. Transferred into a terminological abbreviation, space and time have become the residues and reserves of this narrative of the "I," now exclusively imagined as the skeletal structure necessary for the epistemological process.

In view of Montaigne's project of reconnoitering his own self—a project that pushes the question of how to conceive the "I" to its philosophical extreme—and the Cartesian aporia of a tautological self-constitution of the Ego as *fundamentum inconcussum* demonstrating the difficulty of imagining the "I" as indivisible unit, Kant differentiates the "I" into an empirical and a nonempirical, transcendental "I." If the transcendental "I" accompanies all functions of thought as their necessary form of unity, this fact will necessarily show in the discourse. The double function of the "I" consists on the one hand in the apperceptive activity of knowledge production and on the other hand in forming a discourse about this knowledge production. The autobiographical narrative of the precritical writings addresses exactly this difficulty. There the empirical and the transcendental "I" have not yet fully and clearly emerged as differentiated concepts. The attempt to solve this problem is the underlying motive that makes the use of autobiographical elements necessary in order to create discursive means for the possibility of propelling the differentiation of the "I." The extraordinary difficulty of the Transcendental Deduction reflects the circularity of this differentiation into an empirical and a transcendental form of the "I" as the crucial presupposition for its discursification. The aporia of introducing an "I" that already presupposes such differentiation to prepare the stage for enacting the discourse of the "I" requires the idea of the unity of apperception for its discursive precondition. Screened for its narrative components, the Transcendental Deduction can thus be understood as a highly encoded narrative of the "I." The radical and complicated interwoven process of this narrative is transformed into a theoretical discourse that accounts for the extreme resistance the Deduction exerts against all attempts to translate it into a transparent and simple logic.

The cosmological and the autobiographical narratives are intimately connected. Its classic formulation in the celebrated conclusion of the *Critique of Practical Reason* is expressed with the celebrated phrase "The starry sky above me, and the moral law within me" ("Der bestirnte Himmel über mir, und das moralische Gesetz in mir"). We might call this the crystallized version of the cosmological-autobiographical narrative. And it seems only appropriate that these words have been inscribed in stone on Kant's grave.

The fact of reason (*Factum der Vernunft*) is therefore intimately tied to narrative. Ultimately, propositional assertions cannot constitute themselves. They are always already based on narrative. Kant's critical, or more precisely, transcendental-critical turn attempts the integration of this insight in his precritical essays. As he proceeds to the realization of the architecture of the critique, the theoretical results of this development become building blocks for his critical enterprise. But this takes place at the expense of the disavowal of their intrinsic narrative nature. As Kant recasts his critical philosophical discourse in a new form as methodologically self-reflective procedure, all narrative must become reconstituted within the format of the *Critique*. This means that the critical status of narrative is now at risk of being sacrificed. Reduced to serving as a functional element in the display of the critical discourse, the narrative moment in the formation of the *Critique* is abandoned for a presumably strictly autonomous theoretical self-constitution. The difference between the programmatic declaration and the discursive realization of this claim exposes the problematic nature of the constitution and therefore of the legitimation of Kant's critical project. To discuss this point, two other narratives, the colonial and the world-historical, mentioned previously, must now be examined.

The Island of Truth

It has often been noted that there is a whole complex of seafaring imagery at work in the *Critique* (Garelli). Seafaring is an allegory of long standing (or, rather, floating) in the history of philosophy. And although the elements of that allegorical complex might recall the *Odyssey,* the structure of the exploration and discovery narrative in Kant departs a great deal from the circular (or, alternatively, spiral) progress in the story of Odysseus's homecoming. Odysseus undergoes rites of passage to prepare for his return. In the modern world of newly discovered continents, however, the explorer's and discoverer's account takes a different course. Whereas Odysseus's journey is a tale of visitation where the hero finds himself subject to the fixed rules and mores of the places he visits and where the law of hospitality represents the order of cosmos, the story of the emerging capitalist universe is one of expansion and annexing. For that story shapes its discoveries in the image of the discoverer. It is the fiction of the uncolonized land that awaits its cultivation, the tabula rasa of plain matter, immaculate nature, and virgin land ready for, even yearning for, conquest, occupation, and civilization.[3] For Kant, the colonial narrative works much in the same way that his other narratives work. It is not meant to serve as a fig leaf to cover up a deficit in theory, but designed instead as a clarification device to recapitulate his argument in a transparent way.

However, a close look at Kant's colonial narrative shows that the narrative undermines the discourse it advances. The sheer length and complicated imagery as well as the imaginary power of the passage comprise an overdetermined narrative complex that deviates in astounding ways from the discursive flow of the *Critique*. The passage presents a coming together of the crucial motives of the critical project. It comes at the end of the analytic part of the *Critique of Pure Reason* that Kant prepares for the transition to the dialectic part. Notice that the excursion report starts with us already standing on the Island of Truth. With the narrator already positioned on the island, the narrative takes an unusual turn. But then, this might not necessarily appear so far-fetched, at least for one writing on another island. And certainly, Manhattan once was, if no Tahiti—the paradigm for most eighteenth-century island fantasies—nevertheless an enticing and beautiful place.[4]

> We have now not merely explored the territory of pure understanding, and carefully surveyed every part of it, but have also measured its extent, and assigned to everything in its rightful place. This domain is an island, enclosed by nature itself within unalterable limits. It is the land of truth—enchanting name!—surrounded by a wide and stormy ocean, the native home of illusion, where many a fog bank and many a swiftly melting iceberg give the deceptive appearance of farther shores, deluding the adventurous seafarer ever anew with empty hopes, and engaging him in enterprises which he can never abandon and yet is unable to carry to completion. Before we venture on this sea, to explore it in all directions and to obtain assurance whether there be any ground for such hopes, it will be well to begin by casting a glance upon the map of the land which we are about to leave, and to

---

3. On the dialectics of imagination involved with the occupation of islands see the discussions that have recently emerged around Shakespeare's *The Tempest* and Defoe's *Robinson Crusoe*. For Shakespeare see Nixon and Fernández Retamar; for *The Tempest, Robinson Crusoe,* and additional literary sources see Hulme (*Colonial Encounters*). Taking the clue from Shakespeare's play, discussions often focus on the relationship between Prospero and Caliban. It seems, however, decisive that the first occupant of the island is neither one, but Caliban's mother, "the foul witch Sycorax" (I.2 verse 258). The silent third, then, not only is the mother but emphatically so: the witch whose name contains the name of the sow, a matriarchal symbol for fertility.

4. For a different reading of the Island of Truth passage see Le Doeuff (8f). I thank Susan Shapiro for this reference.

enquire, first, whether we cannot in any case be satisfied with what it contains—are not, indeed, under compulsion to be satisfied, inasmuch as there may be no other territory upon which we can settle; and, secondly, by what title we possess even this domain, and can consider ourselves as secured against all opposing claims. (*Critique of Pure Reason* 257)

The remarkable news of this passage—and a logical consequence of the transcendental-critical vantage point—is that colonization is what we are always already doing when we set out to determine the grounds and limits of reason. Colonization, Kant's narrative illustrates, takes place the moment our epistemological subject acts, that is, produces knowledge. Knowledge is a result of colonization; it takes colonization as its model, even if, and especially if, it aims to be critical of its own procedural ramifications. The enterprise of the critique of reason by itself tacitly implicates what is spelled out only at this juncture in the *Critique:* that the scientific and philosophical production of knowledge can only operate within the limits of an epistemic model that takes as its model the colonization of the world (of experience). Using the discourse of colonization to describe the production of knowledge, Kant flushes out the inner tensions of this discourse. Transposed into the framework of critique, those tensions and contradictions highlight not only the project of critique but expose also the epistemological aporia that haunt the discourse of colonization.

It seems as if, then, colonization were to follow the model of a certain type of cognition. The critical potential seems to consist exactly in opening this perspective that Kant's narrative of the island appears to offer. In a way, the little narrative about the Island of Truth sends us back to other passages in Kant where the imagery of islands and their surrounding waters emerges as a recurrent motif. The ocean of learning, the floods of publications, and the question of directing the flooding and navigating the waters indicate the close affinity of travel by water and the epistemological process in Kant. In his *Observations on the Feeling of the Beautiful and the Sublime* (1764), there are two short passages that, read together with the *Critique*'s island narrative, illustrate the central role that land/water imagery plays in Kant. Lamenting the uncontrolled growth of book production that had, indeed, exponentially exploded in Kant's life time, he notes:

Among the damages incurred by the deluge of books that annually floods our part of the world a not insignificant one is that the really useful volumes that now and again float by on the wide ocean of book-learning are overlooked and must share the fate of perishing with other chaff. (*WW* II: 42)

The use of the hydrokinetic motif returns in the context of the self-regulatory mechanism books and rivers have in common. Censorship, like the artificial construction of dikes, is futile in the face of the forces of nature, or those of the mind, for that matter. Kant's stress on the self-regulatory role of water constructing its own banks is also a comment on the hydrokinetic-like dynamics of the book trade. But the hydrokinetic metaphor also attests to Kant's reserved noninterventionism with regard to a critically comprehended order of nature:

> From now on, no books at all are to be forbidden: that is the single means by which they will eliminate themselves. We have now reached the turning point. Rivers form their own banks on their own if we allow them to flood. The dikes we set against them only serve to make their devastations unceasing. The authors of useless products have as their excuse the injustice of others before them. (*WW* II: 105)

These images assume sharper contours if read in the context of a remark written between 1776 and 1778, when Kant was well on his way to the *Critique*. In a striking image, Kant visualizes the switching of positions with regard to claims on property at the moment land is taken. The instantaneous reversal that takes place in such an action marks an exchange of intentional direction whose epistemological critical implications are not lost on Kant:

> The usual scholastic and doctrinal method of metaphysics stupefies, by effecting a mechanical thoroughness. It constricts the understanding and renders it incapable of accepting instruction; it is not philosophy. Critique, in contrast, expands the concepts and frees up reason. Scholastic philosophers go at it like pirates, who, the moment they set foot on an unoccupied shore, entrench themselves immediately. (Reflexion no. 5089, *Werke* 18: 84)[5]

If pirating is an adventurous occupation, Kant implies, it is one that ultimately turns against itself, especially in the case of "success." Kant's resistance to travel comes to mind here as a refusal to engage in an intellectually dubious adventure that promises experience but, eventually, just stages one's self-fulfilling projection. Taking possession requires or rather

---

5. English translation by Eric Schwab in Goetschel, *Constituting Critique* (119).

produces a discursive shutdown that arrests the discourse, if just for an instant, as it institutes property, that is, the process of taking possession claims to be based on a title that reflects the status quo that it, in fact, has just created, or else changed from a former property regime into another, new arrangement. As Carol Rose so succinctly puts it: "The metaphor of the law of first possession is, after all, death and transfiguration" (*Property* 20). Or as Herman Melville said, we cannot have "our fish both loose and fast" (quoted in Rose 20).

As Kant ridicules the scholastic philosophers' possessive pirate romanticism that picks some island of competence in order to claim it for themselves, he illustrates that the action of taking first possession implies the performance of a paradoxical operation based on a double movement. The trick is to treat this action as if the paradox did not exist but, instead, would represent plain logic—though it be the logic of force. Now, Kant's point is that such practice occurs also in the field of metaphysics. Where titles and entitlements are claimed, his comment suggests, there is always a narrative hidden. This is no accident, for "classic property theory itself has a kind of explanatory glitch" (Rose 27) as Rose expresses it: "The existence of a property regime is not in the least predictable from a starting point of rational self-interest; and consequently, from that perspective, property needs a tale, a story, a post hoc explanation" (38). And more often than not, it may be one that seeks to cover its own blind spot with sheer power and brute force.

If we now return to the Island of Truth in the *Critique of Pure Reason*, its narrative emerges more clearly as a kind of counternarrative. In another context, Kant himself speaks at some point of the poetic imagination of a golden age, of the longing that makes the likes of Robinson and the journeys to the South Sea islands so enticing for those disgusted by civilization ("Mutmaßlicher Anfang der Menschengeschichte" [*WW* XI: 101]). But in the light of enthusiastic reports about the lush and seductive beauty of the newly discovered South Sea islands, the *Critique*'s depiction of the stormy ocean where icebergs and fog banks dominate the scene takes on a rather stark appearance. In 1777, Georg Forster[6] had published *A Voyage round the World* in which he told the story of his trip accompanying Captain Cook on his second journey (1772–75). Published in German in 1778 through 1780, Forster's account became the most important source for the German knowledge of the South Seas (Brunner 120). Its account of the arrival at Tahiti is the more telling when compared to the somber mood in Kant's depiction of the Island of Truth's sorry weather

---

6. Forster was himself an avid reader of Kant who later on involved Kant in a polemical exchange. See Kant (*Briefwechsel* 483).

conditions. In Forster, Tahiti's climate is mild and lush, the island beautifully seductive (see Brunner 121). And so are the people—at least to another visitor, Bougainville, and even more so to Diderot, whose characters are deeply impressed by Bougainville's travelogue. Yet Diderot's *Supplément au voyage de Bougainville* poses in a self-conscious fashion the same epistemological question that the *Critique* systematically addresses. While Diderot gives free rein to his libertine sexual fantasies, he nevertheless indicates the fictional predicament any discussion of islands such as Tahiti poses: the aporia that we only see what we imagine we see. The consequence is that our conceptual tools determine the way, the language, in which the islands talk back. For translation, and this means transference, is always already presupposed even ironically in written form. This, at least, is what we learn from one of the interlocutors in Diderot's *Supplément:* "Just think that this is a translation from the Tahitian language into Spanish, and from Spanish into French. The old man went for the night to Orou whom he had called out to and in whose house the use of Spanish had been preserved from times immemorial. Orou had written in Spanish the complaints of the old man; and Bougainville had recorded a copy during the delivery by the old man."[7] How the old chieftain, who himself apparently does not know any European language, knows how to read the prepared text—and whose text would that be anyway?—is just one of the little complications Diderot throws in the reader's way. How a native from the island would be able to read a text from a manuscript whose alphabet he would not be familiar with and in a language he did not know remains unexplained. Yet rather than a slippage, one might suspect Diderot of playing with the fact that the aporetic adventure of translation resists a simple resolution.

In the *Critique,* the story of the Island of Truth marks the point of transition between the Transcendental Analytic and Dialectic—the focal point between phenomena and noumena, that is, appearances and things in themselves. This was quite literally the crucial "passage" in the Transcendental Doctrine of Elements, the *Critique*'s first part. The considerably shorter, second part—a quarter the length of the first—is called the Transcendental Doctrine of Method. This, Kant's "supplement" to the narrative of the island of truth, complements the earlier "passage." Here, in the concluding part of the *Critique,* firmly settled, as it were, on the island's ground, Kant resumes the metaphor of building with material the

---

7. "Pensez donc que c'est une traduction du tahitien en espagnol, et de l'espagnol en français. [Le vieillard] s'était rendu, la nuit, chez cet Orou qu'il a interpellé, et dans la case duquel l'usage de la langue espagnole s'était conservé de temps immémorial. Orou avait écrit en espagnol la harangue du vieillard; et Bougainville en avait une copie à la main, tandis que le Tahitien la prononçait" (*Oeuvres philosophiques* 472f.).

Transcendental Doctrine of Elements examined and determined to be fit. While the supply of the building material that passed such inspection would just make it possible to erect a house to live in comfortably, the original dreams of a grand tower reaching for the sky must be abandoned:

> We have found indeed that although we had contemplated building a tower which should reach the heavens, the supply of materials suffices only for a dwelling-house, just sufficiently commodious for our business on the level of experience, and just sufficiently high to allow of our overlooking it. The bold undertaking that we had designed is thus bound to fail through lack of material—not to mention the babel of tongues, which inevitably gives rise to disputes among the workers in regard to the plan to be followed, and which must end by scattering them over all the world, leaving each to erect a separate building for himself, according to his own design. (*Critique of Pure Reason* 573: A 707/B 735)

If it is primarily the lack of material that keeps the project from its realization, another no less important reason is named, if only in passing. Yet the quick reminder of the biblical story of the tower of Babel contains more than one might suspect. If *Sprachverwirrung* denotes both linguistic confusion and confusion between languages, unavoidably splitting the workers over the design, it also disperses them all over the world. And here Kant adds a little additional clause to the effect that each would so cultivate his/her spot of land according to his/her own plan.

The fourth narrative operative in Kant's *Critique* is the universal- or world-historical narrative, which in some ways is closely related to the question of colonialism. For any teleological view of historical development poses the question of some kind of interaction that might be viewed in terms of colonization. To the degree that the idea of a universal world history implies some model of how to imagine the world as one, such a vision presupposes the need for political and cultural transfer. The line, however, between such mediation and colonialism is tenuous and difficult to hold if such a distinction is even possible at all. The concluding chapter of the *Critique* is called "The History of Pure Reason." So, at the end of the long and winding course of a critical revision of reason's faculties, the *Critique* concludes with a contextualization of its project within the history of philosophy (and more specifically, of Kant's history of philosophy). Henceforth, as Kant's famous verdict puts it, the critical road alone remains open. The *Critique of Judgment* addresses the question of teleology as *the* systematic problem created by the first two critiques. It is perhaps most clearly in the problem of teleology that the role of narrative for critical thought emerges as the blind spot whose implications can no longer be ignored. To make a world-historical narrative short, its relevance in Kant's thought is stressed in his writings on the philosophy of history. Not only are his philosophical-historical thoughts closely connected to the project of the critique, but it becomes clear that the minimal structure of a universal-historical perspective seems necessary to provide the critical project with a sense of direction that even transcendental idealists need in order to be able to fill a formula like the categorical imperative in a meaningful way.

Conclusion

In his later writings, Kant leaves no doubt where his sympathies lie. His unequivocal condemnation of any kind of rationalization of colonialist claims remains firm and allows for no compromise. In his *On Perpetual Peace* he flatly states that by virtue of "the common property of the surface of the earth," on which nobody has more rights than any other to be on a specific spot, a "visitation right" must be assumed with all the ensuing duties of a guest's behavior. However, if this right is abused and its code violated, Kant maintains, visitors are rightly denied access to foreign markets. China and Japan are commended for having restricted access to their countries by Western visitors precisely for this reason. Kant also does not let pass the chance to point to the ultimately inefficient economic production form colonialism represents (*WW* XI: 214–16; see Cavallar). Two years later, in his *Metaphysics of Morals,* Kant challenges Locke's theory of property. For Kant, labor as such, whether in the form of cultivation or simply the erecting of fences or another kind of demarcation, does not constitute the title to land. Rather, he argues, there is no property outside the civil state, whose contractual fiction establishes the necessary framework for the notion of private property (see Ulemann 549–55). In the state of nature, however, there is only a provisory, fictional entitlement to property. For property can only be assumed under the fiction of a universal civil state; and this, by implication, runs counter to colonialist exploitation (*Metaphysics of Morals* para. 15). In a staging of the question of what makes a contract—a staging that, in its obvious failing to demonstrate the inner logic of the concept of contract, betrays a good moment of slapstick—Kant demonstrates that there is a moment that remains irreducible to empirical explanation. This is the "glitch" Rose refers to (27), the sudden switch that occurs at the moment property is claimed and a contractual agreement is instituted. As Kant's comment illustrates, instituting a contract does not take place on empirical grounds alone. Its nonempirical character points to the transcendental framework the contract presupposes. The constitutive legal act of transfer of claims implies a transcendental moment, and the action of taking first possession presupposes a valid transfer from the whole of humanity's claim unto one's own title. Kant's insight consists in the stress on the not-altogether-trivial fact that this operation attests to the rather intricate structure of the concept of property (*WW* VIII: para. 19).[8]

Kant's theory of property, contrary to Locke's, operates therefore with the argument of a universal human right of all to all territory. This transcendental move introduces a fictional element into the discussion of property that effectively exposes a problematic moral moment in Locke's concept of property, based on a work ethic (see Rose 27). In this respect, Kant's stand remains uncompromising: any legitimation of property hinges on the fact that it is a result of arrangements made by contract, and this, in turn, means within the framework of a civil state of society. As Kant conceives the civil state, it is not exclusive but includes all that are involved in its consequences. As a result, according to Kant (and already according to Rousseau), no one can any longer be thought of as living in the state of nature. Natives, therefore, cannot be excluded, but are legitimate claimants the moment claims are made on their land. Colonizers can only lay claim insofar as they engage in a contract that not only negotiates with those present on the land they wish to take, but is based on the transcendental assumption that all land and water were originally the property of all of humanity. This effectively rules out any form of appropriation that excludes the rest of humanity—whether they are present on a specific piece of land or not. Kant rigorously rejects any attempt to justify occupation of land in any other way. He argues that what cannot be conceived of as happening in the civil state—that is, subjection to others' interests and exploitation—lacks a rational framework. Where there is no civil state, but where the presumed or actual absence of contractual agreements rules, one would, instead, have to speak of it as a situation still in the state of nature.

The crucial point is not so much Kant's categorical denunciation of colonialism, but rather the way he addresses the issue as a principal problem of knowledge production rather than merely one of morality. The point of the *Critique of Pure Reason* can, in this context, be taken in two ways. The *Critique* can be read as a problematic text that brings colonialism to its conceptual expression. But it can also be seen as a critical way to rethink the colonial pattern that informs European thinking even in its least expected aspect, its epistemological critique. As such, it reflects on the conditions of the epistemological project as intrinsically problematic in its

---

8. Paragraph 17 discusses the original common property of all territories. On the precarious notion of what exactly all available land means from the point of physical geography, see Kant's *Geographische und andere naturwissenschaftliche Schriften.*

colonizing moment. In the application of the critique to itself, Kant anticipates to a certain degree much of what contemporary Western critique owes the colonized as well as to itself. In this, as in so many other ways, the outcome of a rigorous critique of Kant depends on the manner in which we fashion our reading of his project. There are good reasons to assume that this project was designed not so much to moralize about the ills of colonialism, imperialism, and exploitation, which were for Kant just different criminal forms of the same disregard of humanity. Instead Kant's philosophical project exposes like no other critique the implications that any grounding of an autonomy of thought faces. Implicated in an infinite regress of legitimation whose end remains contingent and arbitrary, both the production of knowledge and its critique move in territory that is never uncontested. To deny this, Kant's analysis suggests, is itself a form of colonization that is problematic from its very start. The best Kant seems able to offer is to keep critical reflection of this fact awake and resistant against any discursive shutdown.

The "blind spot," that is, the ambiguous state of that enticing Island of Truth and Reason, is then not so much Kant's but ours. The mini-narrative of the critique, to colonize that island, not only implicates all critical activity, but describes as well the only grounds on which we can stand. To pretend there is more would mean to cheerfully head for the high sea of dialectics. And this is exactly what Kant warns against—in the name of critique.

Bibliography

Achelis, T. *Moderne Völkerkunde, deren Entwicklung und Aufgaben.* Stuttgart: Encke, 1896.
Adelson, Leslie. *Making Bodies, Making History: Feminism and German Identity.* Lincoln: U of Nebraska P, 1993.
———. "Migrants' Literature or German Literature? TORKAN's *Tufan: Brief an einen islamischen Bruder.*" *German Quarterly* 63 (1990): 382–89.
———. "There's No Place Like Home: Jeannette Lander and Ronnith Neumann's Utopian Quests for Jewish Identity in the Contemporary West German Context." *New German Critique* 50 (1990): 113–34.
Albrecht, Gerd. *Der Film im 3. Reich.* Karlsruhe: DOKU, 1979.
"Alle hassen die Zigeuner." *Der Spiegel* 3 Sept. 1990: 34–57.
Amman, Ludwig. *Östliche Spiegel: Ansichten vom Orient im Zeitalter seiner Entdeckung durch den deutschen Leser 1800–1850.* Hildesheim: Olms, 1989.
Anderson, Benedict. *Imagined Communities: Reflections on the Origin and Spread of Nationalism.* 1983. Rev. ed. London: Verso, 1991.
Angress, Ruth Klüger. "Gibt es ein 'Judenproblem' in der deutschen Nachkriegsliteratur?" *Neue Sammlung* 1:26 (1986): 22–40.
Appiah, K. Anthony. "Race." *Critical Terms for Literary Study.* Ed. Frank Lentriccia and Thomas McLaughlin. Chicago: U of Chicago P, 1990. 274–87.
Arendt, Hannah. *The Origins of Totalitarianism.* 1951. 2d ed. New York: Harcourt Brace Jovanovich, 1973.
Das Argument. "Postkoloniale Kritik." 38.3 (1996).
Arnold, H. *Die Zigeuner: Herkunft und Leben im deutschen Sprachgebiet.* Freiburg: Olten, 1965.
Ascher, Saul. *Die Germanomanie.* Flugschrift, 1815.
Aschheim, Steven. *Brothers and Strangers: The East European Jew in German and German Jewish Consciousness, 1800–1923.* Madison: U of Wisconsin P, 1982.
Ashcroft, Bill, Gareth Griffiths, and Helen Tiffin, eds. *The Post-Colonial Reader.* London: Routledge, 1995.
Das Ausland: Überschau der neuesten Forschungen auf dem Gebiete der Natur-, Erd- und Völkerkunde. Ed. Friedrich von Hellwald. Stuttgart: Cotta, 1878.
Bachmann, Ingeborg. Ms. 454. Vienna: Nationalbibliothek.
———. *"Todesarten"-Projekt: Kritische Ausgabe.* Ed. Robert Pichl, Monika Albrecht, and Dirk Göttsche. 4 vols. Munich: Piper, 1995.
———. *Werke.* Ed. Christine Koschel, Inge von Weidenbaum, and Clemens Münster. 4 vols. Munich: Piper, 1982.

———. *Wir müssen wahre Sätze finden: Gespräche und Interviews.* Ed. Christine Koschel and Inge von Weidenbaum. Munich: Piper, 1983.
Bader, Wolfgang, and Janos Riesz, eds. *Literatur und Kolonialismus I: Die Verarbeitung der kolonialen Expansion in der europäischen Literatur.* Bayreuther Beiträge zur Literaturwissenschaft 4. Frankfurt am Main: Lang, 1983.
Balibar, Etienne. "Racism and Nationalism." *Race, Nation, Class: Ambiguous Identities.* Ed. Etienne Balibar and Immanuel Wallerstein. Tr. Chris Turner. London and New York: Verso, 1991. 37–67.
Bartels, Adolf. "Heimatkunst." *Heimat: Blätter für Literatur und Volkstum* 1.1 (1900): 1–20.
Barth, Ariane. "Hier steht eine Giftsuppe auf." *Der Spiegel* 14 Oct. 1991: 118–43.
Bathrick, David. "Cultural Studies." *Introduction to Scholarship in the Modern Languages and Literatures.* Ed. Joseph Gibaldi. 2d ed. New York: MLA, 1992. 320–40.
———. *The Powers of Speech: The Politics of Culture in the GDR.* Lincoln: U of Nebraska P, 1995.
Baumgart, Winfried. "German Imperialism in Historical Perspective." Knoll and Gann. 151–64.
Behdad, Ali. *Belated Travelers: Orientalism in the Age of Colonial Dissolution.* Durham: Duke UP, 1994.
Benjamin, Walter. *Illuminations.* Ed. Hannah Arendt. Tr. Harry Zohn. New York: Schocken, 1969.
———. "The Storyteller. Reflections on the Works of Nikolai Leskov." *Illuminations.* Tr. Harry Zohn. New York: Schocken, 1968. 83–109.
Benveniste, Émile. *Problèmes de linguistique générale.* Paris: Gallimard, 1966.
Berger, Peter L., and Thomas Luckmann. *The Social Construction of Reality.* Garden City, N.Y.: Doubleday, 1966.
Bergmann, Peter. *Nietzsche: The Last Antipolitical German.* Bloomington: Indiana UP, 1987.
Bergner, Gwen. "Who Is That Masked Woman? or, The Role of Gender in Fanon's *Black Skin, White Masks.*" *PMLA* 110.1 (Jan. 1995): 75–88.
Berman, Nina. *Orientalismus, Kolonialismus und Moderne: Zum Bild des Orients in der deutschen Kultur um 1900.* Stuttgart: Metzler, 1997.
Berman, Russell A. *The Rise of the Modern German Novel: Crisis and Charisma.* Cambridge: Harvard UP, 1986.
Beste, Konrad. *Das heidnische Dorf.* Berlin: Vier Falken, 1932.
Bhabha, Homi. "DissemiNation: Time, Narrative and the Margins of the Modern Nation." *The Location of Culture.* 139–70.
———. *The Location of Culture.* New York: Routledge, 1994.
———, ed. *Nation and Narration.* London: Routledge, 1990.
———. "Of Mimicry and Man: The Ambivalence of Colonial Discourse." 1987. *The Location of Culture.* 85–92.
———. "The Other Question: Stereotype, Discrimination and the Discourse of Colonialism." 1992. *The Location of Culture.* 66–84.
———. "Postcolonial Criticism." *Redrawing the Boundaries: The Transformation*

of English and American Literary Studies. Ed. Stephen Greenblatt and Giles Gunn. New York: MLA, 1992. 437–65.

———. "Signs Taken for Wonders: Questions of Ambivalence and Authority Under a Tree Outside Delhi, May 1817." 1985. *The Location of Culture.* 102–22.

Birken, Andreas. *Die Wirtschaftsbeziehungen zwischen Europa und dem Vorderen Orient im ausgehenden 19. Jahrhundert.* Wiesbaden: Reichert, 1980.

Bitterli, Urs. *Conrad—Malraux—Greene—Weiss: Schriftsteller und Kolonialismus.* Zurich: Benzinger, 1973.

Bley, Helmut. *South-West Africa under German Rule 1894–1914.* Tr. Hugh Ridley. London: Heinemann, 1971; Evanston: Northwestern UP, 1971.

Bloch, Ernst. *Erbschaft dieser Zeit.* Ca. 1962. Frankfurt am Main: Suhrkamp, 1985.

Blumenberg, Hans. "Wirklichkeitsbegriff und Wirkungspotential des Mythos." *Terror und Spiel: Probleme der Mythenrezeption.* Poetik und Hermeneutik IV. Ed. Manfred Fuhrmann. Munich: Fink, 1971. 11–66.

Bowyer, Alan. "'Narrating the Nation': Homi Bhabha and Gustav Frenssen." *Journal of Literary Studies* 9. 314 (Dec. 1993): 250–65.

Brantlinger, Patrick. "Victorians and Africans: The Genealogy of the Myth of the Dark Continent." *"Race," Writing, and Difference.* Ed. Henry Louis Gates Jr. Chicago: U of Chicago P, 1986. 185–222.

Braun, Christoph. *Carl Einstein: Zwischen Ästhetik und Anarchismus: Zu Leben und Werk eines expressionistischen Schriftstellers.* Munich: iudicium, 1987.

Braun, Georg. *Zur Frage der Rechtsgültigkeit der Mischehen in den deutschen Schutzgebieten.* Diss. U Greifswald, 1912.

Braun, Michael. "Perspektive und Geschichte in Christoph Heins Roman 'Horns Ende.'" *Wirkendes Wort* 42.1 (Apr. 1992): 93–102.

Brennan, Timothy. "The National Longing for Form." *Nation and Narration.* Ed. Homi K. Bhabha. London: Routledge, 1990. 44–71.

Brenner, Michael. *The Renaissance of Jewish Culture in Weimar Germany.* New Haven: Yale UP, 1996.

Bridgman, Jon M. *The Revolt of the Hereros.* Berkeley: U of California P, 1981.

Bröck, Sabine. "Do White Ladies Get the Blues? Nancy Cunard and Desire." Unpublished manuscript.

Brockhaus Enzyklopädie. 17th ed. Vol. 7. Wiesbaden: Brockhaus, 1969.

Brockhaus' Konversations-Lexikon. 14th ed. Vol. 12. Berlin and Vienna: Brockhaus, 1898.

Bronfen, Elisabeth. "Entortung und Identität: Ein Thema der modernen Exilliteratur." *Germanic Review* 69 (1994): 70–78.

Brug, Manuel. "Moritaten, Mordtaten." *Theater heute* 32 (Feb. 1991): 37.

Brunner, Horst. *Die poetische Insel: Insel und Inselvorstellungen in der deutschen Literatur.* Stuttgart: Metzler, 1967.

Bulmahn, Heinz. "Christoph Hein's *Horns Ende:* Historical Revisionism—A Process of Renewal." *Studies in Twentieth-Century Literature* 15.2 (summer 1991): 247–62.

Bülow, Frieda von. *Im Lande der Verheißung: Ein Kolonialroman um Carl Peters.* 1899. Dresden: Carl Reißner, 1914.

———. *Der Konsul: Vaterländischer Roman aus unseren Tagen.* Berlin: Fontane, 1891.

Bürger, Peter. *Theory of the Avant-Garde.* Tr. Michael Shaw. Minneapolis: U of Minnesota P, 1984.

Campt, Tina. *'Afro-German': The Convergence of Race, Sexuality and Gender in the Formation of a German Ethnic Identity, 1919–1960.* Diss. Cornell U, 1996.

Carby, Hazel. "The Multicultural Wars." *Black Popular Culture: A Project by Michele Wallace.* Ed. Gina Dent. Seattle: Bay Press, 1992. 187–99.

Case, Sue-Ellen. *Feminism and Theatre.* New York: Methuen, 1988.

———. "Towards a Butch–Femme Aesthetic." *Discourse* 11.1 (fall/winter 1988–89): 55–73.

Cavallar, Georg. *Pax Kantiana: Systematisch-historische Untersuchung des Entwurfs "Zum ewigen Frieden" (1795) von Immanuel Kant.* Vienna: Böhlau, 1992.

Centre national de la recherche scientifique. *Trésor de la Langue Française.* Paris: Gallimard, 1986.

Chickering, Roger. *We Men Who Feel Most German: A Cultural Study of the Pan-German League, 1886–1914.* London: Allen and Unwin, 1984.

Chow, Rey. *Writing Diaspora: Tactics of Intervention in Contemporary Cultural Studies.* Bloomington: Indiana U P, 1993.

Christoph Hein: Texte, Daten, Bilder. Ed. Lothar Baier. Frankfurt am Main: Luchterhand, 1990.

Chronist ohne Botschaft: Christoph Hein. Ein Arbeitsbuch: Materialien, Auskünfte, Bibliographie. Ed. Klaus Hammer. Berlin: Aufbau, 1992.

Clifford, James. *The Predicament of Culture.* Cambridge: Harvard UP, 1988.

Clifford, James, and George Marcus. *Writing Culture: The Poetics and Politics of Ethnography.* Berkeley: U of California P, 1986.

Cocalis, Susan. "The Politics of Brutality: Toward a Definition of the Critical Volksstück." *The Divided Home/Land.* Ed. Sue-Ellen Case. Ann Arbor: U of Michigan P, 1992. 106–30.

Collits, Terry. "Theorizing Racism." *De-Scribing Empire.* Ed. Chris Tiffin and Alan Lawson. New York: Routledge, 1994. 61–69.

Colonial Discourse and Post-Colonial Theory: A Reader. Ed. Patrick Williams and Laura Chrisman. New York: Columbia UP, 1994.

Condorcet, Antoine Marquis de. *Esquisse d'un tableau historique des progrès de l'esprit humain.* Paris: Librairie de Brissot-Thivars, 1795.

Craig, Gordon. *The Politics of the Prussian Army 1640–1945.* New York: Oxford UP, 1955.

Crowhurst-Bond, Griseldis W. "Volk ohne Raum: Landschaft und Raum bei Hans Grimm." *Acta Germanica: Jahrbuch des Germanistenverbandes im Südlichen Afrika* 17 (1984): 143–57.

Debrunner, Hans-Werner. *Presence and Prestige: Africans in Europe. A History of Africans in Europe before 1918.* Basel: Basler Afrika Bibliographien, 1979.

Dedering, Tilman. "The German–Herero War of 1904: Revisionism of Genocide

or Imaginary Historiography." *Journal of Southern African Studies* 10.1 (Mar. 1993): 80–88.
Delany, Samuel R. "Twilight in the Rue Morgue." Rev. of *Primate Visions: Gender, Race and Nature in the World of Modern Science and Simians, Cyborgs and Women,* by Donna Haraway. *Transition* 54 (1991): 36–57.
Deleuze, Gilles, and Félix Guattari. *A Thousand Plateaus: Capitalism and Schizophrenia.* Tr. and foreword Brian Massumi. Minneapolis: U of Minnesota P, 1987.
Deutsche Rundschau für Geographie und Statistik. Vienna: Hartleben, 1879–1880.
Diderot, Denis. *Oeuvres philosophiques.* Ed. P. Vernière. Paris: Garnier, 1964.
Digre, Brian. *Imperialism's New Clothes: The Repartition of Tropical Africa, 1914–1919.* New York: Lang, 1990.
Diner, Dan. "European Counterimages: Problems of Periodization and Historical Memory." *New German Critique* 53 (1991): 163–74.
———. "Negative Symbiose: Deutsche und Juden nach Auschwitz." *Babylon: Beiträge zur jüdischen Gegenwart* 1 (1986): 9–20.
Djurić, Rajko. *Roma und Sinti im Spiegel der deutschen Literatur: Ein Essay.* Studien zur Tsiganologie und Folkloristik 13. Frankfurt am Main: Lang, 1995.
Doane, Mary Ann. *Femmes Fatales: Feminism, Film Theory, Psychoanalysis.* New York: Routledge, 1991.
Döblin, Alfred. *Journey to Poland.* Tr. Joachim Neugroschel. Ed. Heinz Graber. New York: Paragon House, 1991.
Drechsler, Horst. *Südwestafrika unter deutscher Kolonialherrschaft.* Berlin: Akademie, 1966.
Drewniak, Boguslaw. *Der deutsche Film 1938–45.* Düsseldorf: Droste, 1987.
Dyson-Hudson, Neville. "The Study of Nomads." *Perspectives on Nomadism.* Ed. William Irons and Neville Dyson-Hudson. Leiden: E. J. Brill, 1972.
Ebel, Sabine. *Engagement und Kritik: Carl Einstein—Ein Vermittler zwischen Deutschland und Frankreich.* Diss. U. Bonn, 1989.
Eckart, Wolfgang U. "'Germanin'—Fiktion und Wirklichkeit in einem nationalsozialistischen Propagandafilm." *Medizin im Spielfilm des Nationalsozialismus.* Ed. Udo Benzenhöfer and Wolfgang U. Eckart. Tecklenburg: Burgverlag, 1990. 69–82.
Eichberg, Henning. "The Nazi Thingspiel: Theater for the Masses in Fascism and Proletarian Culture." *New German Critique* 11 (spring 1977): 133–50.
Einstein, Carl. *Fabrikation der Fiktionen.* Ed. Sybille Penkert. Hamburg: Rowohlt, 1973.
———. *Gesammelte Werke.* Ed. Ernst Nef. Wiesbaden: Limes, 1962.
———. *Die Kunst des 20. Jahrhunderts.* Propyläen Kunstgeschichte. Vol. 16. Berlin: Propyläen, 1926 (1928, 1931).
———. *Werke I–III.* Berlin: Medusa, 1980, 1981, 1985.
———. *Werke IV.* Berlin: Fannei und Waltz, 1992.
Eley, Geoff. "Introduction: Is There a History of the Kaiserreich?" *Society, Culture and the State in Germany, 1870–1930.* Ed. Geoff Eley. Ann Arbor: U of Michigan P, 1996. 1–42.
Eliade, Mircea, ed. *The Encyclopedia of Religion.* New York: Macmillan, 1987.

Epstein, Klaus. "Erzberger and the German Colonial Scandals, 1905–1910." *The English Historical Review* 74 (1959): 637–62.

Eyferth, Klaus, Ursula Brandt, and Wolfgang Hawel. *Farbige Kinder in Deutschland: Die Situation der Mischlingskinder und die Aufgaben ihrer Eingliederung.* Munich: Juventa, 1960.

Fabian, Johannes. *Time and the Other: How Anthropology Makes Its Object.* New York: Columbia UP, 1983.

Fanon, Frantz. *Black Skin, White Masks.* Tr. Charles Lam Markam. New York: Grove, 1977.

Fassbinder, Rainer Werner. *Katzelmacher. Preparadise Sorry Now.* Frankfurt am Main: Verlag der Autoren, 1982.

Fernández Retamar, Roberto. *Caliban and Other Essays.* Tr. Edward Baker. Minneapolis: U of Minnesota P, 1989.

Filkins, Peter, tr. *Songs in Flight: The Collected Poems of Ingeborg Bachmann.* New York: Marsilio, 1994.

Fischer, Bernd. *Christoph Hein: Drama und Prosa im letzten Jahrzehnt der DDR.* Heidelberg: Winter, 1990.

Fischer, Eva-Elisabeth. "Eine Frau webt ihr Leben." *Süddeutsche Zeitung* 14 July 1993.

Fischer, Michael, and George Marcus. *Anthropology as Cultural Critique.* Chicago: U of Chicago P, 1986.

Flessner, Bettina. *Asyl.* Unpublished manuscript.

Fonseca, Isabel. *Bury Me Standing: The Gypsies and Their Journey.* New York: Knopf, 1995.

Förster, Bernhard. *Deutsche Colonien in dem oberen Laplata-Gebiete mit besonderer Berücksichtigung von Paraguay: Ergebnisse eingehender Prüfungen, praktischer Arbeiten und Reisen, 1883–1885.* Naumburg: Selbstverlag, 1886.

———. "Ein Deutschland der Zukunft." *Bayreuther Blätter* 6 (1883): 44–56.

Förster, Eli (Elisabeth Förster-Nietzsche). *Dr. Bernhard Förster's Kolonie Neu-Germania in Paraguay.* Berlin: Commissions-Verlag der Actien-Gesellschaft "Pionier," 1891.

Frankenstein, Luise. *Soldatenkinder: Die unehelichen Kinder ausländischer Soldaten mit besonderer Berücksichtigung der Mischlinge.* Ed. Internationale Vereinigung für Jugendhilfe. Geneva, Munich, Düsseldorf: Steinebach, 1954.

Fraser, Angus. *The Gypsies.* 2d ed. Oxford: Blackwell, 1994.

Frenssen, Gustav. *Hilligenlei.* Berlin: Grote, 1905.

———. *Jörn Uhl.* Berlin: Grote, 1931.

———. *Peter Moors Fahrt nach Südwest: Ein Feldzugbericht.* Berlin: 1906. Tr. Margaret May Ward as *Peter Moor's Journey to Southwest Africa.* London: Archibald Constable, 1909.

Fretz, Joseph Winfield. *Immigrant Group Settlements in Paraguay: A Study in the Sociology of Colonization.* North Newton, Kansas: n.p., 1962.

Freud, Sigmund. *The Aetiology of Hysteria. The Standard Edition of the Complete Psychological Works of Sigmund Freud.* Ed. and tr. James Strachey. London: Hogarth and Institute of Psycho-Analysis, 1962. 3: 189–221.

———. *The Question of Lay Analysis. The Standard Edition of the Complete Psychological Works of Sigmund Freud.* 20: 179–250.
———. *Totem and Taboo. The Standard Edition of the Complete Psychological Works of Sigmund Freud.* 13: 1–165.
Friedlander, Saul. *Probing the Limits of Representation: Nazism and the 'Final Solution.'* Cambridge: Harvard UP, 1992.
Friedrich, Walter, and Wilfried Schubarth. "Ausländerfeindliche und rechtsextreme Orientierungen bei ostdeutschen Jugendlichen: Eine empirische Studie." *Deutschland Archiv* (Oct. 1991): 1052–65.
Friedrichsmeyer, Sara. "Romantic Nationalism: Achim von Arnim's Gypsy Princess Isabella." *Gender and Germanness.* Ed. Patricia Herminghouse and Magda Mueller. Providence: Berghahn, 1997. 51–65.
Fuchs-Sumiyoshi, Andrea. *Orientalismus in der deutschen Literatur: Untersuchungen zu Werken des 19. und 20. Jahrhunderts, von Goethes 'West-östlichem Divan' bis Thomas Manns 'Joseph'-Tetralogie.* Hildesheim: Olms, 1984.
Gann, Lewis H. "Marginal Colonialism: The German Case." *Germans in the Tropics: Essays in German Colonial History.* Ed. Arthur J. Knoll and Lewis H. Gann. New York: Greenwood, 1987. 1–17.
Garber, Marjorie. *Vested Interests: Cross-Dressing and Cultural Anxiety.* New York: Routledge, 1992.
Garelli, Gianluca. "L'oceano della metafisica: Una metafora di Kant." *aut aut* 265–66 (1995): 103–32.
Gates, Henry Louis, Jr., ed. *"Race," Writing, and Difference.* Chicago: U of Chicago P, 1986.
Gellner, Ernest. *Encounters with Nationalism.* Oxford: Blackwell, 1994.
———. *Nations and Nationalism.* Oxford: Blackwell, 1983.
Germany and the Middle East 1835–1939. Ed. Jehuda L. Wallach. Tel-Aviv: Institute for German History, University of Tel-Aviv, 1975.
Geyer, Michael. "Postmodern Thought and German History." E-mail to H-German Mailing List. 18 Sept. 1995.
Geyer, Michael, and Miriam Hansen. "German-Jewish Memory and National Consciousness." *Holocaust Remembrance.* Ed. Geoffrey H. Hartman. Oxford: Blackwell, 1994. 175–90.
Gilman, Sander L. *Difference and Pathology: Stereotypes of Sexuality, Race and Madness.* Ithaca: Cornell UP, 1985.
———. *Disease and Representation: Images of Illness from Madness to AIDS.* Ithaca: Cornell UP, 1988.
———. *Jewish Self-Hatred: Antisemitism and the Hidden Language of the Jews.* Baltimore: Johns Hopkins UP, 1986.
———. *The Jew's Body.* New York and London: Routledge, 1991.
———. *On Blackness without Blacks: Essays on the Image of the Black in Germany.* Boston: Hall, 1982.
———. *Sexuality: An Illustrated History.* New York: John Wiley and Sons, 1989.
Gilroy, Paul. "Route Work: The Black Atlantic and the Politics of Exile." *The Post-colonial Question.* 17–29.

Glinga, Werner. "Life Story, Utendi, and Colonial Novel: Literature in 'German East Africa.'" *Afrika und Übersee* 70 (1987): 257–77.
Goetschel, Willi. *Constituting Critique: Kant's Writing as Critical Praxis.* Tr. Eric Schwab. Durham: Duke UP, 1994.
Göttsche, Dirk. "'Die Schwarzkunst der Worte'—Zur Barbey- und Rimbaud-Rezeption in Ingeborg Bachmanns 'Todesarten-Zyklus.'" *Jahrbuch der Grillparzer-Gesellschaft.* Ed. Klaus Heydemann and Robert Pichl. 3. Folge 17 (1987–90): 127–62.
Graudenz, Karlheinz. *Deutsche Kolonialgeschichte in Daten und Bildern.* Documentation and pictures by Hanns Michael Schindler. Munich: Südwest, 1984.
Greenfeld, Liah. *Nationalism: Five Roads to Modernity.* Cambridge: Harvard UP, 1992.
Greenhalgh, Paul. *Ephemeral Vistas: The Expositions Universelles, Great Exhibitions and World Fairs, 1851–1939.* Manchester: Manchester UP, 1988.
Grieser, Dietmar. *Irdische Götter: Idole und ihre Kultstätten.* Munich: Goldmann, 1980.
Grimal, Pierre, ed. *Larousse World Mythology.* New York: Putnam's, 1963.
Grimm, Hans. "Dina." 1913. *Südafrikanische Novellen. Gesamtausgabe.* Lippoldsberg: Klosterhaus, 1975. 1: 7–42.
———. "Die Geschichte vom alten Blut und von der ungeheuren Verlassenheit." 1931. *Lüderitzland: Geschichten aus Südwestafrika. Gesamtausgabe.* Lippoldsberg: Klosterhaus, 1973. 8: 77–136.
Gronemeyer, Reimer, ed. *Zigeuner im Spiegel früher Chroniken und Abhandlungen. Quellen von 15. bis zum 18. Jahrhundert.* Giessen: Focus, 1987.
Grosse, Pascal. *Kolonialmigration in Deutschland, 1885–1945.* Diss. FU Berlin, 1997.
Gründer, Horst. *Christliche Mission und deutscher Imperialismus.* Paderborn: Schöningh, 1982.
———. *Geschichte der deutschen Kolonien.* Paderborn: Schöningh, 1985.
Grunwald, Kurt. "Pénétration Pacifique—The Financial Vehicles of Germany's 'Drang nach dem Osten.'" *Germany and the Middle East 1835–1939.* 85–103.
Gündogar, Feruzan. *Trivialliteratur und Orient: Karl Mays vorderasiatische Reiseromane.* Frankfurt am Main: Lang, 1983.
Habermas, Jürgen. "A Kind of Settlement of Damages (Apologetic Tendencies)." *New German Critique* 44 (1988): 25–39.
Hall, Catherine. "Histories, Empires and the Post-Colonial Moment." *The Postcolonial Question.* 65–76.
Hall, Stuart. "Cultural Identity and Diaspora." *Identity: Community, Culture, Difference.* Ed. Jonathan Rutherford. London: Lawrence and Wishart, 1990. 222–37.
———. "When Was 'The Post-Colonial'? Thinking at the Limit." *The Post-colonial Question.* 242–60.
Hammer, Klaus. "Christoph Hein: Horns Ende." *Weimarer Beiträge* 33.8 (1987): 1358–69.
———, ed. *Chronist ohne Botschaft: Christoph Hein. Ein Arbeitsbuch: Materialien, Auskünfte, Bibliographie.* Berlin: Aufbau, 1992.

———. "'Horns Ende': Versuch einer Interpretation." *Chronist ohne Botschaft.* 121–33.
Hancock, Ian. *The Pariah Syndrome: An Account of Gypsy Slavery and Persecution.* Ann Arbor: Karoma, 1987.
Handelman, Susan. *Fragments of Redemption: Jewish Thought and Literary Theory in Benjamin, Scholem, and Levinas.* Bloomington: Indiana UP, 1991.
Haraway, Donna. *Primate Visions: Gender, Race and Nature in the World of Modern Science.* New York: Routledge, 1989.
Hartsock, Nancy. "Rethinking Modernism: Minority vs. Majority Theories." *The Nature and Context of Minority Discourse.* Ed. Abdul R. JanMohamed and David Lloyd. New York: Oxford UP, 1990. 17–36.
Hartung, Günter. "'Volk ohne Raum' von Hans Grimm." *Weimarer Beiträge* 35. 10 (1985): 1655–76.
Heermann, Christian. *Der Mann, der Old Shatterhand war: Eine Karl-May-Biographie.* Berlin: Verlag der Nation, 1988.
Heid, Ludger. "Ostjüdische Kultur in Deutschland der Weimarer Republik." *Juden als Träger bürgerlicher Kultur in Deutschland.* Ed. Julius H. Schoeps. Stutt-gart: Berg, 1989.
Hein, Christoph. *Als Kind habe ich Stalin gesehen: Essais und Reden.* Berlin and Weimar: Aufbau, 1990.
———. *Horns Ende.* 1985. Frankfurt am Main: Luchterhand, 1987.
———. *Öffentlich arbeiten: Essais und Gespräche.* Berlin and Weimar: Aufbau, 1987.
———. "Worüber man nicht reden kann, davon kann die Kunst ein Lied singen: Zu einem Satz von Anna Seghers." *Öffentlich arbeiten.* 43–56.
Heißerer, Dirk. *Negative Dichtung: Zum Verfahren der literarischen Dekomposition bei Carl Einstein.* Munich: iudicium, 1992.
Heizer, Donna. *Those Other Orientals: The Muslim Orient in the Works of Else Lasker-Schüler, Friedrich Wolf, and Franz Werfel.* Diss. Ohio State U, 1992.
Heller, Agnes. *A Theory of History.* London: Routledge and Kegan Paul, 1982.
Hellwald, Friedrich von, and Ludwig C. Beck, eds. *Die Erde und ihre Völker: Geographisches Hausbuch.* Vols. 1 and 2. Stuttgart: Spemann, 1878.
———. *Die heutige Türkei.* Leipzig: Spamer, 1882.
———. *Die Umgestaltung des Orients als Culturfrage.* Augsburg: Lampart, 1878.
"Helsinki's Island Playgrounds." *New York Times.* Travel section. 25 Aug. 1996: 14.
Hemingway, Ernest. *The Green Hills of Africa.* New York: Scribner, 1935.
Henderson, W. O. *The German Colonial Empire: 1884–1919.* London: Frank Cass, 1993.
———. *Studies in German Colonial History.* London: Cass, 1962.
Henseleit, Felix. "'Carl Peters' in Hamburg erfolgreich uraufgeführt." *Film-Kurier,* 22 Mar. 1941.
Herding, Klaus. "Immer auf der flucht vor einem bindenden milieu." *Merkur* 46 (1992): 717–25.
Hermand, Jost. "Bürger zweier Welten? Arnold Zweigs Einstellung zur deutschen

Kultur." *Juden als Träger bürgerlicher Kultur in Deutschland.* Ed. Julius H. Schoeps. Stuttgart: Burg, 1989.

Herrmann, Hans Peter, Hans-Martin Blitz, and Susanna Moßmann. *Machtphantasie Deutschland: Nationalismus, Männlichkeit und Fremdenhaß im Vaterlandsdiskurs deutscher Schriftsteller des 18. Jahrhunderts.* Frankfurt am Main: Suhrkamp, 1996.

Herzberg, Georg. "Der Kaiser hat entschieden." *Film-Kurier,* 30 Nov. 1940.

Hildebrand, Klaus. *Vom Reich zum Weltreich: Hitler, NSDAP und die koloniale Frage 1919–1945.* Munich: Fink, 1969.

Hillers, Hans Wolfgang. "'Germanin' als Formproblem." *Film-Kurier,* 19 June 1942.

Hirschman, Albert O. *The Rhetoric of Reaction.* Cambridge: Harvard UP, 1991.

Hitler, Adolf. *Mein Kampf.* Tr. Ralph Mannheim. Boston: Houghton Mifflin, 1962.

Hobsbawm, E. J. *Nations and Nationalism since 1780: Programme, Myth, Reality.* Cambridge: Cambridge UP, 1992.

Hoffmann, Hilmar. *Es ist noch nicht zu Ende: Sollen Nazikunst und Nazifilme wieder öffentlich gezeigt werden?* Frankfurt am Main: Frankfurter Bund für Volksbildung, 1988.

Hofman, Inge, and Anton Vorbichler. *Das Islam-Bild bei Karl May und der Islamo-Christliche Dialog.* Vienna: Afro-Pub, 1979.

Hohmann, J. S. *Geschichte der Zigeunerverfolgung in Deutschland.* Frankfurt am Main: Campus, 1981.

Holub, Robert C. *Friedrich Nietzsche.* New York: Twayne, 1995.

———. "Nietzsche and the Jewish Question." *New German Critique* 22.3 (1995): 94–121.

———. "Nietzsche and the Women's Question." *German Quarterly* 68.1 (1995): 67–71.

Horn, Peter. "Fremdheitskonstruktionen weißer Kolonisten." *Perspektiven und Verfahren interkultureller Germanistik.* Akten des I. Kongresses der Gesellschaft für Interkulturelle Germanistik. Ed. Alois Wierlacher. Munich: iudicium, 1987. 405–18.

———. "Die Versuchung durch die barbarische Schönheit: Zu Hans Grimms 'farbigen' Frauen." *Germanisch-Romanische Monatsschrift* 35.3 (1985): 317–41.

Horton, Susan R. *Difficult Women, Artful Lives: Olive Schreiner and Isak Dinesen, In and Out of Africa.* Baltimore: Johns Hopkins UP, 1995.

Hösch, Edgar. *Geschichte der Balkanländer.* Munich: Beck, 1988.

Hulme, Peter. *Colonial Encounters: Europe and the Native Caribbean, 1492–1797.* London and New York: Methuen, 1986.

———. "Polytropic Man: Tropes of Sexuality and Mobility in Early Colonial Discourse." *Europe and Its Others.* Ed. Francis Barker et al. Colchester: University of Essex, 1985. 2: 17–32.

Hurka, Herbert. "Die Mischlingskinder in Deutschland: Ein Situationsbericht auf Grund bisheriger Veröffentlichungen." *Jugendwohl* (1956): 1–19.

Huyssen, Andreas. "The Inevitability of Nation: German Intellectuals after Unification." *October* 61 (summer 1992): 63–73.

———. "The Search for Tradition: Avant-Garde and Postmodernism in the 1970s." *New German Critique* 22 (1981): 23–40.
Jachimczak, Krzysztof. "Wir werden es lernen müssen, mit unserer Vergangenheit zu leben: Gespräch mit Christoph Hein." *Christoph Hein: Texte, Daten, Bilder* 45–67.
Jacobs, Jürgen. "Ein Instrument der Herren." *Frankfurter Allgemeine Zeitung* 24 June 1993.
Jakobson, Roman. "Shifters, Verbal Categories, and the Russian Verb." *Selected Writings.* Vol. II: *Word and Language.* The Hague and Paris: Mouton, 1971. 130–47.
Jannings, Emil. "Gedanken zu meinem Film 'Ohm Krüger.'" *Film-Kurier,* 29 Mar. 1941.
Janz, Curt Paul. *Friedrich Nietzsche: Biographie.* 3 vols. 2d rev. ed. Munich: Hanser, 1993.
Jelinek, Elfriede. "'Ich bin im Grunde ständig tobsüchtig über die Verharmlosung.' Ein Gespräch mit Elfriede Jelinek." Program *Stecken, Stab und Stangl,* Deutsches Schauspielhaus Hamburg, 1996. 11–17.
Jonaitis, Aldona. "Introduction: The Development of Franz Boas's Themes on Primitive Art." *A Wealth of Thought: Franz Boas on Native American Art.* Ed. A. Jonaitis. Seattle and London: U of Washington P, 1995. 3–37.
Kant, Immanuel. *Briefwechsel.* Ed. Otto Schöndörffer. 3d rev. ed. Ed. Rudolf Malter. Hamburg: Meiner, 1986.
———. *Critique of Judgment. Including the First Introduction.* Tr. Werner S. Pluhar. Indianapolis: Hackett, 1987.
———. *Critique of Pure Reason.* Tr. Norman Kemp Smith. New York: St. Martin's, 1929.
———. *Geographische und andere naturwissenschaftliche Schriften.* Ed. J. Zehbe. Hamburg: Meiner, 1985.
———. *Werkausgabe.* Ed. Wilhelm Weischedel. Wiesbaden: Insel, 1958.
Ketelsen, Uwe-K. *Literatur und Drittes Reich.* Schernfeld: Süddeutsche Hochschul-Verlagsgesellschaft, 1992.
Kiefer, Klaus H. *Diskurswandel im Werk Carl Einsteins.* Tübingen: Niemeyer, 1994.
———. "Fonctions de l'art africain dans l'oeuvre de Carl Einstein." *Festschrift zum 60. Geburtstag von Carl F. Hoffmann.* Ed. Franz Rottland. Hamburg: Helmut Buske, 1986. 169–202.
Klaren, Georg C. "Der deutsche Film und unsere Kolonien." *Lichtbild-Bühne,* 24 May 1939.
Klemm, Gustav Friedrich. *Allgemeine Culturgeschichte der Menschheit.* 10 vols. Leipzig: Teubner, 1843–52.
Kline, Linus W. "The Migratory Impulse versus Love of Home." *American Journal of Psychology* 10.1 (Oct. 1898): 1–81.
Klostermaier, Klaus K. *A Survey of Hinduism.* New York: State U of New York P, 1989.
Klotz, Marcia. *White Women and the Dark Continent: Sexuality and Gender in Ger-*

man *Colonial Discourse from the Sentimental Novel to the Fascist Film.* Diss. Stanford U, 1994.
Knoll, Arthur J., and Lewis H. Gann, eds. *Germans in the Tropics: Essays in German Colonial History.* New York: Greenwood, 1987.
Kolodny, Annette. *The Lay of the Land: Metaphor as Experience and History in American Life and Letters.* Chapel Hill: U of North Carolina P, 1975.
Koltès, Bernard-Marie. "Ich fühle mich völlig verraten." *Der Spiegel* 24 Oct. 1988: 234–43.
Kössler, Arnim. *Aktionsfeld Osmanisches Reich—Die Wirtschaftsinteressen des Deutschen Kaiserreiches in der Türkei 1871–1908.* New York: Arno, 1981.
Krafft-Ebing, Richard von. *Psychopathia Sexualis: A Medico-Forensic Study.* New York: Pioneer, 1947.
Kraft, Helga. *Ein Haus aus Sprache: Dramatikerinnen und das andere Theater.* Stuttgart: Metzler, 1996.
Kramer, Carl. *Die "verfluchte Heredität loswerden": Studie zu Carl Einsteins "Bebuquin."* Münster: Kleinheinrich, 1990.
Kratzer, Barbara. "Subject and/or Object of Colonization: German Colonial Women in Southwest Africa." Paper presented at the 1994 MLA Convention in San Diego.
Kristeva, Julia. *Powers of Horror: An Essay on Abjection.* Tr. Leon S. Roudiez. New York: Columbia UP, 1982.
———. *Strangers to Ourselves.* Tr. Leon S. Roudiez. New York: Columbia UP, 1991.
Kromschröder, Gerhard. *Als ich ein Türke war.* Frankfurt am Main: Eichborn, 1983.
Kuhn, Ernst, ed. *Wissenschaftlicher Jahresbericht über die Morgenländischen Studien.* Leipzig: Brockhaus, 1883.
KultuRRevolution. "Tropische Tropen—Exotismus." 32/33 (Dec. 1995).
Kursawe, Karl Heinz. "Farbige Besatzungskinder—auch ein Problem der öffentlichen Fürsorge." *Zeitschrift für das Fürsorgewesen* 22 (1959): 338–39.
LaCapra, Dominick. *Representing the Holocaust: History, Theory, Trauma.* Ithaca and London: Cornell UP, 1994.
Lander, Jeannette. *Jahrhundert der Herren: Roman.* Berlin: Aufbau, 1993.
Langhoff, Anna. "Transit Heimat/Gedeckte Tische." *Theater heute* 3 (Mar. 1994): 45–52.
Layard, A. H. *Ninive und seine Ueberreste, nebst einem Bericht über einen Besuch bei den chaldäischen Christen in Kurdistan und den Jezidi oder Teufelsanbetern.* Tr. Meißner. Leipzig: n.p., 1850.
Lazarus, Moritz, and Hermann Steinthal. "Einleitende Gedanken über Völkerpsychologie." *Zeitschrift für Völkerpsychologie und Sprachwissenschaft* 1 (1860).
Lazarus, Neil. "Marxism and the Idealism of Postcolonial Studies." Paper presented at the 1996 Conference on Politics and Languages of Contemporary Marxism at the U of Massachusetts.
Lebzelter, Gisela. "Die 'Schwarze Schmach': Vorurteile—Propaganda—Mythos." *Geschichte und Gesellschaft* 11 (1985): 37–68.
Le Doeuff, Michèlle. *The Philosophical Imaginary.* Stanford: Stanford UP, 1989.

Lee, Hyunseon. *Günter de Bruyn—Christoph Hein—Heiner Müller: Drei Interviews.* Siegen: Universität Siegen, Fachbereich 3, Sprach- und Literaturwissenschaft, 1996.
Leed, Eric. *The Mind of the Traveller: From Gilgamesh to Global Tourism.* New York: Basic Books, 1991.
Lefebvre, Henri. *The Production of Space.* Tr. Donald Nicholson-Smith. Oxford: Blackwell, 1991.
Lehmann, Joachim. "Christoph Hein—Chronist und 'historischer Materialist.'" *Text und Kritik* 111 (July 1991): 44–56.
Leipziger Illustrierte Zeitung. Vol. 74. Leipzig: Weber, 1880.
Lemke-Muniz de Faria, Yara-Colette. *Prüfstein der Demokratie: Afrodeutsche Kinder in Nachkriegsdeutschland, 1945–1960.* Diss. TU Berlin (in preparation).
Lennox, Sara. "Enzensberger, *Kursbuch,* and Third-Worldism." *"Neue Welt"/ "Dritte Welt": Interkulturelle Beziehungen Deutschlands zu Lateinamerika und der Karibik.* Ed. Sigrid Bauschinger and Susan Cocalis. Tübingen: Francke, 1994. 185–200.
Lester, Rosemarie K. *Trivialneger. Das Bild des Schwarzen im westdeutschen Illustriertenroman.* Stuttgart: Heinz, 1982.
Levinas, Emmanuel. *Outside the Subject.* Stanford: Stanford UP, 1994.
———. "Time and the Other." *The Levinas Reader.* Ed. Sean Hand. Oxford: Blackwell, 1989. 37–58.
———. *Totality and Infinity.* Pittsburgh: Duquesne UP, 1961.
Lindner, Gabriele. "Ein geistiger Widergänger." *Christoph Hein: Texte, Daten, Bilder.* 163–60.
Löffler, Dietrich. "Christoph Heins Prosa—Chronik der Zeitgeschichte." *Weimarer Beiträge* 33.9 (1987): 1484–87.
Lorenz, Dagmar C. G. *Verfolgung bis zum Massenmord: Holocaust-Diskurse in deutscher Sprache aus der Sicht der Verfolgten.* New York: Lang, 1992.
Lott, Eric. *Love and Theft: Blackface Minstrelsy and the American Working Class.* Oxford: Oxford UP, 1993.
Lowe, Lisa. *Critical Terrains: French and British Orientalisms.* Ithaca: Cornell UP, 1991.
Lutz, Catherine A., and Jane Collins. *Reading National Geographic.* Chicago: U of Chicago P, 1993.
Luz, Oskar, and Horst Luz. "Proud Primitives: The Nuba People." *National Geographic* 130.5 (Nov. 1966): 672–705.
Lyotard, Jean François. *The Postmodern Condition: A Report on Knowledge.* 1979. Tr. Geoff Bennington and Brian Massumi. Minneapolis: U of Minnesota P, 1984.
Macintyre, Ben. *Forgotten Fatherland: The Search for Elisabeth Nietzsche.* New York: Farrar Straus Giroux, 1992.
Maier, Donna J. E. "Slave Labor and Wage Labor in German Togo, 1885–1914." Knoll and Gann. 73–91.
Makropoulos, Michael. "Über das Fremde und das Andere." *L' 80* 43 (1987): 5–10.

Mamozai, Martha. *Schwarze Frau, weiße Herrin: Frauenleben in den deutschen Kolonien.* 1982. Reinbek: Rowohlt, 1989.

Mann, Gustav. "Zum Problem der farbigen Mischlingskinder in Deutschland." *Jugendwohl* 37 (1956): 50–53.

Margalit, Gilad. "Antigypsyism in the Politics of the Federal Republic of Germany: A Parallel with Antisemitism?" ACTA 9 (1996): 1–29.

Marks, Sally. "Black Watch on the Rhine: A Study in Propaganda, Prejudice and Prurience." *European Studies Review* 13 (1983): 297–334.

Martin, Biddy, and Chandra Talpade Mohanty. "Feminist Politics: What's Home Got to Do with It?" *Feminist Studies/Critical Studies.* Ed. Teresa de Lauretis. Bloomington: Indiana UP, 1986. 191–212.

Martin, Peter. *Schwarze Teufel—Edle Mohren: Afrikaner im Bewußtsein und Geschichte der Deutschen.* Hamburg: Junius, 1993.

Mason, Otis T. "Migration and the Food Quest." *American Anthropologist* 7 (1894): 275–92.

May, Karl. *Karl Mays Werke: Historisch-Kritische Ausgabe für die Karl-May-Gedächtnis-Stiftung.* Ed. Hermann Wiedenroth and Hans Wollschläger. Zurich: Haffmans, 1990.

McClintock, Anne. *Imperial Leather: Race, Gender and Sexuality in the Colonial Context.* New York: Routledge, 1995.

McKnight, Phil. "Ein Mosaik zu Christoph Heins Roman 'Horns Ende.'" *Sinn und Form* 39.2 (1987): 415–25.

———. *Understanding Christoph Hein.* Columbia: U of South Carolina P, 1995.

Meffre, Lilliane. *Carl Einstein et la problématique des avant-gardes dans les arts plastiques.* Bern: Lang, 1989.

Meyers Konversations-Lexikon: Eine Encyclopädie des allgemeinen Wissens. 4th ed. Vol 12. Leipzig: Verlag des Bibliographischen Institutes, 1890.

Miller, Christopher. *Blank Darkness: Africanist Discourse in French.* Chicago: U of Chicago P, 1985.

Moddelmog, Debra A. *Readers and Mythic Signs: The Oedipus Myth in Twentieth-Century Fiction.* Carbondale/Edwardsville: Southern Illinois UP, 1993.

Mode, H., and S. Wölffling. *Zigeuner: Der Weg eines Volkes in Deutschland.* Leipzig: Koehler and Amelang, 1968.

Moeller van den Bruck, Artur. *Die Zeitgenossen: Die Geister—Die Menschen.* Minden: Bruns, 1906.

Moore, Mick. "Thoroughly Modern Revolutionaries: The JVP in Sri Lanka." *Modern Asian Studies* 27 (1993): 593–642.

MordsWeiber. Tanztheater. Koltès. Ed. Dramaturgische Gesellschaft. Berlin: Dramaturgische Gesellschaft, 1990.

Morel, Edmund. "The Black Plague in Europe: French Sex Horror Unleashed in the Rhine." *Daily Herald* [London] 10 Apr. 1920.

Müller, Elfriede. *Goldener Oktober. Die Bergarbeiterinnen.* Frankfurt am Main: Verlag der Autoren, 1990.

Nair, Supriya. "Partition and After: Religious Fundamentalism and the Gendered Nation in India." Paper presented at the 1994 Conference on Literature, Politics, and Society in Africa at Ohio State U.

N'dumbe, Kuma Alexandre III. *Hitler voulait l'Afrique. Le projet du 3e Reich sur le continent africain.* Paris: Editions l'Harmattan, 1980.

Nelson, Keith. "'The Black Horror on the Rhine': Race as a Factor in Post World War I Diplomacy." *Journal of Modern History* 42 (4 Dec. 1970): 606–27.

Neue Rundschau. "Der postkoloniale Blick: Eine neue Weltliteratur?" 107.1 (1996).

Nietzsche, Friedrich. *Kritische Gesamtausgabe: Briefwechsel.* Ed. Giorgio Colli and Mazzino Montinari. 18 vols. Berlin: de Gruyter, 1975–84.

———. *Sämtliche Briefe.* Kritische Studienausgabe. Ed. Giorgio Colli and Mazzino Montinari. 8 vols. Munich: dtv; Berlin/New York: de Gruyter, 1975–1984.

———. *Sämtliche Werke.* Kritische Studienausgabe. Ed. Giorgio Colli and Mazzino Montinari. 15 vols. Munich: dtv; Berlin/New York: de Gruyter, 1967–77.

Nissan, Elizabeth, and R. L. Stirrat. "The Generation of Communal Identities." Jonathan Spencer. 19–44.

Nissan, Kate. "6000 Mischlingskinder vor der Berufsausbildung." *Unsere Jugend* 11 (1959): 230–31.

Nixon, Rob. "Caribbean and African Appropriations of *The Tempest.*" *Critical Inquiry* 13 (1987): 557–78.

Noyes, John K. "The Capture of Space: An Episode in a Colonial Story by Hans Grimm." *Pretexts* 1.1 (1989): 52–63.

———. *Colonial Space: Spatiality in the Discourse of German South West Africa 1884–1915.* Chur: Harwood, 1992.

———. "Wide Open Spaces and the Hunger for Land: Production of Space in the German Colonial Novel." *Faultline* 1 (1992): 103–17.

Numelin, Ragnar. *The Wandering Spirit: A Study of Human Migration.* London: Macmillan, 1937.

Oberst, Robert C. "A War Without Winners in Sri Lanka." *Current History* 91 (1992): 128–31.

Obeyesekere, Gananath. "Buddhism and Conscience: An Exploratory Essay." *Daedalus* 120 (1991): 219–40.

Oehm, Heidemarie. *Die Kunsttheorie Carl Einsteins.* Munich: Fink, 1976.

Opitz, May, Katharina Oguntoye, and Dagmar Schultz, eds. *Showing Our Colors: Afro-German Women Speak Out.* Foreword Audre Lorde. Tr. Anne Adams. Amherst: U of Massachusetts P, 1992.

Osterhammel, Jürgen. *Kolonialismus: Geschichte, Formen, Folgen.* Munich: Beck, 1995.

Otis, Pauletta, and Christopher D. Carr. "Sri Lanka and the Ethnic Challenge." *Conflict* 8 (1988): 203–16.

Owen, Roger. *The Middle East in the World Economy, 1800–1914.* London: Methuen, 1981.

Özdamar, Emine Sevgi. *Karagöz in Alamania.* Unpublished manuscript. Frankfurt am Main: 1982.

———. *Keloglan in Alamania.* Unpublished manuscript. Frankfurt am Main: 1991.

Partsch, J. *Die Schutzgebiete des deutschen Reiches: Für die Schüler höherer Lehranstalten.* Berlin: Reimer, 1893.

Peck, Jeffrey M. "Minority Discourse in German Studies." *New German Critique* 46 (1989): 203–8.
Peck, Jeffrey, Mitchell Ash, and Christiane Lemke. "Natives, Strangers, and Foreigners: Constituting Germans by Constructing Others." *After Unity: Reconfiguring German Identities.* Ed. Konrad Jarausch. Providence: Berghahn, 1997. 61–102.
Penkert, Sybille. *Carl Einstein: Existenz und Ästhetik: Einführung mit einem Anhang unveröffentlichter Nachlaßtexte.* Wiesbaden: Steiner, 1970.
Peters, Carl. *Gesammelte Schriften.* Ed. Walter Frank. 3 vols. Munich: Beck, 1943.
Peters, H. F. *Zarathustra's Sister: The Case of Elisabeth and Friedrich Nietzsche.* New York: Crown, 1977.
Piyadasa, L. *Sri Lanka: The Holocaust and After.* London: Marram Books, 1984.
Podach, Erich F. *Gestalten um Nietzsche.* Weimar: Lichtenstein, 1932.
Poeschel, Hans. *Die deutsche Kolonialfrage im Frieden von Versailles.* Berlin: Mittler, 1920.
Pogge von Strandmann, Hartmut. "Deutscher Imperialismus nach 1918." *Deutscher Konservativismus im 19. und 20. Jahrhundert.* Ed. Dirk Stegmann et al. Bonn: Neue Gesellschaft, 1983. 281–93.
Pommerin, Reiner. *Die Sterilisierung der Rheinlandbastarde.* Düsseldorf: Droste, 1979.
The Post-colonial Question: Common Skies, Divided Horizons. Ed. Ian Chambers and Lidia Curti. London: Routledge, 1996.
Pratt, Mary Louise. *Imperial Eyes: Studies in Travel Writing and Transculturation.* London: Routledge, 1992.
Preußer, Heinz-Peter. "Hoffnung im Zerfall: Das Negative und das Andere in 'Horns Ende.'" *Chronist ohne Botschaft.* 134–46.
Quast, Antje. *Das Neue und die Revolte.* Frankfurt am Main: Lang, 1994.
Quataert, Jean H. "Introduction 2: Writing the History of Women and Gender in Imperial Germany." *Society, Culture and the State in Germany, 1870–1930.* Ed. Geoff Eley. 43–65.
Raddatz, Fritz J. "In mir zwei Welten." *Die Zeit* 1 July 1994: 13–14.
Ranke, Leopold von. *Weltgeschichte.* Vol. 5. Leipzig: Duncker und Humblot, 1887.
Rathmann, Lothar. *Berlin—Bagdad: Die imperialistische Nahostpolitik des kaiserlichen Deutschlands.* Berlin: Dietz, 1962.
Reichkommissar für die besetzten rheinischen Gebiete (RBRG), Abteilung I/1755, signature no. 1602. Newspaper articles.
Reinders, E. D. "Racialism on the Left: E. D. Morel and the 'Black Horror on the Rhine.'" *International Review of Social History* 12 (1968): 1–28.
Ridley, Hugh. "Hans Grimm and Rudyard Kipling." *Modern Language Review* 68 (1973): 862–69.
Riefenstahl, Leni. Interview in "Cahiers du Cinéma." Tr. in Susan Sontag. "Fascinating Fascism." 24.
———. *The Last of the Nuba.* London: Collins, 1989.
———. *A Memoir.* New York: St. Martin's, 1992.
———. *The People of Kau.* London: Collins, 1976.

———. *Vanishing Africa.* New York: Harmony Books, 1982.
———, dir. *Olympia.* Ufa. 1938.
———, dir. *Triumph of the Will.* Ufa. 1935.
Rimbaud, Arthur. *Oeuvres complètes.* Ed. Antoine Adam. Paris: Gallimard, 1972.
Rogers, John D. "Social Mobility, Popular Ideology, and Collective Violence in Modern Sri Lanka." *Journal of Asian Studies* 46 (1987): 583–602.
Rohrbach, Paul. *Die Kolonie.* Frankfurt am Main: Rütten und Loening, 1907.
Rose, Carol. *Property and Persuasion. Essays on the History, Theory, and Rhetoric of Ownership.* Boulder: Westview, 1994.
Rose, Jacqueline. *States of Fantasy.* New York: Oxford UP, 1996.
Rose, Romani. *Bürgerrechte für Sinti und Roma: Das Buch zum Rassismus in Deutschland.* Heidelberg: Zentralrat Deutscher Sinti und Roma, 1987.
Rosenzweig, Franz. *Franz Rosenzweig: His Life and Thought.* Presented by Nahum Glatzer. New York: Farrar, Straus and Young [1953].
Roth, Joseph. *Juden auf Wanderschaft.* Cologne: Kiepenheuer und Witsch, 1976.
Rubin, William. "Modernist Primitivism: An Introduction." *'Primitivism' in Twentieth-Century Art: Affinity of the Tribal and the Modern.* Ed. William Rubin. New York: Museum of Modern Art, 1984. 1–84.
———. "Picasso." *'Primitivism' in Twentieth-Century Art: Affinity of the Tribal and the Modern.* 241–333.
Rushdie, Salman. *The Satanic Verses.* New York: Viking, 1988.
Rutherford, Jonathan. "Interview with Homi Bhabha: The Third Space." *Identity: Community, Culture, Difference.* Ed. Jonathan Rutherford. London: Lawrence and Wishart, 1990. 207–21.
———. "A Place Called Home: Identity and the Cultural Politics of Difference." *Identity: Community, Culture, Difference.* 9–27.
Said, Edward. "Criticism/Self-Criticism." *Lingua Franca* (Feb./Mar. 1992): 37–43.
———. *Culture and Imperialism.* New York: Knopf, 1993.
———. *Orientalism.* New York: Vintage Books, 1978.
Salih, Tayeb. *Season of Migration to the North.* Tr. Denys Johnson-Davies. 1969. Portsmouth: Heinemann, 1991.
Schiller, Friedrich. *On the Naive and Sentimental in Literature.* 1795. Tr. and introd. Helen Watanabe-O'Kelly. Manchester: Carcanet New Press, 1981.
Schinzinger, Francesca. *Die Kolonien und das Deutsche Reich: Die wirtschaftliche Bedeutung der deutschen Besitzungen in Übersee.* Stuttgart: Steiner, 1984.
Schlosser, Friedrich Christoph. *Weltgeschichte für das deutsche Volk.* 2d ed. Vols. 3 and 5. Oberhausen: Spaarmann, 1876.
Schmidt, Arno. *Sitara und der Weg dorthin.* Karlsruhe: Stahlberg, 1963.
Schmokel, Wolfe W. *Dream of Empire: German Colonialism, 1919–1945.* New Haven: Yale UP, 1964.
Schneckenburger, Eberhardt. "Das farbige Mischlingskind in der Klassengemeinschaft." *Kultus und Unterricht* 6.1 (1957): 8–9.
Schneider, Peter. "All My Foreigners." *World Literature Today* 69.3 (summer 1995): 487–93.
Schöllgen, Gregor. *Imperialismus und Gleichgewicht: Deutschland, England und die orientalische Frage 1871–1914.* Munich: Oldenbourg, 1984.

"Schulaufnahme von Negerkindern." *Jugendwohl* 33.4 (1952): 119–20.

Schulte-Althoff, Franz-Josef. "Rassenmischung im kolonialen System: Zur deutschen Kolonialpolitik im letzten Jahrzehnt vor dem ersten Weltkrieg." *Historisches Jahrbuch* 105 (1985): 52–94.

Schulte-Sasse, Jochen. "Karl Mays Amerika-Exotik und deutsche Wirklichkeit: Zur sozialpsychologischen Funktion von Trivialliteratur im wilhelminischen Deutschland." *Karl May*. Ed. Helmut Schmiedt. Frankfurt am Main: Suhrkamp, 1983. 101–29.

Sedgwick, Eve Kosofsky. *Between Men—English Literature and Male Homosocial Desire*. New York: Columbia UP, 1985.

Sevin, Dieter. *Textstrategien in DDR-Prosawerken zwischen Bau und Durchbruch der Berliner Mauer*. Heidelberg: Winter, 1993.

Shapiro, Susan E. "*Écriture judaïque:* Where Are the Jews in Western Discourse?" *Displacements: Cultural Identities in Question*. Ed. Angelika Bammer. Bloomington: Indiana UP, 1994. 182–201.

Sharpe, Jenny. "The Unspeakable Limits of Rape: Colonial Violence and Counter-Insurgency." *Colonial Discourse and Post-Colonial Theory*. 221–43.

Showat, Ella, and Robert Stam. *Unthinking Eurocentrism: Multiculturalism and the Media*. London: Routledge, 1994.

Sieg, Katrin. *Exiles, Eccentrics, Activists: Women in Contemporary German Theatre*. Ann Arbor: U of Michigan P, 1994.

———. "Wigwams on the Rhine: Race and Nationality on the German Stage." *TheatreForum* 6 (winter/spring 1995): 12–19.

Simons, Alfred. *Maxi unser Negerbub*. Bremen: Eilers und Schünemann, 1952.

Smith, Woodruff. *The German Colonial Empire*. Chapel Hill: U of North Carolina P, 1978.

———. *The Ideological Origins of Nazi Imperialism*. New York: Oxford UP, 1986.

Snitow, Ann, Christine Stansell, and Sharon Thompson, eds. Introduction to "'The Mind That Burns in Each Body': Women, Rape, and Racial Violence" by Jaquelyn Dowd Hall. *The Powers of Desire: The Politics of Sexuality*. New York: Monthly Review Press, 1983. 328.

Sohns, Ekkehard-E. *Der Leser Carl Einsteins*. Frankfurt am Main: Lang, 1992.

Sontag, Susan. "Fascinating Fascism." *New York Review of Books* 2 (6 Feb. 1975): 23–30.

Specht, Kerstin. *Lila. Das glühend Männla. Amiwiesen*. Frankfurt am Main: Verlag der Autoren, 1990.

Spencer, Herbert. *The Principles of Sociology*. Vol. 1. London: Williams and Norgate, 1885.

Spencer, Jonathan, ed. *Sri Lanka: History and the Roots of Conflict*. New York: Routledge, 1990.

Der Spiegel. 23 Dec. 1991: 56–57.

Spitzer, Leo. "Invisible Baggage in a Refuge from Nazism." *Diaspora* 2 (1993): 305–36.

———. *Lives In Between: Assimilation and Marginality in Austria, Brazil, West Africa, 1780–1945*. Cambridge: Cambridge UP, 1989.

Spivak, Gayatri Chakravorti. "Can the Subaltern Speak?" *Marxism and the Inter-*

pretation of Culture. Ed. Cary Nelson and Lawrence Grossberg. London: Macmillan, 1988.
Spraul, Gunther. "Der 'Völkermord' an den Herero." *Geschichte in Wissenschaft und Unterricht* 12 (1988): 713–40.
Stam, Robert, and Louise Spence. "Colonialism, Racism and Representation." *Screen* 24.2 (1983): 2–20.
Stenographische Berichte über die Verhandlungen des deutschen Reichstages. Berlin, 1903–14.
Stern, Frank. "Antagonistic Memories: The Post-War Survival Alienation of Jews and Germans." *Memory and Totalitarianism.* International Yearbook of Oral History and Life Stories. Vol. I. Oxford: Oxford UP, 1992. 21–43.
———. *Im Anfang war Auschwitz: Antisemitismus und Philosemitismus im deutschen Nachkrieg.* Tel Aviv: Institut für Deutsche Geschichte, 1991; Gerlingen: Bleicher, 1991.
———. "The 'Jewish Question' in the 'German Question,' 1945–1990: Reflections in the Light of November 9th, 1989." *New German Critique* 52 (1991): 155–72.
———. *The Whitewashing of the Yellow Badge: Antisemitism and Philosemitism in Postwar Germany.* Tr. William Templer. Oxford: Pergamon, 1992.
Stirrat, R. L. "The Crisis of Sri Lanka and Its Origins." *Ethnic and Racial Studies* 12 (1989): 146–49.
Stobrawa, Ilse. "Mit den deutschen Reitern in Ost-Afrika." *Lichtbildbühne,* 12 Oct. 1934.
Stoecker, Helmuth, ed. *German Imperialism in Africa: From the Beginnings until the Second World War.* Tr. Bernd Zöllner. London: Hurst, 1986.
Stoecker, Helmuth. "The Position of Africans in the German Colonies." Knoll and Gann. 119–29.
Stoecker, Helmuth, and Peter Sebald. "Enemies of the Colonial Idea." Knoll and Gann. 59–72.
Stoler, Ann Laura. *Race and the Education of Desire: Foucault's History of Sexuality and the Colonial Order of Things.* Durham: Duke UP, 1995.
———. "Rethinking Colonial Categories: European Communities and the Boundaries of Rule." *Comparative Studies in Society and History* 31.1 (1989): 134–61 (also in *Colonialism and Culture.* Ed. Nicholas B. Dirks. Ann Arbor: U of Michigan P, 1992. 319–52).
Streese, Konstanze. *"Cric?—"Crac!" Vier literarische Versuche, mit dem Kolonialismus umzugehen.* Bern: Lang, 1991.
———. "Writing the Other's Language: Modes of Linguistic Representation in German Colonial and Anti-Colonial Literature." *Encountering the Other(s): Studies in Literature, History, and Culture.* Ed. Gisela Brinker-Gabler. Binghamton: State U of New York P, 1995. 285–94.
Sudhoff, Dieter, and Hartmut Vollmer, eds. *Karl Mays Orientzyklus.* Paderborn: Igel, 1991.
SWAPO of Namibia Department of Information and Publicity. *To be Born a Nation: The Liberation Struggle for Namibia.* London: Zed Press, 1981.
Tagesspiegel. 19 Jan. 1997.

Taylor, A. J. P. *Germany's First Bid for Colonies: 1884–1885.* New York: Norton, 1970.
Teraoka, Arlene. *East, West, and Others: The Third World in Postwar German Literature.* Lincoln: U of Nebraska P, 1996.
———. "Talking 'Turk': On Narrative Strategies and Cultural Stereotypes." *New German Critique* 46 (winter 1989): 104–28.
Theweleit, Klaus. *Male Fantasies.* 2 vols. Minneapolis: U of Minnesota P, 1987.
"They Couldn't Take Our Thoughts: A Conversation with Ceija Stojka." Interview with Karen Rosenberg. *Women's Review of Books* 12.6 (Mar. 1995): 18–20.
Thomas, Nicholas. *Colonialism's Culture: Anthropology, Travel, and Government.* Cambridge: Polity, 1994.
Thorson, Helga. "Sexual and Racial Differentiation: Two German Colonial Novels." Paper presented at the 1994 MLA Convention in San Diego, Calif.
Tiffin, Chris, and Alan Lawson, eds. *De-Scribing Empire: Post-Colonialism and Textuality.* New York: Routledge, 1994.
Timm, Uwe. *Deutsche Kolonien.* Cologne: Kiepenheuer und Witsch, 1986.
Todorov, Tzvetan. *The Conquest of America: The Question of the Other.* New York: Harper and Row, 1984.
Torgovnick, Marianna. *Gone Primitive: Savage Intellects, Modern Lives.* Chicago: U of Chicago P, 1990.
Townsend, Mary Evelyn. *Origins of Modern German Colonialism 1871–1885.* Diss. Columbia U, 1921.
Trenker, Luis. *Alles gut gegangen: Geschichten aus meinem Leben.* Munich: Bertelsmann, 1979.
Trumpener, Katie. "The Time of the Gypsies: A 'People without History' in the Narratives of the West." *Critical Inquiry* 18 (1992): 843–84.
Trumpener, Ulrich. "German Officers in the Ottoman Empire, 1880–1918." *Germany and the Middle East 1835–1939.* 30–44.
Tschapke, Reinhard. "Der literarische Markt im 19. Jahrhundert: Verlag, Vertriebs- und Verbreitungsformen." *Karl-May-Handbuch.* Ed. Gert Ueding and Reinhard Tschapke. Stuttgart: Kröner, 1987. 39–56.
Ulemann, Jennifer. "Kant on the Right to Property and the Value of Extended Freedom." *Proceedings of the Eighth International Kant Congress.* Memphis: Marquette UP, 1995.
Uyangoda, Jayadeva. "Review Essay: Reinterpreting Tamil and Sinhala Nationalisms." *South Asia Bulletin* 7 (1987): 39–46.
Venkatachalam, M. S. *Genocide in Sri Lanka.* Delhi, India: Gian, 1987.
Verhandlungen des Deutschen Bundestages, Stenographische Berichte, 1. Legislaturperiode, Bd. 10, 198. Sitzung am 12.3.1952.
Volkov, Shulamit. "The Dynamics of Dissimilation." *The Jewish Response to German Culture: From the Enlightenment to the Second World War.* Ed. Jehuda Reinharz and Walter Schatzberg. Hanover and London: UP of New England, 1985. 195–211.
Wagnleitner, Reinhold. *Coca-Colonization and the Cold War: The Cultural Mission*

of the United States in Austria after the Second World War. Tr. Diana M. Wolf. Chapel Hill: U of North Carolina P, 1994.
Wallach, Jehuda L. *Anatomie einer Militärhilfe: Die preußisch-deutschen Militärmissionen in der Türkei 1835–1919.* Düsseldorf: Droste, 1976.
Wallraff, Günter. *Ganz Unten.* Cologne: Kiepenheuer und Witsch, 1985.
Warmbold, Joachim. *"'Ein Stückchen neudeutsche Erd' . . .": Deutsche Kolonial-Literatur. Aspekte ihrer Geschichte, Eigenart und Wirkung, dargestellt am Beispiel Afrikas.* Frankfurt am Main: Haag und Herchen, 1992. Tr. as *Germania in Africa: Germany's Colonial Literature.* New York: Lang, 1989.
Wassermann, Jakob. *My Life as German and Jew.* Tr. S. N. Brainin. New York: Coward-McCann [ca. 1933].
Wegner, Reinhard. *Der Exotismus-Streit in Deutschland: Zur Auseinandersetzung mit 'primitiven' Formen in der bildenden Kunst des 20. Jahrhunderts.* Frankfurt am Main: Lang, 1983.
Weigel, Sigrid. "Die andere Ingeborg Bachmann." *text + kritik Sonderband Ingeborg Bachmann.* Munich: Piper, 1984. 5–6.
———. "'Ein Ende mit der Schrift. Ein anderer Anfang': Zur Entwicklung von Ingeborg Bachmanns Schreibweise." *text + kritik Sonderband Ingeborg Bachmann.* Munich: Piper, 1984. 58–92.
Welch, David. *Propaganda and the German Cinema 1933–1945.* Oxford: Oxford UP, 1983.
West, Cornel. "Habermas's Critical Theory and Eurocentrism." Paper presented at the 1987 MLA Convention in San Francisco.
Westphal, Wilfried. *Geschichte der deutschen Kolonien.* 1984. Bindlach: Gondrom, 1991.
Der Wilde Westen Live: 40 Jahre Karl-May-Spiele Bad Segeberg. Bad Segeberg: Kalkberg GmbH Bad Segeberg, 1992.
Wildenthal, Lora. *Colonizers and Citizens: Bourgeois Women and the Woman Question in the German Colonial Movement, 1886–1914.* Diss. U of Michigan, 1994.
———. "Race, Gender and Citizenship in the German Colonial Empire." *Tensions of Empire: Colonial Cultures in a Bourgeois World.* Ed. Frederick Cooper and Ann Stoler. Berkeley: U of California P, 1997. 263–83.
Williams, Patrick, and Laura Chrisman. "Colonial Discourse and Post-Colonial Theory: An Introduction." *Colonial Discourse and Post-Colonial Theory: A Reader.* New York: Columbia UP, 1994. 1–20.
———. Introduction to "Theorizing Gender." *Colonial Discourse and Post-Colonial Theory.* 193–95.
Wilson, W. Daniel. *Humanität und Kreuzzugsideologie um 1780: Die "Türkenoper" im 18. Jahrhundert und das Rettungsmotiv in Wieland's 'Oberon', Lessings 'Nathan' und Goethes 'Iphigenie'.* New York: Lang, 1984.
Winckelmann, Johann Joachim. *Reflections on the Imitation of Greek Works in Painting and Sculpture.* 1755. La Salle: Open Court, 1987.
Wolf, Christa. *Cassandra: A Novel and Four Essays.* Tr. Jan van Heurck. New York: Farrar Straus Giroux, 1984.
———. *The Reader and the Writer: Essays, Sketches, Memories.* New York: International, 1977.

Wollschläger, Hans. *Karl May—Grundriß eines gebrochenen Lebens.* 1964. Zurich: Diogenes, 1976.
World Brotherhood Association. "Mischlinge und Schule." Nuremberg: July 1952.
———. "Das Schicksal der Mischlingskinder in Deutschland." Wiesbaden: Aug. 1953.
Wulf, Joseph. *Theater und Film im Dritten Reich: Eine Dokumentation.* Frankfurt am Main: Ullstein, 1983.
Young, Robert. *White Mythologies: Writing History and the West.* London: Routledge, 1990.
Zank, Wolfgang. "Panthersprung nach Agadir." *Die Zeit* 19 July 1991: 13–14.
Zantop, Susanne. *Colonial Fantasies: Conquest, Family, and Nation in Precolonial Germany, 1770–1870.* Durham: Duke UP, 1997.
———. "Dialectics and Colonialism: The Underside of the Enlightenment." *Impure Reason: Dialectic of Enlightenment in Germany.* Ed. W. Daniel Wilson and Robert C. Holub. Detroit: Wayne State UP, 1993. 301–21.
———. "Domesticating the Other: European Colonial Fantasies 1770–1830." *The Question of the Other(s).* Ed. Gisela Brinker-Gabler. Albany: State U of New York, 1995. 269–83.
Zeitschrift der Deutschen Morgenländischen Gesellschaft. Leipzig: 1847–.
Zimmermann, Peter. "Kampf um den Lebensraum. Ein Mythos der Kolonial- und der Blut- und Boden-Literatur." *Die deutsche Literatur im Dritten Reich: Themen, Traditionen, Wirkungen.* Ed. Horst Denkler and Karl Prümm. Stuttgart: Reclam, 1976. 165–82.
Zweig, Arnold. *Herkunft und Zukunft.* Vienna: Phaidon, 1929.
———. *Das ostjüdische Antlitz.* Wiesbaden: Fourier, 1988.

Contributors

Leslie A. Adelson is professor of German Studies at Cornell University. She has authored *Crisis of Subjectivity: Botho Strauß's Challenge to West German Prose of the 1970s* (1984), *Making Bodies, Making History: Feminism and German Identity* (1993), and numerous articles on contemporary German literature, feminist cultural theory, minority discourse in the German context, and interdisciplinary German cultural studies. For *Making Bodies, Making History* she was awarded the MLA's first Aldo and Jeanne Scaglione Prize for an Outstanding Scholarly Study in the Field of Germanic Languages and Literatures (1994). For her overall contributions to the study of postwar German culture she received the DAAD Prize for Distinguished Scholarship in German Studies (1996).

Nina Berman is assistant professor of German at the University of Texas at Austin. She has published on German colonialism and orientalism, German minority literature, the self-representation of German Jews, Arabic travel literature and geographical writings, and questions of modernity. Her book entitled *Orientalismus, Kolonialismus, und Moderne: Zum Bild des Orients in der deutschsprachigen Kultur um 1900* (1997) explores the Saidian concept of orientalism in the German context. She is currently working on a monograph on imperialism and culture in modern Germany.

Tina Campt received her Ph.D. in history from Cornell University, where she completed her dissertation entitled "Afro-German: The Convergence of Race, Sexuality and Gender in the Construction of a German Ethnic Identity." She taught for three years at the Technical University of Berlin in the Department of Education and is currently an assistant professor in the Department of Women's Studies at the University of California in Santa Cruz.

Friederike Eigler is an associate professor in the German Department at Georgetown University. She is the author of *Das autobiographische Werk von Elias Canetti* (1988) and has published widely in the areas of late-nineteenth- and twentieth-century literature, in particular on GDR literature and post-*Wende* literature. Having coedited the volumes *Cultural Transformation in the New Germany: American and German Perspectives* (1993, with Peter C. Pfeiffer) and *The Feminist Encyclopedia of German Literature* (1997, with Susanne Kord), Eigler is currently working on a book-length study entitled *The Legacy of the GDR in Contemporary German Literature and Culture.*

Sara Friedrichsmeyer is professor of German and head of the Department of Germanic Languages and Literatures at the University of Cincinnati. Her publications include *The Androgyne in Early German Romanticism* and the coedited volume *The Enlightenment and Its Legacy.* She has published articles on German Romanticism, feminist theory, and various nineteenth- and twentieth-century writers, including Caroline Schlegel-Schelling, Achim von Arnim, Paula Moderson-Becker, Käthe Kollwitz, and Christa Wolf. She has been coeditor of the *Women in German Yearbook* since 1990.

Lisa Gates is currently a Fellow at the W. E. B. Du Bois Institute at Harvard University. She received her Ph.D. in Germanic languages and literatures from Harvard and specializes in the area of race construction in German popular culture.

Willi Goetschel is associate professor of German at Columbia University. His 1990 study of Kant, *Kant als Schriftsteller,* appeared in English translation in 1994 under the title *Constituting Critique: Kant's Writing as Critical Praxis.* He is the editor of a special issue on *Germanistik* in the United States and of the collected works of Hermann Levin Goldschmidt. Having published essays on Fontane, Kafka, Keller, theories of Enlightenment, and German-Jewish identity, he is currently working on a study focusing on Spinoza, Mendelssohn, Lessing, and modernity.

Pascal Grosse received his M.D. and his M.A. in history from the Free University of Berlin. He completed a doctoral dissertation entitled "Colonialism and Eugenics in Germany, 1885–1914" in the history of medicine and is preparing a new project on colonial migration in Germany. He currently works in the Department of Neurology at the Humboldt University of Berlin.

Sabine Hake is professor of German at the University of Pittsburgh. She is the author of *Passions and Deceptions: The Early Films of Ernst Lubitsch* (1992) and *The Cinema's Third Machine: German Writings on Film, 1907–1933* (1993). Her article on colonial film is part of a research project that focuses on the cinema of the Third Reich.

Robert C. Holub teaches German intellectual, cultural, and literary history in the German Department at the University of California, Berkeley. Among his publications are *Friedrich Nietzsche* (1995), *Crossing Borders*

(1992), *Jürgen Habermas: Critic in the Public Sphere* (1992), *Reflections of Realism* (1991), *Reception Theory* (1984), and *Heinrich Heine's Reception of German Grecophilia* (1981). He also coedited several collections of essays, including *Impure Reason: Dialectic of Enlightenment in Germany* (1993) and *Responsibility and Commitment: Ethische Postulate der Kulturvermittlung* (1996), and is currently working on an extended study of Nietzsche and discourses of the nineteenth century.

Yara-Colette Lemke-Muniz de Faria received her M.A. in American Studies from the John F. Kennedy Institute for North American Studies at the Free University of Berlin. She is currently writing her dissertation on Afro-German children in postwar Germany and the United States ("'Prüfstein der Demokratie': Afrodeutsche Kinder in Nachkriegsdeutschland und den USA, 1945–1960") in history at the Institute for Research on Antisemitism at the Technical University of Berlin.

Sara Lennox is professor of Germanic Languages and Literatures and director of the Social Thought and Political Economy Program at the University of Massachusetts, Amherst. She is editor of *Auf der Suche nach den Gärten unserer Mütter: Feministische Kulturkritik aus Amerika* (1982) and coeditor of *Nietzsche heute* (1988). She has published articles on various twentieth-century German and Austrian authors, women's writing in the FRG and GDR, and literary theory, as well as on feminist theory and pedagogy, anti-feminism, and the feminist movement.

Andreas Michel is assistant professor of Germanic Studies at Indiana University. His main areas of research include intellectual history, cultural theory, and philosophical aesthetics. He has published articles on German Studies, (post)modernity, exoticism, and media theory, coedited an anthology on early German Romantic theoretical texts (*Theory as Practice: A Critical Anthology of Early German Romantic Writings*), and is presently finishing a book-length study of Carl Einstein's aesthetics.

Leslie Morris is Assistant Professor of German at the University of Minnesota/ Twin Cities. She has also taught at Bard College, where she served as director of German Studies and of Jewish Studies. In 1998–99 she was a Fullbright Senior Scholar at the Europa-Universität-Viadrina in Frankfurt an der Oder, where she taught Jewish Studies and comparative literature courses. She has published articles on German-Jewish topics, a book on history and memory in the poetry of Ingeborg Bachmann, and is currently working on a book on elegy and the postmodern in French and German poetry.

Having taught at the Free University of Berlin and at the University of California, Berkeley, Thomas Nolden is currently an associate professor of German at Wellesley College. He has published a study of epistolary poetics, *'An einen jungen Dichter': Studien zur epistolaren Poetik* (1995), and a book on young Jewish writers in the gentile cultures and societies of postwar Austria and Germany entitled *Junge jüdische Literatur: Konzentrisches Schreiben in der Gegenwart* (1995). His research focuses on questions of cross-cultural literacy, on eighteenth-century, fin-de-siècle, and contemporary literature and philosophy, and, more recently, on contemporary European Jewish literature.

John K. Noyes is an associate professor in the Department of German Language and Literature and program coordinator in Theory of Literature at the University of Cape Town. He has written on colonial literature, the history of sexuality, and literary theory and is the author of *Colonial Space: Spatiality in the Discourse of German South West Africa, 1884–1914* (1992) and *The Mastery of Submission: Inventions of Masochism* (forthcoming). He is editor of *Acta Germanica: German Studies in Africa*. At present he is working on the production of desire in imperialism.

Katrin Sieg is an assistant professor at Indiana University. She is the author of *Exiles, Eccentrics, Activists: Women in Contemporary German Theater* (1994) and has published in the areas of theater and performance studies, as well as feminist and queer theory and criticism. She is currently working on a second book tentatively titled *Ethnic Drag: Dramaturgies of Race and Nation.*

Helmut Walser Smith is assistant professor of history at Vanderbilt University. The author of *German Nationalism and Religious Conflict: Culture, Ideology, Politics, 1870–1914* (1995), he has published essays on German colonialism, on antisemitism, and on historical writing after the linguistic turn. Currently he is at work on a study of an East German industrial city from the Great Depression to the building of the Berlin Wall.

Susanne Zantop is professor of German and Comparative Literature and currently chair of the Department of German Studies at Dartmouth College. While her earlier books or anthologies deal with history and literature (*Zeitbilder: Geschichte und Literatur bei Heinrich Heine und Mariano José de Larra,* 1987), literature and painting (ed. *Paintings on the Move: Heinrich Heine and the Visual Arts,* 1989), and women's writing (*Bitter Healing: German Women Writers 1700–1830,* coedited with Jeannine Blackwell, 1992), her most recent study focuses on the colonialist imagination (*Colonial Fantasies: Conquest, Family, and Nation in Precolonial Germany, 1770–1870,* 1997).

Index

Achelis, T., 98n
Adelson, Leslie, 28, 261, 262
Adorno, Theodor, 154
Africans: images of, 72, 95, 108, 163–87, 233–46, 248–62. *See also* Blackness
Afro-Germans. *See* Blacks in Germany
Alterity, 194–95, 200–201, 270
Amman, Ludwig, 51
Anderson, Benedict, 18, 19, 84–85, 90, 120, 125, 127, 266n. 3, 268, 284
Animism, 83
Antisemitism, 156, 165, 173–78, 180, 181, 186–87, 302; and philosemitism, 224, 302, 305; and racism, 225; in Karl May, 64; in Friedrich Nietzsche, 64. *See also* Colonialism, and antisemitism; Racism; Xenophobia
Appiah, Anthony, 246n
Arabs, images of, 60–63, 72–73
Arendt, Hannah, 4, 29, 81n. 15, 82n. 16, 110, 122, 208
Ascher, Saul, 302n. 12
Ashcroft, Bill, 2
Auschwitz. *See* Holocaust

Bachmann, Ingeborg, 27, 247–63
Balkankrise, 54
Balkans: history of the, 65–66; images of the, 65
Barckhausen, Joachim, 183
Bartels, Adolf, 90, 93
Barth, Ariane, 281
Bataille, Georges, 142, 155n
Bathrick, David, 265, 292
Bauer, Bruno, 44n
Baumgart, Winfried, 11, 14, 22
Bebel, August, 107, 110–11, 118, 122
Beethoven, Ludwig van, 44n
Behdad, Ali, 251

Benjamin, Walter, 102, 141, 248
Benveniste, Émile, 88
Berger, John, 246
Berger, Peter, 222
Bergmann, Peter, 45
Bergner, Gwen, 259
Berlin Conference, 10, 168
Berman, Nina, 1, 26
Besson, Benno, 313
Beveridge, Ray, 213
Bhabha, Homi, 4, 58, 63, 74n. 8, 85, 101, 105, 125, 163, 265, 267, 270–71, 271n. 13, 283
Bismarck, Otto von, 8–11, 45, 46, 70, 168
Black body: female, 165, 186, 240; male, 211, 241; the "primitive," 244–45; sexualization of, 186, 242. *See also* Blackness; Exoticism
Black Horror on the Rhine, 208–14, 219. *See also* Blacks in Germany
Blackness: in colonial film, 176–82; in photography, 234–46
Blacks in Germany, 205–29, 297n. 4
Bley, Helmut, 29, 108nn. 2–3, 109
Bloch, Ernst, 100
Blood as racial marker, 103, 207
Boas, Franz, 150n
Bonaparte, Marie, 257
Bougainville, Louis Antoine de, 332
Bowyer, Alan, 93
Braband, Carl, 121
Brandes, Georg, 44n
Brandt, Ursula, 223
Braque, Georges, 142, 149
Brennan, Timothy, 125
Bridgman, Jon, 108n. 3, 110
Bröck, Sabine, 258
Bronfen, Elisabeth, 266
Brug, Manuel, 312

363

Buch, Hans Christoph, 25
Bulmahn, Heinz, 283n. 7
Bülow, Frieda von, 22, 24, 26, 69–85, 181
Bülow, Hans von, 44n
Bürger, Peter, 148n. 10
Burton, Sir Richard, 57
Butler, Judith, 317
Byron, Lord, 57

Campt, Tina, 27
Carby, Hazel, 297
Carl Peters, 170, 171, 178–83
Carr, Christopher D., 277n. 19
Case, Sue-Ellen, 299
Chickering, Robert, 8
Chow, Rey, 187n, 266n. 3
Chrisman, Laura, 3, 80n. 13, 283n. 7
Citizenship, German, 313, 316n. 22. *See also* Identity, German
Clifford, James, 146n, 236
Cocalis, Susan, 304n
Colonial fantasies, 19–25, 163–87, 220, 222, 254, 281, 314, 332
Colonial film, 163–87
Colonialism: and antisemitism, 181; British, 54, 273–74, 280; British vs. German 165, 181; and desire, 76, 91, 134, 185; and disease, 76, 171, 173–74; eastward, 173, 187; as epistemology, 329–36; feminist critique of, 71, 297–98; French, 54; and gender, 23, 59, 71–85, 183–84; history of German, 7–18, 33–50, 53–55, 87, 107–23, 168–69, 175n, 184, 216; ideologies of, 94; after 1918, 218; after 1933, 175; and sexuality, 23–24, 75, 76, 182, 185; theory of, 175n, 321–36
Colonial literature, 130, 167, 175; by female writers, 22, 69–85; by male writers, 87–105, 125–38. *See also* Postcolonial literature
Colonization, German, in Latin America (*Nueva Germania*), 33–49
Congo Conference. *See* Berlin Conference
Conrad, Joseph, 127, 253
Cook, Captain James, 331
Critical Volksstück, 304, 309
Cross-dressing, 313
Cubism, 12, 151–55; vs. Expressionism, 149. *See also* Space, in art
Cunard, Nancy, 258–59

Darwinism, 134, 171, 301
Das ostjüdische Antlitz, 189–203
Decolonization, 3, 5, 6, 18
Dedering, Tilman, 110n. 6
Defoe, Daniel, 328n. 3. *See also Robinson Crusoe*
Deleuze, Gilles, 93
Dérain, André, 149
Der Fall Franza, 249–55, 259
Der Konsul, 69–86
Dernburg, Bernhard, 109, 111, 113
Derrida, Jacques, 2
Descartes, René, 325, 326
Desire. *See* Black body; Colonialism, and desire; Colonialism, and sexuality
Deutsch, Helene, 257
Deutsche Kolonialgesellschaft. See German Colonial Society
Diderot, Denis, 332
Die Brücke, 149
Die Nuba, 233–46
Die Nuba von Kau, 233–46
Die Reiter von Deutsch-Ostafrika, 184–86
Digre, Brian, 217
Diner, Dan, 269
Dinesen, Isak, 78
Disease. *See* Colonialism, and disease; *Germanin;* Race, and disease; Whiteness, and disease
Doane, Mary Ann, 248
Drechsler, Horst, 14, 108nn. 2–3
Drewniak, Boguslaw, 163
Droop, Marie-Luise, 185n
Duden, Anne, 262
Dyson-Hudson, Neville, 97

Eberhardt, Isabelle, 57
Eichberg, Henning, 301
Eigler, Friederike, 26
Einstein, Carl, 26, 141–61
Eley, Geoff, 7
Emigration, German, 42, 53
Empire: British, 3, 6, 7, 11, 271; French, 3, 6, 11; German, 3, 11, 53; Habsburg, 3, 53, 263; Ottoman, 52, 65
Enlightenment, 5, 6, 282
Erzberger, Matthias, 118, 119n. 39, 120
Ethnicity. *See* Race
Ethnography, 165; theory of, 234–36
Europeanness, 5, 41, 48

Exile, 271
Exoticism: discourse of, 243, 253. *See also* Colonialism, and sexuality; Racism
Eyferth, Klaus, 24, 223, 226

Fabian, Johannes, 122, 157
Fanon, Frantz, 2, 85, 100, 250, 257, 259
Fantasies. *See* Colonial fantasies
Fascism, 4, 6; and art, 155; and patriarchy, 249
Fassbinder, Rainer Werner, 297, 303–7, 315
Femininity under patriarchy, 299
Feminism, 5. *See also* Colonialism, feminist critique of; Colonialism, and gender
Fernández Retamar, Roberto, 328n. 3
Film. *See* Colonial film
Fischer, Eva-Elisabeth, 273
Fischer, Michael M. J., 146n
Fleißer, Marieluise, 304–5
Flessner, Bettina, 307n. 15
Fonseca, Isabel, 281n. 1, 282, 291n. 18
Formalism: in the plastic arts, 144; social function of, 150
Förster, Bernhard, 34–39
Forster, E. M., 168
Förster, Elisabeth, née Nietzsche, 38, 39
Forster, Georg, 9, 331
Foucault, Michel, 2, 260
Frank, Walter, 82n. 18
Fraser, Angus, 282n. 3
Frenssen, Gustav, 26, 70, 87–105
Freud, Sigmund, 2, 155, 156, 254, 257, 260, 317
Friedlander, Saul, 269
Friedrichsmeyer, Sara, 28
Frisch, Max, 251
Frobenius, Leo, 150n, 220
Fuchs-Sumiyoshi, Andrea, 51

Gandhi, Mahatma, 280
Gann, Lewis, 29
Garber, Marjorie, 57
Gates, Lisa, 27
Geertz, Clifford, 236
Gellner, Ernest, 19, 84, 125
Genoveva Legend, 272, 280
German African Show. *See Völkerschau*
German Colonialism: in Cameroon, 10, 11–12, 15, 168, 172, 206, 214; in German East Africa, 10, 12, 15; in Kiachow and the Pacific colonies, 10, 11, 113–15, 168; in Southwest Africa, 10, 11, 12–13, 15, 107–23, 125–38, 168; in Togo, 10, 11, 15, 168, 206, 214. *See also* Colonialism, history of German
German Colonialism, racial policy under, 206. *See also* Miscegenation
German Colonial Society, 8, 10, 11, 13, 16, 168
German Democratic Republic: and "the culture question," 292n. 20, 293; reflected in novel, 289, 289n. 16
Germanin, 164–75
Germanness. *See* Identity, German
German Studies, 1; critique of, 270; practice of, 266–67
Geschichten aus Südwestafrika, 125–39
Geyer, Michael, 5, 269
Giacometti, Alberto, 145
Gilman, Sander, 94n, 206, 208
Gilroy, Paul, 6
Glinga, Werner, 70
Gobineau, Comte de, 61, 120
Goethe, Johann Wolfgang von, 44n, 61
Goetschel, Willi, 28, 323n
Göttsche, Dirk, 250
Gramsci, Antonio, 2
Graudenz, Karlheinz, 8
Greenfeld, Liah, 19
Grieser, Dietmar, 300n. 8
Griffith, Gareth, 2
Grimm, Hans, 16, 23, 24, 26, 125–38, 169
Gris, Juan, 149
Gröber, Adolf, 119, 120
Grosse, Pascal, 27
Grosz, George, 142
Gründer, Horst, 8n. 2, 11, 12, 16
Guattari, Félix, 93
Gypsies, 28, 83, 99, 281–94; images of, 281–94; and Nazi persecution, 288n. 15; prejudice against, 283, 284

Habermas, Jürgen, 4–6
Hall, Catherine, 7
Hall, Stuart, 7, 266
Hammer, Klaus, 283n. 7, 292
Hansen, Miriam, 269
Hartsock, Nancy, 59
Hartung, Günter, 136

Hawel, Wolfgang, 223
Hebbel, Friedrich, 270, 273
Heimatkunst, 90. *See also* Bartels, Adolf
Hein, Christoph, 28, 281–93
Heine, Heinrich, 44n
Heizer, Donna, 51
Heller, Agnes, 268
Hemingway, Ernest, 233
Henderson, W. O., 8
Herder, Johann Gottfried, 61, 246
Herero and Nama Wars, 13–14, 87, 103–4, 107–8, 109–23, 125–38
Herrmann, Hans Peter, 18–19
Herzberg, Georg, 164n
Hitler, Adolf, 176, 303. *See also* National Socialism
Hobsbawm, Eric, 52, 84, 85
Hohmann, J. S., 290n. 18
Holocaust, 4, 5, 81n. 15, 82nn. 17–18; German memory of, 269, 301, 303; politics of restitution, 224. *See also* National Socialism
Holub, Robert C., 26
Homoeroticism, 306
Horn, Peter, 136
Horns Ende, 281–93
Horton, Susan, 78–79
Horvath, Ödön von, 304
Hulme, Peter, 59, 328n. 3
Humboldt, Alexander von, 9, 22
Hurka, Herbert, 226
Huyssen, Andreas, 5, 6

Identity: European vs. Asian, 42, 272; European vs. non-European, 105; and gender, 24, 59; German ("Germanness"), 5, 6, 7, 10, 18–20, 23, 26, 28, 74, 75, 92, 102, 104, 186, 279, 302n. 12; German vs. *Indianer,* 295; German vs. Jewish 84–85, 99, 279; German vs. "natives," 95; German vs. "oriental," 63; German vs. Turkish, 4, 64–65, 318; national, in West Germany, 295, 301; as performance, 91, 316; visual representations of Germanness, 163–87
Imagination, fascist, 138
Im Lande der Verheißung, 69–86
Imperialism: British, 172, 173, 175, 186; European, 25; French, 209; German, in the Balkans, 55; and the novel, 126; U.S., 254. *See also* Empire; Vietnam War

India. *See* Colonialism, British
Indians, 300–303. *See also* Identity, European vs. Asian

Jahrhundert der Herren, 265–80
Jakobson, Roman, 88
Jelinek, Elfriede, 307, 307n. 15, 315
Jews. *See* Antisemitism; Identity; Holocaust; National Socialism

Kaffernwirtschaft, 135
Kant, Immanuel, 28, 321–36; and colonialism, 321–22, 324; concepts of space and time, 325
Karagöz in Alamania, 312–18
Karl May Festspiele, 299n, 300
Katzelmacher, 303–7
Keller, Gottfried, 44n
Keloglan in Alamania, 312–18
Kimmich, Max, 170
Kipling, Rudyard, 57, 127, 168
Klee, Paul, 145
Kleine, Friedrich Karl, 171
Klemm, Gustav Friedrich, 98n
Kline, Linus W., 99
Klotz, Marcia, 51
Klüger, Ruth, 312
Knoll, Arthur, 29
Kolodny, Annette, 77
Kolonialschuldlüge, 16, 217
Koltès, Bernard-Marie, 295, 307, 319
Köselitz, Heinrich, 36
Krafft-Ebing, Richard, 99, 100
Kraft, Helga, 307n. 15
Kratzer, Barbara, 70n. 4
Krieger, Arnold, 183
Kristeva, Julia, 85, 260
Kritik der reinen Vernunft, 321–36
Kromschröder, Gerhard, 297, 297n. 5
Kulturnation, 169
Kurds, images of, 64
Kürschner, Joseph, 67

LaCapra, Dominick, 269
Lander, Jeannette, 28, 265–80
Lang, Alexander, 295, 299, 306, 315
Langhof, Anna, 307n. 15, 311n. 19
Lattmann, Wilhelm, 115
Laude, Jean, 149
Lavater, Johann Kaspar, 61

Lawrence, D. H., 258
Lawrence, T. E., 57, 254
Lazarus, Neil, 5
Lebzelter, Gisela, 209
Ledebour, Georg, 113, 118
Le Doeuff, Michelle, 328n. 4
Lefèbvre, Henri, 127–28, 137
Leiris, Michel, 142, 144, 155n
Lemke-Muniz de Faria, Yara-Colette, 27
Lenau, Nikolaus, 283n. 5
Lennox, Sara, 25, 27
Lettow-Vorbeck, Paul von, 184
Levinas, Emmanuel, 194–95, 200–201
Lichtenberg, Georg Christoph, 61
Lila, 297, 304–12
Lindner, Gabriele, 283n. 7
Lindquist, Friedrich von, 113, 214, 221
Literature, colonial. *See* Colonial fantasies; Colonial literature
Locke, John, 317, 334, 335
Lohenstein, Daniel Casper von, 64
Lott, Eric, 298–99
Lowe, Lisa, 52
Luckmann, Thomas, 222
Lukács, György, 125
Luther, Martin, 64
Luxemburg, Rosa, 71
Luz, Horst, 240
Luz, Oskar, 234, 240–44
Lyotard, Jean-François, 125, 255

Macintyre, Ben, 36
Maier, Donna J. E., 11
Maji-Maji Revolt, 12
Makropoulos, Michael, 63
Mamozai, Martha, 70, 71, 74, 74n. 7, 79n. 11, 137
Mann, Klaus, 303
Mann, Thomas, 283n. 5
Marcus, George E., 146n
Margalit, Gilad, 284n. 9
Martin, Biddy, 259
Marx, Karl, 148
Marxism, 2
Masculinity, 22, 80, 81; and blackness, 248; vs. femininity, 177; and race, 211. *See also* Black body, male; Colonialism, and gender
Mason, Otis T., 98
May, Karl, 26, 51–67, 180, 297, 299–303

McClintock, Anne, 3, 22, 247, 260
McKnight, Phil, 283n. 7, 284n. 8
Mehr, Mariella, 282n. 4
Melville, Herman, 331
Mendel, Gregor Johann, 213
Michel, Andreas, 26
Migrants, 312–18; African, 206; literature by/on, 265–80; in relation to Jewish thematic, 270; Turkish, 297. *See also* Nomadism
Miller, Christopher, 250
Minority literature, 299
Minstrelsy, 298
Miscegenation, 107–23, 137, 176, 185, 216, 222; and disease, 121; in Germany, 212. See also *Mischlingsfrage*
Mischlingsfrage, 223
Modernity, 6, 147, 238, 247
Moeller van den Bruck, Artur, 94n
Mohanty, Chandra, 259
Montaigne, Michel, 326
Morel, Edmund D., 207
Morgan, Henry Lewis, 150n
Morris, Leslie, 27
Mosse, George, 19
Mulattisierung. See Miscegenation
Müller, Elfriede, 307n. 15
Müller-Meiningen, Ernst, 114, 115
Multiculturalism, 267, 297
Mumm, Reinhard, 120

Napoleon, 41, 44
Nationalism, 22, 83, 84, 186; and gender, 80; German, 8; and racism, 176
National Liberation movements. *See* Decolonization
National Socialism, 4, 8, 16–18, 77n, 82nn. 17–18; race policies under, 218–22; self-representation of, 163–87. *See also* Antisemitism; Hitler, Adolf; Racism
National stereotypes. *See* Identity
Nation, and narration, 125–27
Naumann, Friedrich, 22
N'dumbe, Kuma Alexandre III, 215
Nef, Ernst, 141n. 2
Negerplastik, 141–61
Nietzsche, Friedrich, 25, 33–49, 64, 147, 148
Nixon, Rob, 328n. 3
Nolden, Thomas, 26

Nomadism, 87–105; idealized, 290; vs. *Wanderlust*, 100–101. See also Gypsies; Migrants
Noyes, John, 26, 51
Numelin, Ragnar, 100
Nuremberg Laws, 218

Obeyesekere, Gananath, 278n
Ohm Krüger, 178–84
Opitz, May, 297
Orientalism, 2, 51, 52, 251, 256, 314–15, 317; and gender, 76
Orientzyklus, 51–67
Osterhammel, Jürgen, 18
Otis, Pauletta, 277n. 19
Özdamar, Emine Sevgi, 298, 299, 312–19

Paasche, Hermann, 113
Pan-German League, 8
Patriotism. See Nationalism
Peck, Jeffrey, 6
Penkert, Sybille, 141n. 2
Performance: of ethnicity, 295–319; of gender, 299
Persians, images of, 64
Peter Moors Reise nach Südwest., 87–105
Peters, Carl, 10, 12, 24, 69, 73, 183
Picasso, Pablo, 145, 149
Pollack, Sydney, 58
Pornography, 234
Positionality, 266n. 5
Postcolonialism: and disease, 253; German, 3, 8; in literature and film, 24; in Shri Lanka, 273–80; theory of, 1–7
Postcolonial literature, 3. See also Postcolonialism, in literature and film
Postmodernism and poststructuralism, 5
Pratt, Mary Louise, 60
Preußer, Heinz-Peter, 283n. 7
Primitivism, 143–61, 178, 237; in Nazi film, 165
Puccini, Giacomo, 298, 313, 318

Quataert, Jean, 8
Queer Studies, 295–319

Race: and disease, 213; and eroticism, 317; and fantasy, 247–63; in the Federal Republic of Germany, 121, 222–29; fictions of, 166; and gender, 247–63; and nation, 319; relations during the Empire, 107–23, 215; theories of, 174. See also Antisemitism; Colonialism; Identity; Miscegenation; Racism
Racism, 28, 75, 81n. 15, 83, 84, 98, 108–9, 121, 165, 173–77, 186–87, 205–29, 302; in the Critical Volksstück, 304, 305; feminist critique of, 307–19; and gender, 74; in Nietzsche, 41; in postwar Germany, 295–304; and religion 120; and sexuality, 305, 306; and space, 136. See also Black body; Whiteness
Raddatz, Fritz J., 265
Rationality, critique of, 250–51
Ratzel, Friedrich, 114
Realism, African vs. European, 153
Reeducation, 222, 224
Regionalism, 90, 91
Restitution, fantasies of, 301, 302, 312. See also Colonial fantasies
Reventlow, Graf Ludwig zu, 107, 112
Richthofen, Freiherr Hartmann von, 116, 121
Riefenstahl, Leni, 27, 183, 233–46, 302
Riehl, Alois, 141n. 1
Rimbaud, Arthur, 250, 252
Robinsonades. See *Robinson Crusoe*
Robinson Crusoe, 20–21, 23, 331
Rohrbach, Paul, 114
Roma, 307. See also Gypsies
Rose, Carol, 331, 334, 335
Rose, Jacqueline, 18, 19
Rose, Romani, 282
Rosenzweig, Franz, 200–201
Roth, Joseph, 198–99
Rousseau, Jean-Jacques, 335
Rubin, William, 144–46
Rushdie, Salman, 93

Said, Edward, 2, 3, 7, 51, 52, 60, 76, 126, 127, 142n. 6, 265, 291
Schiller, Friedrich, 237
Schindler, Hanns Michael, 8
Schlieffen, Count von, 110
Schmokel, Wolfe, 8, 17
Schneckenburger, Eberhardt, 228
Schneider, Peter, 6
Schopenhauer, Arthur, 44n. 147
Schrader, Karl, 112

Schreiner, Olive, 78
Sculpture, African. See *Negerplastik*
Sebald, Peter, 22
Sedgwick, Eve Kosofsky, 59
Seghers, Anna, 281n. 1
Selpin, Herbert, 180, 184
Sexuality: female, 164; white female, 260, 261. *See also* Black body, female; Colonialism, and gender; Colonialism, and sexuality
Shakespeare, William, 314, 328n. 3
Shapiro, Susan, 255
Showat, Ella, 2
Sieg, Katrin, 28
Simmel, Georg, 141n. 1, 148, 154
Sinti. *See* Gypsies; Roma
Smetana, Bedrich, 314
Smith, Robert Walser, 26
Smith, Woodruff, 8, 10, 11, 12, 14, 17
Socialists: and colonialism, 10; and *Kultur,* 292; and race question, 107–23
Solf, Wilhelm, 117, 118, 121n. 47
Sontag, Susan, 27, 234–39, 244
Space, 125–38; in art, 152
Spahn, Peter, 118
Specht, Kerstin, 297, 304, 307–18
Spence, Louise, 187n
Spencer, Herbert, 150n
Spiesser, Fritz, 170n. 5
Spitzer, Leo, 268, 269
Spivak, Gayatri, 311
Spraul, Gunther, 110n. 6
Stalinism, 4
Stam, Robert, 2, 187n
Stendhal (Henri Beyle), 44n
Stereotypes. *See* Identity; Racism
Sterilization. *See* Racism; Miscegenation
Stern, Frank, 224–25, 269, 302
Stobrawa, Ilse, 185n
Stoecker, Adolf, 113
Stoecker, Helmuth, 16, 17, 22, 137
Stojka, Ceija, 282n. 4
Stoler, Ann Laura, 108, 260
Streese, Konstanze, 24, 25
Struck, Hermann, 27, 189–203
Subjectivity, 105; and mobility, 102
Surrealism, 155

Taine, Hippolyte, 44n
Taylor, A. J. P., 9, 14

Teraoka, Arlene, 1, 307n. 14
Theweleit, Klaus, 19, 91
Third Reich. *See* Holocaust; National Socialism
Thomas, Nicholas, 108n. 2
Thorson, Helga, 70n. 4
Tieck, Ludwig, 270, 273
Tiffin, Helen, 2
Timm, Uwe, 18, 24, 25
Todesarten, 247–63
Todorov, Tzvetan, 115
Torgovnick, Marianna, 27, 143–47, 160
Triangulation: as a discursive strategy, 169, 174, 180; *Indianer* as Jews, 303
Triumph des Willens, 233, 236
Trotha, Lothar von, 13–14, 112, 113, 118
Trumpener, Katie, 99, 282
Turks, 312–18; in Germany, 4, 305, 306. *See also* Identity, German vs. Turkish
Tylor, E. B., 150n

Unger, Hellmuth, 171n
Universalism, 5
Uyangoda, Jayadeva, 278n

Valentino, Rudolph, 57
Versailles, Treaty of, 15–16, 168, 172, 209, 217; impact on colonial idea, 168. *See also* World War I
Vietnam War, 4, 5, 256
Vlaminck, Maurice de, 149
Völkerschau, 218–22

Wagner, Richard, 34, 35, 44n
Wagnleitner, Reinhold, 254
Wallraff, Günter, 297, 307n. 14
Warmbold, Joachim, 23, 70, 70n. 4
Wassermann, Jakob, 199–200
Weigel, Sigrid, 249
Weimar Republic, 16, 172, 208–18; and gender, 186. *See also* Colonialism, after 1918
Welch, David, 163
West, Cornel, 6
Westermarck, Edward, 99
Whiteness, 247, 252; and blackface, 298; and disease, 255; and female identity, 252, 263; and female sexuality, 211, 256, 262; male fantasies, 254
Wiedergutmachung. See Restitution, fantasies of

Wildenthal, Lora, 7, 22, 23, 51, 116n. 31
Williams, Patrick, 2, 80n. 13, 283n. 6
Wilson, W. Daniel, 64
Winckelmann, Johann Joachim, 245
Wolf, Christa, 266
Wölfflin, Heinrich, 141n. 1
Wollschläger, Hans, 56
World War I, 15–16, 168. *See also* Versailles, Treaty of
World War II, 164, 170

Xenophobia, 122; in the GDR 289, 293; vs. xenophilia, 293. *See also* Antisemitism; Racism

Young, Robert, 5, 6

Zantop, Susanne, 1, 8n. 2, 20, 21, 51, 77, 277n. 21
Zürn, Johannes, 120
Zweig, Arnold, 27, 189–203